South Africa Under Apartheid

South Africa Under Apartheid

A Select and Annotated Bibliography

Jacqueline A. Kalley

Meckler

Westport • London

This edition is published in North America, Japan, and
Australia by special arrangement with Shuter and Shooter (Pty)
Ltd., Pietermaritzburg, South Africa.

Library of Congress Cataloging-in-Publication Data

Kalley, Jacqueline A. (Jacqueline Audrey)
    South Africa under apartheid : a select and annotated bibliography
/ Jacqueline A. Kalley.
        p.   cm.
    Bibliography : p.
    Includes index.
    ISBN 0-88736-506-X (alk. paper) : $
    1. Apartheid--South Africa--Bibliography. 2. South Africa--Race
relations--Bibliography.   I. Title.
Z3608.R3K34   1989
[DT763]   89-31983
                                                    CIP

Meckler Corporation, 11 Ferry Lane West, Westport, CT 06880.

Printed on acid free paper.
Printed in the United States of America.

For Paul and Joshua

CONTENTS

PREFACE

1   AIM AND SCOPE

The literature on South Africa's crisis is enormous and ever
burgeoning.   This bibliography seeks to provide the user
with a representative selection of literature on all aspects
of the South African issue. Its canvas is wide, illustrating
apartheid's permeation of all political, economic, social
and religious facets of the country's life.   The
preponderance of entries are in English, and where this is
not the case, a free translation of their titles into
English is offered.

2   ARRANGEMENT

The annotated entries are alphabetically arranged by author
or title, in accordance with current cataloguing procedure
as determined by the Anglo-American Cataloguing Rules, 2nd
edition, AACR II. It was decided to present the material in
one sequence, and not in specific subject categories; most
writing on South Africa is multidisciplinary.

The author index, which includes names of editors,
compilers, authors, sponsoring bodies and institutes, refers
to relevant item numbers.

The subject index has been compiled as an information
retrieval tool. It provides quick and in-depth access to all
topics in the text.

3   ANNOTATIONS

These provide the researcher with a succinct guide to the
content and relevance of the material presented. I have
refrained from making value judgements, and intend only to
alert the user to contents and special features of the
selected article.

4   SOURCES

A list of periodicals cited can be found on page   xi . The
libraries used in the compilation of this bibliography
include the holdings of the University of the Witwatersrand,
the South African Institute of International Affairs and the
Johannesburg Public Library.

5   ACKNOWLEDGEMENTS

This project was initiated by the Director of the Institute
of Social and Economic Research, Rhodes University.   Peter
Vale and Elna Schoeman, respectively Director of the
Institute of Social and Economic Research, Rhodes University,
and International Organizations Librarian, University of the
Witwatersrand, deserve particular mention and my grateful
thanks for their important role in this project, and for
their friendship and steadfast support of my work.   My
thanks are also due to Carol Leigh of the Johannesburg
Public Library and Carol Archibald, Jan Smuts Library, for
their willing assistance, Tom Lodge of the Department of
Political Studies, University of the Witwatersrand for
reading the manuscript, and to Renee Vroom and Kathy Holton
for typing this work so efficiently.   The Institute of
Social and Economic Research sponsored the typing of the
manuscript.

Jacqueline A. Kalley
Jan Smuts House Library

JOURNALS CITED

Africa Perspective

Africa Report

Africa Today

African Affairs

African Communist

African National Congress. ANC Weekly News Briefings

African Review

African Studies

Afrika

American Academy of Political and Social Sciences. Annals

American Historical Review

American Journal of Sociology

Annual Report on Labour Relations in South Africa

Annual Survey of South African Law

Anti-Apartheid News

Australian Outlook

Bank of Lisbon. Economic Focus

Black Who's Who in Southern Africa

British Journal of Sociology

Bulletin on Islam and Christian-Muslim Relations

Canadian Journal of African Studies

Capital and Class

Chatham House Papers

Civilisations

Communications in Africa

Comparative and International Law Journal of Southern Africa

Comparative Education

Comparative Studies in Society and History

Conflict Studies

Contemporary Review

Country Report: South Africa

Current Bibliography on African Affairs

Current History

Development Southern Africa

Economy and Society

Ethnic and Racial Studies

Facts and Reports

Finance and Trade Review

Focus on Political Repression in South Africa

Foreign Affairs

Foreign Policy

Government and Opposition

Harvard Educational Review

Index on Censorship

Indicator South Africa: a Barometer of Social Trends

Insurgent Sociologist

International Affairs

International Affairs (Moscow)

International Affairs Bulletin

International Committee against Apartheid, Racism and
    Colonialism. ICSA Bulletin

International Journal

International Journal of African Historical Studies

International Journal of the Sociology of the Law

International Political Science Review

International Security

International Social Science Journal

Johns Hopkins University. School of Advanced and International
    Studies. SAIS Review.

Journal for Contemporary History

Journal of African History

Journal of African Studies

Journal of Asian and African Studies

Journal of Black Studies

Journal of Commonwealth and Comparative Politics

Journal of Contemporary African Studies

Journal of Development Studies

Journal of International Affairs

Journal of Modern African Studies

Journal of Politics

Journal of Southern African Affairs

Journal of Southern African Studies

Journal of World Trade Law

Kroniek van Afrika

Leadership South Africa

Marxism Today

Minority Rights Group. Report

Monthly Review

Mozambican Studies

New Left Review

Nigerian Journal of International Affairs

Optima

Orbis

Plural Societies

Political Studies

Politikon

Quarterly Economic Review of South Africa

Race

Race and Class

Race Relations

Reality

Register

Research in African Literatures

Review

Review of African Political Economy

Round Table

Sash

Sechaba

Social Dynamics

South Africa International

South African Historical Journal

South African Institute of Race Relations. Quarterly Countdown

South African Journal of African Affairs

South African Journal on Human Rights

South African Labour Bulletin

South African News Summary

South African Outlook

South African Review

South African Yearbook of International Law

Southern Africa Record

Southern African Update: a Bibliographical Survey

Survival

Third World Quarterly

TransAfrica Forum

Ufahamu

Umsebenzi: the Voice of the South African Communist Party

United Nations. Centre Against Apartheid. Notes and Documents

University of Durban-Westville. Journal

Washington Quarterly

Who's Who of Southern Africa

Work in Progress

World Marxist Review

World Today

1   ABRAHAMS, Trevor
            "Coloured politics" in South Africa: the
            quislings' trek into the abyss. Ufahamu, vol.
            12, no. 3, 1983. p. 245-255

        Evaluates the reaction to the Botha government's
        proposal that Coloureds be coopted into the Presidents'
        Council, and the decision of some members of the Labour
        Party to participate. Set within the historical context
        of Coloured politics, the author demonstrates that the
        constitutional proposals should be viewed within the
        collaborationist/anti-collaborationist struggles.

2   ABRAHAMS, Trevor
            State policy, militarization, and the
            liberation movement in contemporary South
            Africa. Ufahamu, vol. 11, no. 3, Spring 1982.
            p. 94-120

        The author clarifies his objective: I thus hope to
        examine the current Botha regime's policies and the
        ancillary developments in the fortification of white
        South Africa as conscious policy decisions occurring in
        the confines of the economic changes being experienced
        in virtually every sector of the economy, and the
        renewed and increasingly militant struggle waged
        against the State by black South Africans. Includes
        useful statistical tables.

3   ACCELERATED development in Southern Africa, edited by
            John Barratt (and others). London: Macmillan,
            1974, 706 p.

        Based on papers delivered at a conference in 1972
        entitled: Accelerated Development in Southern Africa,
        sponsored by the Foundation for Foreign Affairs, the
        Rand Afrikaans University and the South African
        Institute of International Affairs. In this interaction
        of ideas, opinions and attitudes of experts from South
        and Southern Africa, the United States, United Kingdom

and Germany, the basic dimensions of development are
discussed, together with development problems of multi-
ethnic societies. International aspects and an
evaluation conclude the work. Chapters of particular
relevance to South Africa are those by W.B. Vosloo on
the policy of separate development as a framework for
development in South Africa; agriculture and economic
development in Southern Africa by Simon Brand; and
background to planning the development of the homelands
by Jan A. Lombard, amongst others.

4   ADAM, Heribert
     Conquest and conflict in South Africa.
     Journal of Modern African Studies, vol. 13,
     no. 4, December 1975, p. 621-640

A Professor of Sociology at the Simon Fraser
University, British Columbia, attempts to clarify over-
simplified perceptions of white rule in South Africa.
Examines white domination in its historical context and
expands on its four means of control - coercive,
ideological, political and economic which should also
be viewed as response to protest and resistance from
the dominated.

5   ADAM, Heribert
     Minority monopoly in transition: recent
     policy shifts of the South African state.
     Journal of Modern African Studies, vol. 18,
     no. 4, December 1980, p. 611-626

Reviews the history and nature of the South African
ruling group, prior to assessing the chances of its
transformation with reference to unfulfilled political
aspirations. Looks not only at organizations and their
programmes but also at actual and potential black
constituencies and their strategies. These he
distinguishes as opportunistic collaborators, strategic
collaborators, Inkatha, non-collaborators, and black
unions.

2

6   ADAM, Heribert
     Modernising racial domination: South Africa's
     political dynamics. Berkeley: University of
     California Press, 1971, 203 p.

Author states that this study differs from the vast
political literature on Southern Africa in respect of
its focus on the political economy and specific
dynamics of the South African scene, and secondly, that
it tries to avoid the tone of moral indignation
frequently present in writings on South Africa.
Examines reasons for racist South Africa's continued
functioning and indicates the unlikelihood of imminent
revolutionary change. By analysing apartheid in its
existing format, he attempts to explain its future
direction. Concludes that change could be instrumented
given past responses to South Africa's racial policies
in a changing internal and international environment.

7   ADAM, Heribert
     Outside influence on South Africa:
     Afrikanerdom in disarray. Journal of Modern
     Studies, vol. 21, no. 2, June 1983. p. 235-
     251

Initially explores the role of external investment in
the Republic, and South Africa's growing stake in North
America. Adam states that for external intervention to
have effective impact, divisions between the ruling
group must be clarified. He itemizes four competing
definitions of Afrikaner policy, namely, the labour
racists, the orthodox ideologues, the ruling
technocrats, and the critical moralists. Their
differing perceptions of crisis and relevant strategies
are assessed, as is their actual or potential political
power and susceptibility to outside influence.

8   ADAM, Heribert
      Racist   capitalism versus capitalist non-
      racialism in South Africa. Ethnic and Racial
      Studies, vol. 7, no. 2, April 1984, p. 269-
      282

      Assesses   the relationship between capitalism   and
      racism. Elaborates on the anomalous situations of the
      former's relatively easy adjustment to a racially
      structured society determined by legislation, noting
      however that its future depends on a radical departure
      from the past. Prospects for its deracialization are
      discussed, highlighting the key role of the Black
      bourgeoise. Stresses   that only the dismantling of all
      legal racial categorizations, access to the accumulated
      wealth by broad-based black middle class and political
      power-sharing would change the emphasis from race to
      class.

9   ADAM, Heribert and GILIOMEE, Hermann
      The rise and crisis of Afrikaner power. Cape
      Town: Philip, 1979, 308 p.

      Heribert Adam and historian Hermann Giliomee provide an
      in-depth investigation of interrelated aspects of South
      Africa's white ruling group, which the authors argue
      cannot be studied in isolation from both internal and
      external pressures. The authors summarize the scope of
      their study: 'With an emphasis on historical process,
      chapters, 4, 6, and 7 discuss the evolving self-concept
      of the Afrikaners and their economic   advance,
      highlighting the extent to whcih specific interests
      rather than an inimitable ideology condition Afrikaner
      strategies. Chapter 8 describes the political
      structures of the ruling National Party and the
      processes of decision making and legitimation. Chapter
      2 critically evaluates the diverse perspectives in the
      vast literature on South Africa. The concept of ethnic
      mobilization (chapter 3) is explored in order to
      understand the present ideological redefinition

(chapter 5). Finally, the failure of political liberalism (chapter 9) is analyzed in conjunction with the current debate on political alternatives (chapter 10) in South Africa.

10   ADAM, Heribert
     The rise of black consciousness in South Africa. Race, vol. 15, no. 2, October 1973, p. 149-165

Assesses the Black Consciousness Movement which he traces from the break of the blacks from the National Union of South African Students (NUSAS) to form their own exclusive South African Student Organisation (SASO). Although Black Consciousness ideas are not new to South Africa, the author indicates differing facets covered by the movement, and its goals and strategies as viewed against South Africa's social structure and resistance history.

11   ADAM, Heribert and MOODLEY, Kogila   ·
     South Africa without apartheid: dismantling racial domination. Berkeley: University of California Press, 1985, 300 p.

Studies the power configurations in South Africa and in the emerging post-apartheid state. The authors demonstrate the feasibility of power-sharing, averring that neither the status quo nor revolutionary transfer is likely. They analyze reform rhetoric, cleavages in opposition politics, the African National Congress, the unions, Inkatha, and splits within the National Party. Authors conclude that a non-racial democracy has a better chance of success than believed by sceptics.

12   ADDRESSING the nation: studies on the South African media, edited by Keyan Tomaselli, Ruth Tomaselli and Johan Muller. Durban: Richard Lyon, 1986, 3 vols.

Volume 1 entitled: Narrating the crisis: hegemony and the South African press, examines the print media and their role in the maintenance of the apartheid system, introduces and utilizes analytical tools for the mass media investigated. Volume 2: Currents of power: state broadcasting in South Africa, studies the role of both radio and television, illustrating their part in continued domination by the Nationalist Party. Volume 3: The limits of dissent: resistance, community and the press, focusses on the 'alternative press' in particular a Western Cape publication entitled Grassroots. Includes an appraisal of the commercial press.

13   AFRICAN Communist
        1959 –
        London: Inkuleleko Publications

The theoretical organ of the South African Communist Party, this journal is a quarterly of reviews and comments, written in the interest of African solidarity and as a forum for Marxist-Leninist thought on the continent. Each issue is individually and sequentially numbered, comprising approximately 112 pages.

14   AFRICAN crisis areas and U.S. foreign policy, edited by
        Gerald J. Bender, James S. Coleman and
        Richard L. Sklar. Berkeley: University of
        California Press, 1985, 373 p.
        Southern Africa: p. 27-157

Contains the following contributions relevant to South Africa: United States policy towards South Africa – is one possible? by William J. Foltz; South African policy and United States options in Southern Africa, by Sam C. Nolutshungu; creating new political realities – Pretoria's drive for regional hegemony, by Robert M. Price; and Congressional initiatives on South Africa, by Anne Forrester Holloway.

15   AFRICAN NATIONAL CONGRESS OF SOUTH AFRICA
        ANC Weekly News Briefings
        1 -   ,(1977?) -
        London: The Congress

        Based on clippings from the South African press
        Formerly: Weekly News Briefings

16   AFRICAN NATIONAL CONGRESS OF SOUTH AFRICA
        Strategy and tactics of the African National
        Congress IN: REVOLUTIONARY thought in the
        20th century, edited by B. Turok. London:
        Zed, 1980, p. 145-156

        Adopted in Morogoro in 1969, this document elaborates
        on its methodological principles.

17   AFRICAN NATIONAL CONGRESS OF SOUTH AFRICA
        Unity in action: a photographic history of
        the African National Congress. London: ANC,
        1982, 156 p.

        Provides a pictorial record of the African National
        Congress for the period 1912 to 1982 thus commemorating
        its seventieth anniversary. Contains little or no text
        but is clearly captioned.

18   AFRICAN perspectives on South Africa: a collection of
        speeches, articles and documents, edited by
        Hendrik W. van der Merwe (and others). Cape
        Town: Philip in association with the Centre
        for Intergroup Studies, 1978, (Black and
        white perspectives on South Africa), 612 p.

        The speeches of various black leaders, manifestos and
        documents of black political parties and organizations,
        as well as those of cultural and educational bodies are
        included under the following headings: historical and
        traditional background, political aspirations - the
        federal idea, dignity and consciousness, economic

development, education, religion, community
development, and the homelands, both 'independent' and
'non-independent'.

19   ALEXANDER, Neville
        Sow   the   wind: contemporary   speeches.
        Johannesburg: Skotaville, 1985, 180 p.

        John Samuel, in providing the foreword to this book,
        states: 'the single thrust that runs through much of
        Neville   Alexander's writings is   the   dynamic
        relationship he perceives between the national struggle
        for liberation in South Africa and the future political
        vision.' Speeches include the following topics: the
        need for unity; Jean Naidoo's funeral oration; the
        crisis of white supremacy and their strategies; racial
        capitalism and the need for its destruction; the role
        of the student; careers in apartheid South Africa;
        education; the role of liberation of women; background
        to the Nkomati Accord; race, ethnicity and nationalism;
        and the implication of the elections for the tricameral
        parliament.

20   AMERICAN FRIENDS SERVICE COMMITTEE. Southern
        Africa Working Party.
        South Africa: challenge and hope. Philadelphia:
        The Committee, 1982, 146 p.

        By providing an examination of the apartheid system and
        methods of promoting peaceful change to a just South
        African society, the growth of black resistance is
        traced as is South Africa's political and economic
        inter-relationship with the rest of the world and with
        international organizations. Assesses the ability of
        these relationships to promote internal change. Of
        especial note in this connection is Chapter Six which
        concerns international pressure on apartheid, in which
        the   following are explored – the Organization of

African Unity, the United Nations, religious organizations, corporations, divestment, arguments both for and against economic pressure, and liberation groups.

21   The AMERICAN people and South Africa: publics, elites, and policymaking processes, edited by Alfred O. Hero and John Barratt. Lexington: Lexington Books, 1981, 225 p.

Intended as a sequel to: Conflict and compromise in South Africa (1980) q.v., this study focusses on the American aspect of South Africa's relationship with the West. Details the evolution of American public attitudes, and the role and interaction of interest groups with governmental policy-making. Describes analytically perceptions of corporations, churches, universities and other private institutions pertinent to the issue.

22   ANATOMY of apartheid, edited by Peter Randall. Johannesburg: Sprocas, 1970, (Study Project on Christianity in Apartheid Society. Sprocas occasional publication, no. 1), 88 p.

As part of the working papers prepared for the Sprocas commissions, the political conditions prevalent at the time of writing are briefly examined prior to the presentation of the following contributions: the factors underlying apartheid by L. Schlemmer; some aspects of culture and apartheid, by André Brink; economics of separate development, by Robin Siedle; and modernization and apartheid, by F. van Zyl Slabbert.

23   ANC speaks: documents and statements of the African National Congress, 1955-1976. (Lusaka): African National Congress of South Africa, 1977, 224 p.

Comprises speeches by the leaders of the African National Congress on important issues for the period under review. Provides an overview of organizations allying themselves with the Congress, its aims and armed struggle. Includes both the Freedom Charter and resolutions adopted at the Morogoro Conference in 1969.

24   ANDOR, Lydia Eve
      South Africa's chrome, manganese, platinum and vanadium: foreign views on the mineral dependency issue, 1970-1984. A select and annotated bibliography. Johannesburg: South African Institute of International Affairs, 1985, (South African Institute of International Affairs. Bibliographical series, no. 13), 222 p.

Supplemented by an extensive author and subject index, the compiler of this bibliography brings together, in 587 entries, the views expressed by individuals and by spokesmen of organizations and governments on the mineral dependence or non-dependence of the West on South African minerals. The emphasis is on resources, reserves and production capacities in South Africa and, in comparison with the same factors in the rest of the world, on export-import relationships, including economic interdependence with the industrialized countries of the West.

25   ANDREWS, Penelope E.
      Corporate codes of conduct under apartheid: an assessment. TransAfrica Forum, vol. 3, no. 3, Spring 1986, p. 21-28

Assesses the corporate codes of conduct employed by foreign international corporations in expressing their recognition of changes in the Republic's economy, particularly since the 1979 change in industrial relations.

26   ANNUAL Report on Labour Relations in South Africa
      1984/5 -
      Johannesburg: Andrew Levy and Associates

      Critically analyzes South African labour relations over
      a twelve month period, indicating what may become
      important focal points in the year ahead. The 1985/86
      Report is based heavily on papers presented at a
      conference held in Johannesburg and entitled: Labour
      Horizons 1986. This report contains a review of 1985
      including trade union activity; labour and politics,
      patterns of industrial action; and legislative and
      court review. It further contains a prognosis for 1986,
      and annexures itemizing the current structure of the
      union movement, statistical data detailing economic and
      demographic parameters, and an analysis of strike
      activities.

27   ANNUAL Survey of South African Law
      1 -   , 1947 -
      Johannesburg: University of the Witwaters-
      rand, School of Law

      Formerly published by the University's Faculty of Law,
      this publication reviews change and developments which
      have taken place in the law for the year under review.

28   ANTI-Apartheid News
      March 1964 - 10 p.a.
      London: British Anti-Apartheid Movement

      Provides information on both suppression and
      exploitation in Southern Africa and international
      action against apartheid. Previously known as : World
      Campaign for the Release of South African Political
      Political Prisoners, and Apartheid News.

11

29   APARTHEID and education: the education of black South
      Africans,   edited   by   Peter   Kallaway.
      Johannesburg: Ravan, 1984, 494 p.

      Published in association with the Education Policy Unit
      and Centre for African Studies at the University of
      Cape Town, this collection of essays aims at providing
      analytical perspectives on South African educational
      history which, of necessity, have to be placed in the
      broader context of social, political and economic
      change. This study is made up of four parts which
      include the origins of black education; apartheid and
      education; education beyond the schools; and   the
      current   crisis.   Concludes   with   an   extensive
      bibliography on the education of black South Africans.
      Reviewed by Cynthia Kros in Africa Perspective, no. 24,
      1984, p. 112-116

30   APARTHEID   and   health.   Geneva: World   Health
      Organization, 1983, 258 p.

      Contains two parts: Part 1 comprises a report of an
      International Conference held at Brazzaville, People's
      Republic of the Congo, 16-20 November 1981. The main
      themes of this conference were the choice between
      health or apartheid,   an analysis of health care
      delivery,   and the relationship between apartheid and
      maternal, child, workers' and mental health. In Part
      II, an analytical report to the conference on the
      health implications of racial discrimination and social
      inequalities is presented.

31   APARTHEID and the church, edited by Peter Randall.
      Johannesburg: Sprocas, 1972. (Study Project
      on Christianity in Apartheid Society. Sprocas
      publication, no. 8), 91 p.

The Church Commission appointed by Sprocas, reflected a wide range of denominations, but for reasons beyond their control was comprised mainly of white ministers and theologians '. . . and therefore our report is to this extent sectional . . . Our approach to change is gradualist while seeking to be radical, that is to go to the roots . . . The main thrust of our report is critical both of the Church and the norms of the South African society which influence it.' Prior to offering its Recommendations, the Commission investigates the effects of apartheid on the Church; disunity and discrimination; and the mission of the Church.

32   APARTHEID in the Republic of South Africa, edited by A.G. Mezerik. New York: International Review Service, 1967, 154 p.

A survey of apartheid identifying its manifestations, implications, and subsequent international action against it, as evidenced particularly by United Nations resolutions.

33   APARTHEID is a heresy, edited by John W. de Gruchy and Charles Villa-Vicencio. Cape Town: Philip, 1983, 184 p.

A collection of essays written by theologians of differing denominations and cultural backgrounds. Compiled with the intention of enabling South Africans to look critically at themselves in the light of the decision taken by the World Alliance of Churches to declare apartheid a heresy. Contributors include Allan Boesak, Chriss Loff, David Bosch, Desmond Tutu, Simon Maimela, Charles Villa-Vicencio, John de Gruchy, Willem Vorster and Douglas Bax. Appendix contains documents pertinent to the debate.

34   The APARTHEID regime: political power and racial
domination, edited by Robert M. Price and
Carl G. Rosberg. Cape Town: Philip, 1980,
376 p.

Dominated by the confrontation between Afrikaner and
African nationalisms, contemporary South Africa is
assessed from the following standpoints: Emerging
strategies for political control - nationalist
Afrikanerdom (Andre du Toit); the National Party and
the Afrikaner Broederbond (Hermann Giliomee); the
failure of political liberalism in South Africa
(Heribert Adam); contemporary African political
organizations and movements (Roland Stanbridge);
observations on Inkatha and other black political
organizations (Lawrence Schlemmer); urban blacks
(Martin E. West); labour (Francis Wilson); black trade
unions (Philip Bonner); the homelands (Newell M.
Stultz); minority anxiety (Kogila A. Moodley); change
in South Africa (Lawrence Schlemmer); South Africa in
the contemporary world (Colin Legum); and the meaning
of government-led reform (Robert M. Price).

35   APARTHEID, South Africa and international law, edited
by Enuga S. Reddy. New York: United Nations,
1985, (United Nations. Centre against
Apartheid. Notes and documents, 13/85), 136
p.

In order to make more widely known the implications of
the new norms of international law for the struggle
against apartheid, the following papers, some of which
have been condensed, are presented: Declaration of the
Seminar on the Legal Status of the Apartheid Regime and
other Legal Aspects of the Struggle against Apartheid
(Lagos, 1984); Report of the Unitar Colloquim on the
Prohibition of Apartheid, Racism and Racial
Discrimination and the Achievement of Self-
Determination in International Law (Geneva, 1980);
Apartheid as an international crime is discussed, by

Albie Sachs, I.E. Sagay and Kader Asmal; the legal status of the apartheid regime and national liberation movements, by Albie Sachs and Kader Asmal; the laws of armed conflict and apartheid, by Keith D. Suter; self-determination and the 'independent bantustans', by Niall MacDermot; international action against apartheid, by Gay J. McDougall, Kader Asmal, and G. Brahme, Annexures include the International Convention on the Suppression and Punishment on the Crime of Apartheid, and extracts from declarations and resolutions of the United Nations General Assembly and the Security Council.

36   APARTHEID: the facts. London: International Defence and
      Aid Fund for Southern Africa in cooperation
      with the United Nations Centre against
      Apartheid, 1983, 111 p.

Presents information on apartheid South Africa under main headings. For speeches and writings of representative South Africans such as Mandela, Tutu, P.W. Botha and Andries Treurnicht, see: APARTHEID in crisis, edited by Mark A. Uhlig. New York: Vintage Books, 1986, 334 p.

37   ARCHER, Robert and BOUILLON, Antoine
      The South African game: sport and racism.
      London: Zed, 1982, 352 p.

An attempt is made 'to present the point of view of the modern non-racial sports movement within the country, and to describe the historical and social context with which it came into being'. This examination of sport as a political issue includes a chronology of South Africa's sporting history, the sports policies of the South African Council on Sport and the 'multinational' sports policy of the South African government. Appendix 5 comprises a table of South Africa's position in sport in 1980. First published in 1981 under the title: Sport et apartheid, by Albatros. Reviewed by J.A. Distefano in Ufahamu, vol. 13, no. 2/3, 1984, p. 345-347

38   ARKIN A.J.
        The relative contribution of the Indians to the South African economy, 1860-1970. University of Durban-Westville. Journal, vol. 4, no. 2, 1983. p. 164-175

Based on the author's doctoral thesis entitled: The contribution of the Indians in the economic development of South Africa 1960-1970: an historical income approach. (University of Durban-Westville, 1981). By calculating the contribution of the Indians to South Africa's Gross Domestic Product in 1911, 1946 and 1970, and relating these figures to the actively economic South African population, the author ascertains the improved Indian contribution since 1911.

39   ARMS embargo against South Africa: a bibliography of United Nations resolutions, documents and other publications. New York: United Nations, 1985, (United Nations. Centre against Apartheid. Notes and documents, 15/85), 18 p.

As indicated by the title, this work lists both Security Council and General Assembly resolutions, from 1962 onwards, reports of the Special Committee against Apartheid, perinent issues of Notes and Documents of the Centre against Apartheid, as well as other United Nations documents.

40   ASHERON, Andrew
        Race and politics in South Africa. New Left Review, no 53, January/February 1969, p. 55-67

Discusses the reformist thesis as applied to the South African situation. Takes cognizance of the dominant white minority attitudes by assessing their flexibility under changing political, social and economic cirumstances. The analysis '. . . leaves little room for illusions about the likelihood of the dominant white group undertaking the reforms, and the re-evaluation of their original definition of the situation, that economic rationality would apparently demand of them – that is, a definition that requires a complete break from dominance based simply on race'.

41   ASPECTS of black housing in South Africa Johannesburg: South Africa Foundation, 1981, 116 p.

Intends to promote understanding of black housing issues, by a presentation of papers delivered by experts reflecting various competing interests in this field. These include the state, private industry and local authorities. Contributors are Pauline Morris, Professor Wallace van Zyl, Dr Graeme J. Hardie, Dr C.F. Swart, Mark Louden, Bob Stevenson, A. Rabie, and T.P. Davis.

42   ATTWELL, Michael
        South Africa: background to the crisis.
        London: Sidgwick and Jackson, 1986, 224 p.

Based on research carried out for the current affairs programme 'Weekend World', this work examines the developing conflict in South Africa. From a study of the country's history, Attwell argues that the conflict is deeper than race alone. The roles of the Afrikaner and the British are analyzed, as are race relations, Western policy and interests. A scenario of the future is presented.

43   AUSTIN, Dennis
            Birds of a feather? The Commonwealth and
            South Africa, 1985. Round Table, 297, January
            1986, p. 14-21

            Comments on discussion by the Commonwealth Heads of
            Government Meeting at Nassau, October 1985 over South
            Africa and the question of sanctions. Decision has been
            deferred for six months until the committee urging
            reform on the P.W. Botha government has tabled their
            report.

44   AUSTIN, Dennis
            Britain and South Africa. London: Oxford
            University Press under the auspices of the
            Royal Institute of International Affairs,
            1966, 191 p.

            In view of the condemnation of the Verwoerd government,
            Austin states as his aim 'to measure the extent of
            British interests in South Africa, and the degree to
            which they are likely to influence United Kingdom
            policy towards the Republic'. Includes defence
            interests, trade, investments, gold, and a comparative
            examination of British involvement in Africa as a
            whole. Policy towards the Protectorates and the
            Namibian settlement issue is assessed, as well as the
            crisis in Rhodesia.

45   AUSTIN, Dennis
            South Africa 1984. Chatham House Papers, 26,
            1985, (entire issue: 80 p.)

            Provides a critical analysis of current developments
            and future prospects for a political settlement which
            embraces the black majority. He takes cognizance of the
            role Western powers could play and their choices with
            respect to South Africa's future; domestic factors such
            as the right-wing threat to the Nationalist government,
            the tricameral parliament, and the Republic's regional

role, including an interpretation of the Nkomati Accord. Reviewed by John Edward Spence in World Today, vol. 42, no. 1, January 1986, p.17; James Barber in International Affairs, vol. 62, no. 1, Winter 1985/86, p. 95

46   AUSTIN, Dennis
        The trinitarians: the 1983 South African constitution. Government and Opposition, vol. 20, no. 2, Spring 1985, p. 185-195

Provides an analysis of the constitution, which he describes as 'a constitutional form of apartheid tempered by necessity'.

47   AZEVEDO, Mario
        'A sober commitment to liberation?' Mozambique and South Africa 1974-1979. African Affairs, vol. 79, no. 317, October 1980, p. 567-584

Reviews the ties between the two countries, particularly in the field of trade, labour, harbour and railways, the Cahora Bassa Dam and notes the 'Mozambique would commit economic suicide if she were to sever ties with South Africa.'

48   BAKER, Donald G.
        The impact of regional events on whites in Rhodesia and South Africa. Plural Societies, vol. 10, no. 1, Spring 1979, p. 27-58

Describes events since the 1974 Portuguese coup d'etat and the sense of heightened threat experienced by whites in both countries. White attitudes and actions are surveyed, based mainly on the analyzes of Heribert Adam and R.W. Johnson. H.E. Dickie-Clark comments on Baker's perceptions in an article entitled: Do the South African whites need racial discrimination? Plural Societies, vol. 11, no. 1. Spring 1979, p. 27-58

49   BAKER, Donald
        Race, ethnicity and power: a comparative
        study. London: Routledge and Kegan Paul,
        1983, 243 p.

        Race and power in South Africa and Rhodesia: p. 79-113

        Describes the continued white hegemony which he
        accounts for by identifying three types of dominance:
        coercive, structural and psychosocial. Discusses
        political, social and economic structures which deprive
        blacks of resources and their mobilization capacities
        reviewed as strategies designed to preserve white power
        and privilege.

50   BALLINGER, Margaret
        From union to apartheid: a trek to
        isolation. Cape Town: Juta, 1969, 499 p.

        Records the author's personal impressions as a member
        of the South African Parliament in her capacity as a
        representative of the Africans, from the 1938
        Parliamentary session until the abolishment of African
        representation in 1960. Political events and
        developments are traced for the period under review
        illustrating the increasing entrenchment of apartheid
        policies.

51   BANTON, Michael
        Race relations. London: Tavistock, 1967,
        434 p.

        Chapter Eight: White supremacy in South
        Africa, p. 164-192

20

The South African case is seen against a background
outlining the political functions of racist ideology.
The author thereafter discusses ethnic and class
alliances among the whites; the inhibition of alliances
between subordinate groups, interpersonal relations,
and the economic dysfunctions of racism.

52   BARBER, James
        Afrikanerdom in disarray. World Today, vol.
        38, nos 7/8, July/August 1982, p. 288-296

Examines the split within the National Party which
Barber places in historical perspective. Major
confrontation over power sharing is discussed, as are
regional and class factors. Assesses future options.

53   BARBER, James
        BOSS in Britain. African Affairs, vol 82, no.
        328, July 1983, p. 311-328

Examines the activities of the South African Bureau of
State Security in Great Britain. Information is derived
from published sources, evidence from opponents of the
system, court cases and confessions of ex-spies. Case
studies are presented on the Republic's attempts to
infiltrate anti-apartheid groups and political parties
in exile.

54   BARBER, James
        South Africa: a society at war with itself.
        World Today, vol. 41, no. 7, July 1985, p.
        129-132

In a brief article, Barber considers the unrest
instigated by the Uitenhage shootings. The subsequent
breakdown of order in black urban areas and the renewed
vigour evident in black politics is examined, as are
the consequences of the tricameral constitution. The
status of white politics, as well as the government's
reform policy concludes this overview.

55   BARBER, James
        South Africa: the regional setting. <u>World Today</u>, vol. 42, no. 1, January 1986, p. 8-12

Concentrates on South Africa's position in Southern Africa. Illustrates that, although the Republic remains predominant within the region, its internal problems have affected regional issues, and that no clear overall policy is evident.

56   BARBER, James
        South Africa's foreign policy, 1945-1970. London: Oxford University Press, 1973, 325 p.

Author states that his decision to commence this study in 1945, and not in 1948 when the National Party came to power is 'because there are common characteristics in South Africa's international position and her foreign policy which stretch across the whole post-war period. These characteristics were not substantially altered by changes of government inside South Africa.' The work is chronologically divided into four parts: 1945 to 1948, the aftermath of war; 1948 to 1959 - the early years of National Party rule; 1960 to 1966 - the years of crisis and doubt, which saw the acceptance of isolation; 1966 to 1970, which Barber terms the years of confidence. Included in the latter chapter is an examination of the outward policy, dialogue in Africa, the limits of international cooperation, the ambivalence of western contacts, and the broad goals of the Republic's foreign policy.

57   BARBER, James
        The uneasy relationship: Britain and South Africa. London: Heinemann Educational Books for the Royal Institute of International Affairs, 1983, 142 p.

22

Emphasizes the British view of Anglo/South African relations and related topics including economic interests, British links with South Africa's neighbouring states, the interchange of people, organizations and diplomatic contacts. Examines Britain's vulnerability to international pressure resulting from its South African connections, and the role of British pressure groups is assessed. Appendix includes an analysis of both French and West German relations with the Republic, by Christopher R. Hill. Reviewed by Lucy Mair in African Affairs, vol. 82, no. 329, October 1983, p. 592-593

58   BARBER, James
      White South Africa - into the political unknown. World Today, vol. 39, no. 12, December 1983, p. 490-499

Identifies pertinent features of the 1983 constitutional proposals and illustrates that the government's victory is tempered by the divisions manifest in Afrikanerdom, black opposition, and the uncertainty generated as to the country's future political and constitutional developments.

59   BARKAT, Anwar M.
      Churches combating racism in South Africa. Journal of International Affairs, vol. 36, no. 2, Fall/Winter 1982/83, p. 297-305

Briefly identifies the role played by the World Council of Churches in promoting an awareness of racism in general, prior to focussing on the South African problem which he states 'provides a model for racism everywhere'. Assesses the contribution made by the Program to Combat Racism in working towards a just society.

60   BARRATT, John
       South African diplomacy at the UN IN:
       DIPLOMACY at the UN, edited by Geoff R.
       Berridge and A. Jennings. London: Macmillan,
       1985, p. 191-203

       Illustrates the failure of the United Nations to
       resolve the issues of South Africa's race policies and
       a settlement for Namibia through diplomatic means,
       within the conference context. Subsequently assesses
       the broader diplomatic value of the United Nations to
       South Africa through its continued representation at
       the organization. Although unable to attend formal
       meetings, being able to act as a 'listening post',
       disseminating information, and some bilateral contact
       are considered practical advantages.

61   BARRELL, Howard
       The United Democratic Front and National
       Forum: their emergence, composition and
       trends. South African Review, 2, 1984, p. 6-
       20

       Traces the origins and strategies of the United
       Democratic Front (UDF), placing in perspective its
       relations with other political and trade union
       organizations. The structure and programmes of both the
       UDF and the National Forum, seen as 'mechanisms for
       consultation and/or coordinated action between existing
       organisations' prompted debate as to how the issue of
       state power should be addressed.

62   BEINART, William
       The political economy of Pondoland, 1860-
       1930. Cambridge: Cambridge University Press,
       1982, 220 p.

Drawing extensively on the papers of officials administering the Transkeian Territories, and complemented by fieldwork conducted in Pondoland during 1976 and 1977, this work focusses on the process of colonization, with an emphasis on Eastern Pondoland. The influence of the developing South African industrial capitalism on the formerly independent Mpondo chiefdom is assessed under five headings. See also the book which he co-authored with Colin Bundy entitled: Hidden struggles in rural South Africa: policies and popular movements in the Transkei and Eastern Cape, 1890-1930. Berkley: University of California Press, 1986.

63   BEKKER, Simon and HUMPHRIES, Richard
        From control to confusion: the changing role of Administration Boards in South Africa, 1971-1983. Pietermaritzburg: Shuter & Shooter in association with the Institute of Social and Economic Research, 1985, (Rhodes University, Institute of Social and Economic Research, Occasional paper, no. 29), 258 p.

Traces the origins of Administration Boards in South Africa, taking cognizance of changes in their structure and function during the period 1971 to 1982. Features of the black population residing under the jurisdiction of Administration Boards in the decade 1970 to 1980 are presented, and their role in the black labour market, influx control, housing and local government is assessed. Finances of these Boards are scrutinized particularly from 1979 onwards. Appendices contain useful statistics.

64   BEKKER, Simon
        The plural society and the problem of order. Cape Town: University of Cape Town, 1974, 175 p.

        Thesis: Ph.D.

25

The author describes his thesis: 'This study focuses upon pluralism and the problem of order in society. Hereby, a new pluralist perspective is developed which avoids the pitfalls of the traditional approach, on the one hand, and yet retains the valid emphasis on pluralism, on the other.' Within this context, Bekker analyzes the work of four major pluralists J.S. Furnivall, M.G. Smith, Leo Kuper and Pierre van den Berge, amongst others. Possibilities for directions of change in a plural society are presented.

65   BELL, Trevor
       Industrial decentralisation in South Africa.
       Cape Town: Oxford University Press, 1973,
       304 p.

The author clarifies and elucidates on the regional distribution of economic activity in the Republic which he describes: 'The peculiar feature of planned industrial decentralisation in South Africa is that it forms an important part of the attempt to bring about racial separation on a regional basis. It is claimed that industrial decentralisation would in any case be desirable for social and economic reasons, but racial separation appears to be the overriding consideration.'

66   BELL, Trevor
       Unemployment in South Africa. Durban:
       University of Durban-Westville, Institute for
       Social and Economic Research, 1984,
       (University of Durban-Westville. Institute
       for Social and Economic Research. Occasional
       paper, 10), 54 p.

Considers theoretical and empirical issues on the nature and extent of unemployment. Investigates tendencies and causes evident in unemployment patterns, rates and the scope for government policies aimed at job creation.

67   BENCH, Bryan
        'Constructive engagement': the confused art
        of regional foreign policy. South African
        Review, 2, 1984, p. 197-210

Analyzes the policy as advocated by Chester Crocker,
the academic, and its subsequent adjustment into
potentially workable policies on his appointment as
Assistant Secretary of State for African Affairs.
Assesses effects on the policy, particularly on South
Africa.

68   BENSON, Mary
        Nelson Mandela. Harmondsworth: Penguin, 1986,
        269 p.

A largely updated version of the earlier work published
by Panaf in 1981, approximately half of which deals
with Mandela's career until his arrest in 1962 by the
South African police, and the Rivonia Trial. Thereafter
Benson concentrates on his prison period and the
development of the Mandela campaign in the 1970s and
80s. The biography quotes extensively from Mandela's
writings and correspondence, and was written with the
help of his family. Contains ten photographs, all pre-
dating 1963.

69   BENSON, Mary
        South Africa: the struggle for a birthright.
        Rev. ed. Harmondsworth: Penguin African
        Library, 1966, 314 p.
        Original Title: The African patriots

Reprinted in 1985 by the International Defence and Aid
Fund for Southern Africa, this work provides an account
of the African National Congress from its beginnings in
1912 until 1965. Based on many personal interviews, she
provides insight into the social, historical and
political contexts into which the liberation struggle
belongs.

70   BERGER, Iris
Sources of class consciousness: South African
women in recent labor struggles. International Journal of African Historical Studies,
vol. 16, no. 1, 1983, p. 49-66.

Describes women's participation in labour issues
especially over the past ten years. In order to assess
more fully the nature and sources of their class
consciousness, the author concentrates on the garment
and textile industries, which have the highest
concentration of women workers.

71   BERNSTEIN, Hilda
For their triumphs and for their tears: women
in apartheid South Africa. Rev. ed. London:
International Defence and Aid Fund for
Southern Africa, 1985, 136 p.

Laws, customs and circumstances of black women are
examined and their struggle against oppression and
exploitation in the apartheid system is documented.
Recounts how the movement of women to free themselves
has always been an integral part of the national
liberation process.

72   BHANA, Surendra and MESTHRIE, Uma S.
Passive resistance among Indian South
Africans: an historiographical survey.
South African Historical Journal, vol. 16,
November 1984. p. 118-131

Focusses on the historiography of three movements:
Satyagraha, 1906 to 1914, Passive Resistance, 1946 to
1948, and the 1952 Defiance Campaign.

28

73   A BIBLIOGRAPHICAL guide to South African economic
        development, edited by A.B. Lumby and M.D.
        North-Coombes. Durban: University of Natal,
        Department of Economic History, 1984, 520 p.

        Comprises over 8 000 items grouped into twelve major
        sections, with fifty-four subsections. The major topics
        include economic development, population and
        urbanization, labour, industrial relations and living
        standards; land and agriculture, mining, industrial
        development; aspects of the domestic economy; services
        including transportation, posts and communications,
        energy, water resources, education, health care and
        social services, tourism; banking and finance; role of
        the state; South Africa in the international economy,
        science, technology and the role of research.

74   BIBLIOGRAPHIES on South African political history,
        compiled by O. Geyser, P.W. Coetzer and J.H.
        Le Roux. Boston: Hall, 1978- (Bibliographies
        and guides in African studies) - vols

        Volume 1:   Register of private document collections on
                    the political history of South Africa since
                    1902
        Volume 2: General resources on South African
                    political history since 1902
        Volume 3: Index to periodical articles on South
                    African political history since 1902

75   BIKO, Steve
        Black Consciousness and the quest for a true
        humanity. Ufahamu, vol. 11, no. 1, Summer
        1981, p. 133-142

        This article, first published in Ufahamu, vol. 8, no.
        3, 1978, presents the tenets and development of the
        Black Consciousness Movement within the South African
        setting.

76   BIKO, Steve
            Black Consciousness in South Africa, edited
            by Millard Arnold. New York: Random House,
            1978, 298 p.

            Records Steve Biko's testimony, delivered on 3 to 7 May
            1976, at a trial in which defendants, all members of
            either the South African Students Organization or of
            the Black People's Convention, were accused of
            'endangering the maintenance of law and order in the
            Republic.' Biko's testimony reveals the nature and
            evolution of his political thinking, the formation and
            rationale of the Black Consciousness Movement, and
            other aspects of contemporary South African life
            including investment, and the need for a non-racial
            society.

77   BIKO, Steve
            I write what I like. Ufahamu, vol. 11, no. 1,
            Summer 1981, p. 143-148

            Reprint of an article first published in Ufahamu, vol.
            8, no. 3, 1978, in which Biko expounds on the dimension
            of fear as a determinant in South African politics,
            with regard to both blacks and whites.

78   BIKO, Steve
            I write what I like, edited by Aelred Stubbs.
            London: Bowerdean, 1978, 216 p.

            Comprises a selection of Biko's writings, which reflect
            his opinion on the South African Students'
            Organization, fragmentation of black resistance, Black
            Consciousness; Bantustans and some African cultural
            concepts. Concludes with a personal memoir on Biko
            written by Aelred Stubbs.

79   BISSELL, Richard E.
        Apartheid and international organizations.
        Boulder: Westview Press, 1977, 231 p.

        Investigates the impact of black African states,
        utilizing international forums, to press for a change
        in South Africa's racial policies.

80   BLACK leaders in Southern African history, edited by
        Christopher Saunders. London: Heinemann,
        1979, 160p.

        Presents biographical information on nine black leaders
        each placed within an historical framework - Ngqika,
        Mzilikazi, Mpande ka Senzangakhona, Mswati II,
        Cetshwayo ka Mpande, Masopha, Adam Kok, Tiyo Soga, and
        John Tengo Jabavu.

81   BLACK migration to South Africa: a selection of policy
        oriented research, edited by W.R. Böhning.
        Geneva: International Labour Office, 1981,
        184 p.

        Editor states that two key objectives dominated this
        research, firstly, methods in which the working and
        living conditions of both migrants and their families
        could be improved, and secondly, ways of reducing their
        dependency on South African employment opportunities
        under the migrant labour system, as constituted by the
        white ruling minority. Contributions include the
        following: Migrant labour supplies, past, present and
        future: with special reference to the gold-mining
        industry by C.W. Stahl; labour migration in Swaziland
        by F. de Vletter, and others; conditions affecting
        black migrant workers in South Africa: a case-study of
        the gold-mines by F. de Vletter; easing the plight of
        migrant workers' families in Lesotho by Elizabeth
        Gordon; computer simulation and migration planning, by

W. Woods, and others; reducing dependence on migration in Southern Africa by C.W. Stahl and W.R. Böhning. This latter paper was reprinted in STUDIES in international labour migration, edited by W.R. Böhning. London: Macmillan, 1984, p. 191-223.

82   The BLACK People's Convention (BPC) - South Africa: historical background and basic documents, edited by Sipho Buthelezi. New York: Black Liberation Press, 1978, 32 p.

This booklet carries a message of tribute to Steve Biko prior to sketching the history of the movement. The remainder consists of the BPC constitution.

83   BLACK RENAISSANCE CONVENTION, 1984
      Black renaissance, edited by Thoalane Thoalane. Johannesburg: Ravan, 1986, 75 p.

Comprises the 1984 conference papers which can be regarded as crucial to the understanding of Black Consciousness. Includes the following: G.M. Nkondo on education, Manas Buthelezi on Black Theology, M.P. Gwala on Black Consciousness, Fatima Meer on Black women, Sam Motsuenyane on Black Consciousness and the economic position of the black man, Harold Nxasana and Foszia Fisho on the labour situation, the Reverend M.H. Zwane on social communications, and Professor J.H. Cone focusses on the black church.

84   BLACK trade unions in South Africa: core of a new democratic opposition movement? Bonn: Friedrich Ebert Stiftung, 1983, 120 p.

Proceedings of a workshop organized in November 1983 by the Friedrich-Ebert-Stiftung, focussing particularly on the status of trade unions in South Africa post the 1979 reforms, and the development of the emerging unions. The following papers were contributed: Weiner Puschra's presentation of a brief history of trade unionism in South Africa: organizational trends, achievements and potential of the labour movement in South Africa in the post Wiehahn period (1979 to 1983) by Eddie Webster; the changing labour market of the seventies and state strategies of reform, by Robert V. Lambert; developments in South African labour legislation since Wiehahn, by Charles Nupen; and some problems of international labour policies towards South Africa, by Mike Murphy.

85   BLACK viewpoint, edited by B.S. Biko. Durban: Sprocas Black Community Programmes, 1972, 67 p.

Contains the following contributions, listed under their chapter headings: Black development, by Ngabulo Ndebele; the new day, by C.M.C. Ndamse; Kwa-Zulu development by M.G. Buthelezi: the new Black, by Bennie A. Khoapa.

86   BLACK villagers in an industrial society: anthropolo- gical perspectives on labour migration in South Africa, edited by Philip Mayer. Cape Town: Oxford University Press, 1980, 369 p.

Based on extensive fieldwork conducted under the auspices of the Migrant Labour Project, undertaken at Rhodes University in the period 1976 to 1979, the contributors demonstrate the effect on the lives and families participating in the migrant labour system. Contributors include Philip Mayer, William Beinart, Andrew D. Spiegel, C.W. Manona, P.A. McAllister, M.C. O'Connell, J.K. McNamara.

87   The BLACK who's who of Southern Africa today, compiled and edited by Sheila Keeble. 2nd ed. Johannesburg: African Business Publications, 1982, 336 p.

Preceded by a general reference section noting incumbents of ministerial, parliamentary and university posts, profiles follow in alphabetical sequence.

88   BLOCH, Graeme
        Sounds in the silence: painting a picture of
        the 1960s. Africa Perspective, no. 25, 1984,
        p. 3-23

In what Bloch states is a discursive rather than academic essay, he defines the major characteristics of the 1960s in South Africa 'as an example of a brief era of social stability and ruling class confidence. It holds lessons in terms of understanding the state, but also the inevitability of social contradictions in a class and racially divided nation'. Takes cognizance of restructuring the repressive apparatuses and the changing nature of economic conditions.

89   BLOCH, Robin and WILKINSON, Peter
        Urban control and popular struggle: a survey
        of state urban policy, 1920-1970.
        African Perspective, no. 20, 1982, p. 2-40

Intended essentially as a survey of the fifty-year period of the South African state's urban policy, this paper is largely based on Bloch's B.A. Honours dissertation entitled: The state in the townships: state, popular struggle and urban crisis in South Africa, 1970-1980, (Johannesburg: University of the Witwatersrand, 1981).

90   BLUMENFELD, J.P.
        The South African economy: potential and
        pitfalls. World Today, vol. 36, no. 9,
        September 1980, p. 334-342

34

Identifies the nature and extent of economic changes during the late 1970s, and assesses both strengths and weaknesses evident in the economy. Elaborates on the possible problem areas which he categorizes into inflation, imports and exports, black unemployment, trade unions, and skilled labour.

91   BOESAK, Allan
      Black and reformed: apartheid, liberation and the Calvinist tradition. Johannesburg: Skotaville in association with Orbis Books, 1984, (Black theology series, no. 2), 176 p.

Mainly comprises a collection of addresses delivered by Dr Boesak during the period 1974 to 1983 illustrating his own position and the experience of black South Africans.

92   BOESAK, Allan
      Farewell to innocence: a socio-ethical study of black theology and black power. Johannesburg: Ravan, 1977, 140 p.

Originally submitted for the degree of Doctor of Divinity at the Theological Academy of the John Calvin Foundation, Kampen in the Netherlands, this study examines the relationship between black power and black theology, after a definition of the two concepts. Concludes with a directive for an ethic of liberation as an ethic for black theology.

93   BÖHMER, E.W.
      A bibliographical and historical study of left radical movements and some alleged left radical movements in South Africa and Namibia, 1900-1981. Stellenbosch: University of Stellenbosch, Institute for the Study of Marxism, 1985, 1 250 p.

Awarded a Master's Degree cum laude, this bibliographical study comprises 5 039 entries with the concentration of material being available in South Africa. Historical overviews and five indexes - author, subject, name, journals and court cases complement this research tool. It also includes two addenda - on the subject-terms and a list of all persons, organizations and journals banned in the Republic. Main topics covered include black resistance movements, communist organizations, Trotskyite organizations, multiracial organizations, trade unions, political unrest, and international anti-apartheid organizations.

94   BOOTH, D.G.
        International sporting tours of South Africa:
        a critical comment. Transafrica Forum, vol.
        3, no. 2, Winter 1986, p. 25-42

Presents the viewpoints of a diverse selection of people in an attempt to assess the differing opinions of both pro-sporting tour supporters and anti-tour demonstrators. Illustrates the complexity of multiracial sport in South Africa, the role of sports tours, and assesses the degree of support amongst South Africans for international sporting boycotts against the country.

95   BOOYSEN, Susan and KOTŹE, Hennie
        The political socialization of isolation: a
        case study of the Afrikaner student youth.
        Politikon, vol. 12, no. 2, December 1985, p.
        23-46

The premise of this article is that politically the Afrikaner youth is socialized into isolation. On the one hand, homogeneity of political influences resulting from socialization agents furthers isolation. On the other hand, through lack of political participation, Afrikaner youth does not come into contact with infuences which may effect political change. To test

this premise, survey data were drawn from a research
project conducted among Afrikaner student youth. The
following facets of their socialization process were
analyzed: homogeneity of partisan identification among
socialization agents, low levels of political
participation which reinforce isolation from political
realities, the effect of political trust and efficacy.
(Author's abstract: Booysen and Kotzé were members of
the Department of Political Studies at the Rand
Afrikaans University, Johannesburg at the time of
writing.)

96   BOTHA, P. Roelf
        South Africa: plan for the future; a basis
        for dialogue. Johannesburg: Perskor, 1978,
        250 p.

Seeks to contribute to the debate on South Africa's
development by drawing up a plan for the future, based
on a synthesis of alternative strategies. Adhering to
established planning methodology 'this book seeks to
synthetise a vision for the future of South Africa, a
Plan for the Future, which, while emphasising spatial
organisation in the physical sense, nevertheless may
also suggest social, economic and political structures
which will fit into the spatial structure to produce a
harmonious dispensation for the future'. Advocates a
policy of pluralism necessitating territorial units.

97   BOTHA, P.W.
        Manifesto for the future. Pretoria:
        Department of Foreign Affairs, 1985, 14 p.

President Botha outlined his manifesto for South Africa
in an address to the annual congress of the National
Party in Durban on 15 August 1985.

98   BOTHA, P.W.
         Peace initiatives in Southern Africa. South
         Africa International, vol. 15, no. 2, October
         1984, p. 66-72. (With a response by S.
         Manyane, p. 73-75.)
         Text of an address delivered to the German Foreign
         Policy Association in Bonn on 5 June 1984 in which he
         discusses current South African regional policy as far
         back as the early 1960s. In the reply by an Account
         Executive at TWS Public Relations, Manyane refutes many
         of the Prime Minister's statements and draws attention
         to South Africa's destabilization policies.

99   BOTTARO, Jean
         Education   and   development: Carnegie
         Commissions   and   South   Africa.   Africa
         Perspective, no. 26, 1985, p. 3-28

         Examines   reasons   for   the   Carnegie   Corporation's
         involvement   with   African   education,   and   their
         relationship with South Africa. This information is
         provided against the background of their Investigation
         into the Poor White Problem, 1929-1932, and the Inquiry
         into Poverty and Development in Southern Africa, 1982-
         1985, which are analyzed in some detail.

100   BOUCH, Richard
         Aspects of party organization in the Cape
         Province, 1910-1924. South African Historical
         Journal, vol. 15, 1983, p. 105-124

         Provides a political history of the South African
         National Party, known as the South African Party (SAP)
         when the National Party was formed in 1914. Reasons for
         schism within the SAP are detailed. The establishment
         of the Cape National Party, as one of the new parties
         established in each province, is described, together
         with reasons for its entrenchment.

101 BOULLE, L.J.
South Africa and the consociational option: a
constitutional analysis. Cape Town: Juta,
1984, 270 p.

Focusses on constitutional developments in South Africa
which are placed in historical context. Western
constitutionalism in the guise of British
parliamentarism and American presidentialism are
described and compared. Thereafter the theories of
pluralism and consociationalism are analyzed as factors
within the emerging constitutional arrangements. The
constitutions of 1977 and 1983 are assessed, as is the
role of the President's Council in this process.
Appendix contains the Republic of South Africa
Constitution Act, 110 of 1983.

102 BOWMAN, Larry W.
The strategic importance of South Africa to
the United States: an appraisal and policy
analysis. African Affairs, vol. 81, no. 323,
April 1982, p. 159-191

Divided into two sections, this paper initially
propounds arguments both for and against the Republic's
strategic significance. Thereafter the policy
implications for the United States are assessed.
Suggests that the United States will follow a
vacillating policy for about five years in their
reluctance to relinquish their preference for peaceful
change. He forsees however, that they will ultimately
have no recourse but to impose severe measures
including oil sanctions and disinvestment.

103 BOZZOLI, Belinda
The political nature of a ruling class:
capital and ideology in South Africa, 1890-
1933. London: Routledge & Kegan Paul, 1981
384 p.

Uses the South African case to illustrate the relationship between the political and ideological features of particular capitalist societies. Studies the role of those concerned in shaping the processes of state and class formation from the days dating from the emergence of a mining bourgeoisie. Reviewed by Baruch Hirson in an article entitled: Marxists, neo-Marxists and labour history in South Africa. Journal of Commonwealth and Comparative Politics, vol 21, no. 1, March 1983, p. 80-85.

104   BRADFORD, Helen
        Lynch law and labourers: the ICU in Umvoti, 1927-1928. Journal of Southern African Studies, vol. 11, no. 1, 1984, p. 128-149

Provides a detailed account of the mass support achieved by the Industrial and Commercial Workers' Union in the Greytown area of the Umvoti county. Presents historical background on the ICU, reasons for its support by blacks, the role of the farmers and details of the ensuing friction.

105   BRANDEL-SYRIER, Mia
        Reef town elite: a study of social mobility in a modern African community on the Reef. London: Routledge & Kegan Paul, 1971, 335 p.

The life and career histories of sixty African men, considered the elite of Reeftown during the period 1960-1962, are chronicled in detail in order to assess reasons for their upward social mobility.

106   BREWER, John D.
        The membership of Inkatha in KwaMashu. African Affairs, vol. 84, no. 334, January 1985, p. 111-135

Author states that in this article, an empirical study of Inkatha membership in KwaMashu township in KwaZulu is reported and relevant data extracted, prior to reviewing existent knowledge on Inkatha membership. Thereafter, this information is presented within its empirical context. The author, at the time of writing, is at the Department of Social Studies, Queen's University of Belfast.

107   BREWER John D.
        Official ideology and lay members' belief in Inkatha. Politikon, vol. 12, no. 1, June 1985, p. 57-63

The author presents an abstract of his work as follows: 'The size, loyalty and commitment of Inkatha's members is seen as a vital element to Inkatha's importance in current South African politics. It is claimed to strengthen Buthelezi's bargaining position with the state and to differentiate Inkatha's support from the much less committed support of affiliate-based organizations like the United Democratic Front. Yet this assumption about Inkatha's lay members cannot be taken for granted, given the paucity of the empirical data on Inkatha membership. One measure of this commitment is the extent to which lay members have internalized the movement's official ideology. It is thus evident in the degree of coherence between official ideology and the beliefs of lay members. This paper reports on empirical research amongst a sample of Inkatha's members in Kwa Mashu in order to assess this coherence.'

108   BREYTENBACH, W.J.
        Bantoetuislande, verkiesings en politieke partye (Bantu homelands, elections and political parties.) Pretoria: Africa Institute of South Africa, 1974, (Africa Institute of South Africa. Mededelinge, no. 23), 147 p.

Traces the historical background to the homeland concept, constitutional and political developments, particularly in Transkei. Includes the manifestoes of the various political parties.

109   BREYTENBACH, W.J.
The new South African constitution and its implications for development. <u>Development Southern Africa</u>, vol. 1, no. 1, May 1984, p. 66-74

As then Senior Constitutional Planner, Department of Constitutional Development and Planning, Pretoria, Dr Breytenbach summarizes this article as follows: The new constitutional dispensation will stimulate development activities for the Coloureds and Indians through community development and basic needs programmes which are mainly categorized as "own affairs". Local government institutions will become important additional instruments in this respect. The development backlog of Coloureds and Indians and its implications are sketched and expectation is expressed that the dynamics of the new situation will lead to greater public expenditure for these needs. However, political demands for the realisation of development goals, could outpace societal progress in terms of community development approaches, while the demographic distribution of Coloureds and Indians militates somewhat against their optimal drawing of benefit from decentralisation policies.

110   BRIDGE or barricade? The constitution: a first appraisal, edited by Fleur de Villiers. Johannesburg: Ball in association with the Sunday Times, 1983, 141 p.

Series of short newspaper articles in which the new dispensation was debated from various standpoints. Reproduces the Constitution Bill in full prior to the presentation of sixteen contributions by the following:

Marinus Wiechers, Lawrence Schlemmer, Willie Esterhuyse, Bhadra Ranchod, Otto Krause, David Welsh, Sampie Terreblanche, Harry Schwarz, André Thomashausen, Robert Schrire, Hermann Giliomee, R.E. van der Ross, Oscar Dhlomo, Peter Collins, Andre du Pisani, and Fleur de Villiers.

111   BROOKES, Edgar H. and MACAULAY, J.B.
        Civil liberty in South Africa. Cape Town:
        Oxford University Press, 1958, 175 p.

        Traces the decline of civil liberty in South Africa.
        Considers the rule of law, the police force, the
        franchise and whether racial discrimination is
        fundamental in South African law. Analyzes freedom from
        the viewpoint of movement, expression, economic,
        educational, religious and social aspects. Highlights
        the relevant legislation which curtails these freedoms.

112   BROOKES, Edgar H.
        History of native policy in South Africa:
        from 1830 to the present day. 2nd ed.
        Pretoria: van Schaik, 1927, 524 p.

        Presents an investigation of the institutional aspect
        of this policy derived from primary sources, and based
        on an assessment of the study, an attempt to deduce
        what direction future policy should take. Among others,
        chapters include information pertinent to history,
        policy and law, administration, segregation and the
        land question, land tenure, agriculture, labour and
        industry, religion and education.

113   BROOKES, Edgar H.
        White rule in South Africa, 1830-1910:
        varieties in governmental policies affecting
        Africans. Pietermaritzburg: University of
        Natal Press, 1974, 223 p.

An extensive revision of: The History of Native policy in South Africa, 1924 (2nd ed: 1927), q.v., in which the author attempts to delineate ways in which white governments, both colonial and republican, governed blacks within their jurisdiction for the six decades under review. Concludes with a brief summary of post-Union policies.

114   BROOKS, Alan and BRICKHILL, Jeremy
       Whirlwind before the storm: the origins of the uprising in Soweto and the rest of South Africa, from June to December 1976. London: International Defence and Aid Fund for Southern Africa, 1981, 368 p.

As indicated by the title, this work extensively provides both reasons for the 1976 uprising with a focus on the crisis in the schools, as well as details of events.

115   BROTZ, Howard
       The politics of South Africa: democracy and racial diversity. Oxford: Oxford University Press, 1977, 164 p.

An American sociologist examines the possibilities for change by constitutional means. He assesses apartheid South Africa from the aspects of its political history, the relationship between economics and politics, and within its social framework. He concludes with an analysis of Chief Justice H.A. Fagan's practical contribution to the debate on South African race relations, and also to the guide-lines indicated in the 1948 Native Laws Commission Report.

116   BROUARD, Pierre
         African rights and the 1986 Parliamentary
         Session.   Johannesburg: South   African
         Institute of Race Relations, 1986, (South
         African Institute of Race Relations. Topical
         briefing), 11 p.

         Highlighted by township unrest, both external and
         internal   pressure,   and   the government's   reform
         programme,   author states that these rights will be one
         of the 1986 Parliamentary Session's major issues. Draws
         together various statements on political change made by
         the government in 1985, and indicates those to which no
         answer has yet been forthcoming.

117   BROUGHTON, Morris
         Press and politics of South Africa. Cape
         Town: Purnell, 1961, 306 p.

         Divided   into   two   separate   sections,   the   author
         initially focusses on the press, concentrating on   the
         role   and   significance   of   the   English   press.
         Demonstrates   that the 'ethical and actual value of the
         freedom   of   the press has   become   vitiated'.   In   the
         second part entitled - Politics, Broughton presents an
         analysis   covering   such topics as   the   Englishman   and
         Afrikaner; the collapse of liberalism, the two parties,
         blacks, and apartheid, amongst others.

118   BROWN, Douglas
         Against   the   world: a study of white   South
         African   attitudes. London: Collins,   1966,
         222 p.

         A distillation of conversations illustrating   attitudes
         and   opinions   of 'white Africans' and describing   what
         this means in the South African context.

45

119   BRUTUS, Dennis
       South Africa and the Olympics: an interview
       ... by Ed Ferguson. Ufahamu, vol. 13, no 2/3,
       1984, p. 40-59

       An interview with Professor Brutus in his capacity as
       President of the South African Non-Racial Olympic
       Committee, and Chairperson of the International
       Committee against Racism in Sport.

120   BUCKLAND, Peter
       The education crisis in South Africa:
       restructuring the policy discourse.
       Social Dynamics, vol. 8, no. 1, 1982, p. 14-
       28

       Examines, compares and places in context, three key
       education policy documents, namely the de Lange, Syncom
       and Buthelezi reports. Argues that the education issue
       is a manifestation of South Africa's deeper structural
       crisis.

121   BUDLENDER, Debbie
       A critique of poverty datum lines. Cape Town:
       Southern Africa Labour and Development
       Research Unit, 1985, (Southern Africa Labour
       and Development Research Unit. Saldru working
       paper, no. 63), 22 p.

       Provides a brief history of poverty datum lines in
       South Africa, and critically discusses levels and
       theoretical foundations.

122   BUIS, Robert
       Religious beliefs and white prejudice.
       Johannesburg: Ravan, 1975, 71 p.

Based on the results of a survey, the author attempts to provide an explanation of certain aspects of racial attitudes in South Africa. The particular emphasis of his study is to establish whether there are links between certain religious beliefs held by whites and their attitudes towards black South Africans.

123   BUNDY, Colin
       Land and liberation: the South African national liberation movements and the agrarian question, 1920s-1960s. Review of African Political Economy, no. 29, 1984, p. 14-29

As stated in the author's abstract: 'This paper asks how the national movements viewed rural issues between the 1920s and 1960s, what attention they devoted to rural mobilisation, and how their perceptions and efforts altered over time. It suggests that, given a society which saw wars of conquest and territorial dispossession in the 19th century, given the Land Acts of 1913 and 1936, and given the different forms of expropriation and exploitaiton historically visited upon peasants, labour tenants, farm labourers and migrant workers, the agrarian question has not been accorded the theoretical or practical attention one might have anticipated.' Focusses particularly on the rural struggle in the Transkei against aspects of state policy in the 1940s and 1950s. Specific attention is paid to the role of the African National Congress, the All African Convention, Govan Mbeki and the Transkeian Organised Bodies.

124   BUNDY, Colin
       Resistance in the reserves: the A.A.C. and the Transkei. Africa Perspective, no. 22, 1983, p. 51-61

Focusses on the local struggles in the Transkei, the rural grievances which shaped them and the role of the All African Convention in co-ordinating and broadening this resistance in the late 1940s and 1950s. Stresses in particular, the part played by I.B. Tabata.

125   BUNDY, Colin
        The rise and fall of the South African
        peasantry. Berkeley: University of California
        Press. 1979, (Perspectives on Southern
        Africa, no. 28), 276 p.

With particular emphasis on conditions in the Cape, Bundy concentrates on the period 1870 to 1913 in this analysis of African agriculture, illustrating the transformation from pastoralist cultivators to proletarians and providing an explanation of South Africa's development and level of underdevelopment. For a review see: Peasants, capitalists, and historians: a review article. Journal of Southern African Studies, vol. 7, no. 2, April 1981, p 284-314. A further substantial critique and reassessment of this work is presented by Jack Lewis, Journal of Southern African Studies, vol. 11, no. 1, October 1984, p. 1-24. Attention too, should be drawn to Bundy's important article entitled: The rise and decline of a South African peasantry. African Affairs, vol. 71, 1972, p. 369-388.

126   BUNTING, Brian
        Apartheid: the road to poverty. Cape Town:
        Real Printing and Publishing, 1959, 12 p.

Reprint of articles published in the issues of New Age, 18 June, 25 June and 2 July 1959.

48

127   BUNTING, Brian
       Education for apartheid. London: Christian
       Action for the Southern Africa Education
       Fund, 1971, 34 p.

       An overview which takes the following points into
       consideration: segregation policies, ten years of Bantu
       education, state expenditure, African teachers,
       mother-tongue education, matriculation results, equal
       standards, university apartheid, staff unequality,
       student enrolment, university standards, vocational
       training, and student disturbances.

128   BUNTING, Brian
       Moses Kotane: South African revolutionary.
       London: Inkululeko Publications, 1973, 309 p.

       Written by a political colleague in honour of Kotane's
       birthday in 1973, this is a detailed biographical
       history of the General Secretary of the Communist Party
       of South Africa, who held the position from 1939 until
       his death in 1979. Contains frequent excerpts of his
       writing and is based largely on Party documentation,
       reports in the Party press, and personal reminiscences.

129   BUNTING, Brian
       The rise of the South African reich. rev. ed.
       Harmondsworth: Penguin African Library, 1969,
       552 p.

       Based on considerable original research, the author
       provides a general history of South African politics.
       Argues that the state became fascist with the National
       Party's accession to power.

130   BUNTING, Brian
       Who runs our newspapers: the story behind the
       non-white press. Cape Town: Pioneer Printers,
       1959, 9 p.

Indicates that the press is dominated by big business which reflects their interests, prior to assessing general circulation. Discusses The World in terms of African readers, as well as Drum and Zonk; the National Party orientated paper Bona, the papers reflecting Coloured interests - Torch and Golden City Post; the African National Congress paper Ikhwezi Lomso; and Indian readership. Stresses the importance of New Age which, although not specifically for blacks, advocates equal rights.

131   BUNTING, Sidney Percival
        Imperialism and South Africa. Johannesburg:
        Communist Party of South Africa, 1928, - p.

Unseen.

132   BURCHELL, David E.
        Adams College, Natal, c. 1920-1956: a criti-
        cal assessment. University of Durban-West-
        ville. Journal. New Series, 1, 1984, p. 151-
        159

Investigates the origins, objectives, and achievements of the College, highlighting its trend-setting role. Consequences of the government take-over and its transformation to a Zulu Training School are discussed, and a brief evaluation of its importance in missionary education is presented.

133   BUREAU FOR ECONOMIC RESEARCH RE BANTU DEVELOPMENT
        Bophuthatswana at independence. Pretoria:
        Benbo, 1977, 133 p.

A general survey divided into two sections: the country, its people and economy, and secondly, national economy and development programmes. Contains numerous statistical tables.

134   BUREAU FOR ECONOMIC RESEARCH RE BANTU DEVELOPMENT
       Transkei economic review, 1975. Pretoria:
       Benbo, 1975, 76 p.

       A general survey, including numerous tables, on the
       following topics: historical review, political
       development, physiography, population, national
       accounts, employment and income, development of human
       potential, social services, government administration,
       and infrastructure. Reviews based on the same format
       are also available for Ciskei, Gazankulu, Kangwane, and
       QwaQwa.

135   BUSINESS in the shadow of apartheid: U.S. firms in
       South Africa, edited by Jonathan Leape, Bo
       Baskin and Stefan Underhill. Lexington:
       Lexington Books, 1985, 242 p.

       This analysis is based mainly on the proceedings of a
       conference entitled: U.S. Firms in South Africa, held
       during 1982. The role of these firms and their
       activities to effect change is critically examined by a
       group comprising mainly South African politicians,
       scholars and businessmen within the framework of United
       States economic interests, and the relationship between
       these and those of black South Africans. Includes
       useful appendices on South African statistics; the
       United States business presence in the Republic;
       disinvestment; divestment; the Sullivan Principles;
       federal and state actions; and United States
       contributions to black South African development.

136   BUTHELEZI COMMISSION
       The requirements for stability and
       development in KwaZulu and Natal. Durban: H &
       H Publications, (1982), 2 vols

       Presents the findings of a forty-five person Commission
       established on black initiative which was 'asked to

explore the possibility of finding a way, within the overall framework of the Republic of South Africa, of developing a regional constitutional arrangement which might provide an alternative to the programmes to which the white political parties have become committed'. Complemented by substantial statistical data and maps.

137   BUTHELEZI, Mangosuthu Gatsha
        Power is ours. New York: Books in Focus, 1979, 198 p.

A compilation of speeches providing insights into the complexities of South Africa by Buthelezi in his capacity as chief executive officer of the KwaZulu homeland, president of the National Cultural Liberation Movement (Inkatha) and chairman of the South African Black Alliance. Attention should be drawn to a critical assessment of Buthelezi and the Inkatha movement by Gerhard Maré and Georgina Stevens entitled: Appetite for power: Buthelezi's Inkatha and the politics of loyal resistance. Johannesburg: Ravan, 1986, 320 p.

138   BUTHELEZI, Qedusizi
        Bilingual education and segregation in South Africa: with special reference to black education. Ufahamu, vol.11, no. 3, Spring 1982, p. 169-187

Examines the bilingual education experienced in South Africa as compared to universally acknowledged bilingual typologies. Indicates the urgent need to evaluate the bilingual programmes in black schools given the nature of education, conditions within the schools, and the level of teacher-training.

139   BUTLER, Jeffrey (and others)
The Black homelands of South Africa: the
political and economic development of
Bophuthatswana and KwaZulu, by Jeffrey
Butler, Robert I. Rotberg and John Adams.
Berkeley: University of California Press,
1977. (Perspectives on Southern Africa, no.
21), 250 p.

This critique of the South African government's
balkanization policy is presented with special
reference to pre-'independent' Bophuthatswana and
KwaZulu which has refused to accept this
'independence'. The policy is examined within its
political, economic and legislative framework, as well
as a study of the administration of these homelands.
Biographical information is provided on the leaders –
Lucas Mangope and Gatsha Buthelezi, and their policies
and programmes are discussed. All aspects of the two
homelands' economies are assessed, and the study
concludes with a prognosis for the future.

140   BUZAN, Barry and NAZARETH, H.O.
South Africa versus Azania: the implications
of who rules. International Affairs, vol. 62,
no. 1, Winter 1985/86, p. 35-40

Provides a scenario of features relevant to Azania when
it finally emerges, and insight into how it could fit
into the set of international relations now occupied by
South Africa. Bases his assumptions on an Azania
emerging from a political settlement to avoid full-
scale civil war, as experienced in Zimbabwe.

141   CACHALIA, Firoz
The state, crisis and restructuring: 1970-
1980. Africa Perspective, no. 23, 1983, p. 3-
45

Written before the formation of the United Democratic Front, this paper as stated by the author,is an attempt to theorize the relevance and importance of the forum that an alliance such as the UDF would represent. Based on the final chapter of his Honours dissertation, entitled: Indian representation, popular struggle and the state, 1860-1980: an historical perspective. (Johannesburg: University of the Witwatersrand, 1983), the author focusses both on the nature of the capitalist South African state, the deepening economic crisis, and changes in the labour system. A detailed examination of changes in the state's political processes is given. Specific attention is paid to the changing mode of Indian representation, and in particular on the President Council's recommendations.

142   CALLINICOS, Alex and ROGERS, John
        Southern Africa after Soweto. 2nd ed. London:
        Pluto, 1978, 246 p.

Central to the analysis of the changing political situation within Southern Africa, is the role of Western domination of the region, operative through the South African capitalist system. Examines regional politics since the Portuguese coup of 25 April 1974, with special reference to the then Rhodesia, Zambia, Angola, the 1976 Soweto riots and the United States role. Assesses future prospects.

143   CALPIN, G.H.
        Indians in South Africa. Pietermaritzburg:
        Shuter and Shooter, 1949, 310 p.

Discusses the history of Indian immigration to South Africa, their contribution and relevant government policies up to the time of the 1949 African revolt against the Indians.

144   CALPIN, G.H.
        There are no South Africans. London: Nelson,
        1941, 412 p.

        Examines the white minority in South Africa from the
        earliest times, presenting a picture of their role,
        attitudes and differences.

145   CARRIM, Yunus
        Cosatu: working-class politics to the fore.
        Work in Progress, no. 40, 1986, p. 4-13

        Examines the formation of the largest ever trade union
        federation in South Africa's history, the Congress of
        South African Trade Unions. It represents unions in
        almost all economic sectors, including mining, metals,
        automobiles, chemicals, textiles, food, transport, wood
        and paper, municipal services, commercial and catering.
        Concludes it will have much political weight, despite
        differences within the federation.

146   CARTER, Gwendolen Margaret
        The politics of inequality: South Africa
        since 1948. London: Thames and Hudson, 1958,
        535 p.

        In this political study of South Africa after the
        National Party came to power in 1948, Gwendolen Carter
        broadly examines Afrikaner nationalism in all its
        facets with special reference to the 1953 election.
        Useful appendices include the programmes of principles
        and objectives of South African political parties and
        groups.

147   CARTER, Gwendolen Margaret (and others)
        South Africa's Transkei: the politics of
        domestic colonialism, by Gwendolen Margaret
        Carter, Thomas Karis and Newell M. Stultz.
        Evanston: Northwestern University Press,
        1967, (Northwestern University. African
        studies, no. 19), 200 p.

Examines, as background, both external and internal pressures which resulted in the implementation of territorial separate development. Application of the policy in its various stages and the government's motives forms the basis of this study.

148   CARTER, Gwendolen Margaret
        Which way is South Africa going? Bloomington:
        Indiana University Press, 1980, 162 p.

Interwoven within this analysis of South African politics and economics, Carter explores the formation of both Afrikaner and African nationalism, Black Consciousness and the role of the homelands within the policy of separate development.

149   CASSAR, Paul
        Dr F. van Zyl Slabbert: the emergence of a
        key figure. Journal of Contemporary History,
        vol. 10, no. 3, December 1985, p. 1-24

Concentrates on the development of van Zyl Slabbert's political life which led him from his upbringing as part of traditionally Afrikaner nationalist family to the leadership of the official opposition, the Progressive Federal Party. Details his transition from academic life to active party politics, formative influences on his thinking, and reasons for his rise to prominence.

150   CATHOLIC INSTITUTE FOR INTERNATIONAL RELATIONS
        South Africa in the 1980s. rev. ed. London:
        The Institute, 1983, 51 p.

Updates the 1980 edition and includes an additional section on trade unions. Divided into two parts, this study discusses the national security of the state and apartheid which includes discussion on the origins of the latter, national security ideology and industrial and commercial interests. The second section comments on the prospects for black nationalism. This includes discussion on the Black Consciousness Movement during the decade of 1966-77; class, race and national liberation; Inkatha; the ANC; radicalization of black nationalism, and the black trade unions.

151   CATHOLIC INSTITUTE FOR INTERNATIONAL RELATIONS
       War and conscience in South Africa: the churches and conscientious objection. London: The Institute and Pax Christi, 1982, 112 p.

Demonstrates the increasing militarization of South Africa, the role of war resisters and the response of Christian Churches. Highlights the increasing rift between these churches and the South African government.

152   CELL, John W.
       The highest stage of white supremacy: the origins of segregation in South Africa and the American south. Cambridge: Cambridge University Press, 1982, 320 p.

Concentrating on the period 1890 to 1925, the author compares 'the evolving matrix of race and class relations in two societies that are regarded as the most pervasively racist in the world, South Africa and the Southern United States.' In particular, he considers the origins and ideology of segregation and concludes by gauging reactions to the system. Based mainly on a combination of secondary and contemporary published sources.

153   CHALLENGE to the church: a theological comment on the political crisis in South Africa - the Kairos Document. Johannesburg: Kairos Theologians, 1986, 28 p.

Preface states '. . . it is a critique of the current theological models that determine the type of activities the Church engages in to try to resolve the problems of the country. It is an attempt to develop, out of this perplexing situation, an alternative biblical and theological model that will in turn lead to forms of activity that will make a real difference to the future of our country'.

154   CHANGE in contemporary South Africa, edited by Leonard M. Thompson and Jeffrey Butler. Berkeley: University of California Press, 1975, (Perspectives on Southern Africa, 17), 447 p.

Considers in detail the process of change, both within the white and black communities themselves, the instruments of coercion utilized by the dominant white ruling class; the role of the Indians and an examination of major group interaction. External factors are taken into consideration, including the impact of change on the Republic both within surrounding territories and internationally.

155   CHANGE in South Africa, edited by D.J. van Vuuren (and others). Durban: Butterworths, 1983, 483p.

Seventeen aspects of socio-economic and political change and their implications are analyzed in an attempt to provide the reader with an insight to developments within the Republic at the time of writing. The following topics are included: constitutional law, the political system, administration, urbanization, black local government, industrial relations, manpower development, education, sport, social indicators for change, the roles both of the church and the press, a case study of Coloured and Indian perceptions of change, strategy and tactics for change, security legislation, and theoretical and practical implications of change in South Africa's foreign policy.

156 CHANGE, reform and economic growth in South Africa, edited by Lawrence Schlemmer and Eddie Webster. Johannesburg: Ravan, 1978, 244 p.

Divided into two parts, this work initially highlights the debate on economic growth as a contributory factor to political and social change within the Republic, supported by analyses relevant to the issue. The latter includes broad topics such as income and employment; employers, and the workers.

157 CHARNEY, Craig
The politics of changing partners: control and co-option in the new South African constitution. Review of African Political Economy, no. 29, 1984, p. 122-131

Provides background to the new constitution and assesses its implications under the heading: White politics - Government by default, and black politics - co-option on the cheap.

158 CHARNEY, Craig
Restructuring white politics: the transformations of the National Party. South African Review, 1, 1983, p. 142-154

Considers the 1982 split in the National Party which he views in terms, not of ideological clashes between 'verligtes' and 'verkramptes', but as part of the process of class realignment.

159 CHARNEY, Craig
Towards rupture or stasis? An analysis of the 1981 South African general election IN: WORKING papers in Southern African studies, edited by D.C. Hindson. Johannesburg: Ravan, 1983, p. 173-190

See also: African Affairs, vol. 81, no. 325, October 1982, p. 527-545

Provides background information to the election, taking into account reforms envisaged by the Botha government prior to assessing the election results and the emerging class division as manifest by the strategies of the political parties. The trends evidenced by the results and the implications for the future of white politics concludes this analysis. Contains useful tables comparing the 1977 and 1981 elections.

160   CHARTON, Nancy C.J.
        Black elites in the Transkei. Politikon, vol. 3, no. 2, October 1976, p. 61-74

Attempts to answer the question as to who will dominate post-independent Transkei, how they became rulers and their relationship both to the ruled, and the South African government. Initially examines the tribal elite, prior to the modern elites as represented by the teachers, bureaucrats and entrepreneurs.

161   CHAZAN, Naomi
        The fallacies of pragmatism: Israeli foreign policy towards South Africa. African Affairs, vol. 82, no. 327, April 1983, p. 169-199

Examines the continued relationship between the two countries, given its problematic and paradoxical nature for Israeli policy-makers. Assesses Israeli interests in the Republic, including its Jewish population, economic co-operation, trade and investment, and military exchange.

162 . CHETTLE, John H.
        Economic relations between South Africa and black Africa. Johns Hopkins University. School of Advanced and International Studies. SAIS Review, vol. 4, no. 2, Summer/Fall 1984, p. 121-133

The Director for North and South America of the South Africa Foundation considers the economic strength of South Africa within the region. Discusses institutions established both to strengthen and diminish its influence, trade relations - the countries involved, types of goods, patterns of trade and transportation, in an attempt to determine the nature and extent of South Africa's economic relationship with black Africa.

163   CHILDREN under apartheid. London: International Defence and Aid Fund for Southern Africa, 1980, 119 p.

Commissioned by the Belgian Government in commemoration of both the International Anti-Apartheid Year and the International Year of the Child, this compilation of 110 photographs depicts manifestations of apartheid as it affects children. The photographs are categorized into eleven sections.

164   CHIMUTENGWENDE, Chenhamo C.
South Africa: the press and the politics of liberation. London: Barbican, 1978, 197 p.

States that this book is about the mass media of communication, information work and the politics of liberation, dealing more with the printed than broadcast media. Argues that the media's role as a tool of political change is limited, tending to reinforce existing beliefs, rather than changing them. Analyzes why the press is a sensitive area in politics, how it serves as a barometer of the dominant centres of power within the ruling classes, and to what extent the media can be used as an instrument for liberation or preserving the status quo.

165   CHISHOLM, Linda
From revolt to a search for alternatives: broadening the education base. Work in Progress, 42, May 1986, p. 14-19

Provides a survey of the changing nature of the education struggle, highlighting its intensification since the 1976 Soweto uprising and analyzing increased state control.

166   CHISHOLM, Linda
Redefining skills: black education in South Africa in the 1980s. Comparative Education, vol. 19, no. 3, 1983, p. 357-371

As indicated in the title, the author analyzes the status of black education, taking cognizance of the de Lange Report, skills shortage, state initiatives in technical education, and intervention by monopoly capital. In this way, she aims to illustrate 'how processes of legitimation for altered conditions of exploitation change, how this renegotiated legitimation takes place and is modified in the context of already-existing class and national forces.'

167   CHISHOLM, Linda and CHRISTIE, Pamela
Restructuring in education. South African Review, 1, 1983, p. 254-263

The authors discuss educational reform. This they indicate should be analyzed within the political and economic framework in which it is operative, and that the restructuring of educational control 'is one aspect of the wider restructuring of racial capitalism'. Focus particularly on the de Lange Report; skill shortages; expansion of technical and vocational education; the increase in private sector involvement in education; and challenges to existing educational structures.

168   CHOSACK, Hilary R.
The African homelands of South Africa: a list of material held by the Jan H. Hofmeyr Library. Johannesburg: South African Institute of Race Relations, 1975, (South African Institute of Race Relations. RR. 99/75), 35 p.

Traces publications on the homelands dating from the establishment of reserves until the mid-seventies. As indicated by the title, the bibliography is not comprehensive, but reflects the holdings of the Institute's library. Omits newspapers and government publications. Organized according to general literature, followed by material on individual homelands and arranged in alphabetical order.

169 CHRISTIE, Renfrew
Electricity, industry and class in South Africa. Albany: State University of New York Press, 1984, 241 p.

Provides an insight into an important aspect of industrialization by examining the relationship between electricity supply, industrialization and capital accumulation. The effects of electricity supply development on the accumulation of capital both in South Africa and abroad are analyzed and set within their historical perspective. Reviewed by Fred Curtis of the Drew University in the The Review of African Political Economy, no. 34, December 1985, p. 109-110.

170 CHURCH and nationalism in South Africa, edited by Theo Sundermeier. Johannesburg: Ravan, 1975, 152 p.

Fourteen papers delivered to the 1974 Consultation on Church and Nationalism Conference are edited by the former Director of the Missiological Institute at the Lutheran Theological College, Mapumulo, Natal, the Conference's sponsoring body. Philosophical, sociological and historical views are depicted on nationalism as manifested in South Africa, especially in the form of Afrikaner Christian-Nationalism. Reviewed in Social Dynamics, vol. 2, no. 1, June 1976, p. 71-72.

171   CILLIERS, Stephanus Petrus
       Appeal to reason. Stellenbosch: University
       Publishers and Booksellers, 1971, 81 p.

       A Professor of Sociology at Stellenbosch presents a
       selection of his papers on various aspects of the South
       African social structure. They include discussion on
       the border industries but concentrate mainly on the
       Coloured community, their socio-economic status and
       implications for education, economic future and
       utilization in Western Cape industry.

172   CILLIERS, Stephanus Petrus and GROENEWALD, C.J.
       Demographic analysis of urbanisation, 1936-
       2000. Stellenbosch: University of
       Stellenbosch, Research Unit for Sociology and
       Development, 1982, 38 p.

       Provides a demographic overview of urban growth and the
       movement of the different population groups to urban
       areas. Analyzes factors affecting these processes and
       develops alternative scenarios of future growth
       patterns.

173   CISKEI. Commission
       The Quail Report. Pretoria: Conference
       Associates, 1980, 328 p.

       Chairman: George Philip Quail

       This seven-man body was appointed by the Ciskei
       Government in terms of Government Notice, no. 14,
       Ciskei Official Gazette, vol. 6, no. 177, 4 August
       1978, to assess the feasibility of 'independence' for
       the territory. Provides an in-depth study of the area,
       complemented by substantial tables, maps, and a variety
       of appendices, including a bibliography on Ciskei. The
       Report which rejected independence as contrary to the
       wishes of the Ciskeian people is analyzed by Simon

64

Bekker in an article entitled: Report of the Ciskei
Commission - a review. Development Studies Southern
Africa, vol. 2, no. 3, April 1980, p. 391-412.

174   CISKEI: economics and politics of dependence in a South
        African homeland, edited by Nancy Charton.
        London: Croom Helm, 1980, 253 p.

States that the research project from which this book
emerged, 'was conceived as a unit with a single focus:
the interrelationship of the Ciskei homeland with its
environment, geographical, economic, and political'.
Accordingly, the following topics are covered: economic
development, urbanization, agriculture, the constitution, the administrative system, ethnic relations,
political parties, the legislature, mass communication,
the relevance of Maqoma to Ciskeian politics, and
dependence on South Africa.

175   CLARKE, Liz and NGOBESE, Jane
        Women without men: a study of 150 families in
        the Nqutu District of Kwazulu. Durban:
        Institute for Black Research, 1975, 95 p.

Depicts daily life of the peasant people in this
district as being fairly typical of a homeland area.
Presents findings of their research into income,
expenditure and livestock ownership. Endeavour to
assess a poverty datum line. Heavily illustrated and
substantiated by statistical data.

176   CLASS, race and gender: domestic workers in South
        Africa, by Deborah Gaitskell (and others).
        Review of African Political Economy, no.
        27/28, 1984, p. 87-108

Observes domestic service from conceptual, historical
and contemporary viewpoints noting how race, class and
gender have shaped the character of this service.
Implications of the new trend towards unionization are
assessed.

177   CLASS struggle and the periodization of the state in
South Africa, by Robert H. Davies (and
others). Review of African Political Economy,
no. 7, September/December 1976, p. 4-30

As stated in the author's abstract: This article
represents an attempt to periodise the South African
state through an analysis of political class struggle.
The analysis draws heavily on the theoretical work of
Nicos Poulantzas. The changing patterns of conflict and
alliance between the different classes and "fractions"
in the "power bloc" are traced in an attempt to
identify changes in the form of state and form of
regime. The analysis, concentrating on three historical
periods - the Pact period, the Fusion period and the
period between 1940 and 1948 - thus provides a
fundamental reinterpretation of South African history,
and shows how the ground was cleared for the capture of
state power in 1948 by those class forces represented
by the Nationalist Party.

Different critiques on this article are developed by
Belinda Bozzoli in an article entitled: Capital and
state in South Africa. Review of African Political
Economy, no. 11, January/April 1978, p. 40-50; and
secondly by Duncan Innes and Martin Plaut in: Class
struggle and the state. Review of African Political
Economy no. 11, January/April 1978, p. 51-61. From this
emanated a further article, by David Kaplan analyzing
limitations in the Innes/Plaut contribution on their
alternative analysis of the South African state between
the world wars. Review of African Political Economy,
no. 15/16, May/December 1979, p. 135-144; this provoked
a reply by Duncan Innes, p. 144-146.

178   COCK, Jacklyn
         Maids and madams: a study of the politics of
         exploitation. Johannesburg: Ravan, 1980,
         410 p.

Documents the exploitation of domestic workers in South Africa's unequal society. Notes that they are situated at the convergence of three lines along which social inequality is generated - class, race, and sex, which are related to the Republic's capitalist system of production.

179   COCKRAM, Gail-Maryse
      Constitutional law in the Republic of South Africa. Cape Town: Juta, 1975, 86 p.

Briefly presents fundamental constitutional principles prior to providing an explanation of Parliament, Executive and Provinces as based on the Constitution Act 32 of 1961, as amended by Act 79 of 1973. Devotes brief chapters to the homelands, Namibia and public safety.

180   COETZEE, Johann J.L.
      Industrial relations in the Republic of South Africa: a critical overview. South Africa International, vol. 15, no. 1, July 1984, p. 19-25

The author, Professor in the School of Management at Potchefstroom University for Christian Higher Education, delivered this paper to the Dallas Chamber of Commerce and at the University of Texas at Dallas in May 1984. Describes the process of change from the system of job reservation and discriminatory labour practice to a more democratized industrial community. Special attention is paid to the role of the Wiehahn Commission.

181   COETZEE, W.A.J.
      Development of local government and administration in Coloured and Indian group areas. University of Durban-Westville. Journal, vol. 3, no. 4, 1981, p. 281-299

Reviews the development of local government and administration for both Indians and Coloureds, noting the application of legislative and administrative measures and outlining contemporary proposals for local government under the 'new dispensation'.

182   COETZEE, W.A.J.
Political realities in South African public administration.University of Durban-Westville. Journal, vol. 3, no. 3, 1980, p. 159-196

The main issue discussed here is the roles played by political and public administrators in the formulation and execution of public policy-making, with special reference to their awareness of and responsiveness to current political realities in South Africa. Emphasis is placed, among other things, on the recent efforts of the South African government towards devising and obtaining a new constitutional dispensation acceptable to all population groups in the country. An assessment is also made of the South African public administrator concerning his role in policy-making and his contributions towards realising and solving political realities. It is pointed out, inter alia, that whereas today government and administration are even more complicated demanding professional politicians and professionally trained public administrators, the greatest problem the modern public administrator grapples with is change. To obtain, equip and retain the sorely needed eminent and talented public functionaries, the political administrator (minister), public administrator and, to a great measure, also the academic have important roles to play. Accordingly these roles are discussed towards meeting the said objective. (Author's abstract).

183   COETZER, Piet
Allan Hendrickse: awaiting trial. Alberton (Transvaal): Librarius, 1984, 208 p.

Within this biography of Hendrickse's life and political contribution as leader of the Labour Party, the author chronicles living conditions and experiences of the Coloured community. Appendix includes the Constitution of the Labour Party of South Africa.

184   COHEN, Robin
        Endgame in South Africa? London: James Currey/Unesco Press, 1986, 128 p.

The author, Director of the Centre for Research in Ethnic Relations and Professor of Sociology at the University of Warwick, provides an analysis of the ideology of apartheid which he relates to key social institutions and practices. Identifies four key pillars of apartheid including white monopoly of political power, the attempt to make 'race coincide with space', labour regulation, and the maintenance of social control. Assesses prospects should white political power become dislodged but concludes that there will be more continuity than expected.

185   COHN, William
        Influx control and black resistance in apartheid South Africa. TransAfrica Forum, vol. 3, no. 2, Winter 1986, p. 53-78

Conflict between the state and squatters in the Western Cape is examined historically, taking cognizance of the Coloured Labour Preference policy; influx control and African women in the Cape; exclusionary control over Africans, the position of the informal commercial sector, and employers' attitudes. Resistance tactics are chronicled.

186   COKER, Christopher
        Bophuthatswana and the South African homelands. World Today, vol. 39, no. 6, June 1983, p. 231-240

Achievements six years after 'independence' are assessed with particular reference to agriculture and mining. This success is examined within the framework of South Africa's homelands policy, the Republic's future options and the attitude of the West. Notes that and understanding of all three may help to explain 'why international recognition is more unlikely now than ever'.

187   COKER, Christopher
        South Africa: a new military role in Southern
        Africa. Survival, vol. 25, no. 2, March/April
        1983, p. 59-67

Investigates the role of the South African Defence Force within the Southern African region since 1968, especially in the then Rhodesia and Angola. Concentrates on South Africa's subsequent destabilization policy and its significance for the region. It is the author's opinion that the United States failure to prevent the Soviet Union intervening in Southern Africa resulted in the development of South Africa as an independent military power.

188   COKER, Christopher
        The South African elections and neo-
        apartheid. World Today, vol. 37, no. 6, June
        1981, p. 235-242

Identifies trends evident from the April 1981 election results which he states may mark a watershed year in South African history.

189   COLEMAN, Max and WEBSTER, David
        Repression and detentions in South Africa.
        South African Review, 3, 1986, p. 111-136

Presents an overview of security legislation providing statistical information on state repression in the form of detentions, torture, bannings, deportations in both 1984 and 1985. This includes action taken under the state of emergency.

190   COLLINGE, Jo-Anne
        The United Democratic Front. South African
        Review, 3, 1986, p. 248-266

Comprising a largely descriptive account of events within the UDF during the period early 1984 to mid-1985, in which the author takes cognizance of campaigns and issues; structures and policy-relations with other organizations - including the African National Congress, AZAPO, and Inkatha; and its relationship with the international community.

191   COMMONWEALTH EMINENT PERSONS GROUP ON SOUTH AFRICA
        Mission to South Africa: the Commonwealth
        Report. Harmondsworth: Penguin, 1986, 176 p.

Preceded by biographical details on members of the Group, a note on the Commonwealth, and the Letter of Transmittal, the material in this report is organized as follows: Apartheid - dismantling or reform? This is further subdivided into apartheid in perspective, the government's programme, and attitudes among the whites. In the second section, the issue of violence is addressed under the headings: the apartheid state - origins of violence, violence during the visit of the Eminent Persons Group, and the position after the state of emergency. The Group further elucidates on the release of Nelson Mandela and other political prisoners, the establishment of political freedom and prospects for negotiation. Presents the position of both the South African government, and of other parties and organizations; the Group's proposals; the regional dimension before providing their conclusion. Annexures include the Commonwealth Accord on South Africa; a letter dated 13 December 1985 from the Group's co-chairmen to the State President, and the former's reply dated 24 December 1985; the Group's programme of visits and meetings; the Freedom Charter of South Africa; banning orders on Mrs Winnie Mandela; announcement of the State President to the President's Council on constitutional developments on 15 May 1986.

192   CONDITIONS of the black worker, by W.H. Thomas (and others). London: Africa Publications Trust for the Study Project on External Investment in South Africa and Namibia (South West Africa), 1975, 298 p.

As explained by Professor Gwendolen Carter in the overview, these papers fall into two closely related sections: the position of the blacks within the economy in relation to job structure and wages; and their living conditions in both rural and urban areas. The study includes the following contributions: the structure of the South African economy and the nature of its ties with the international economy, by W.H. Thomas; current labour utilization and underemployment by Johann Maree; industrial decentralisation by W. Beinart; constraints on both black workers and white employees by Benjamin Pogrund; South Africa's rural black population is viewed in two studies by J.H. Moolman and P. Smit, and secondly by Elizabeth Clarke and Anthony Barker. A banned leader of the S.A. Students' Organisation presents a black South African's view of the urban, rural and industrial situation in the Republic at the time of writing; and Constance Ntshona concludes by depicting various facets of Soweto and life within its confines.

193   CONFERENCE ON CONSTITUTIONAL MODELS AND CONSTITUTIONAL CHANGE IN SOUTH AFRICA. Pietermaritzburg, 1978
Constitutional Change in South Africa, edited by John A. Benyon. Pietermaritzburg: University of Natal Press, 1978, 297 p.

The editor in his introduction to this work on constitutional alternatives, describes the structure of the conference: 'The papers and discussions were designed to lead through in logical sequence from the short and long-term forces of African and European history and background to matters of legal principle and practice; thence to questions of political analysis and proposed alternatives'. Consequences and applying certain of these alternative models were considered in their strategic, fiscal, economic, social and demographic dimensions.

194   CONFERENCE ON HISTORY OF OPPOSITION IN SOUTH AFRICA, Johannesburg, 1978.
        (Papers). Johannesburg: University of the Witwatersrand, (Students') Development Studies Group, 1978, 312 p.

Included are the following papers: The conceptual determination of class-conflict as opposition (Glen Moss); Towards a periodisation of the South African social formation (Susan M. Brown); Production, trade and labour migration from the Delagoa Bay hinterland in the second half of the 19th Century (Patrick Harries); The role of tributary labour in the Zulu political economy, 1865-1879 (Charles Ballard); Migrant labour and Nquthu District of Zululand, 1879-1910 (Elaine Unterhalter); Dr Philip, the 'spread of civilisation' and liberalism in South Africa (Andrew Nash); Black peasants and Ethiopianism in South Africa: 1895-1915 (Paul B. Rich); The ideology of self help in the Natal Native Congress from 1910 to the early 1920s (R. Cloete); The opposition to General Hertzog's segregation bills, 1929-1934 (Richard Haines); The Federation of South African Women, 1954-1962 (Cherryl Walker); Natal 1959 - the women's protests (Joanne Yawitch); The rival struggle: Poqo and Transkei resistance, 1960-1965 (Tom Lodge); Class, continuity and change in black South African literature 1948-60

(Kelwyn Sole); Opposition politics in Venda and Gazankulu (David Dison); Class conflict and ideology among the petty bourgeoisie in the 'Homelands': Inkatha - a study (Gerhard Maré)

195   CONFLICT and compromise in South Africa, edited by Robert I Rotberg and John Barratt. Cape Town: Philip, 1980, 209 p.

A conference held under the auspices of the World Peace Foundation and the South African Institute of International Affairs, held in Rustenburg, South Africa during 1978. Issues concerning the Republic's future and its relations with the West form the basis of this publication, which is divided into four sections. In Part I Robert Rotberg writes on creating a more harmonious South Africa. Part II entitled: The Contemporary Crisis offers political options for South Africa and implications for the West by C. John R. Dugard, and John Barratt interviews Nthato Motlana in a chapter headed From South Africa to Azania. Part III comprises evolutionary options. Arend Lijphart considers federal, confederal, and consociational options; Walter Dean Burnham discusses electoral regimes and their relevance to South Africa; Gavin Maasdorp examines forms of partition, while Percy Qoboza queries the possibility of an open society. Harald Pakendorf examines whether separate development can evolve, and Gibson Thula concludes this section by providing a basis for the country's constitutional transformation. In Part IV; South Africa and the West, Hedley Bull concentrates on Western interests and objectives, their bearing on South Africa's alternative political future, and its possible definition. Robert C. Good offers an 'outsider's' personal reflection on the Republic's future.

196   CONFLICT and progress: fifty years of race relations in
       South Africa, edited by Ellen Hellmann and
       Henry Lever. Johannesburg: Macmillan South
       Africa, 1979, 278 p.

In order to commemorate the fiftieth anniversary of the
South African Institute of Race Relations, ten
authorities in their respective fields were selected to
provide an analytical survey of the period under
review. Essays include the following: fifty years of
the South African Institute of Race Relations (Ellen
Hellmann); South African politics: the rising tide of
colour (René de Villiers); black politics in
transition (Patrick Laurence); racial legislation and
civil rights (John Dugard); the changing face of the
economy (Sheila T. van der Horst); conflict and
progress in education (E.G. Malherbe); urbanisation in
South Africa, 1929-1979 (David Welsh); changing racial
attitudes (Henry Lever); South Africa in a changing
world (John Barratt); in the crucible: a situation of
change for South African literature (Adam Small).

197   CONGRESS of South African Trade Unions. Review of
       African Political Economy, no. 35, May 1986,
       p. 68-83

Reproduces an abridged version of Jon Lewis and Estelle
Randall's Trade Union Survey, taken from South African
Labour Bulletin, vol. 11, no. 2, October/December 1985,
and published under the title: The State of the Unions,
in which South African labour relations are analyzed,
with particular reference to the consequences for
bargaining and union organization of the recession. The
second contribution, extracted from the South African
Labour Bulletin, vol. 11, no. 3, January 1986, relates
to the launch of the Congress of South African Trade
Unions, and includes the opening speech delivered by
Cyril Ramaphosa.

198   The CONSTITUTION, (articles by) Chris Heunis, Gatsha
        Buthelezi and Allan Hendrickse. Leadership
        South Africa, vol. 2, no. 2, Winter 1983
        p. 6-24

        Presents three viewpoints on the controversial
        Constitution Bill. Chris Heunis, Minister of
        Constitutional Development and Planning elaborates on
        the government's argument for its implementation,
        namely the evolution of the South African
        constitutional structure by providing for increased
        participation in the decision-making process; Gatsha
        Buthelezi, Chief Minister of KwaZulu, President of
        Inkatha and Chairman of the South African Black
        Alliance, explains why the exclusively racial focus of
        the new constitution makes it a specific act of
        agression directed at the majority of South Africans;
        Allan Hendrickse, leader of the Labour Party details
        reasons why his party has decided to participate in
        the planned new dispensation.

199   CONSTITUTIONAL change in South Africa: the next five
        years, edited by W.H.B. Dean and Dirk van Zyl
        Smit. Cape Town: Juta, 1983, 124p.

        Offers various perspectives on the constitutional
        debate taking political, economic and psychological
        factors likely to influence change, into consideration.
        The possible direction of constitutional change is
        assessed and the proposals of 1982 are analyzed in
        detail. Other contributors include A. du Toit, C.E.W.
        Simkins, D.H. Foster, and L.J. Boulle.

200   The CONSTITUTIONAL law implications of the Buthelezi
        Commission Report. Comparative and
        International Law Journal of Southern Africa,
        vol. 15, no. 3, 1982, p. 257-298

Five papers were presented at a seminar held at the University of South Africa, Pretoria on 21 June 1982, where some of the implications of the Buthelezi Commission Report recommendations for South African constitutional law were assessed. Contributors include Marinus Wiechers, L.J. Boulle, John Hund, Francois Venter and A.J.G.M. Sanders.

201   The CONSTITUTIONS of Transkei, Bophuthatswana, Venda and Ciskei, edited by M.P. Vorster, Marinus Wiechers and D.J. van Vuuren. Durban: Butterworths, 1985, 269 p.

Provides an analysis of their post 'independence' constitutions, set against an introductory chapter reviewing historical, institutional, comparative and political perspectives. Thereafter each constitution is studied in detail and followed by a presentation of the official English version of the Constitution, together with amendments until the end of 1984.

202   CONTEMPORARY South Africa: social psychological perspectives, edited by Stanley J. Morse and Christopher Orpen. Cape Town: Juta, 1975, 299 p.

Comprises a compilation of reading relevant to social psychology, sociology and political science courses in South Africa. Sections comprise an analysis of white attitudes in South Africa, those of blacks, and factors relating to change and stability, including the significance of the 1970 general election.

203   CONTENDING ideologies in South Africa, edited by James Leatt; Theo Kneifel and Klaus Nürnberger. Cape Town: Philip, 1986, 318 p.

Findings of a national study commission, promoted by the National Conference of the South African Council of

Churches to examine conflicting ideologies in South Africa and to gauge possible theological responses. This study is divided into five main parts, which are then subjected to further subdivision: capitalism; race power and ideology; socialism; Marxism; and ideology and theology.

204   COOPER, Carole
        Bantustan attitudes to trade unions. South African Review, 2, 1984, p. 165-184

Pays particular attention to the Ciskei, which has the most notorious record of trade union oppression, and Bophuthatswana which is prepared to accept trade unions, although subjecting them to strict controls. Implications for workers are assessed.

205   COOPER, Carole
        The established trade union movement. South African Review, 1, 1983, pp. 204-217

Examines the responses of the established trade union movement to important changes in labour relations which have involved the official recognition of trade union rights for blacks and the abolition of job reservation. In particular, analyzes the responses of the white industrial unions affiliated to the South African Confederation of Labour (SACLA), mixed industrial unions affiliated to the Trade Union Council of South Africa (TUCSA); and the craft-diluted unions.

206   COOPER, Carole and ENSOR, Linda
        Pebco: a black mass movement. Johannesburg: South African Institute of Race Relations, 1981, 58 p.

Chronicles the history of the Port Elizabeth Black Civic Association, known as Pebco, from its inception in 1979 to its decline in 1980. Intended both to represent the aspirations of blacks and to air their grievances with the authorities, its structure, policies and strategies are outlined, prior to the presentation of a chronology illustrating both its involvement in the Ford strike, and its development.

207   COOPER, Saths and NTLOKO, Lusiba
       'Engaged in debate and struggle': National
       Forum, interview by Susan Brown. Work in
       Progress, 42, May 1986, p. 20-24

The National Forum convenor and publicity secretary provides information on the Forum's organizational structure, operations and perceptions of the United Democratic Front. Lists organizations participating in the National Forum.

208   COWEN, D.V.
       The foundations of freedom: with special
       reference to Southern Africa. Cape Town:
       Oxford University Press, 1961, 258 p.

Part One of this work by Cowen, Professor of Comparative Law at the University of Cape Town, focusses particularly on South Africa and the problems encountered within this racially diverse country. The evolution of apartheid and erosion of civil rights are discussed prior to a presentation of the author's concept of alternative policies.

209   CRANKSHAW, Owen
       Theories of class and the African "middle
       class" in South Africa, 1969-1983. Africa
       Perspective, New Series, vol. 1, nos 1 and 2,
       1986, p. 3-33

Specifies his aims as follows: firstly to examine contemporary Marxist theories of class in order to establish criteria by which different occupations can be assigned to the "middle class". Secondly, to apply these criteria to an analysis of the African "middle class", using the data collected in the Manpower Surveys over the period 1969-1983.

210   CRAPANZANO, Vincent
       Waiting: the whites of South Africa. London:
       Grenada, 1985, 377 p.

Crapanzano, Professor of Anthropology and Comparative Literature at the City University of New York concentrates on the beliefs and attitudes, particularly of a racial nature, of white South Africans. His study is compiled from the perspective of a participant-observer in the daily life of an agricultural village near Cape Town, which he calls Wyndal. Provides general information on South African history, culture, and politics which he intersperses with extracts from interviews with some thirty-five English and Afrikaans-speaking whites, arranged under headings including past, marriage, workers and the future. Reviewed in: New Republic, 23 December 1985, p. 31-32.

211   CRIME and power in South Africa, critical studies in
       criminology, edited by Dennis Davis and Mana
       Slabbert. Cape Town: Philip, 1985, 138 p.

Addresses the following issues: criminology in South Africa by Davis; problems specific to criminological research by Slabbert; Coloured gangs and family structure - an indictment of forced removals by Don Pinnock; political trials by Davis; liquor, the state and urban blacks by Wilfred Schäf; sexism in South African law and its application, studied by Andrea Durbach; Mark Sher considers the pass laws; Slabbert on violence on cinema and television and in the streets; Sch'narf on shebeens in the Cape Peninsula; and Cathi Albertyn on drugs and drug abuse.

212   CROCKER, Chester
South Africa: a strategy for change. Foreign
Affairs, vol. 59, no. 2, Winter 1980/81,
p. 323-351

Written in Crocker's capacity as Director of African
Studies at the Center for Strategic and International
Studies at Georgetown University, and shortly before he
became Assistant Secretary of State for African
Affairs, this is regarded as a seminal article
articulating the United States policy of constructive
engagement towards Southern Africa. This he felt, would
lead to enhanced American prestige in the region, a
solution to the Namibian issue, and the withdrawal of
Cuban advisers from Angola. With reference to South
Africa he elaborates on the United States role of
achieving change and to '... steer between the twin
dangers of abetting violence in the Republic and
aligning ourselves with the cause of white rule'.

213   CURTIS, Fred
Contradiction and uneven development in South
Africa: the constrained allocation of African
labour-power. Journal of Modern African
Studies, vol. 22, no. 3, September 1984, p.
381-391

Confined mainly to the period 1948 to 1978, the author
illustrates that the relationship of apartheid and the
associated cheap labour system does not fall either
into a neo-classical or Marxist analysis but '. . . is
uneven and contradictory, and not reducable to a
simple, essential result.' Substantiated by an
exploration of ways in which African labour power has
been cheapened by concentrating on the role of the
labour bureaux, the taxation of wage income, state
housing and transportation commodities, food and
housing provided 'in kind' by employers, and uneven
effects in male and female labour-powers.

214   DAG HAMMARSKJOLD LIBRARY
Apartheid: a selected bibliography on the
racial policies of the Government of the
Republic of South Africa. New York: United
Nations, 1968, (ST/LIB/22), 52 p.

Concentrates on material which deals exclusively or
primarily with racial aspects, arranged under the
following headings: apartheid; treatment of people of
Indo-Pakistan origin; economic aspects, Tomlinson
Report; educational aspects; legal aspects; Treason
Trial; United Nations and racial powers; sanctions;
national attitudes and reaction; biographies and
personal narratives. This bibliography was updated in
1970: (ST/LIB/22/Rev.1)

215   DAG HAMMARSKJOLD Library
Apartheid: a selective bibliography on the
racial policies of the Government of the
Republic of South Africa, 1970-1978. New
York: United Nations, 1979, (ITS: Bibliographical series, no. 2,) (ST/LIB/SER.B/28),
50 p.

Compiled in observance of International Apartheid Year,
this bibliography is a supplement to the 1970 edition,
and includes all the references cited in the 1974
supplement. It is a select work reflecting the holdings
of the Dag Hammarskjold Library, and covers the
following aspects: general works on apartheid, economic
facets including trade unions; education; legal; social
which is further subdivided into churches, sport, youth
and students; bantustans; United Nations and apartheid;
sanctions; national attitudes and reactions;
biographies and personal narratives. Subsequent to
these references, is a list of United Nations
documents, arranged to correspond with most of the
above categories.

216   DAG HAMMARSKJOLD LIBRARY
Legal aspects of apartheid: a selective bibliography of books and articles and United Nations documentation in English, 1950-1983. New York: United Nations Secretariat, 1984, (ST/LIB/SER.B/34), 49 p.

A selection of references commenting on those South African laws pertaining to apartheid, and to the consideration of this question under international law.

217   DAG HAMMARSKJOLD LIBRARY
Sanctions against South Africa: a selective bibliography. New York: United Nations, 1981, (ITS: Bibliographical series, no. 32), (ST/LIB/SER.B/32), 28 p.

Encompassing the period 1962 to 1980, this bibliography considers all aspects of sanctions against the Republic. It is divided into five main categories: sanctions including general works, arms, diplomatic relations, investments, loans, nuclear-weapon capability, oil, shipping and airline connections, sports, and trade; action by inter-governmental organizations; action by non-governmental organizations; national attitudes and reaction; bibliographies.

218   DAG HAMMARSKJOLD LIBRARY
Selective bibliography on apartheid. New York: United Nations 1974, (United Nations. Unit on Apartheid. Notes and documents, 10/74), 14 p.

Compiled as a supplement to: Apartheid: a selected bibliography on the racial policies of the Government of South Africa, q.v., this bibliography focusses on material published in the period 1970 to 1973.

219   DANAHER, Kevin
          The political economy of U.S. policy toward
          South Africa. Boulder: Westview, 1985, 331 p.

          Analyzes both United States corporate and government
          motives for maintaining the political status quo in
          South Africa.

220   DANAHER, Kevin
          Sanctions against South Africa: strategy for
          the anti-apartheid movement of the 1980s.
          Ufahamu, vol. 10, nos. 1 and 2, Fall and
          Winter 1980/81, p. 5-18

          Analyzes reasons why the United States has long
          resisted imposing sanctions on South Africa, noting its
          key role and similar obstacles confronted by other
          anti-apartheid forces. Drawing on this information,
          Danaher concludes with strategic suggestions for the
          anti-apartheid movement in its attempt to isolate white
          South Africa.

221   DANAHER, Kevin
          South Africa and the United States: an
          annotated bibliography. Washington, D.C.:
          Institute for Policy Studies, (1979?), 27 p.

          Produced with the needs of the anti-apartheid movement
          in mind, this bibliography contains references
          primarily pertaining to the United States; involvement
          of the corporations, the Central Intelligence Agency,
          the Soviet Union and Cuba; liberation movements,
          mercenaries, military affairs, minerals and mining
          companies; nuclear issues; South African economy,
          politics and history; the Southern Africa region;
          theory and United States government policy. The 221
          references contain succinct annotations and the broad
          subject index relates to the above-mentioned
          categories. C Tsehloane Keto's bibliography should

also be noted. It is entitled American-South African relations, 1784-1980: review and select bibliography. It is published as Africa series, no 45, Ohio University monographs in international studies, 1985, 165 p. Contains material published before July 1983 which describes and analyzes developments up to 1980. He also cites American and South African groups, organisations, research centres and libraries with extensive collections in this field.

222   DANIEL, John
        A comparative analysis of Lesotho and Swaziland's relations with South Africa.
        South African Review, 2, 1984, p. 228-238

Argues, that although both countries are dependent on South Africa, in neither case can their relationship be described as 'accommodationist' and that the geopolitical and economic dependence is not the major influence. Delineates the differences in their general foreign policy stance, and towards the Republic.

223   DANIEL, John
        Radical resistance to minority rule in South Africa: 1906-1965. Ann Arbor: University Microfilms International, 1975, 399 p.

        Thesis: Ph.D. (State University of New York at Buffalo)

The primary focus of the thesis is to account for the failure of the political efforts of the black majority and the perpetuation of minority rule in South Africa. Focusses on the role of the radical opposition to discrimination and oppression, which he examines for the period under review in three parts. These he delineates as follows: Part One (1906-1949) details the gradual evolution and development in the late nineteen-forties of coherent radical ideology which moved the resistance movement out of its liberal phase into the period of radical struggle; Part Two (1949-1961) examines the translation of this radical ideology into a non-violent political programme, while Part Three (1961-1965) focusses upon the climactic years of the radical effort during which organized violence was used for the first time and which ended in failure and the collapse of the internally-based radical movement.

224   DANZIGER, K.
        Ideology and Utopia in South Africa: a methodological contribution to the sociology of knowledge. British Journal of Sociology, vol. 14, 1963, p. 59-76

An investigation of cognitive styles in South Africa with findings based on an essay given to 53 Afrikaans-speaking white pupils, 251 English-speaking whites, 51 Indians, and 84 blacks, written during the periods 1956-7 and 1960-2. Topic of the essay was on the future of South Africa - an actual history of the period 1960 to 2010 was required.

225   DAVENPORT, T.R.H.
        The Afrikaner Bond: the history of a South African political party, 1880-1911. Cape Town: Oxford University Press, 1966, 431 p.

The history of the first real political party to emerge in South Africa is analyzed from the viewpoints of its origin, aims, achievements and influence. The roles of Jan Hofmeyer and S.J. du Toit are highlighted in this work which attempts to shed new perspectives on the South African history for the period under review.

226   DAVENPORT, T.R.H.
       South Africa: a modern history. Johannesburg:
       Macmillan South Africa, 1977, 432 p.

Written by the Professor of History and Head of
Department at Rhodes University, Grahamstown, this book
covers the entire spectrum of South African history. It
dates from the early Stone Age to 1976, but its main
focus is on the Twentieth Century. The study is divided
into two main parts: the prelude to white domination
and secondly, the consolidation of a white state,
concluding with an examination of South Africa's socio-
economic conditions.

227   DAVIDSON, Basil
       Southern   Africa: progress   or   disaster?
       London: British Defence and Aid Fund for
       Southern   Africa,   1984,   (Canon   Collins
       memorial lecture), 34 p.

Argues that South African policy is aimed both at
safeguarding the apartheid system and the maintenance
of its regional military, political and economic
domination. Discusses future prospects and suggests
ways in which change could be achieved.

228   DAVIES, John
       United   States   foreign policy and   the
       education of black South Africans. Africa
       Perspective, no. 26, 1985, p. 61-79

Explains why both the Reagan Administration and South
African-based American corporations foster an
educational policy towards the Republic. Bases his
study on a brief review of the Administration's South
Africa policy as a whole. Concludes however, that these
policies actually re-inforce anti-capitalist and anti-
American sentiment among black students.

229   DAVIES, Robert H.
        Capital, state and white labour in South
        Africa 1900-1960: an historical materialist
        analysis of class formation and class
        relations. Atlantic Highlands, N.J.:
        Humanities Press, 1979, 414 p.

        Presents a Marxist analysis of state intervention
        during the period under review, in order to promote
        understanding of South Africa's class formation
        revealing the relationship between capitalism and
        apartheid. Part One considers the white wage earners
        and the hegemony of mining capital; Part Two
        concentrates on the white wage earners and the hegemony
        of national capital, 1924-1939; while Part Three
        examines the status of the white wage-earners and
        Afrikaner nationalism during the period 1934 to 1960.
        This study is based on the author's D.Phil thesis
        presented to the University of Sussex in 1977.

230   DAVIES, Robert H.
        Mining capital, the state, and unskilled
        white workers in South Africa, 1910-1913.
        Journal of Southern African Studies, vol. 3,
        no. 1, October 1976, p. 41-69

        Supportive of the view that mining capital profitted
        from the policy of non-employment of whites in general
        unskilled labour. This resulted in labour being
        racially divided and its subsequent entrenchment in
        law. The subjection of blacks to 'exploitation colour
        bars' proved to be a vital determinant.

231   DAVIES, Robert H.
        South African strategy towards Mozambique in
        the post-Nkomati period: a critical analysis
        of effects and implications. Uppsala:
        Scandinavian Institute of African Studies,
        1985, (Scandinavian Institute of African
        Studies. Research report, no. 73), 71 p.

The author concentrates on the Republic's strategy towards Mozambique within the context of its regional policy. Written a year after the signing of the Nkomati Accord, Davies also includes historical background prior to analyzing the significance of the Accord, its impact both within the Southern African region and internationally, as well as its effect on the struggle within South Africa itself.

232   DAVIES, Robert H. and O'MEARA, Dan
       The state and analysis of the Southern
       African region: issues raised by South
       African strategy. Review of African Political
       Economy, no. 29, 1984, p. 64-76

Reviews some of the literature on the concept of South Africa's Total Strategy and its implications both within the Republic itself and regionally. Thereafter analyses the development, meaning, limits, possibilities, and implications for struggles within the region, with particular reference to the Southern African Development Coordination Conference (SADCC).

233   DAVIES, Robert H (and others)
       The struggle for South Africa: a reference
       guide to movements, organizations and
       institutions, by Robert H. Davies, Dan
       O'Meara and Sipho Dlamini. London: Zed, 1984,
       2 vols.

Designed to provide both information on specific organizations involved in the struggle for power and an indepth analysis from a Marxist perspective, of this struggle. The authors link this to the historical development and current operation of the apartheid system. As defined by the authors, 'the book is fundamentally concerned with the interlinked processes of, and contradictions around, capital accumulation, class struggle and national liberation in South Africa'.

234   DAVIES, Robert H. and O'MEARA, Dan
        Total strategy in Southern Africa: an
        analysis of South African regional policy
        since 1978. Journal of Southern African
        Studies, vol. 11, no. 2, 1985, p. 183-211

        As indicated by the title, the authors analyse P.W.
        Botha's regional strategy and its effects in its
        different phases. Results and prospects, limits and
        possibilities of this strategy are assessed 'from a
        perspective different from much of the existing
        literature.'

235   DEANE, Dee Shirley
        Black South Africans: a who's who, 57
        profiles of Natal's leading blacks. Cape
        Town: Oxford University Press, 1978, 210 p.

        Aided by five black trustees, selection was made on the
        following specified criteria: willingness to sacrifice
        self in the interests of others, dedication to the
        black community and contributions made, leadership
        qualities, personal, vocational, avocational and
        educational achievements.

236   DE BEER, Cedric
        The South African disease: apartheid health
        and health services. Johannesburg: Southern
        African Research Service, 1984, 86p.

        An employee in the Department of Community Health at
        the University of Witwatersrand's Medical School,
        examines apartheid South Africa as a determinant of
        ill-health. Presents five case studies in support of
        his thesis. Asserts that until South African society
        has been transformed, medical science alone cannot
        achieve the best health services for all.

237   DE CONING, Christo and FICK, Johan
      Menslike verbrandings: 'n sosio-politieke
      ondersoek na die aard en impak van
      kataklismiese geweld in Suid Afrika (Human
      burnings: a socio-political investigation
      into the nature and impact of cataclysmic
      violence in South Africa) Politikon, vol. 13,
      no. 1, June 1986, p. 22-53

Increased polarisation and escalating cataclysmic
violence in South Africa, especially since 1984, have
dramatically been brought to the attention of all
segments of society as well as the international
community through the phenomenon of the burning of
people by way of the so-called "necklace-method". An
effort is made in this article to explain human
burnings in terms of certain vital societal parameters
such as the relevance of traditional beliefs and
practices, the concept of "instant justice", the role
of the media and rumours, group dynamics in which the
process of "scapegoating" figures prominently, as well
as political phenomena such as the deprivation -
frustration - aggression hypothesis and aspects of
rational choice, such as the functionality of
intimidation in order to make society ungovernable in
terms of revolutionary strategy. Various alternatives
for future research in this vital field are suggested.
(Author's abstract)

238   DE GRUCHY, John W.
      Cry justice! Prayers, meditations and
      readings from South Africa. London: Collins,
      1986, 261 p.

Focussing particularly on the South African context,
this is a collection of thirty-one readings, selected
for their link to Christian spirituality and the need
for the social transformation of the apartheid society.

239   DE KIEWIET, C.W.
       History of South Africa: social and economic.
       London: Oxford University Press, 1941, 292 p.

The main focus of this work is on South Africa's development - both social and economic - which the author traces from earliest times. Chapters include discussion on industry, the Witwatersrand and the Boer War, Union, gold, poor whites, poor blacks, and labour. Appendix contains useful list of principal officials from 1795 to time of writing.

240   DE KLERK, Michael
       Seasons that will never return: the impact of farm mechanization on employment, incomes and population distribution in the Western Transvaal.Journal of Southern African Studies vol. 11, no. 1, 1984. p. 84-105

Based on the author's unpublished M.A. thesis entitled: Technological change and employment in South African agriculture: the case of maize harvesting in the Western Transvaal, 1968-1981 (Cape Town: University of Cape Town, 1983), this article focusses particularly on the nature and strength of the link between changes in technology and employment. De Klerk states as his specific objectives the assessment of the degree to which certain forms of mechanization have occurred on maize farms; changes in the labour process, the level of employment and the characteristics of farm workers; and whether the decline in employment has led to unemployment. With an emphasis on empirical findings, the author makes a number of deductions concerning the changes in geographical distribution and the incomes of the black rural population.

241   DE KLERK, W.A.
The puritans in Africa: a history of Afrikanerdom. Harmondsworth: Penguin, 1975, 376 p.

Traces the history of the Afrikaners from the earliest times, illustrating the development of their thinking and attitudes. As stated by the author 'this is a book about the attempt by a small people, totalling no more than the population of an average-sized American or European city, to remake their particular world to the concept of a rational plan from the radical Right. In no other way can the modern Afrikaners be understood'.

242   DE KLERK, Willem
The second (r)evolution: Afrikanerdom and the crisis of identity. Johannesburg: Ball, 1984, 81 p.

Assesses the changing stance of the Afrikaner within the framework of political attitudes and policy, religious attitudes, Afrikaner organizations and the press. De Klerk is a journalist, academic and political commentator.

243   DE KOCK, Wessel
A manner of speaking: the origins of the press in South Africa. Cape Town: Saayman & Weber, 1982, 150 p.

The aim of this book in the centenary year of the Newspaper Press Union, is to contribute to an understanding of the men and motives involved in securing for South Africa what the pioneer John Fairbairn called the "inestimable privilege" of a free press. While a controversial topic, the press is also one about which most people know little. Newspapers did not "happen" overnight. Their history in this country is turbulent, rich and varied and cries out for research. The following chapters touch fleetingly on some of the milestones which have made the press what it is. (Author's foreword)

244   DE LA HARPE, Jean and MANSON, Andrew
       The U.D.F. and the development of resistance
       in South Africa. Africa Perspective, no. 23,
       1983, p. 58-74

Places the United Democratic Front within its historical context and analyzes its principles and practice in an attempt to explain its emergence as a major force in the democratic movement. Argues that its formation is a logical step in the development of resistance by melding together the multitudinous grass roots structures, and that its strategy should be perceived as such.

245   DELIUS, Peter
       The land belongs to us: the Pedi polity, the
       Boers and the British in the Nineteenth
       Century Transvaal. Johannesburg: Ravan, 1983,
       278 p.

An in-depth history of the Pedi polity covering mainly the period 1820 to the 1870s. Interwoven in this analysis of the Pedi political system is their interaction with the missionaries, the Trekkers and their role as migrant labourers. Examines the influence of the initial stages of South Africa's industrial revolution, and the factors leading to the destruction of their independence.

246   DENOON, Donald
       Settler capitalism: the dynamics of dependent
       development in the Southern Hemisphere.
       Oxford: Clarendon Press, 1983, 280 p.

A comparative study on economic development in six settler societies in the Southern Hemisphere - New Zealand, Australia, South Africa, Uruguay, Argentina and Chile. Commentates mainly on the period 1890 to 1914.

247   DESMOND, Cosmas
        Christians or capitalists? Christianity and politics in South Africa. London: Bowerdean Press, 1978, 160 p.

Addresses the issue from the viewpoint of both theology and politics, including options advocated by the nationalists, enlightened capitalists and socialists. The role of socialism is assessed.

248   DESMOND, Cosmas
        The discarded people: an account of African resettlement. 3rd ed. Johannesburg: Christian Institute of South Africa, (1969?), 268 p.

Father Cosmas Desmond presents first-hand information on specific resettlement schemes throughout South Africa illustrating 'what apartheid means in practice'.

249   DESMOND, Cosmos
        Sanctions and South Africa. Third World Quarterly, vol. 8, no. 1, January 1986, p. 78-99

Describes and analyzes both the causes and effects of the growth in the campaign for divestment and the increasing calls for sanctions against South Africa which are evident in the United States and elsewhere in the world.

250   DETENTIONS Project: list of material in Resource Centre. Cape Town: University of Cape Town, Institute of Criminology, 1984, 16 p.

With reference to South Africa, material has been organized into the following categories: detention and security legislation, psychological effects, personal testimonies, torture; security legislation, trials, views from Robben Island, organizations opposing detention, banning and inquests.

251   DEVENISH, G.E.
        A critical evaluation of the theoretical and political justifications of the new constitutional proposals. Bellville: University of the Western Cape, 1979, 35 p.

Investigates the proposals in some detail but indicates the serious flaws evidenced by the total exclusion of blacks and the autocratic method of its presentation. States however that they deserve serious consideration for their principle of 'institutionalised and quasi-consociational joint decision-making with its potential for constitutional and political reform'.

252   DE VILLIERS, Dirk and DE VILLIERS, Johanna
        PW. Cape Town: Tafelberg, 1984, 376 p.

A biographical account of P.W. Botha taking into account both his personal life and political career until the signing of the Nkomati Accord. Set against the background of world politics and clashes within the Afrikaner nation, this study reveals the Prime Minister's (now President's) attitudes towards previous premiers, western diplomats, African and world leaders.

253   DE VILLIERS, Richard
        UDF: front or political party? Work in Progress, no. 40, 1986, p. 14-17

Considers the nature of the United Democratic Front. Assesses the implications of the question posed by the title, particularly for its affiliate organizations.

254   DEWAR, D. (and others)
Urbanisation and settlement policy in South
Africa: some findings and recommendations, by
D. Dewar, A. Todes and V. Watson. Cape Town:
University of Cape Town, Urban Problems
Research Unit, 1985, (University of Cape
Town. Urban Problems Research Unit, Working
paper, no. 32, and Occasional paper, no. 19),
53 p.

Broadly, the theme of this work concentrates on influx
control, decentralization, rural growth and development
framework.

255   DICKIE-CLARK, H.E.
Do the South African whites need racial
discrimination? Plural Societies, vol. 11,
no. 1, Spring 1980, p. 47-54

Comments on Donald G. Baker's: The impact of regional
events on whites in Rhodesia and South Africa. Plural
Societies, vol. 10, no. 1, Spring 1979, p. 27-58.
Addresses the question whether the Afrikaners would be
prepared to make concessions which would mean the end
of their present dominance.

256   DICKIE-CLARK, H.F.
The marginal situation: a sociological study
of a Coloured group. London: Routledge and
Kegan Paul, 1966, 226 p.

Considers both theoretically and empirically, the
situation of the marginal man, taking into
consideration both 'marginal' personality traits and
the effect of this situation on the structure and
functioning of groups. The Coloureds of the Sparks
Estate in Durban were interviewed in this respect.

257   DITSHWANTSHO TSA RONA STU
       'They like our hands, not us': a study of
       policy bearing on Alexandra from 1948 to
       1963, Africa Perspective, no. 21, 1982, p.
       29-43

       The Group has provided its own abstract:
       This paper was delivered at the "Urbanisation
       Conference" of the SAIRR in October 1982. It has its
       origin, however, in a lively interest by people from
       Alexandra, in the events and conditions of the
       township. The quotation comes from a worker. We
       pondered this sentence which cuts to the heart of
       political economy, trying to understand as fully as
       possible the mechanisms and the implications of the
       separation of labour from labourer. It is our
       provisional conclusion that a main technique in this
       strategy has been the construciton of urban
       segregation. We have tried to support this hypothesis
       by analysing the 1963 decision to make Alexandra a
       hostel dormitory.

258   DIVIDED or united power: views on the new
       constitutional dispensation by prominent
       South African political leaders, edited by
       J.A. du Pisani. Johannesburg: Lex Patria,
       1986, 362 p.

       Represents five basic viewpoints on the 1983
       constitutional dispensation divided as follows:
       Creators of the new constitution - P.W. Botha, A.L.
       Schlebusch, P.C.J. Koornhof, J.C. Heunis, J.D. du
       Basson; Supporters of the new constitution - W.M.
       Sutton, A.J. Hendrickse, D.M.G. Currey, J.A. Rabie, A.
       Rajbansi; Right wing opponents of the new constitution
       - J.A. Marais, A.P. Treurnicht, F. Hartzenberg, C.P.
       Mulder, H. Booysen; Opposition parties in the tri-
       cameral parliament - F. van Zyl Slabbert, H. Suzman,
       N.J.J. Olivier, D.T. de la Cruz, A.P. Booysen, J.N.

Reddy, M. Rajab; Extra-parliamentary left-wing opponents of the new constitution - M.G. Buthelezi, D.M. Tutu, Natal Indian Congress, S. Cooper.

259   A DOCUMENTARY history of Indian South Africans, edited Surendra Bhana and Bridglal Pachai. Cape Town, Philip, 1984, (Black and white perspectives on South Africa, 2) 306 p.

A selection of eighty-eight documents are placed in broader context by means of an explanatory preface, with each section of the work being proceeded by a brief historical introduction. These documents serve to illustrate the history of Indian South Africans from the arrival of the first indentured labourers in 1860 to their involvement in the contemporary political issues of the 1970s and 1980s.

260   DOCUMENTS of the second National Consultative Conference of the African National Congress, Zambia, 16-23, June 1985. London: Caledonian Press, 1985, 60 p.

Proceedings of the Kabwe Conference providing an overview of the struggle.

261   D'OLIVIERA, John
Botha's gamble. Washington Quarterly, vol. 6, no. 1, Winter 1983, p. 146-151

Assesses the effect of the 1983 political dispensation, particularly on South Africa's white political structure. Problems encountered by P.W. Botha are identified and the author notes that 'he has taken action that will mean the beginning of the end of Afrikaner nationalism as a dominant force in South African politics'.

262   D'OLIVEIRA, John
       Vorster - the man.   Johannesburg: Ernest
       Stanton, 1977, 292 p.

       An analysis of Vorster's personality and nature set
       within his own cultural and historical framework forms
       the basis of this study. Written in his capacity as a
       reporter, D'Oliveira bases his book largely on
       Vorster's own views and explanations, as well as the
       observations of those who knew him. It covers the
       period from his early life until he became Prime
       Minister in 1971.

263   DOLLIE, Na-iem
       The National Forum. South African Review, 3,
       1986, p. 267-277

       Provides details of issues at National Forum meetings,
       its relations with other organizations, and future
       prospects.

264   DOSTAL, Elizabeth
       The future of South Africa: a survey among
       leaders of the major South African
       institutions. Stellenboach: University of
       Stellenbosch, Institute for Futures Research,
       (1984?), (University of Stellenbosch.
       Institute for Futures Research. Occasional
       Paper, no. 1) 50 p.

       Based on the findings of a questionnaire, the text of
       which is reproduced, this study focusses on both the
       ideals and threats to political, economic and social
       development.

265   DOUWES DEKKER, Loet C.G.
       Aspects of the labour market in: SOUTH Africa
       in the world economy, edited by Jacqueline
       Matthews. Johannesburg: McGraw-Hill, 1983, p.
       53-95

Enlarges on both the statistical characteristics of South Africa's segmented labour market and the criticism of the system by the international community. Annexure A, p. 87-89 comprises the European Economic Community's Code of Conduct for companies with subsidiaries, branches or representation in South Africa.

266   DOUWES DEKKER, Loet C.G.
       Notes on international labour bodies and their relevance to South Africa in: The SOUTH African labour scene in the 1980s, edited by Deon Johannes Geldenhuys. Johannesburg: South African Institute of International Affairs, 1980, (South African Institute of International Affairs. Study group series, no. 3), p. 1-16

Previously published in: South African Labour Bulletin, vol. 5, no. 8, May 1980

An annexure describing South Africa's status (or lack of it) within International Trade Secretariats for the year 1976 complements an analysis of these secretariats, international federations of national co-ordinating bodies, national co-ordinating bodies and international regulations.

267   DOXEY, G.V.
       The industrial colour bar in South Africa. Cape Town: Oxford University Press, 1961, 205 p.

The author, who was then Senior Lecturer in Commerce and Applied Economics at the University of the Witwatersrand, Johannesburg, reviews the industrial labour market. The period under review dates from the discovery of diamonds in 1870, and Doxey seeks to provide reasons for the pattern depicted by the labour market. Both the underlying factors and the content of legislation affecting the growth of legal rigidity in the labour market are explained.

268   DOXEY, G.V.
        The South African problem: a conflict of
        nationalism. International Journal, vol. 18,
        no. 4, Autumn 1963, p. 501-512

        Illustrates the status of both Afrikaner and African nationalism in the 1960s set against an historical overview of white politics. Briefly sketches the black political movements but notes that at the time of writing there has been no trial of strength between black and white. States, however, that as a result of the government's policies, South Africa faces a crisis in its foreign relations and poses a severe problem for the international community.

269   DRUCKER, José
        Twentieth century South Africa: source
        material on South African history. Cape Town:
        Oxford University Press, 1984, (Creative
        history series), 95 p.

        Although designed principally for senior high school pupils, this study provides information on migrant labour, industrialization and urbanization, politics and apartheid. Contains an extensive bibliography of both primary and secondary sources.

270   DUBE, Ernest F.
        The relationship between racism and education
        in South Africa. Harvard Educational Review,
        vol. 55, no. 1, February 1985, p. 86-100

        The author traces the relationship between racism and education in South Africa in light of the numerous racist policies and practices that the South African government has pursued and continues to implement. He postulates that, contrary to a general belief that racism is practiced primarily by the Afrikaners, the English-speaking South Africans have also been racist. Dube describes the introduction of Bantu Education and draws attention to the intended and unintended outcomes of this system. He offers his insights into the gravity of the situation and forecasts that serious consequences will result from the oppressive educational practices that exist today. (Journal abstract)

271   DUBOW, Saul
       Land, labour and merchant capital in the pre-industrial rural economy of the Cape: the experience of the Graaff-Reinet district, 1852-72, Cape Town: University of Cape Town, Centre for African Studies, 1982, (University of Cape Town. Centre for African Studies. Communications, no. 6/1982), 95 p.

Originally submitted in partial fulfilment of the requirements for a B.A. Honours degree in History at the University of Cape Town, this study depicts the political economy of the Graaff-Reinet district between 1852 and 1872. Analyzes the incorporation of Graaff-Reinet into the world economy, discusses relevant land and labour legislation, labour processes and what the author considers most important, squatting on the 'Crown Lands and develops the analysis of social stratification in the light of the transition from quasi-feudal to capitalist relations of production'.

272   DUGARD, John
       Human rights and the South African legal order. Princeton: Princeton University Press, 1978, 470 p.

103

Describes and explains the features of South Africa's legal order which have aroused the opposition both of the international community and domestically within South Africa. The study is divided into five main sections: the legal framework, human rights and the law; the political trial; the judicial process and human rights; and a new approach to law.

273   DUGARD, John
       Silence is not golden. Foreign Policy, no.
       46, Spring 1982, p. 37-48

The implications of the Reagan Administration's policy towards South Africa are assessed and some tentative conclusions drawn. Pays particular attention to the status of reform and human rights within the Republic. Author is the Director of the Centre of Applied Legal Studies, University of the Witwatersrand, Johannesburg.

274   DURBAN WOMEN'S BIBLIOGRAPHY GROUP
       Women in Southern Africa: a bibliography, by
       Jill Burning, Heather Hughes and Judith Shier
       (and others). Durban: University of Natal,
       Department of African Studies, 1985, 107 p.

Comprising a general foreword, and sixteen sections, each with its own introduction, this bibliography covers South Africa, Botswana, Lesotho, Swaziland and Namibia. Mainly sociologically-orientated, topics include: Growing up female; domestic division of labour and child-rearing; migrant labour; women's associations; the law; education; biographies and personalities.

275   DU TOIT, A.B.
       Politics and ethics in South Africa: a study
       in the identification and evaluation of
       political alternatives. Stellenbosch:
       University of Stellenbosch, 1974, 362 p.

Thesis: Ph.D.

Defines the scope of his work, as a case study in the relation between politics and ethics. Chapter headings are as follows: The ethical framework - justice, equality and freedom as normative principles for the evaluation of political alternatives; traditional and popular formulations of the problem of political alternatives and their academic variants - a preliminary investigation; the crucial issues underlying the alternatives; domination and discrimination - a critique of separate development; democratic stability and consensus in a divided plural society - a critique of liberal constitutionalism, the structure of political conflict - democratic alternatives to the 'Westminster' Model?

276   DU TOIT, André and GILIOMEE, Hermann
       Afrikaner political thought: analysis and
       documents. Berkeley: University of California
       Press, 1983-, (Perspectives on Southern
       Africa, 22),- vols.

Presents documents germane to Afrikaner political thinking dating from the Eighteenth Century, and designed ultimately to extend to the present. Volume One covers the period 1780 to 1850. Subsequent to placing early Afrikaner thought in its historical context and thereafter assembling documents which serve to illustrate the discussion presented on each section, the work is divided into the following sub-sections: the colonial crisis, labour and slavery, 1780-1840; law, order and equality, 1780-1860; the politics and morality of frontier conflict, 1780-1870; settlement, conquest and trek, 1800-1860; and colonial grievances, civil liberties and self-government, 1778-1854. These have all been translated into English.

277   DU TOIT, André
        Captive to the nationalist paradigm: Prof.
        F.A. van Jaarsveld and the historical
        evidence for the Afrikaner's ideas on his
        calling and mission. South African Historical
        Journal, vol. 16, November 1984, p. 49-80
        (With a reply by van Jaarsveld: p. 81)

        Focusses on the seminal essays of F.A. van Jaarsveld,
        stating that his work reveals in-depth and influential
        utilization of relevant primary evidence in the modern
        literature.

278   DU TOIT, André
        Facing up to the future: some personal
        reflections on the predicament of Afrikaner
        intellectuals in the legitimation crisis of
        Afrikaner nationalism and the apartheid
        state. Social Dynamics, vol. 7, no. 2, 1981,
        p. 1-27

        Examines the relationship between Afrikaner
        intellectuals and Afrikaner nationalism in the light of
        a changing South Africa. Describes and explores what he
        terms the 'inner crisis' of Afrikaner intellectuals.
        Utilizes imaginative projection based on personal
        experience and discussion placed within the relevant
        social and historical framework.

279   DU TOIT, André
        No chosen people: the myth of the Calvinist
        origins of Afrikaner nationalism and racial
        ideology. American Historical Review, vol.
        88, no. 4, October 1983, p. 920-952

        Author defines his study: 'the present essay will be
        limited to a critical survey of the relevant secondary
        evidence for the existence of a "primitive Calvinism"
        and of the ideology of a Chosen People among early

Afrikaners during the crucial period from the mid-eighteenth to the mid-nineteenth century'. This complements the author's survey of the relevant evidence in the primary sources for the history of early Afrikaner thinking prior to 1880 in his: Captive to the Nationalist paradigm, q.v.

280   DU TOIT, Bettie
        Ukubamba amadolo: workers' struggles in the
        South African textile industry. London: Onyx,
        1978, 145 p.

The author, for many years a worker and trade union organizer in South African secondary industries, provides, says Nadine Gordimer in the foreword '. . . in an informal way fascinating even to general readership a politico-historical microcosm of the black workers' struggle'. Covering the period from the early 1930s, du Toit chronicles the struggles over forty years of South African textile workers for better working conditions.

281   DU TOIT, Darcy
        Capital and labour in South Africa: class
        struggles in the 1970s. London: Kegan Paul,
        1981, 495 p.

Concentrates on the class nature of South Africa's social struggle during the 1970s set within its historical background, legal regulations, political and industrial organization. He thereafter concentrates on the strikes of that period as manifestations of the rising movement of the black working class. Examines the role of the Black Consciousness Movement, the South African Communist Party, the South African National Congress and the South African Congress of Trade Unions. Reviewed by Baruch Hirson in an article entitled, Marxists, neo-Marxists, and labour history in South Africa. Journal of Commonwealth and Comparative Politics, vol. 21, no. 1, March 1983, p. 80-85.

282   DU TOIT, M.A.
        South African trade unions: history,
        legislation, policy. Johannesburg: McGraw-
        Hill, 1976, 198 p.

        Set against a detailed theoretical framework, which
        includes among others, factors such as functions,
        organizational structure, member participation, reasons
        for joining, origins and growth, acceptance and
        recognition, economic development, the author
        thereafter examines pertinent legislation and National
        Party government policy. The origin and development of
        black trade unions is highlighted, and Du Toit provides
        a detailed analysis of the Bantu Labour Act of 1953.
        Surveys South African trade unionism since 1950, the
        Trade Union Council of South Africa, mine workers'
        unions and black labour. Concludes by providing
        extensive information on the structure of trade unions
        as at 1974.

283   DVORIN, Eugene P.
        Racial separation in South Africa: an
        analysis of apartheid theory. Chicago:
        University of Chicago Press, 1952. 256 p.

        Analyzes the apartheid policy of the National Party and
        related events, providing the reader with discussion on
        pre-apartheid racial policy, the forces shaping it as
        well as apartheid and political theory. He thereafter
        studies the effects on both urban and rural blacks, the
        Indians and Coloureds, and implications for
        neighbouring states.

284   ECONOMY and society in pre-industrial South Africa,
        edited by Shula Marks and Anthony Atmore.
        London: Longman, 1980, 385 p.

As stated by the editors, the objective of these case studies is 'to explore three crucial areas in South Africa's nineteenth-century history: the nature of precapitalist social formations; the ways in which these were affected, if not necessarily yet restructured, by colonial penetration and mercantile capital; and the impact on Africans of the colonial experience and methods of social control'. The work comprises a detailed introduction by the editors followed by thirteen essays depicting various aspects of the socio-economic basis of diverse area studies. Reviewed by Baruch Hirson in an article entitled: 'Marxists, neo-Marxists and labour history in South Africa. Journal of Commonwealth and Comparative Politics, vol. 21, no. 1, March 1983, p. 80-85.

285   EDELSTEIN, Melville Leonard
        A sociological study of the Coloured Community of Johannesburg with special reference to attitude analysis. Pretoria: University of Pretoria, 1973, 359 p.

        Thesis: Ph.D.

        As the third largest Coloured Community in the Republic, a study was conducted in Johannesburg based on a sample of 500 residents, utilizing the results of a questionnaire. Various facets of their social structure and attitudes towards their role and position in South Africa's socio-political structure were ascertained.

286   EDELSTEIN, Melville Leonard
        What do Coloureds think? An attitude study of the Coloured Community of Johannesburg. Johannesburg: Labour and Community Consultants, 1974, 153 p.

        Thesis: Ph.D. (City University of New York)

Investigates aspects of their social structure and specific attitudes such as political and social to other groups and stereotyped concepts of South African ethnic groups. Their grievances are assessed. The questionnaire is reproduced in the appendix. This study is substantiated by numerous tables.

287   EDELSTEIN, Melville Leonard
        What do young Africans think? An attitude
        survey of urban African Matric pupils in
        Soweto with special reference to stereotyping
        and social distance: a sociological study.
        Johannesburg: South African Institute of Race
        Relations, 1972, 122 p.

In order to determine a more knowledgeable perception of black attitudes, this study was conducted amongst 200 Soweto students. The purpose was to determine their attitudes towards thirteen ethnic groups, themselves and their situation. The study further determined whether the subjects' attitude were affected by the following: the intermarriage of their parents; birthplace of their parents; education of their father; occupation of their father; their sex; their religious affiliation; the local chiefdom to which they belong; and their period of residence in a city. Findings summarized in various tables.

288   EDUCATION: control and resistance. Africa Perspective,
        no. 24, 1984 (entire issue: 116 p.)

Comprises the following contributions: redefining education – the White Paper on the Provision of Education (Michael Gardiner); education and training in the homelands: a separate development? A case study of Bophuthatswana (Francine de Clerq); the historical roots of Bantu education; what school students think – Matric pupils' attitudes in the Mafikeng Region (Monty Roodt and Mike Lawrence); an interview with Azaso students, with Cosas activists, and with Kate Phillip, president of Nusas; worker education in the 1970s (Lisa Seftel); formal education programmes of the Congress Alliance.

289   EDUCATION, race and social change in South Africa, edited by John A. Marcum for the Study Team of the United States-South Africa Leader Exchange Program. Berkeley: University of California Press, 1982, 251 p.

The educational needs of black South Africans are explored and assessed as a result of various visits to South Africa by a team of American educationalists, sponsored by the United States-South Africa Leader Exchange Program. Dr Marcum presents an historically-orientated introduction and collates the findings of the USSALEP team, prior to offering a selection of eighteen documents, South African-based, with one exception, which contribute to the debate on the Republic's educational present and future.

290   EDWARDS, Jan
       Migrant labour: a select bibliography. Johannesburg: South African Institute of Race Relations, 1974, 35 p.

Compiled for a one-day Black Sash Conference on Migrant Labour, held in Johannesburg in August 1974, the compiler states that this work is fairly comprehensive but should not be regarded as exhaustive. It relies mainly on material from the South African Institute of Race Relations, University of the Witwatersrand, and published catalogues. Entries are divided into three main sections, individually numbered: South Africa; other African countries; and other countries. There are no additional author or subject indexes.

291   EDWARDS, Jan and HORNER, Dudley
        A select bibliography on the poverty datum
        line in South Africa. Johannesburg: South
        African Institute of Race Relations, 1974,
        22 p.

        Contains 228 entries on the subject. Part I
        concentrates on the pre-1950 period while Part II
        focusses on 1951 to 1974. Also contains references to
        the then Rhodesia. No additional author or subject
        index included.

292   EISELEN, W.W.M.
        Harmonious multi-community development.
        Optima, vol. 9, no. 1, March 1959, p. 1-15

        Dr Eiselen, Secretary of the Department of Bantu
        Administration and Development, outlines government
        policy towards the blacks, taking into account human
        rights, Bantu Authorities, and their political,
        practical, educational, and economic development.

293   EISELEN, W.W.M.
        The meaning of apartheid. Race Relations,
        vol. 15, no. 3, 1948, p. 69-86

        Propounds the view that race separation . 'offers the
        only solution, provided the task is undertaken in an
        honest and constructive spirit'. Outlines the common
        arguments advanced against the system prior to briefly
        describing the positive aspects of apartheid as he sees
        them.

294   EL-KHAWAS, Mohammed A. and HOPE, Constance Morris
        A bibliographical essay on U.S. diplomatic
        relations with South Africa. Journal of
        Southern African Affairs, vol. 4, no. 1,
        January 1979, p. 81-115

Provides initially, a general overview of the literature, prior to presenting a brief review of the major works on United States policy towards South Africa under the Democratic and Republican Administrations for the period 1960 to 1978. The bibliography subsequently presented, is unnumbered, and follows an alphabetical arrangement.

295   EL MAHMUD-OKEREKE, N. Enuma
        OAU: time to admit South Africa. (Lagos?):
        El-Mahmud Mass Communication of Nigeria
        (EMMCON), 1983, 93 p.

Advocates his reasons for promoting South Africa's application for membership to the Organisation of African Unity.

296   EMDON, Erica
        Co-option and control: TUCSA and the African unions in the sixties. Africa Perspective, no. 25, 1984, p. 40-63

Defines the scope of the article as a description of strategies adopted by the Trade Union Council of South Africa in the 1960s to protect its members, given the factors which were beginning to undermine white privileged position in particular. Central to TUCSA's functioning during this period was its approach to black workers, causing tension and several splits, and changes to its constitution.

297   ENGLISH-SPEAKING SOUTH AFRICA: AN ASSESSMENT.
        Conference, Grahamstown, 1974.
        English-speaking South Africa, edited by André de Villiers. Cape Town: Oxford University Press, 1976, 387 p.

Critically assesses the achievements of English-speaking South Africans in the fields of public affairs, population and community, the economy, religion, education, language and literature, and the media.

298   ENTERPRISE and exploitation in a Victorian colony: aspects of the economic and social history of colonial Natal, edited by Bill Guest and John Sellers. Pietermaritzburg: University of Natal Press, 1985, 360 p.

A collection of twelve essays based on extensive original research, this work records information on wide-ranging topics such as the Port Natal harbour; railway development; the impact of white settlers on the natural environment; external exchange and the Zulu kingdom; colonial agriculture; the woolled-sheep industry; indentured and free Indians; Indian trade; African economic experiments; the impoverishment of the Natal peasantry; and the pre-Union coal industry.

299   ESSAYS in Southern African labour history, edited by Eddie Webster. Johannesburg: Ravan, 1978, 248 p.

Divided into five sections, this history details control and resistance on the mines; classes, the state and industrial relations; early African trade unionism; class and Afrikaner nationalism, and organized labour under apartheid. Comprising articles originally published in the South African Labour Bulletin, contributors include Philip Bonner, Robert Davies, Linda Ensor, Jeff Lever, David Lewis, Jon Lewis, John Mawbey, Sean Moroney, Dan O'Meara, Ian Phimister, Mark Stein, Peter Warwick and Eddie Webster.

300   EVANS, Gavin
        The role of the military in education in
        South Africa. Cape Town: University of Cape
        Town, 1983, 285 p.

        Dissertation: BA (Hons)

        Provides an analysis of the militarization of education
        in South Afria, addressing the relationship between
        repressive and ideological state apparatus. Commences
        by examining the South African state, the economic
        crisis, political restructuring, upsurge of the masses,
        the "Total Strategy" and the rise of the military. The
        role of the South African Defence Force in white
        schools, universities and black education is critically
        assessed.

301   FACT Paper on Southern Africa
            no. 1 -   , 1976 -   Irregular
            London: International Defence and Aid Fund
            for Southern Africa

        Titles include, among others: African worker and
        apartheid by David Davis, (no. 5); The apartheid war
        machine: the strength and deployment of the South
        African armed forces (no. 8); Apartheid's army in
        Namibia: South Africa's illegal military occupation
        (no. 10); Akin to slavery: prison labour in South
        Africa, by Allen Cook (no. 11); Massacre at Maseru:
        South African aggression against Lesotho (no. 12).

302   FACTS and Reports
            1972 -   Bi-monthly
            Amsterdam: Holland Committee on Southern
            Africa

        Comprises press cuttings on Southern Africa covering
        wide-ranging political and economic developments.

303 FATTON, Robert
   The African National Congress of South Africa:
   the limitations of a revolutionary strategy.
   Canadian Journal of African Studies, vol. 18,
   no. 3, 1984, p. 593-608

   This critical analysis of the revolutionary strategy
   and ideology of the African National Congress of South
   Africa (ANC) seeks to show that despite its socialist
   rhetoric the ANC is fundamentally a populist movement
   which has yet to go beyond the confines of petty-
   bourgeois radicalism. Its petty-bourgeois radicalism is
   embedded in the creation of an all-class common front
   rather than in the determined mobilization of the black
   proletariat and peasantry. Not surprisingly, the ANC
   still espouses the old and cautious Freedom Charter of
   the 1950s as its revolutionary programme of the 1980s.
   Accordingly, in spite of its adoption at Morogoro in
   1969 of a "Revolutionary Programme," the ANC has failed
   to develop a truly socialist revolutionary strategy as
   well as a programmatic and ideological vision of a
   post-apartheid South Africa. Indeed it has eschewed
   class analysis and opted for the more "pragmatic" and
   all embracing politics of nationalism. In addition, the
   exigencies and viscissitudes of exile which were forced
   on the ANC by the repressiveness of the apartheid
   regime also limited its revolutionary character. They
   contributed to a certain alienation of the masses from
   the leaders and engendered for many years the relative
   primacy of the military over the political struggle.
   (Journal abstract)

304 FATTON, Robert
   Class and nationalism in South Africa: a
   study in the radicalization of black politics
   (1952-1976). Ann Arbor: University Microfilms
   International, 1981, 331 p.

   Thesis: Ph.D. (University of Notre Dame)

Set against an analytical background assessing the following theories: liberal/capitalist, cultural/ pluralist, radical/neo-Marxist, Fatton procedes to a periodization of African resistance dating from 1652. Says of his work: I concentrate on the two most important means of African resistance to white supremacy: the African National Congress (ANC) representing the oldest and most prestigious black organization, and the more recent but equally prestigious Black Consciousness Movement. My thesis is that the ideological manifestations of black nationalism are essential to any understanding of contemporary South Africa, for the content of this nationalism has and will have a decisive impact on the unfolding political and revolutionary struggle as well as on the institution of a "liberated" South Africa . . .' Attention should be drawn to Fatton's book entitled: Black Consciousness in South Africa. Albany: State University of New York, 1986, 195 p.

305   FEIT, Edward
       South Africa: the dynamics of the African
       National Congress. London: Oxford University
       Press under the auspices of the Institute of
       Race Relations, 1962, 73 p.

Anaylzes reasons why, as at the time of the 1956-1961 Treason Trial, the African National Congress could not be regarded as an effective mass movement. In this context, internal and external pressures on the Congress are examined.

306   FEIT, Edward
       Urban revolt in South Africa, 1960-1964: a
       case study. (n.p.): Northwestern University
       Press, 1971, 365 p.

Author states that his work is intended as a case study of attempted urban insurgency - its organization, limited success and ultimate failure. He introduces the study with a survey of African resistance in South Africa, followed by a theoretical framework of protest. Although the role of the African National Congress, the South African Communist Party and Umkonto we Sizwe are featured, the main emphasis is on the role played by the average person. Based largely on the trials of those who participated in the insurgency, the appendices include a record of acts of sabotage during the period under review, and select biographies.

307   FEIT, Edward
      Workers without weapons: the South African
      Congress of Trade Unions and the Organization
      of African Workers. Hamden, Conn: Archon
      Books, 1975, 230 p.

Set against an historical background providing information on the first of the African trade unions - the Industrial and Commercial Workers' Union, this work concentrates mainly on the South African Congress of Trade Unions. The organization is explored in detail and reasons for its failure are advanced. Chronicles current developments and assesses future propsects for trade unions.

308   FENRICK, Joseph C.
      South African politics and race relations:
      selected bibliography of books and articles
      published since 1961. Washington D.C.:
      Library of Congress, Legislative Reference
      Service, 1966, 16 p.

Separately lists books and articles published during the period under review. Material is unnumbered but alphabetically arranged index under the subdivisions of history; government/politics; race relations/apartheid;

Bantustans; the United States and South Africa; the United Nations and South Africa. Concludes with a brief list of references on Namibia.

309   FIG, David
        South African interests in Latin America.
        South African Review, 2, 1984, p. 239-255

Presents an overview of the role of the South African state and monopoly capital in Latin America. Pays particular attention to two major South African investments - that of the Anglo American Corporation mainly in Brazil, and of the fishing industry with a focus on Chile, which the author has placed in their political and social contexts.

310   FINE, Alan and RAFEL, Robyn
        Trends in organised labour. South African Review, 3, 1986, p. 1-19

Reviews the 1984 to 1985 period under the following headings: unity talks, the split union phenomenon, the International Mineworkers Federation, the Trade Union Council of South Africa, legislation, and the National Manpower Commission.

311   FIRST, Ruth
        Black gold: the Mozambican miner, proletarian and peasant. Brighton: Harvester Press, 1983, 256 p.

Documents and analyzes the Mozambican migrant labour system. States that the purpose of this in-depth study 'is to contribute to the process of breaking out of colonialism and capitalism; of restructuring the South African economy; of transforming production, and especially labour's part in it'. The appendices include information on the conventions on mine labour between Portugal and South Africa; questionnaires presented to miners, and to selected households; the Agreement of Service between mineworkers and the Employment Bureau of Africa; and the Charter of Rights for Migrant Workers in Southern Africa.

312   FIRST, Ruth (and others)
        The South African connection: Western investment in apartheid, by Ruth First, Jonathan Steele, and Christabel Gurney. London: Temple Smith, 1972, 352 p.

In this study of South Africa's political economy, the issue of investment or disengagement facing British and Western multinational companies is addressed. Illustrates that blacks have not benefitted from the industrial boom, the wage gap is widening, and unemployment is widespread.

313   FIVE African states: responses to diversity, edited by Gwendolen M. Carter. Ithaca: Cornell University Press, 1963, 643 p.

South Africa, by Thomas Karis, p. 471-616

Providing a background of the people and political history of the country, Karis discusses the four interacting but conflicting developments which he states are important to the understanding of contemporary South Africa. These are: the spread of racial integration in the economy, the failure of liberalism, the rise of Afrikaner nationalism, and the emergence of African nationalism.

314   FOCUS on Political Repression in Southern Africa no. 1 -, November 1975 - 6 p.a. London: International Defence and Aid Fund, Research, Information and Publications Department

Provides coverage of political trials and imprisonment, detentions, banning and state security measures in both South Africa and Namibia. As a supplement to this serial publication, five Briefing Papers are produced annually with the aim of providing detailed but succinct information on a specific topic including a summary of the year's events. Supersedes: Southern Africa Information Service.

315   FOLTZ, William J.
        The security situation in Southern Africa: an interpretive essay IN: AFRICAN regional security and the OAU's role in the next decade, edited by Nosakhare O. Obaseki. New York: International Peace Academy, 1984, p. 28-36

In this report of the International Peace Academy Workshop held in New York, 1983, Professor Foltz, Director of International and Area Studies at Yale University, assesses the increasing militarization of the South African state. He analyzes the effect of South Africa's policy of destabilization within the region which he indicates originates fundamentally from the Republic's internal policies.

316   FRANKEL, Philip
        The dynamics of a political renaissance: the Soweto Students Representative Council. Journal of African Studies, vol. 7, no. 3, Fall 1980, p. 167-180

An evaluation of this urban black political organization comprised of the township's youth, is presented to demonstrate the political meaning of the 1976 riots and the forces which have fuelled a new black authenticity.

317   FRANKEL, Philip
       Political   culture and revolution in   Soweto.
       Journal of Politics,   vol. 43, no. 3, August
       1981, p. 831-849

       Given the constraints in defining political culture in
       Soweto,   Frankel states that 'it is important to
       delineate   the perceived political world   in   the
       townships in order to come to grips with the major
       issues of contemporary South African politics; in doing
       so, it is equally important to treat the emerging
       parameters in a broadly cautious manner'. Traces the
       basic contours of township political culture upon which
       he elaborates his statement that 'South Africa is
       entering (or has in fact entered) an   incipient
       revolutionary situation'.

318   FRANKEL, Philip
       Pretoria   praetorians: civil   military
       relations   in   South   Africa.   Cambridge:
       Cambridge University Press, 1984, 207 p.

       A study of the increased role of the military in   South
       African politics, not only in public decision-making
       but in the economy, in the education of young people
       and in a variety of social relations generally. Sources
       of militarization in recent South African history and
       developments over the last fifteen years are analyzed.
       Includes   a   study of the current status of
       militarization and an evaluation of whether this is a
       realistic response to South Africa's problems.

319   FRANKEL, Philip
       Race and counter-revolution: South Africa's
       'total strategy' Journal of Commonwealth and
       Comparative Politics, vol. 18, no.   3,
       November 1980, p. 272-292

Provides an analysis of the 'total strategy' concept, illustrating factors which have sensitized whites 'to the necessity of carefully coordinating energies and resources in the face of majority demands for political change'. Identifies a number of features indicative of this policy's utilization as an instrument of counter-revolution, and to what degree it has been viable.

320 FREDERIKSE, Julie
South Africa: a different kind of war - from Soweto to Pretoria. Johannesburg: Ravan, 1986, 192 p.

Based on interviews and excerpts from the media this illustrated work chronicles from 1976 the history of the struggle against white minority rule. Material is organized into the categories of resistance, reform, repression and war.

321 FREDMAN, Sandra (and others)
The narrow margin: how black and white South Africans view change by Sandra Fredman, Marian Nell and Peter Randall. Cape Town: Philip, 1983, 127 p.

Compiled by the Human Awareness Programme from the research of the Arnold Bergstraesser Institute of Socio-Political Research, this study provides information on the feelings and attitudes of black and white South Africans in the search for peaceful change. Topics covered include the politics of apartheid; the 'homeland' policy; white support for apartheid; the economic reality, the social reality; black resistance to white domination; alternative political solutions; and strategies for the future. Appendices include both the urban black sample and that of the whites.

322 FREDRICKSON, George M.
White supremacy: a comparative study in American and South African history. New York: Oxford University Press, 1981, 356 p.

In this comparative study of race relations, the William Smith Mason Professor of American History at Northwestern University explains the historical development of white supremacy in the United States and South Africa by concentrating on attitudes, beliefs, and policies in both societies. These he compares by breaking down the history of white supremacy into parallel phases or aspects revealing both similarities and differences.

323   FREER, Pamela A. and SAMSON D.
        South Africa: business prospects re-assessed.
        London: Economist Intelligence Unit, 1982,
        107 p.

Written by the Economist Intelligence Unit's Southern African representatives, these economic consultants review and assess opportunities and prospects within the various sectors of the economy - mining, manufacturing, agriculture, commerce, finance, property, tourism, and the public sector. Chief characteristics of the economy are itemized, recent economic history is reviewed as well as changes which have occurred in the Republic. Useful tables included.

324   FREER, Pamela A.
        South Africa to 1990: growing to survive.
        London: Economist Intelligence Unit, 1986,
        (Economist Intelligence Unit. Special report,
        no. 239), 121 p.

The author, an economist and business consultant, focusses on an economic prognosis for South Africa over a five year period. She also discusses likely political developments. Chapter headings include the following: recent economic developments; the urbanization issue; political change; labour trends; foreign trade and

124

investment; both world and domestic assumptions behind the central forecast, 1986-1990; and alternative scenarios. Useful appendices provide a guide to South African political groups (including anti-apartheid and trade union groups), and basic information on regional structures and policies.

325   FREUND, W.M.
Forced resettlement and the political economy of South Africa. Review of African Political Economy, no. 29, 1984, p. 49-63

Author aims to provide a generalized and analytical assessment placing the policy and programme of forced population removal within its political and historical context. This he does by examining the scope of the removals, both urban and rural; the significance of this policy and the fate of the resettled. Concludes with a substantial bibliographical note.

326   FREUND, W.M.
Race in the social structure of South Africa, 1652-1836. Race and Class, vol. 18, no. 1, Summer 1976, p. 53-67

Examines the role played by race in the Cape during the Eighteenth and Nineteenth Centuries. He illustrates that the Cape before the Great Trek was not a society based primarily on racial distinctions, despite certain prejudices. This proved to be in direct contrast to the later developments of rigidity and controlled discrimination.

327   FRIEDLAND, Elaine Alice
A comparative study of the development of revolutionary nationalist movements in Southern Africa - Frelimo (Mozambique) and the African National Congress of South Africa. Ann Arbor: University Microfilms International, 1980, 722 p.

Thesis: Ph.D. (City University of New York)

Author states 'the purpose of this political historical
study is to examine the dialectical inter-relationship
between the factors of socio-economic class and of
specific historical circumstances, existing in Southern
Africa which influence the ideologies of the African
National Congress of South Africa (ANC) and the Frente
de Libertacao de Mocambique (FRELIMO), as well as
Frelimo's antecedents'. With reference to the ANC,
particular emphasis is placed on the period post-1949,
although its ideological evolution from 1912 to the
1970's is also covered.

328   FRIEDLAND, Elaine Alice
        South Africa and instability in Southern
        Africa. American Academy and Political and
        Social Sciences. Annals, vol. 463, September
        1982, p. 95-105

        Linkages between South Africa and UNITA in Angola, and
        the Mozambique National Resistance Movement are
        scrutinized. Their reliance on the Republic is
        identified, and their utilization by South Africa for
        its own ends, is examined.

329   FRIEDMAN, Stephen
        Black politics at the crossroads.
        Johannesburg: South African Institute of Race
        Relations, 1986, (South African Institute of
        Race Relations. Topical briefing), 20 p.

        Processes the unrest .prevalent in black townships
        during 1985. Presents background information on the
        turmoil, its features and examines the depth of the
        threat to the system. The strengths and weaknesses of
        the key organizations are identified and the prospects
        for both national and local negotiations are reviewed.

330   FRIEDMAN, Steve
       Political implications of industrial unrest
       in South Africa in: WORKING papers in
       Southern African studies, vol. 3, edited by
       D.C. Hindson. Johannesburg: Ravan, 1983, p.
       123-148

       Provides an historical overview of black unionism and
       traces developments including the implications of the
       Wiehahn Commission. Further developed in his:
       Building tomorrow today: African workers in trade
       unions, 1970-1984. Johannesburg: Ravan, 1987, 300 p.

331   FROM protest to challenge: a documentary history of
       African politics in South Africa, 1882-1964,
       edited by Thomas Karis and Gwendolen M.
       Carter. Stanford: Hoover Institution Press,
       1972-1977, 4 vols.

       A compilation of documents placed within their
       background and setting, reflect the stuggle of the
       African nationalist organizations, engaged in political
       protest and activity. Volume One is entitled: Protest
       and hope, 1882-1932. It comprises three sections, viz
       African politics and the pre-Union political order,
       1882-1909; the establishment of the African National
       Congress, accelerated protest and appeals abroad, 1910-
       1920; and new groupings for effective organization and
       representation, 1921-1932. Volume Two is entitled: Hope
       and challenge, 1935-52, and again comprises three parts
       - Africans under the threat of disenfranchisement,
       1935-1937; moderation and militancy, 1937-1949; joint
       action and the Defiance Campaign, 1950-1952. Volume
       Three: Challenge and violence 1953-1964 encompasses the
       Congress Movement, 1953-1956; the last stage of non-
       violence, 1957- May 1961; and the turn to violence
       since 31 May 1961. Volume four consists of political
       biographical profiles for the period under review.

332   FROM shantytown to township: an economic study of African poverty and rehousing in a South African city; edited by Gavin Maasdorp and A.S.B. Humphreys. Cape Town: Juta, 1975, 157 p.

A comparative study on the poverty and rehousing of Durban's black community spanning a fifteen year period, beginning with a survey conducted by the Durban Corporation in 1958 and complemented by research conducted by the University of Natal's Department of Economics. The earlier study reflects conditions in Cato Manor, and thereafter the economic conditions of blacks, later resettled, are assessed. This work is placed within the framework of rural-urban migration and urban growth in Africa, as well as political, social and economic conditions prevalent in South Africa.

333   GANN, Lewis H. and DUIGNAN, Peter
Why South Africa will survive. Cape Town: Tafelberg, 1981, 299 p.

In this expanded version of: South Africa: war, revolution or peace? (1978) the authors state 'we know that our views are unpopular within the academic establishment but are convinced that an interpretation different from the "gloom, guilt and doom" school deserves to be heard'. Discusses the peoples of South Africa, prior to examining the country's politics, economics, strategic and defence potential. Assesses its vulnerability to revolution. In a section devoted to foreign relations, he focusses primarily on United States relations with the Republic and briefly assesses Russian policy towards the region. Investigates the concept of South Africa as pariah state and provides various policy options which the United States could employ towards the Republic.

334   GASTROW, Shelagh
        Who's who in South African politics.
        Johannesburg: Ravan, 1985, 347 p.

        Contains biographical information on 112 people of
        diverse political persuasion selected by the author
        for their influence on both the political direction and
        events in South Africa at the time of compilation. In
        addition, includes a few entries on those with a long
        political involvement, thus providing a perspective of
        political history dating from the mid-nineteen forties.
        Tom Lodge, in a substantial introduction, provides an
        analysis of the sociology of political leadership
        within the South African context.

335   GELB, Stephen and INNES, Duncan
        Economic crisis in South Africa: monetarism's
        double bind. Work in Progress, 36, 1985, p.
        31-39

        Assesses the recession in the Republic at the time of
        writing, examining both international and local causes.
        The crisis in the long-term is probed, taking
        cognisance of the government's monetarist principles in
        their attempt to resolve the issue.

336   GELDENHUYS Deon Johannes and KOTZÉ, Hennie
        Aspects of political decision-making in South
        Africa. Politikon, vol. 10, no. 1, June 1983,
        p. 33-45

        Presents a succinct survey of the Republic's most
        noteworthy decision-making structures from which the
        importance of the State Security Council and its
        substructures become apparent. The political
        implications of these are identified, as well as five
        additional avenues for further research into the
        decision-making processes.

337   GELDENHUYS, Deon Johannes
        The diplomacy of isolation: South African
        foreign policy making. Johannesburg:
        Macmillan for the South African Institute of
        International Affairs, 1984, 295 p.

        The making of South African foreign policy under Prime
        Ministers Vorster and Botha, forms the focus of this
        study which encompasses the period 1966-1981. Based on
        many personal interviews, the material is arranged as
        follows: background is presented in both chapters 1 and
        2 in order to provide an overview of the development of
        foreign policy making in the period 1910-1966; the most
        important features in South Africa's domestic and
        external environment are then highlighted to clarify
        the setting of its foreign policy making. This is
        examined from various angles - the roles of the
        legislature, the political office holders in the
        executive, the government departments, and that of the
        public.

338   GELDENHUYS, Deon Johannes and GUTTERIDGE, William
        Instability and conflict in Southern Africa:
        South Africa's role in regional security.
        Conflict Studies, no. 148, 1983 (entire
        issue: 26 p.)

        Divided into two sections, William Gutteridge analyzes
        the content, and places in context, the reasons for re-
        publishing an article by Deon Geldenhuys and stresses
        the gravity of South Africa's destabilization policies
        for the region, the West, and South Africa itself.
        Professor Geldenhuys' article entitled: The destabili-
        sation controversy and analysis of a high risk foreign
        policy option for South Africa, was originally
        published in Politikon, vol. 9, no. 2, December 1982,
        p. 16-31. Considers questions relevant to the avoidance
        of major regional conflict, and the future of the

Republic itself. Examines the stability of neighbouring states, and the role of Soviet influence. Concludes that South Africa can respond in alternative ways to perceived threats.

339   GELDENHUYS, Deon Johannes
Internasionale isolasie: Suid-Afrika in vergelykende perspektief. (International isolation: South Africa in comparative perspective). Johannesburg: Rand Afrikaans University, 1986, (Randse Afrikaanse Universiteit. Publikasie. C41, 1986), 106 p.

In a shortened version of the author's Inaugural Lecture delivered in October 1985, Geldenhuys considers the concept of the international isolation of states in international politics, both self and externally imposed. Four areas are identified - diplomatic, economic, military and socio-cultural. Twenty specific indicators of isolation within the four specified areas are introduced in order to assess and compare isolation among states. South Africa is utilized as a case study and a comparison with Taiwan, Israel, Chile and 'normal states' is included.

340   GELDENHUYS, Deon Johannes and KOTZÉ, Hennie
Man of action. Leadership South Africa, vol. 4, no. 2, 1985, p. 30-49

As a product of wide-ranging interviews, this article is an attempt by the authors to reflect the personality of President Botha. Interspersed with biographical information, P.W. Botha's political development is chronicled, together with an assessment of his leadership style.

341   GELDENHUYS, Deon Johannes and KOTZÉ, Hennie
P.W. Botha as decision maker: a preliminary study of personality and politics. Politikon, vol. 12, no. 1, June 1985, p. 30-42

This article starts with a review of the literature on political decision making in South Africa. It is pointed out that the existing studies devote considerable attention to identifying the key role players in top-level decision making. However, very little research has been done on the effects of leaders' personal characteristics on the making of public policy in South Africa. This study focuses in particular on the personal political style of P.W. Botha. It applies Hermann's conceptual scheme to analyse Botha's decision and interpersonal style. The authors conclude by stressing that this field of research still poses many challenges. (Authors' abstract)

342   GELDENHUYS, Deon Johannes
       Some foreign policy implications of South
       Africa's 'Total National Strategy' with
       particular reference to the '12-point plan'.
       Johannesburg: South African Institute of
       International Affairs, 1981, 63 p.

With its scope succinctly defined: how will the total national strategy affect South Africa's present international standing, Geldenhuys considers the South African government's perception of this concept, as its official counter-strategy. The 12-point plan, the text of which is reproduced for the user's convenience, is analyzed in some detail and several observations drawn.

343   GELDENHUYS, Deon and VAN WYK, Koos
       South Africa in crisis: a comparison of the
       Vorster and Botha eras.   South Africa
       International,   vol. 16, no. 3, January 1986,
       p. 135-145

Compares the crisis periods of 1976-78, and 1984-85 which reveal analogies in both the nature of the challenges presented to the government, and responses.

The following aspects are considered: situations of crisis, response to domestic and international pressures, challenges from the right, breakdowns after breakthroughs, styles of decision-making, and the Namibian settlement issue.

344   GELDENHUYS, Deon Johannes
       South Africa's black homelands: past objectives, present realities and future developments. Johannesburg: South African Institute of International Affairs, 1981, (South African Institute of International Affairs. Special study), 104 p.

Examines the political future of the South African homelands. Scenarios together with their salient features are presented, based on the past objectives of the homelands policy, and the position at the time of writing.

345   GELDENHUYS, Deon Johannes
       South Africa's security since the Second World War. Johannesburg: South African Institute of International Affairs, 1978, 19 p.

Identifies and elaborates on the characteristics of South Africa's search for security which, states Geldenhuys, have remained remarkably consistent. Utilizing a chronological and thematic approach, these five characteristics are analyzed within their political concept.

346   GELDENHUYS, Deon Johannes
       What do we think? A survey of white opinion on foreign policy issues. Johannesburg: South African Institute of International Affairs, 1982, 32 p.

A survey, in the form of a questionnaire was sent to a representative sample of some 2 400 adult whites, the findings of which reveal their comprehension of South African foreign affairs. Opinion on threat perception and how to meet it was then assessed, as were correlations between opinion and certain contentious political issues. A copy of the questionnaire is included. Updated in numbers 2 and 3, published in 1984 and 1986 respectively.

347   GERHART, Gail M.
        Black power in South Africa: the evolution of
        an   ideology.   Berkeley: University   of
        California   Press,   1978,   (Perspectives   on
        Southern Africa, no. 19), 364 p.

The   development of African nationalism since   1945   is
the basis of this work ' ... its primary emphasis is on
the   intellectual dimension of black political history,
and in particular on the interplay of ideologies   which
has   marked the post-war era and which has brought many
present-day African   intellectuals   to   their   present
Black Power perspective'.

348   GEYSER, Ockert
        Watershed   for   South   Africa,   London   1961.
        Durban: Butterworths, 1983, 117 p.

Written   by a Professor of History at the University of
the   Orange Free State,   and   incorporating   interviews
with   leading   political   personalities,   this   work
examines   South Africa's role within the British Empire
and factors leading to its ultimate withdrawal from the
Commonwealth.

349   GIBSON, Richard
       African liberation movements: contemporary
       struggles against white minority rule.
       London: Oxford University Press for the
       Institute of Race Relations, 1972, 350 p.
       South Africa: p. 17-105

Set against an introductory chapter discussing the
concept of national liberation in Africa and providing
background information on South Africa, Gibson examines
the African National Congress, Unity Movement, and the
Pan Africanist Congress. Provides a detailed political
history of each movement.

350   GIDLOW, Roger
       Balance of payment trends and economic
       policies IN: SOUTH Africa in the world
       economy, edited by Jacqueline Matthews.
       Johannesburg: McGraw-Hill, 1983, p. 97-120

Author analyzes the implications for South Africa's
domestic economic policy of a strengthened balance of
payments, prior to focussing on the suitability of the
current exchange rate and exchange control policies.
Gold sale policies are discussed with especial
attention to cushioning the impact of the volatile
patterns of gold price movements upon the gold mining
industry and the economy.

351   GIDLOW, Roger
       The impact of the foreign debt standstill.
       Bank of Lisbon. Economic Focus, no. 30,
       November 1985, (entire issue, 6 p.)

Elaborates on South Africa's decision of September 1985
to impose a partial standstill on foreign debt
repayments, by providing background to the financial
measures. Thereafter discusses implications for the
position of the rand, and the future development of the
foreign exchange market.

352   GILIOMEE, Hermann
        The parting of the ways: South African
        politics 1976-82. Cape Town: Philip, 1982,
        165 p.

Mainly essays written for newspapers, this collection
traces political events after the 1976 Soweto Riots
until the split in National Party during 1982.
Illustrates that this can be regarded as a distinctive
period in South African politics with the demise of the
Verwoerdian political concept, a substantial challenge
by blacks to white domination, and an attempt by the
ruling Afrikaners to extend their power base.
Interwoven in this study is an examination of pertinent
issues including these of the free market, press
freedom, reform attempts, the Namibian issue, and the
prospects for political realignments. Reviewed by Lucy
Mair in African Affairs, vol. 82, no. 329, October
1983, p. 592-593.

353   GINWALA, Frene
        Indian South Africans. Minority Rights Group
        (London). Report, no. 34, 1977, (entire
        issue: 20 p.)

In this survey, consideration is paid to historical
background, their position at the time of writing –
economically, educationally and politically, and a
prognosis for the future is offered. New edition
published in 1985, 20 p.

354   GINWALA, Frene
        The press in South Africa. Index on
        Censorship, vol. 2, no. 3, 1973, p. 27-43

An edited and shortened version of a paper prepared for
the United Nations Unit on Apartheid. Author states
that a free press can only exist in a free society.
Surveys the status of the press in South Africa,

dividing the study into African, Afrikaans and the English language papers, press policy, and censorship. Lists legislation governing the latter.

355   GOEDHUYS, D.W.
       The Rand Monetary Area IN: ALTERNATIVE structures for Southern Africa interaction: a collection of addresses presented at a seminar given by the Institute of Foreign and Comparative Law, University of South Africa. Pretoria: Africa Institute of South Africa, 1982, p. 18-21

       Sketches the background to the Rand Monetary Area agreement of 1974 prior to elaborating on its main provisions. Implications for the area are assessed.

356   GOLDBERG, Melvin
       The nature of Afrikaner nationalism. Journal of Modern African Studies, vol. 23, no. 1, March 1985, p. 125-131

       Chronologically examines Afrikaner nationalism viewed in terms of its class character, while taking into consideration the approach attempted by Dan O'Meara in his book: Volkskapitalisme: class, capital and ideology in the development of Afrikaner nationalism, q.v.

357   GOLDIN, Ian
       Aspects of the dialectic of class and race in South Africa: a deviation IN: SOUTHERN African studies - retrospect and prospect. Edinburgh: University of Edinburgh, Centre of African Studies, 1983, p. 31-45

       Reviews the relevant literature, focussing particularly on the short-comings in some of the well-known works, and highlighting lesser-known ones which could be utilized to provide more insights into the debate.

358   GOODWIN, June
           Cry amandla!: South African women and the
           question of power. New York: Africana, 1984,
           252 p.

           Elizabeth Schmidt in reviewing this book for Africa
           Today, vol. 31, no. 2, 1984, p. 52-54 says the author
           . . . explores 'the vast nuanced terrain that separates
           individuals of a single gender within and between
           racial groupings. A correspondent in South Africa for
           the Christian Science Monitor (1976-1979), Goodwin
           tells an intensely personal story, portraying the pain
           and degradation, the anger and resistance to apartheid
           through the lives of individual South African women'.

359   GOOL, Selim Y.
           Mining capitalism and black labour in the
           early industrial period in South Africa: a
           critique of the new historiography. Lund:
           Ekonomisk-Historiska Förening, 1983, 239 p.

           Critically examines the achievements of the 'new
           school' of South African historiography with its
           utilization of Marxist or materialist methodology.
           Concentrates mainly on migrant labour, mining
           capitalism and black labour in the early
           industrialization phase.

360   GORDON, Suzanne
           A talent for tomorrow: life stories of South
           African servants. Johannesburg: Ravan, 1985,
           294 p.

           Portrays the biographies of twenty-three domestic
           workers living in or around Johannesburg. Based on
           edited versions of taped interviews. Experiences and
           views expressed are common to those elsewhere in the
           country.

361   The GOVERNMENT and politics in South Africa, edited by
       Anthony de Crespigny and Robert Schrire. Cape
       Town: Juta, 1978, 260 p.

       An analysis of political institutions and processes
       forms the basis of this work. It comprises a series of
       original essays by fifteen authorities, placed within
       the context of South African politics by Robert
       Schrire.

362   GREEN, Pippa and HIRSCH, Alan
       The impact of resettlement in the Ciskei:
       three case studies. Cape Town: Southern
       Africa Labour and Development Research Unit,
       1983, (Southern Africa Labour and Development
       Research Unit. Saldru working paper, 49),
       133 p.

       Provides an analysis of the relocation concept as
       'possibly one of the most monstrous aspects of
       apartheid' prior to providing an historical
       introduction to the Ciskei, taking into account its
       population and economy. Presents as case studies,
       conditions in Sada, Elukhanyweni and Dimbaza, in order
       to assess longer term implications for those concerned,
       the district and region.

363   GREENBERG, Stanley B.
       Race and state in capitalist development:
       South Africa in capitalist development.
       Johannesburg: Ravan in association with Yale
       University Press, 1980, 489 p.

       Central to this study is persistent racial conflict and
       domination, which Greenberg examines in the primary
       research settings of South Africa and Alabama, although
       the emphasis is upon the former. The main focus is on
       farmers, businessmen and workers. A section is devoted
       to each including an introductory chapter in which

Greenberg 'examines the role of the particular class actors during capitalist development and . . . considers as a logical and theoretical question the probable impact of these actors in a multiracial context'.

364   GREST, Jeremy <u>and</u> HUGHES, Heather
         State strategy and popular response at the local level. <u>South African Review</u>, 2, 1984, p. 45-62

Enlarges on the state's policy with respect to black local government, identifying its contradictory effects on relations between blacks. Events in Lenasia and Lamontville are used to illustrate trends and tensions.

365   GRINKER, David
         Inside Soweto. Johannesburg: Eastern Enterprises, 1986, 133 p.

As former Town Secretary to the Diepmeadow Town Council, Grinker provides 'the inside story of the background to the unrest' based on the record of his own experiences.

366   GRUNDY, Kenneth W.
         A black foreign legion in South Africa? <u>African Affairs</u>, vol. 80, no. 318, January 1981, p. 101-114

Discusses the developing role of blacks in the South African Defence Force. 21 Battalion is examined from various aspects: structure, rank and status of recruits, force levels, training programme and combat duties, pay, benefits and conditions of service. Evaluates the existence of the Battalion as a public relations exercise.

367   GRUNDY, Kenneth W.
        Defence legislation and communal politics:
        the evolution of a white South African nation
        as reflected in the controversy over the
        assignment of armed forces abroad, 1912-1976.
        Athens, Ohio: Ohio University, Center for
        International Studies, 1978, (Ohio
        University. Center for International Studies.
        Papers in international studies, Africa
        series, no. 33), 51 p.

Various facets of South African defence legislation
dating from 1912 are examined and discussed within the
context of a relatively united 'white' nation.

368   GRUNDY, Kenneth W.
        The militarization of South African politics.
        London: Tauris, 1986, 160 p.

Examines the rise of the South African Defence Force
and demonstrates how it has become a participant in
policy making. The effect of this increased power on
the educational system, press, political parties and
the economy is evidenced. The use of blacks in the
Defence Force and problems experienced in homelands
defence are documented.

369   GRUNDY, Kenneth W.
        On domesticating transnational corporations:
        South Africa and the automotive industry.
        Journal of Commonwealth and Comparative
        Politics, vol. 19, no. 2, July 1981, p. 157-
        173

Author describes his study ' . . . in a way, a combined
case study for protectionism for infant industry,
mercantilism or economic nationalism, import
substitution, and the subtle enlistment of non-state
actors to develop positive protective foreign
linkages'.

370   GRUNDY, Kenneth W.
       Pax   Pretoriana: South   Africa's   regional
       policy. Current History, vol. 84, no. 501,
       April 1985, p. 150-154

       Surveys South Africa's regional destabilization policy
       which preceded the Nkomati Accord, illustrating that
       'the diplomatic picture leading up to the Nkomati was
       confusing; even contradictory'. States that the civil
       unrest in the Republic 'calls into question the
       elaborate but frail edifice of regional order'.

371   GRUNDY, Kenneth W.
       A review of scholarly literature on
       Pretoria's homelands scheme. Journal of
       Southern African Affairs, vol. 3, no. 2,
       April 1978, p. 225-234

       Briefly places the homelands policy into its political
       context prior to analyzing Cosmas Desmond's The
       discarded people, q.v.; Paul Giniewski's Bantustans: a
       trek towards the future (1961); Christopher Hill's
       Bantustans: the fragmentation of South Africa (1964);
       South Africa's Transkei (1967) by Gwendolen M. Carter,
       Thomas Karis and Newell M. Stultz, q.v.; The African
       Reserves of South Africa by Muriel Horrell (1969); ee
       South Africa: the Bantu Homelands (1972) and Barbara
       Roger's Divide and Rule (1976) q.v.; Transkei: a study
       in economic regression by Jeff Leeuwenburg (1977),
       q.v.; Patrick Laurence's The Transkei: South Africa's
       politics of partition (1976), q.v.; and The Black
       homelands of South Africa by Jeffrey Butler and Robert
       I. Rotberg (1977), q.v.

372   GRUNDY, Kenneth W.
       The rise of the South African security
       establishment: an essay on the changing locus
       of state power. Johannesburg: South African
       Institute of International Affairs, 1983,
       (Bradlow paper, no. 1), 39 p.

Describes the changing power alignments in an attempt to illustrate the security establishment's increasing role in policy-making. Diverse regional and strategic perspectives of government and other agencies are assessed within this framework and the militarization of whites is demonstrated.

373   GRUNDY, Kenneth W.
        Soldiers without politics: blacks in the South African armed forces. Berkeley: University of California Press, 1983, (Perspectives on Southern Africa, no. 33), 416 p.

Reveals the manpower needs which have led to the incorporation of blacks into the Republic's armed services - the police, homelands armies, Namibian and South African Defence Forces. Examines issues such as relationship between military and government leaders, race relations in the military, and the impact of black military service on South African society.

374   GRUNDY, Kenneth W.
        South Africa in the political economy of Southern Africa IN: INTERNATIONAL politics in Southern Africa, edited by Gwendolen M. Carter and Patrick O'Meara. Bloomington: Indiana University Press, 1982, p. 148-178

States that although South Africa may continue to enjoy regional economic co-operation, its internal political system accounts for the failure of co-operative ideas being successfully implemented. Within this context, the author examines the concept of a Constellation of Southern African States and its denunciation in black Africa, as well as the role of the Southern African Development Co-ordination Conference (SADCC) as a viable means of lessenning the black states' dependence on the Republic and of co-ordinating regional development. South Africa's agressive regional military policy which has resulted from this. He concludes that it is ultimately bound to fail.

375   GRUNDY, Kenneth W.
        South Africa's domestic strategy. Current History, vol. 82, no. 482, March 1983, p. 110-114; 132-133

Reflects on constitutional developments in South Africa which he sees as a 'natural by-product of the drift into greater internal and external violence, unrest and dissatisfaction, a corollary of the "total national strategy" born out of the official South African perception of "total onslaught". They reflect P.W. (Botha's) leadership style and experience: organizational, managerial and tempered by 14 years as Minister of Defence.

376   GRUNDY, Kenneth W.
        South Africa's regional defense plans: the homeland armies IN: SOUTH Africa in Southern Africa; the intensifying vortex of violence, edited by Thomas M. Callaghy. New York: Praeger, 1983, p. 133-151

Elaborates on the role expected of the homeland armies as part of a regional defence system 'the exact content of which has never been made public'. Grundy describes the formation of these armies and concentrates particularly on relations between the South African government with the homelands governments and the interaction between their forces and the South African Defence Force. Shortcomings in the homelands policy are revealed by the attempted implementation of a homelands defence policy.

377   GUELKE, Adrian
      Change in South African politics. <u>Political</u>
      <u>Studies</u>, vol. 31, no. 3, September 1983, p.
      479-485

      Provides a critical insight into the literature on
      South African politics noting that 'one might have
      expected all the talk of change to have had an impact
      on the study of South African politics, but at first
      glance little seems to have changed'.

378   GUTTERIDGE, William
      South Africa: evolution or revolution?
      <u>Conflict Studies</u>, no. 171, (1984), (entire
      issue: 38 p.)

      Surveys the political and economic situation in South
      Africa in 1984 which he considers a 'watershed year'
      for the country. Reasons for violence and boycotts are
      discussed, as is the 'total' national strategy;
      relations with neighbouring states; the introduction of
      the new constitution; economic crisis; education and
      unrest; and the homelands policy, which Gutteridge
      describes as a recipe for instability.

379   GUTTERIDGE, William
      South Africa: strategy for survival. <u>Conflict</u>
      <u>Studies</u>, no. 131, June 1981, (entire issue:
      32 p.)

      Considers P.W. Botha's post-1981 election agenda, and
      his ability to persuade the whites to accept enough
      reform to satisfy black aspirations. The Namibian issue
      and prospects for settlement are discussed and the
      impact of possible sanctions imposition assessed.
      Concludes that the success of P.W. Botha in laying the
      foundations for a new and generally acceptable order by
      1985 'are objectively not good'.

380   GUTTERIDGE, William
        The South African crisis: time for
        international action. Conflict Studies, no.
        179, 1985, (entire issue: 22 p.)

        Provides an analysis of the crisis in South Africa
        which resulted in the declaration of a state of
        emergency in 1985. Takes into account the situation
        under the headings: riot, repression and reform; the
        role of the African National Congress, agenda for
        change; international pressures and interests,
        sanctions and disinvestment; towards a non-violent
        future to which end the author advocates the need for
        positive initiative from concerned nations to defuse
        the crisis, suggesting perhaps the implementation of a
        'postwar Marshall Plan' for Southern Africa.

381   GUY, Jeff
        The destruction of the Zulu kingdom: the
        Civil War in Zululand, 1879-1884. London:
        Longman, 1979, 273 p.

        Details the destruction of the Zulu's political
        independence and material strength, basing much of his
        research on documentary sources of the period written
        by the Bishop of Natal, John William Colenso and
        members of his family, political allies of the Zulu.
        Places this within a deeper historical framework in an
        attempt to reveal '. . . the inexorable drive to divert
        the surplus supporting one society and use it to serve
        the interests of another intrusive one'.

382   GUY, Jeff and THABANE, Motlatsi
        The Ma-rashea: a participant's perspective
        IN: CLASS, community and conflict: South
        African perspective, edited by Belinda
        Bozzoli. Johannesburg: Ravan, 1987, (History
        workshop, 3), p. 436-456

146

Within a wider study, encompassing eighteen papers reflecting research in social history, the authors examine the Basuto gang, the Ma-rashea (the Russians) through the oral evidence of Johannes Rantoa.

383   HAARLOV, Jens
        Labour regulation and black workers' struggles in South Africa. Uppsala: Scandinavian Institute of African Studies, 1983, (Scandinavian Institute of African Studies. Research report, no. 68), 80 p.

Chronicles the use rise in workers' organization and militancy since the early 1970s, and the state's response to these developments. Takes into account mass strikes held in Durban (1973), the Soweto strikes (1976) and the strikes of 1981. Both labour organization and labour market regulation are examined. Stresses the importance of an analysis of these labour struggles, as they reveal both the core of the apartheid issue, the potential economic power of the workers, and their influence on future South African politics.

384   HACHTEN, William A. and GIFFARD, C. Anthony
        Total onslaught: the South African press under attack. Johannesburg: Macmillan, 1984, 336 p.

Trace the roots of the conflict between the press and the government. Take cognizance of the Press Council, the Steyn Commission, legal restraints on newspapers, the suppression of the black press, censorship and the transformation of the Afrikaans press. Highlight the role of the South African Broadcasting Corporation as the propaganda arm of the National Party, 'Muldergate' scandal, and speculate on the future of the press. Also published in 1984 under the title: The press and apartheid, by the University of Wisconsin Press.

385   HACKLAND, Brian
           The economic and political context of the
           growth of the Progressive Federal Party in
           South Africa, 1959-1978. Journal of Southern
           African Studies, vol. 7, no. 1, October 1980,
           p. 1-16

           Concentrates on the relationship between the policies
           of the Progressive Federal Party and capital within the
           context of wider changes in the system of social
           relations.

386   HAHLO, H.R. and KAHN, Ellison
           The Union of South Africa: the development of
           its laws and constitution. London: Stevens,
           1960, 900 p.

           Assisted by specialist contributors, Hahlo and Kahn
           present an in-depth examination of the development,
           basic doctrines and institutions of South Africa's laws
           and constitution. Title varies slightly in other
           editions.

387   HAIGH, Bruce
           The Black Consciousness Movement in South
           Africa. Australian Outlook, vol. 35, no. 2,
           August 1981, p. 169-180

           Indicates that very little has been written on the
           Movement and its influence on students, particularly
           during the 1976-7 outbreaks. In order to place in
           perspective the influence of the Movement, and to
           provide a basis for discussion on its role and aims,
           Haigh presents a brief critique of some of the claims
           and facts emanating from Baruch Hirson's book entitled:
           Year of fire, year of ash - the Soweto revolt: roots of
           a revolution? q.v.

148

388   HALE, Frederick
        South Africa: defending the laager. <u>Current
        History</u>, vol. 84, no. 501, April 1985, p.
        155-158, 184-186

        Hale, Scholar in Residence, Department of History,
        University of California at Berkeley provides an
        overview of South Africa's political history,
        concentrating on the role of the whites, the
        development of apartheid, and the conflicting attitudes
        towards reform in the 1980s.

389   HALLETT, Robin
        Desolation on the veld: forced removals in
        South Africa. <u>African Affairs</u>, vol. 83, no.
        332, July 1984, p. 301-320

        Provides a detailed analysis of the Surplus People
        Project Reports on Forced Removals in South Africa,
        q.v. This review goes beyond the normal length as the
        author aims to present information for those unable to
        consult the original documentation. Hallet stresses the
        importance of the Project for its thorough examination
        of the basic structure of apartheid. The reports are
        given greater significance for having been produced in
        South Africa itself.

390   HAMMOND-TOOKE, W.D.
        Boundaries and belief: the structure of a
        Sotho world-view. Johannesburg: Witwatersrand
        University Press, 1981, (Human Sciences
        Research Council. Publication series, no.
        74), 170 p.

        As stated by the author: 'This study of the
        cosmological system of a Sotho people was prompted by a
        desire to understand the values and symbols that
        underlie Sotho worldview in general'. The main focus of
        this work is on their idea system as a cultural
        pattern.

391   HAMMOND-TOOKE, W.D.
       Command or consensus: the development of
       Transkeian local government. Cape Town:
       Philip, 1975, 240 p.

       Examines local government as it existed during the pre-
       colonial system of independent chiefdoms, the period
       1894 to 1955 of 'Direct Rule' under the magistrates,
       and the system of Bantu Authorities. The particular
       focus is on the role of the location headman
       illustrated by detailed case studies. The work is
       placed within the context of an introductory chapter on
       the Transkei and its people. The author is Professor of
       Social Anthropology at the University of the
       Witwatersrand, Johannesburg.

392   HANDBOOK on race relations in South Africa, edited by
       Ellen Hellmann. Cape Town: Oxford University
       Press for the South African Institute of Race
       Relations, 1949, 778 p.

       Thirty-one contributors present an in-depth analysis of
       South Africa's racial structure in order to heighten
       perception of changes and developing patterns taking
       place within the country. Chapters include the
       following topics: population; government and
       administration; the land and its administration;
       labour; trade unions; land and agriculture both within
       and outside the black reserves; Indian land
       legislation; Indian agriculture; urban areas; the pass
       laws; taxation; the national income and the non-
       European; non-European education; health services;
       social welfare; physical education, sport and
       recreation; non-European co-operative societies; non-
       European press; politics; non-European war record in
       South Africa; African religion; religion among Indians;

religion of Cape Malays; African literature; music, arts and crafts; Cape Malay arts and crafts; inter-racial co-operation; race attitudes; the High Commission Territories; and the Mandated Territory of South West Africa.

393   HANF, Theodor (and others)
        South Africa, the prospects of peaceful change: an empirical enquiry into the possibility of democratic conflict resolution, by Theodor Hanf, Heribert Wieland and Gerda Vierdag. London: Collings, 1981, 492 p.

        Translation of: Südafrika, friedlicher Wandel? Based on empirical social research, the authors study the prospects for changing the existing system in order to promote a fully democratic state and social justice. Divided into five parts; the work initially evaluates conditions for peaceful change 'from unilateral to democratic conflict regulation; Part Two scrutinizes the white power centre and its approach to change; Part Three concentrates on the black majority's expectations; Part Four considers the prospects for consociation, while Part Five offers some conjectures on the immediate future. Reviewed in Africa Today, vol. 31, no. 2, 1984, p. 43-44, by Leslie Rubin.

394   HANLON, Joseph
        Beggar your neighbours: apartheid power in Southern Africa. London: Catholic Institute for International Relations in collaboration with James Currey, 1986, 352 p.

        Provides details of South Africa's military attacks on its neighbours and relates these to the control the apartheid state exercises through its economic power and domination of transport links. Examines differences in South Africa's policy towards its surrounding states, illustrating both how and why these countries have reacted in different ways. A popular version of this study was published under the title: Apartheid's second front. (Harmondsworth: Penguin, 1986)

395   HARRIES, David
        Daniel Koza: a working class leader. Africa Perspective, no. 19, 1981, p. 2-38

Provides some biographical information on Daniel Koza, but concentrates mainly on the early trade union movement and Koza's role in organizing the African Distributive Worker's Union, the most powerful black union on the Witwatersrand in the early 1940's. He led two strikes to successful conclusion in the early years of the war, and was furthermore associated with the All African Convention, and the short-lived African Democratic Party.

396   HARRIS, Laurence
        South Africa's external debt crisis. Third World Quarterly, vol. 8, no. 3, July 1986, p. 793-817

Indicates the significance held by political developments making South Africa's debt crisis a special case. Investigates causes, assessment and prospects.

397   HARRIS, P.B.
        Interest groups in South African politics. Salisbury: University College of Rhodesia, 1968, (Monographs in political science, no. 1), 105 p.

One of the earliest accounts of South African interest groups assessing particularly their impact on the Nationalist government, then in the second decade of its power. Characteristics are analyzed pertaining to group involvement in communications, the economic sector, alcohol and hotel interests, trade unions and promotional groups.

398   HARRIS, P.B.
        Studies in African politics: a study of the political process. London: Hutchinson University Library, 1970, 181 p.
        Chapter 5: South Africa - a study of a political process, p. 99-126

Investigates the internal political mechanics of the Republic, with particular focus on the country's major interest groups.

399   HARRISON, David
        The white tribe of Africa: South Africa in perspective. Berkeley: University of California, 1981, (Perspectives on Southern Africa, no. 31), 307 p.

Provides information on the attitudes and aspirations of Afrikaners, dating from the Anglo-Boer War. This work illustrates their transformation into the ruling elite. Based on a series of interviews and originally utilized as material for a television documentary, it includes chapters on contemporary issues such as suppression of dissent, relocation of population, 'Muldergate' and the Prime Ministership of P.W. Botha.

400   HARRISON, Nancy
        Winnie Mandela: mother of a nation. London: Gollancz, 1985, 181 p.

The author states . . . 'I have merely to tell the story of a quite remarkable woman'.

401   HARSCH, Ernest
        South Africa: white rule,   black revolt. New
        York: Monad, 1980, 352 p.

        Divided into two sections, this work initially provides
        an examination of capitalism and oppression in all its
        manifestations including   land,   labour,   homelands
        policy, and education. In the second section, the
        struggle for freedom is documented, tracing the roots
        of resistance, class and colour, African nationalism,
        the rise of Black Consciousness, the 1976 Soweto
        uprising, and the struggle towards Azania.

402   HART, Gillian Patricia
        Some   socio-economic   aspects   of   African
        entreneurship: with special reference to the
        Transkei and Ciskei. Grahamstown: Rhodes
        University, Institute of Social and Economic
        Research, 1972, (Rhodes University. Institute
        of Social and Economic Research. Occasional
        paper, no. 16), 237 p.

        Examines the role of the entrepreneur in economic
        development   substantiated by interviews with some
        eighty black businessmen in Transkei,   Ciskei and
        several urban locations. Entrepreneurship is analyzed
        within the   framework of economic   theory,   with
        particular reference to Africa, prior to extensively
        defining the South African position. Supplemented by
        numerous tables.

403   HASTINGS, Adrian
        The Christian churches and liberation move-
        ments in Southern Africa. African Affairs,
        vol. 80, no. 320, July 1981, p. 345-354

Records the various facets of this complex relationship, including social, intellectual and institutional elements. Focusses particularly on the decades of the 1950s, 60s and 70s, and indicates the differing attitudes within the specified time spans.

404   HATTINGH, P.S.
Bophuthatswana: a select and annotated bibliography. Pretoria: African Institute of South Africa, 1973, (Africa Institute of South Africa. Occasional paper, no. 36), 32 p.

Comprises 294 entries focussing mainly on Bophuthatswana's resources and development. Commences by listing ten bibliographies relevant to the Tswana followed by both general and regular publications. Further categories include history; anthropology; administration and politics; demography; labour; education and social services; finance; settlement and infrastructure; agriculture; mining; industry; commerce; a selection of statutes pertaining to occupation and administration in areas occupied by blacks; proclamations, government notices; and unclassified material. Succinct annotations but contains no author or additional subject index.

405   HAUCK, David (and others)
Two decades of debate: the controversy over U.S. companies in South Africa, by David Hauck, Meg Voorhes and Glenn Goldberg. Washington, D.C.: Investor Responsibility Research Center, 1983, 163 p.

Concentrates on the history and development of the debate in the United States and the South African involvement of American firms. This, the authors trace from the early 1950s through its escalation in the late 1970s, to its status in the early 1980s. The debate is examined from the viewpoint of the activist, government, shareholders and institutional investors. The response of the corporations is identified, and the campaign against loans to South Africa scrutinized. Appendices include: Statement of Principles of U.S. Firms with Affiliates in the Republic of South Africa; and Signers and Endorsers of the Sullivan Principles.

406   HAYSOM, Nicholas
        The Industrial Court: institutionalising
        industrial conflict. South African Review, 2,
        1984, p. 108-124

Indicates the increasing role of the Industrial Court, which was introduced by the Industrial Conciliation Amendment Act 94 of 1979. Notes that as a result, some areas of managerial power are subjected to the supervision of an institution outside the traditional collective bargaining forum. Impact is assessed in some detail.

407   HAYSOM, Nicholas
        The Langa shootings and the Kannemeyer
        Commission of Enquiry. South African Review,
        3, 1986, p. 278-289

Analyzes in detail the findings of Justice Donald Kannemeyer's commission of enquiry, and in evaluating the report concludes that he 'brought with him subconscious perceptions of what probably took place, his own perceptions of the likely role and behaviour of policemen, and his own beliefs about the behaviour pattern of township residents'. Notes that attention was not really paid to more general standards which should be applied before lethal weapons are used, and that 'the right to life' is not central to the report as indicated by the fact that only one of the twenty people killed was shot directly from the front.

408   HAYSOM, Nicholas
       Mabangalala: the   rise   of   right-wing
       vigilantes   in   South   Africa.   Johannesburg:
       University   of the Witwatersrand,   Centre for
       Applied Legal Studies,   1986,   (University of
       the Witwatersrand.   Centre for Applied Legal
       Studies. Occasional paper, no. 10), 141 p.

       Compiled   at the request of the Transvaal Rural   Action
       Committee and the Black Sash,   this report is based   on
       affidavits,   statements,   reports   and   interviews
       conducted in thirteen communities or regions. Documents
       the   emergence   of vigilantes in 1985 and   attempts   to
       reveal   common characteristics and the relationships in
       which these groups are involved.

409   HAYSOM, Nicholas
       Ruling with   the   whip: a   report   on   the
       violation   of   human rights   in   the   Ciskei.
       Johannesburg: University   of   the
       Witwatersrand,   Development Studies Group   in
       conjunction   with   the   Southern   African
       Research Service, 1983, 90 p.

       Reports   on   the scale of violation of human rights   in
       the Ciskei based on the results of numerous interviews.
       Provides   detailed background information   on   Ciskeian
       politics   and   constitution,   President Sebe,   and   the
       state security apparatus.

410   HEARD, Kenneth A.
       General elections in South Africa, 1943-1970.
       London: Oxford University Press, 1974, 269 p.

       Illustrates   the power struggles prevalent   within   the
       political   structures of white South Africa by his   in-
       depth analysis of the 1943,   1948,   1953,   1958,   1961,
       1966   and 1970 elections,   and the 1960 referendum.   In
       general,   the   examination of each decision follows   an
       introduction,   information   regarding the   contestants,
       the turn-out and the results.

157

411   HEATH, Edward
        The changing world around South Africa.
        International Affairs Bulletin, vol. 5, no. 2,
        1981, p. 6-17

        Comprises the text of Mr Heath's keynote address at the
        first International Political Outlook Conference
        organized by the South African Institute of
        International Affairs entitled: Southern Africa in the
        World, held in Johannesburg on 31 August to 1 September
        1981. Elucidates on the interwoven destinies of South
        Africa and the West and explains that features within
        the international environment such as the concern for
        human rights, the emergence of black rule in Angola,
        Mozambique and Zimbabwe and the policies of the Soviet
        Union, all contribute to the conclusion that the
        eventual granting of full political rights to South
        African blacks has become vital.

412   HEMSON, David
        Trade unionism and the struggle for
        liberation in South Africa. Capital and
        Class, no. 6, Autumn 1978, p. 1-41

        The political and industrial organization of the black
        working class in South Africa has always been central
        to the struggle against exploitation and racial
        oppression. This paper examines the relationship
        between mass strikes, trade unionism, and revolutionary
        strategy in the liberation struggle. The 'stay at home'
        strategy of the 1950s has grown in the period of mass
        resistance to apartheid into mass strikes and
        insurrectionary action by workers and students. While
        black trade unionism is not openly revolutionary, trade
        unions are essential in defence of black workers, in
        supporting strike action, and in advancing the demands
        of the workers. (Author's abstract)

413   HENDLER, Paul (and others)
Rethinking housing questions in South Africa,
by Paul Hendler, Alan Mabin and Sue Parnell.
South African Review, 3, 1986, p. 195-207

Two main questions are considered: firstly, the history
of state involvement in housing including both
segregation and shortage, and secondly, housing as a
form of capital accumulation. The role of the private
sector, and trends in the delivery of housing are
examined. The article concludes with a brief discussion
of the relevance of the housing question to other
political concerns.

414   HEPPLE, Alex
Censorship and press control in South Africa.
Johannesburg: The Author, 1960, 78 p.

Illustrates that this subject cannot be divorced from
the National Party's history, thinking and their
objective of political censorship. Itemizes the
pertinent laws, reproduces clauses and articles
specific to the subject, and other methods of control.

415   HERBSTEIN, Denis
White man, we want to talk to you. New York:
Africana Publishing Company, 1979, 270 p.

In reviewing this work in Social Dynamics, vol. 5, no.
1, June 1979 on pages 68-70 in an essay entitled: The
uprising of 16 June (1976), Frank Molteno says of this
book's contents: 'Herbstein opens with a racy,
journalistic coverage of the first four days of the
uprising. Going back to Sharpeville and the suppression
of resistance in the early 1960s, he looks at the
doldrum years that followed. Here he includes a
superficial description of government legislation,
examples of its application, and a sketch of what
apartheid involves. He looks in turn at Black

Consciousness and the system of education, and then examines the factors leading up to June 1976 in a chapter entitled "From Lisbon to Soweto". An account of the uprising itself is given before concluding with a discussion of the reaction and present position of the white rulers.

416   HEXHAM, Irving
        Dutch Calvinism and the development of Afrikaner nationalism. African Affairs, vol. 79, no. 315, April 1980, p. 195-208

Divides his article into three parts. The author initially outlines the 'received opinion' on the relationship between Calvinism and Afrikaner nationalism, prior to indicating why this opinion is mistaken. Concludes by suggesting an alternative understanding of this relationship.

417   HEXHAM, Irving
        The irony of apartheid: the struggle for national independence of Afrikaner Calvinism against British imperialism. New York: Edwin Mellen Press, 1981, (Texts and studies in religion), 239 p.

Studies the development of Afrikaner nationalism from its origins and takes into account its religious aspects and traditions in an attempt to understand the evolution of apartheid South Africa. The author is Assistant Professor of Religion at the University of Manitoba.

418   HILL, Christopher R.
        Change in South Africa: blind alleys or new directions? London: Collings, 1983, 224 p.

Written by Hill in his capacity as Director of the Centre of Southern African Studies, University of York, this study concentrates on recent trends of thought propounded by various South African elites, and aims to assess any real change emanating from them. Initially examines three approaches to the South African issue – separate development, liberalism and revolutionary change, prior to assessing the role of business pressure groups; industrial relations and trade unions; attitudes of Afrikaner academics; the role of student politics as well as the prospects for constitutional change. Reviewed by Newell M. Stultz in Journal of Modern African Studies, vol. 23, no. 1, March 1985, p. 162-164.

419   HINDSON, D.C. and LACEY, Marian
       Influx control and labour allocation: policy
       and practice since the Riekert Commission.
       South African Review, 1, 1983, p. 97-113

Provides a summary of the Riekert Commission recommendations and practical steps taken after its publication. Reviews the two sets of Koornhof Bills of 1980 and 1982 respectively. Traces the fate of the 1980 Bills which were referred to the Grosskopf Committee, and two of the 1982 Bills, the Community Development and Orderly Movement and Settlement Bills, which similarly failed to pass into legislation. Illustrates that the consequent stalling of the Riekert proposals into legislation means little change over the policies of the previous thirty years.

420   HINDSON, D.C.
       The pass system and the formation of an
       African proletariat in South Africa: a
       critique of the cheap labour - power thesis.
       Brighton: University of Sussex, 1983, 394 p.

Thesis: PhD.

Hindson defines the pass system prior to explaining its use as a method of securing a permanent industrial workforce. He further elucidates on the aim of his study by saying 'My basic thesis is that the system has functioned to reproduce differentiated forms of labour - power, some but no means all, of which are associated with the phenomenon of temporary migration. The functions and development of the system reflect the need on the part of capital, in the circumstances of its development in South Africa, to man and reproduce a differentiated workforce. This argument is advanced in the thesis with reference to the urban branch of the pass system and the urban African proletariat in the period from the Second World War until the end of the 1970s.'

421   HINDSON, D.C.
       The role of the labour bureaux in South
       Africa: a critique of the Riekert Commission
       Report IN: WORKING Papers in Southern African
       Studies, vol. 3, edited by D.C. Hindson.
       Johannesburg: Ravan, 1983, p. 149-172

Author states that the object of his paper 'is to advance the understanding of the role of the labour bureaux system in South Africa through an analysis and critique of the Riekert Report and especially those of its recommendations which deal with the labour bureaux and legislation governing their operation'. Divided into four parts, this study demonstrates the class intentions behind, and the contradictory nature of the Commission's proposals casting limitations on the proposed reforms.

422   HINDSON, D.C.
       Union unity. South African Review, 2, 1984,
       p. 90-107

Presents findings of six unity talks held from 1981 to 1983 called to discuss methods of promoting ties between unions. In the second part of the study, obstacles to union unity are reviewed under the headings of policies and principles, industrial and general unions, and levels of organization.

423   HIRSCH, Alan
        'Banking on discipline': the Development Bank
        of Southern Africa. South African Review, 3,
        1986, p. 372-380

The Bank, as the central development funding body in South Africa, is seen by the author as wielding a great deal of financial power and likely to play an important role in shaping the nature and direction of economic and political power. For these reasons he describes its establishment, structure, approach, practices, political intervention, and cost. The dissolution of the Corporation for Economic Development and the fate of BENSO (Bureau for Economic Research Re Bantu Development) is examined.

424   HIRSCH, Alan
        The study of industrial decentralisation in
        South Africa - some comments IN: SOUTHERN
        African Studies - retrospect and prospect.
        Edinburgh: University of Edinburgh, Centre of
        African Studies, 1983, p. 131-160

Reviews some of the important contributions to the study of industrial decentralization, taking cognisance of shortcomings in approach. Brief history of various programmes and the author's suggestions are included.

425   HIRSON, Baruch
        Language in control and resistance in South
        Africa. African Affairs, vol. 80, no. 319,
        April 1981, p. 219-237

Examines the language problem from the missionary times until the Soweto uprising in 1976, indicating the reopening of the debate in 1953. Author states that this problem is one still to be confronted by liberation movements.

426   HIRSON, Baruch
        Year of fire, year of ash: Soweto - roots of
        a revolution? London: 2ed, 1979, 348 p.

Factors analyzing the 1976 Soweto revolt are presented. Chapter headings include the following: black schools, Bantu education, 1954-1976; university students, 1960-1969; Black Consciousness; secondary schools; black workers; strike waves spread; state repression; the Soweto revolt, and an anatomy of the revolt.

427   The HISTORICAL roots of Bantu education. Africa
        Perspective, no. 24, 1984 p. 41-64

Summarizes the debate over black education, going back to the missionary period of the early nineteenth century, the significance of Sir George Grey's educational policy, the effect of the discovery of gold and the status of education post the establishment of Union. Demonstrates the effect of the Nationalist Party election to power in 1948, the significance of both the de Villiers and the Eiselen Commissions, prior to analyzing the Bantu Education Act of 1953 and subsequent legislation.

428   HOAGLAND, Jim
        South Africa: civilization in conflict.
        Boston, Mass.: Houghton Mifflin, 1972, 428 p.

Part I focusses on South Africa, providing a survey of the country's complexities. Attempts to understand the durability of white power in the country and the implications of the apartheid policies, its economic power and the future of the black majority. Describes its relations with neighbouring states.

429   HODDER-WILLIAMS, Richard
Well, will South Africa survive? A review article. African Affairs, vol. 80, no. 320, July 1981, p. 405-416

Pays particular attention to R.W. Johnson's How long will South Africa survive, (1977); Lewis Gann and Peter Duigan's Why South Africa will survive, (1981); Ethnic power mobilised: can South Africa change by Heribert Adam and Hermann Giliomee (1979) and Which way is South Africa going? by Gwendolen M. Carter (1980).

430   HOERNLÉ, R.F. Alfred
Race and reason: being mainly a selection of contributions to the race problem in South Africa, edited with a memoir by I.D. MacCrone. Johannesburg: Witwatersrand University Press, 1945, 182 p.

A compilation of writings brought together posthumously in honour of Professor Hoernlé, the selection being made ' . . . with a view to illustrating and preserving the liberal spirit to which Professor Hoernlé had dedicated himself'. Included are chapters on the race problem, miscegenation, future of both the whites and the blacks, education, trends in race relations, and suggestions for the improvement in the economic conditions of urban blacks, among others.

431   HOERNLÉ, R.F. Alfred
South African native policy and the liberal
spirit: being the Phelps-Stokes Lectures,
delivered before the University of Cape Town,
May 1939. Cape Town: University of Cape Town
on behalf of the Phelps-Stokes Fund, 1939,
190 p.

Intended as an interpretation of South Africa's inter-
racial situation, the author analyzes the policy
towards blacks prevalent at the time of writing, taking
into account trusteeship, the 'liberal spirit' and
'liberty' which the author evaluates within the South
African context.

432   HOFMEYER, Willie
Rural popular organisation and its problems:
struggles in the Western Cape, 1929-1930.
Africa Perspective, no. 22, 1983, p. 26-49

Highlights the problems faced by rural organizations,
particularly the African National Congress, in this
preliminary study which focusses on attempts by the
popular classes to organize themselves and consequent
efforts made to suppress them.

433   HOLDT, Karl von
The economy: Achilles Heel of the new deal.
South African Review, 3, 1986, p. 303-319

Analyzes the recession, current at the time of writing,
illustrating that it is a result of an economic crisis
which has been maturing for a decade. States that it is
no ordinary slump. 'It combines cyclical factors with
more profound and serious structural contradictions and
can only be overcome by restructuring capitalist
production'.

434   HOLLAND, Martin
        The European Community and South Africa:
        economic reality or political rhetoric.
        Political Studies, vol. 33, no. 3, September
        1985, p. 399-417

This article examines the economic and political
relationship between the European Community (EC) and
the Republic of South Africa (RSA). From the economic
perspective, the Community's objective of securing
economic independence for the region, trends in EC-RSA
trade and the arguments pertaining to mineral
dependency are discussed. From the political
perspective, Community statements on apartheid are
compared with its foreign policy record. In particular,
the Code of Conduct for European firms operating in the
Republic is analysed within the framework of European
Political Cooperation (EPC). The achievements,
failures, future role and alternatives to the Code are
considered and the limitations imposed by EPC in
realizing a collective foreign policy are recognized.
(Journal abstract).

435   HOLLE, Ulrike
        The conflict in South Africa: international
        settlement strategies and internal change.
        Afrika, vol. 22, no. 7/8, 1981, p. 3-4

Focusses on the Republic's internal problems as
discussed at a conference organized by the Friedrich
Ebert Foundation. Gauges the possibilities for reform,
with particular attention being paid to the role of the
Federal Republic of Germany in promoting change. The
possibility of sanctions, either total or selectively
applied was raised, and the need for urgency in
preventing civil war is stressed in the interests of
all South Africans.

436   HORRELL, Muriel
        The African homelands of South Africa.
        Johannesburg: South African Institute of Race
        Relations, 1973, 176 p.

An in-depth study of the homelands and conditions
prevalent at the time of writing, this work encompasses
the following categories: physical description;
population; government and administration; development;
agriculture; mining; border industries and
decentralization; commerce and industry; technical and
vocational education; townships; health services; and
social welfare services. Contains useful maps.

437   HORRELL, Muriel
        Laws affecting race relations in South Africa
        (to the end of 1976). Rev. ed. Johannesburg:
        South African Institute of Race Relations,
        1978, 529 p.

An expanded version of her: Legislation and race
relations, q.v. in which the pre-1948 section has been
reproduced but the subsequent period has been augmented
to include not only Parliamentary legislation affecting
race relations, but also relevant proclamations by the
State President, ministerial policy statements and
action, as well as pertinent court cases, in its
thirty-six chapters. Apart from general legislative
measures, population and administration, the following
aspects are detailed: representation - on central
governing bodies, separate representation for Coloureds
and Indians, and homeland representation of Africans;
local government, control of urban blacks; racial
zoning of land and premises; housing; public transport;
separate amenities; general matters affecting
Coloureds, Indians and the status of Chinese and
Japanese persons; homeland status of black women;
taxation; employment; industrial relations; education -

for the Africans, Coloureds, Indian, Chinese, white and tertiary; health and health services; sport; legal aid; administration of justice and prisons; and security measures.

438   HORRELL, Muriel
Legislation and race relations: a summary of the main South African laws which affect race relationships. rev. ed. Johannesburg: South African Institute of Race Relations, 1971, 121 p.

Presents a factual summary of the laws that bear on race relations, including legislation to the end of 1971. Earlier editions of this work published in 1963 and 1966.

439   HORRELL, Muriel
Race relations as regulated by law in South Africa, 1948-1979. rev. ed. Johannesburg: South African Institute of Race Relations, 1982, 349 p.

A revised edition of her: Laws affecting race relations in South Africa, 1948-1976, q.v. It includes subsequent legislation and laws enacted by 'independent' black states.

440   HORRELL, Muriel
South African trade unionism: a study of a divided working class. Johannesburg: South African Institute of Race Relations, 1961, 150 p.

Demonstrates the effect of race on the trade union movement. Based on the views of participants, the author illustrates the lack of unity by examining the diverse directions of the whites, Coloureds, Asians and blacks prior to the entrenchment of the Nationalist Party's separate development policies, as well as their effects.

441   HORWITZ, Ralph
        The political economy of South Africa.
        London: Weidenfeld and Nicolson, 1967, 522 p.

Says Horwitz of his book: 'It's aim is a realistic account of the economic development of a country, whose social experience may be as instructive for the theory of economic development as it is dehumanizing for political idealism'. The dominating role and aims of Afrikanerdom are interwoven in this study, chapters in which highlight, among others, problems of poor whites and the black proletariat, and the political economy of land, food and labour.

442   HOUGHTON, D. Hobart
        The South African economy. 3rd ed. Cape Town:
        Oxford University Press, 1973, 297 p.

Covers all facets of the South African economy including farming, migrant labour, mining, manufacturing, labour, wages and standards of living, foreign trade and balance of payments, in an attempt to describe the development of the national economy. Complemented by extensive statistics and figures, updated to 1970.

443   HUDDLESTON, Trevor
        Naught for your comfort. London: Collins,
        1956, 256 p.

Records the implications of South Africa's racial policies on the daily lives of black South Africans in Sophiatown in particular, where he was parish priest. Father Huddleston describes the removal of sixty thousand people.

444   HUDSON, Peter and SARAKINSKY, Mike
          Class interests and politics: the case of the
          urban African bourgeoisie. South African
          Review, 3, 1986, p. 169-185

As indicated by the title, this analysis focusses on the urban African bourgeoisie, in an attempt to ascertain whether the colonial model can elucidate the current relationship between this bourgeoisie, white capital and the state, and the way in which class and national relations are developing. Within this context, examines the formation of the National African Federated Chamber of Commerce, the Urban Foundation, the Riekert Commission, the Small Business Development Corporation, the 1983 investigation into the Group Areas Act, and its subsequent amendment in 1984. Findings of the 1984 President Councl's Report, and freehold title for blacks in urban areas outside the 'national states' are included.

445   HUDSON, Peter
          The Freedom Charter and socialist strategy in
          South Africa. Politikon, vol. 13, no. 1, June
          1986, p. 75-90

The author, a Lecturer in the Department of Political Studies at the University of the Witwatersrand, abstracts his contribution as follows: In this paper several interpretations of the Freedom Charter are examined. Particular attention is paid to the South African Communist Party's interpretation of it in terms of the theory of national-democratic revolution. The origins of this theory are identified in the analysis of the underdeveloped world advanced by the international communist movement during the 1950's. In conclusion some criticisms of the application of the theory of national-democratic revolution to South Africa are identified and discussed.

446   HUDSON, William (and others)
           Anatomy of South Africa: a scientific study
           of present day attitudes by William Hudson,
           Gideon Francois Jacobs and Simon Biesheuvel.
           Cape Town: Purnell, 1966, 140 p.

           Also published in Afrikaans under the title: Suid-
           Afrikaners onder die soeklig. Interpretations and
           conclusions are drawn on the facts and results of an
           opinion survey and interviews in order to ascertain
           'what the man next door is thinking'. In this way,
           various portraits and images were compiled - of the
           reactionary, the evolutionary, the moderate, concept of
           the black man and vision of the future.

447   HUGHES, Heather and GREST, Jeremy
           The local state. South African Review, 1,
           1983, p. 122-141

           Analyzes both the community councils and the
           consultative management and local affairs committees as
           organs of racially determined local level government.

448   HUGO, Pierre
           Quislings or realists: a documentary study of
           'Coloured' politics in South Africa.
           Johannesburg: Ravan, 1978, 744 p.

           Provides initially a theoretical discussion of the
           socio-economic status of the Coloureds and their
           prospects viewed from a comparative perspective. This
           is followed by an examination of the franchise question
           prior to a presentation of documents and speeches on a
           wide variety of topics, thus providing an insight into
           Coloured politics.

449   HUGO, Pierre
           Race and class in South Africa. Politikon,
           vol. 2, no. 2, December 1975, p. 140-151

Considers in the main the relevance of pluralist analysis to South Africa '. . . and in doing so to raise the sort of questions with which theoretical work on South Africa is faced'. In particular, examines the finding of Kuper, Smith, and the Marxist analyzes of Simons, Legassick, Wolpe and Trapido.

450   HUGO, Pierre and KOTZÉ, Hendrik
       Suid-Afrika: oorlewing in politieke perspektief. (South Africa: survival in political perspective). Johannesburg: Ball, 1978, 203 p.

Provides background informatin on separate development, an examination of colour and ethnicity, the reactions of the blacks and the Coloureds - from limited vote to limited power-sharing. Concludes by presenting political alternatives for the country, with particular reference to federation.

451   HUMAN rights: the Cape Town Conference, edited by C.F. Forsyth and J.E. Schiller. Cape Town: Juta, 1979, 304 p.

In these proceedings of the First International Conference on Human Rights in South Africa held on 22 to 26 January 1979, the main focus is on South Africa although several papers are theoretical or reflect comparative studies from elsewhere. Papers from nine panel discussions on human rights are incorporated. These are on the concept of human rights and the social foundations thereof, the rights of the wage earner, prodecural human rights and state security, rights in the administrative, state and municipal, humanitarian law, the International Red Cross, the European Convention on Human Rights, the freedom of the press, and human rights in retrospect and their prospects for the future.

452   HUMAN SCIENCES RESEARCH COUNCIL. Investigation into
        Intergroup Relations
        The South African society: realities and
        future prospect. Pretoria: The Council, 1985,
        182 p.
        Chairman: H.C. Marais

As stated in the Preface, this final report issued by
Main Committee 'represents a comprehensive
interdisciplinary attempt to address the intergroup
relations issue in all its facets in a scientifically
accountable way'. The study was divided, for
operational reasons, into subfields briefly identified
as: historical, demographic, anthropological, socio-
psychological, communications, religion, perspectives
of development administration, economic influences,
juridical field, an evaluation of constitutional,
political, and administrative matters, a sociological
view, and presented under the following categories
concerning intergroup relations: general background to
the problems; the experience of intergroup relations;
its structuring; and evaluation; and fundamental
prerequisites for constructive relationships.

453   HUND, John and VAN DER MERWE, Hendrik W.
        Legal ideology and politics in South Africa:
        a social science approach. Cape Town: Centre
        for Intergroup Studies published with the
        University Press of America, 1986, 144 p.

Examine the Marxist interpretation of law, arguing that
Marxism itself is an ideology located in the
superstructure which the authors term the law of power.
Illustrate how South Africa's legal ideology has shaped
attitudes towards concepts such as African socialism, a
bill of rights and international law. Pose the question
whether the Republic has the option of moving from its
repressive legal system to a legal philosophy enabling
all its inhabitants to be drawn into the constitutional
arena.

454   HUNTINGTON, Samuel P.
Reform and stability in a modernizing, multi-
ethnic society. Politikon, vol. 8, no. 2,
December 1981, p. 8-26

The author, Clarence Dillon Professor of International
Affairs and Director, Center for International Affairs,
Harvard University, abstracts this article as follows:
The problems of reform and stability in a modernizing,
multi-ethnic society can be dealt with in broad
theoretical terms, or one could focus on the specific
problems of a particular "multi-ethnic society." In
this article, the author attempts to combine these
approaches, on the one hand setting forth some general
concepts and propositions, and on the other, attempting
to suggest what could be their relevance to South
Africa.

455   HUNTINGTON, Samuel P.
Reform and stability in South Africa.
International Security, vol. 6, no. 4, Spring
1982, p. 3-25

Set within a theoretical framework defining multi-
ethnic political systems, Huntington identifies and
elaborates on significant possible changes in the South
African case. The analytical, prescriptive and
strategic components of movements proposing reform are
discussed, as is the nature of political leadership,
strategy and tactics, timing, power, issue selection
and sequence. The possibility of reform coalitions is
explored prior to the author's conclusion in which he
states '. . . the days of minority dominated vertical
multi-ethnic societies are numbered'.

456   HUTMACHER, Barbara
In black and white: voices of apartheid.
(n.p.): University Publications of America,
1982, 197 p.

A series of interviews conducted post Soweto 1976, with people residing in the Border Area, centred around East London. Provides insight into their attitudes, fears, hopes - a microcosm of South Africa under apartheid.

457   IDENTITEIT en verandering: sewe opstelle oor die Afrikaner vandag (Identity and change: seven essays on the Afrikaner today), edited by Hendrik W. van der Merwe. Cape Town: Tafelberg, 1975, 152 p.

A compilation of papers originally presented, in May 1974, to the Centre for Intergroup Studies at the University of Cape Town. The identity of the Afrikaner, changes in the Afrikaans community, and attitudes towards other racial groups form the basis of this study, which also includes papers on the Afrikaner in the political power structure, the economic factor in the Afrikaner community, as well as the role of the church.

458   An ILLUSTRATED history of South Africa, edited by Trewhella Cameron. Johannesburg: Ball, 1986, 320 p.

Aimed at the general reader, this work encompasses the spectrum of South African history from pre-historic times until 1984. The political restructuring of the country evident from the Boer War until Union is described. Thereafter, its political history is chronicled with contributions by S.B. Spies, B.K. Murray, A.W. Stadler, P.W. Coetzer, H.J. van Aswegan, and T.R.H. Davenport.

459   INDICATOR South Africa: a barometer of social trends vol. 1 -   , 1983 -   Quarterly
        Durban: University of Natal, Centre for Applied Social Sciences, Indicator Project South Africa

Each volume is published in five separate parts: economics monitor, industrial monitor, political monitor, racial monitor, and urban monitor.

460   INDUSTRIAL relations in South Africa, 1982-1984: a comparative review of statistics and trends, edited by Graham Howe. Durban: University of Natal, Centre for Applied Social Sciences, Indicator Project South Africa, 1984, 73 p.

Comprises three articles: a data base on strike activity in the period 1982 to 1984 by Graham Howe; an interpretation of industrial relations trends in 1983 by Sonja Bendix, and a comparative analysis of twenty-five commentators' opinions on labour trends. Substantiated by statistical data.

461   INDUSTRIALISATION and social change in South Africa: African class-formation, culture and consciousness, 1870-1930, edited by Shula Marks and Richard Rathbone. Essex: Longman, 1982, 383 p.

Intended as a preliminary attempt to come to terms with some facets of the African experience of the industrial revolution as it was manifest in South Africa. It comprises fourteen contributions presented under the following chapter headings: Kimberley: labour and compounds, 1871-1888 (Rob Turrell); labour in the South African gold mining industry, 1886-1914 (Peter Richardson and Jan-Jacques van-Helten); the impact of the diamond discoveries on the Kimberley hinterland: class formation, colonialism and resistance among the Tlhaping of Griqualand West in the 1870s (Kevin Shillington); labour migration in Basutoland, c. 1870-1885 (Judy Kimble); kinship, ideology and the nature of pre-colonial labour migration: labour migration from the Delagoa Bay hinterland to South Africa, up to 1895 (Patrick Harries); the destruction and reconstruction

of Zulu society (Jeff Guy); the sharecropping economy,
African class formation and the Natives' Land Act of
1913 in the highveld maize belt (Tim Keegan); the life
story of Nkgono Mma-Pooe: aspects of sharecropping and
proletarianisation in the northern Orange Free State,
1890-1930 (Ted Matsetela); an African in Kimberley, Sol
T. Plaatjie, 1894-1898 (Brian Willan); mine married
quarters: the differential stabilisation of the
Witwatersrand workforce, 1900-1920 (Sean Moroney); the
Transvaal Native Congress, 1917-1920: the
radicalisation of the black petty bourgeoisie on the
Rand (Philip Bonner); moralizing leisure time: the
transatlantic connection and black Johannesburg, 1918-
1936 (Tim Couzens); 'wailing for purity': African
mothers and adolescent daughters, 1912-1940 (Deborah
Gaitskell); the emergence of African working class
culture (David Caplan).

462   INNES, Duncan
        Anglo: Anglo American and the rise of modern
        South Africa. Johannesburg: Ravan, 1984,
        358 p.

The nature, role, and extent of Anglo American
Corporation's power is analyzed with relation to both
South Africa's political and economic history. Reviewed
by Ieuan L. Griffiths in International Affairs, vol.
62, no. 1, Winter 1985/86, p. 154

463   INNES, Duncan
        Monetarism and the South African crisis.
        South African Review, 3, 1986, p. 290-302

Chronicles the failure of the government's monetarist
economic policies which were exacerbated by the
political conflict that arose partly in response. Gives
details of the 1984 measures, the recession taking

effect, state expenditure and inflation, damage to the industrial base, impediments to social restructuring, and the effect of P.W. Botha's mid-August 1985 'Rubicon' speech.

464   INNES, Duncan
         Monopoly capitalism in South Africa. South African Review, 1, 1983, p. 171-183

Traces the historical development of monopolization with special reference to the role of mining capital, especially Anglo American. The importance of state monopolies within the South African economy and their close cooperation with private capital is examined. The implications of the concentration of economic power within every major sector is indicated by giving the implications for employers, workers and their organizations.

465   INSTITUUT VIR SUID-AFRIKAANSE POLITIEK
         Perspektief op ons partypolitiek en politieke partye. (Perspectives on our party politics and political parties), Potchefstroom: Potchefstroom University for Christian Higher Education, 1976, 216 p.

Contributions in English and Afrikaans include chapters on the National Party by Willem de Klerk; the United Party by W.A. Röseman; Progressive Party by Alwena Meintjies (with an addendum on the Progressive Reform Party) the Herstigte Nasionale Party by J.H.P. Serfontein; the Democratic Party by H. Pakendorf. Voting behaviour is assessed by H. Lever; R.M. de Villiers elucidates on liberalism; Denis Worrall on English-speaking South Africans and the political system; Willem van Heerden probes into the South African racial question.

466   INTERGROUP accommodation in plural societies: a selection of conference papers with special reference to the Republic of South Africa, edited by Nic Rhoodie, assisted by Winifred Crum Ewing. London: Macmillan for the Institute for Plural Societies, University of Pretoria, 1978, 482 p.

Twenty-six contributions focussing on the multi-faceted issues raised by ethnic and socio-political pluralism revealing trends, options, and theoretical perspectives with especial reference to South Africa.

467   INTERNAL education in the Congress Alliance. Africa Perspective, no. 24, 1984, p. 99-111

Analyzes the content and organization of the formal education programmes of the Congress Alliance in the training of activists. Content is examined under the headings of five widely used examples of seminar, lecture or discussion notes: elementary course in politics and economics; discussion notes for the Multi-Racial Conference in 1957; the world we live in; the country we live in; discussion and speakers' notes on passes.

468   INTERNATIONAL COMMISSION OF JURISTS South Africa and the rule of law. Geneva: The Commission, 1960, 236 p.

Investigates problems created by the implementation of apartheid policies within the framework of political, social, and cultural rights. Includes an examination of its effect on the administration of justice and on the legal profession. Chapters include racial classification; movement and residence; work and trade unions; rights and freedoms; marriage; equality before the law; arbitrary unrest and detention; freedom of opinion and expression; peaceful assembly and expression; education; and South West Africa, now known as Namibia.

469   INTERNATIONAL COMMITTEE AGAINST APARTHEID, RACISM AND COLONIALISM
ICSA bulletin
1979 -
London: The Committee

The Committee was founded in 1977 at the instance of liberation movements and promotes international support for freedom struggles both in Namibia and South Africa. Supersedes: World Conference against Apartheid, Racism and Colonialism in Southern Africa. Continuation Committee. Bulletin

470   INTERNATIONAL LABOUR CONFERENCE
Special report of the Director-General on the application of the Declaration Concerning the Policy of Apartheid in South Africa
1965- ,Annual.
Geneva: International Labour Office.

Based on the provisions of the Declaration Concerning the Policy of Apartheid of the Republic of South Africa adopted unanimously by the International Labour Conference on 8 July 1964, this annual report assesses labour matters and recommends measures which should be adopted with the view of bringing about the end of apartheid. The 1985 Special Report is divided into three chapters. Chapter 1 details recent developments in labour and social matters, including labour relations, admission to employment and access to training, apartheid, and influx control. Chapter 2 contains information supplied by governments and both employers' and workers' organizations on action taken against apartheid, while Chapter 3 chronicles international measures against apartheid. One section is devoted to the International Labour Organisation, and the second to action within the framework of the United Nations and other intergovernmental organizations.

471   INTERNATIONAL LABOUR OFFICE
        Apartheid and labour: a critical review of the effects of apartheid on labour matters in South Africa. Geneva: International Labour Office, 1983, 56 p.

In this updated version of the ILO and apartheid (1977), the effects of apartheid on labour matters and the consequences for workers and their families are examined under the following headings: what apartheid means; choice of employment; access to employment and training; freedom of association and collective bargaining; ILO action against apartheid. Appendices include the ILO Declaration concerning the Policy of Apartheid in South Africa, 1981; Declaration adopted by the International Conference of Trade Unions on Sanctions and other Actions against the Apartheid Regime in South Africa (1983); Statement of the Executive Committee of the International Organisation of Employers on the policy of apartheid of the Republic of South Africa.

472   INTERNATIONAL sports against apartheid. Ufahamu, vol. 13, nos 2/3, 1984, p. 60-96

Comprises excerpts from papers delivered at the International Conference on Sanctions Against Apartheid Sport, held in London from 27-29 June 1983. It was organized by the United Nations Special Committee against Apartheid in co-operation with the South

African Non-Racial Olympic Committee. Among others, includes comment from Shridath S. Ramphal, Kader Asmal, Bruce Kidd, and the London Declaration on Apartheid Sports.

473   An INTRODUCTION to local government, edited by W.D. Hammond-Tooke. Johannesburg: Witwatersrand University Press, 1977, 94 p.

Based on a course of lectures delivered to the University of the Witwatersrand during August 1977, this collection of essays is intended as an introduction itemizing problems encountered by civic leaders, and examining skills essential to the conduct of efficient local government. It is designed to fill a gap in the literature on local government management skills.

474   IRELAND, Ralph C.
        Racism and desegregation: recent developments in the Republic of South Africa. Plural Societies, vol. 12, no. 1/2, Spring/Summer 1981, p. 107-117

Examines attempts by the South African government in the latter 1970s 'to come to grips with the reality of racism so that the hopes and aspirations of its various racial and ethnic groups may be fulfilled'. These are assessed from political, economic and educational viewpoints.

475   IRVINE, Douglas McKinnon
        Pluralism, ideology and analysis: the South African case. Civilisations, vol. 32, no. 2/vol. 33, no. 1, 1982/83, p. 153-179

Notes certain general features in the changing policy of the government prior to presenting a consideration of pluralism, both theoretically and within the South African context.

183

476   IRVINE, Douglas McKinnon
        South   Africa: federal   potentialities   in
        current developments. International Political
        Science Review,   vol. 5, no. 4, 1984, p. 491-
        506

Federal   potentialities   in   the   South   African
government's constitutional plans are discussed in
terms   of   territorial   arrangements   regarding   the
homelands, and the consociation of corporate groups in
white   South   Africa.   While   the   notion   of   total
independence   for   the   homelands   is   now   discredited,
their underdeveloped condition makes any confederal   or
federal   scheme   highly problematic unless the   regions
are   to be redrawn to incorporate   metropolitan   areas,
rendering   them   multiracial.   In   the   white   Republic,
coloureds   and   Indians   are   being   brought   into   a
consociational frame, albeit one which is controversial
and   seriously   flawed.   Urban Africans still   have   no
adequately   defined place in these plans.   Despite such
manifest   shortcomings   there   are   constitutional
potentialities   that   might suit South Africa's   plural
character   better than a unitary state.   However,   any
acceptable   scheme   would   have to be   based   on   self-
defined   groups,   not official racial   categories,   and
must permit a real reallocation of resources.   At best,
present   arrangements   are   transitional.   (Journal
abstract)

477   ISAACS, Henry
        Struggles within the struggle: an inside view
        of   the   PAC of South   Africa.   London: Zed,
        1985, 416 p.

The   author   was   one   of the   founders   of   the   Black
Consciousness Movement and later President of the South
African   Students Organisation.   After   self-exile,   he
became a member of the Pan Africanist Congress' Central
Committee until 1982.   He describes the inside   history

of the PAC's disintegregation during the years 1978 to 1983 as a means of obviating similar problems. Assesses constraints and prospects of the liberation struggle.

478   JACKSON, John David
        Justice in South Africa. London: Secker & Warburg, 1980, 239 p.

Written from his personal experience as an attorney, Jackson provides an exposition of South Africa's legal system. This insight into the law, particularly as it affects blacks, contains chapters on the judiciary, statutes, the rise of Black Consciousness and Steve Biko, trials, children on Robben Island, and police brutality.

479   JAFFEE, Georgina
        The retrenchment process. South African Review, 2, 1984, p. 125-132

The effects of the recession and the consequent decrease in production led to the retrenchment of thousands of black workers. Although accurate figures are not available, she provides statistics based on reports. The role of the Industrial Court, and the effect of the retrenchment, particularly on unskilled contract and migrant workers are surveyed.

480   JARVIE, Grant
        Class, race and sport in South Africa's political economy. London: Routledge and Kegan Paul, 1985, 107 p.

Aims to use 'class conflict, ideology and cultural struggle as axial principles for analysing the nature, meaning and political significance of South African sports policy' placing it within Gramsci, the Italian Marxist's framework for analysis.

481   JASTER, Robert S.
           Politics and the 'Afrikaner Bomb'. <u>Orbis</u>,
           vol. 27, no. 4, Winter 1984, p. 825-851

Briefly examines the technical evidence of South
Africa's nuclear development, prior to analyzing the
major political factors which define its nuclear
strategy.

482   JASTER, Robert S.
           South Africa in Namibia: the Botha strategy.
           Lanham, Md.: University Press of America and
           Harvard University, Center for International
           Affairs, 1985, 114 p.

In this comprehensive study of President Botha's
policy, Jaster analyzes the major factors shaping South
African goals and strategies in the Namibian conflict.
Focusses on the role of the military and the
implications of developments in Namibia on South
African domestic politics. Argues that 'in spite of
astute diplomacy and dramatic military iniatives, South
African policy has been weak and irresolute'.

483   JASTER, Robert S.
           South African defense strategy and the
           growing influence of the military IN: ARMS
           and the African: military influences on
           Africa's international relations, edited by
           William J. Foltz and Henry S. Bienen. New
           Haven: Yale University Press, 1985, p. 121-
           152

Argues that it was only in the late seventies,
following a shift in the balance of power in Southern
Africa, that South Africa's deteriorating relations
with the West and within its own external security
position, that the South Africa military establishment
has attained political significance. The military's

major, and at times decisive influence on policy is examined under the headings of: strategy and survival; future constraints and viabilities; prospects and future strategies.

484   JASTER, Robert S.
       South Africa's narrowing security options.
       Adelphi Papers, no. 159, 1980, (entire issue:
       51 p.)

Security strategies under the rule of the National Party are assessed; itemizes the factors forming its perception of internal and external threats and discusses responses made with especial reference to Angola, the Soweto Riots of 1976 and the moves towards a garrison state. Concludes with an analysis of South Africa's security options for the 1980's and their implications for the West.

485   JEEVES, Alan H.
       Migrant labour in South Africa's mining economy: the struggle for the gold mines' labour supply, 1890-1920. Johannesburg: Witwatersrand University Press, 1985, 323 p.

The author describes his work as an examination of the development of the migrant labour system in South Africa's premier industry, the gold mines of the Witwatersrand. Mining company archives and government records provide much of the information on which this study is based. With a focus on the interests which created the system and became its principal beneficiaries, the author provides a complement to local studies on the complexities of the system and the extent of its regional variations.

486   JEPPE, W.J.O.
       Bophuthatswana land tenure and development.
       Cape Town: Maskew Miller, 1980, 285 p.

Primarily a descriptive and evaluative report based on the findings of a research project undertaken from 1976 to 1978. It was commissioned by the Committee for Development Research of the Department of Co-operation and Development, with the co-operation of the Bophuthatswana government. Examines 'the systems of rights to land in Bophuthatswana, the bearing these have on rural development, especially on agriculture, and the possibilities of changing or reforming the systems of rights to land chiefly to improve agricultural production. Information on government policy, legislation and administration relevant to the issue are included.

487   JOB advancement in South Africa, compiled and edited by Willie Breytenbach. Johannesburg: South Africa Foundation, 1980, 174 p.

Limited to· the post-War era, and the last two decades in particular, this compilation of essays is intended as an assessment of black job advancement. Contains a chapter on overseas attitudes and issues including codes of conduct, the role of multinational corporations, disinvestment, and sanctions. Scope encompasses an assessment of economics versus ideology, problems experienced in the work, entrepreneurial and public sector situation as well as posing the question whether or not black advancement is a threat to white employment security.

488   JOCHELSON, Karen
        1960-1985: the emergency continues. Work in Progress, 38, 1985, p 14-18

Concentrates mainly on the March 1960 emergency in this brief comparative study which takes into account popular resistance and emergency regulations.

489   JOHNSON, R.W.
         How long will South Africa survive?
         Johannesburg: Macmillan South Africa, 1977,
         327 p.

         Using a journalistic style, the author traces the
         development of the deepening crisis in South Africa
         from 1960 Sharpeville, through the events of the early
         1970s, the implications of both Mozambican and Angolan
         independence, to the 1976 Soweto riots. The emphasis is
         on economic considerations and the role played by the
         West, especially those of the United States, in
         determining South Africa's survival. For an in-depth
         review of this book see Simon Clarke's contribution to
         the Journal of Southern African Studies, vol. 4, no. 2,
         April 1978, p. 261-265

490   JOHNSON, Robert E.
         Indians and apartheid in South Africa: the
         failure of resistance. Ann Arbor: University
         Microfilms International, 1973, 161 p.

         Thesis: PhD. (Political Science, University of
         Massachusetts)

         Evaluates the contribution made by the Natal Indian
         Congress to the multi-racial anti-apartheid campaigns
         of the 1950s. The origins of Indian politics are
         examined and within this context, the revival and
         subsequent failure of passive resistance is assessed.

491   JOHNSTONE, Frederick A.
         Class, race and gold: a study of class
         relations and racial discrimination in South
         Africa. London: Routledge and Kegan Paul,
         1976, 298 p.

189

Concentrates on the First World War period in an attempt to explain, in terms of class, the system of racial discrimination prevalent in South African gold mines and relevant historical developments. Reviewed by K. Kolbe in South African Labour Bulletin, vol. 3, no. 3, October 1976.

492   JOHNSTONE, Frederick A.
        White prosperity and white supremacy in South Africa today. African Affairs, vol. 69, no. 275, April 1970, p. 124-140

In this revised version of a paper presented at St Anthony's College, Oxford, the author defines its purpose as an assessment of the relations between economic development, apartheid labour policies and white supremacy, and to develop a critique of this thesis.

493   JONES, Robert A.
        Collective bargaining in South Africa. Johannesburg: Macmillan, 1982, 89 p.

Written principally for students of commerce at first- and second-year university level, this booklet elucidates on the concepts, procedures and legal provisions of collective bargaining in the Republic. This includes an analysis of the Labour Relations Act , 28 of 1958, as amended in 1981. The historical development of racial exclusion, registration, the emergent black unions, settlement of disputes, strikes, the Industrial Court and unfair labour practices are central to this work.

494   JONES, Robert A. and GRIFFITHS, Howard R.
        Labour legislation in South Africa. Johannesburg: McGraw Hill, 1980, 208 p.

Presents chronologically since 1900, statutes which have affected labour issues. Information is complemented by succinct analyzes detailing social, political and economic conditions for each period under review.

495   JORDAN, Pallo
Zemk' inkomo Magwalandini: the life and times of W.B. Rubusana (1858-1936). Sechaba, January 1984, p. 4-13

Provides biographical information on one of the founder members of the African National Congress who was, for nearly forty years, actively engaged in the most important political and social struggles.

496   JOSEPH, Helen
Side by side. London: Zed, 1986, 272 p.

The autobiography, published on the occasion of her eighty-first birthday, of a noted campaigner against apartheid and author of two books: If this be treason (London: Deutsch, 1963, 192 p.) and Tomorrow's sun: smuggled journals from South Africa (London: Hutchinson, 1968, 310 p.)

497   JUBBER, Ken
Sociology and its social context: the case of the rise of Marxist sociology in South Africa. Social Dynamics, vol. 9, no. 2, December 1983, p. 50-63

Challenges the validity of the claim that both university teaching and South African research in sociology further the interests of the dominant groups. Reviews the history of sociology in South Africa including the rise of Marxist sociology in the 1970s. Author suggests a variety of factors influencing its now prominent position, which the determination by immediate social context is but one.

498   KADALIE, Clements
My life and the ICU: the autobiography of a
black trade unionist in South Africa, edited,
with an introduction by Stanley Trapido.
London: Cass, 1970, (South African studies,
no. 3), 230 p.

As founder of the Industrial and Commercial Workers'
Union of Africa (ICU), the first black mass movement in
South Africa and one which numbered ten thousand
members by the time of its disintegration, Kadalie's
autobiography is germane to the understanding of trade
unionism in South Africa.

499   KAGAN, Alfred
The African National Congress of South
Africa: a bibliography. New York: United
Nations, 1982. (United Nations. Centre
against Apartheid. Notes and documents,
special issue, March 1982), 40 p.

Compiled in observance of the Congress' Seventieth
Anniversary, and in compliance with General Assembly
resolution 34/93 J of 12 December 1979, this
bibliography is divided into the following sections:
general reference works; works authored by ANC and key
leaders; books, articles and papers; current audio-
visual material; current periodicals; back issues of
ANC and ANC-related periodicals; and United Nations
Centre against Apartheid documents.

500   KAHN, Ellison
The new constitution. London: Stevens, 1962,
69 p.

Being a supplement to: South Africa: the development of
its laws and constitution by H.R. Hahlo and Ellison
Kahn, in which the author provides an explanation of
South Africa's republican constitution. Includes text

of the Republic of South Africa Constitution Act, no. 32 of 1961 and comparative tables of this Act, the South Africa Act and earlier provisions.

501   KALLAWAY, Peter
        Apartheid and education: selected paper on black education in South Africa IN: SOUTHERN African studies - retrospect and prospect. Edinburgh: University of Edinburgh, Centre of African Studies, 1983, p. 343-366

Reviews the crisis in black education as highlighted by the 1976 riots. Considers the nature of the problem under the headings: Soweto and the Seventies; the search for reformist options; the response by the state; the response by monopoly capital. He concludes with a critique of the de Lange Commission Report.

502   KALLAWAY, Peter and KALLAWAY, Jackie
        A preliminary select bibliography of education for black South Africans. Cape Town: University of Cape Town, 1983, 181 p.

Alphabetically arranged by author, this select bibliography is not annotated. It is preceded by a list of published bibliographies relevant to the study of education and pertinent research in South Africa. It also contains a useful list of black or non-racial teachers organizations.

503   KALLEY Jacqueline Audrey
        Bophuthatswana politics and the economy: a select and annotated bibliography.Johannesburg South African Institute of International Affairs, 1978, (South African Institute of International Affairs. Bibliographical series, no. 4), 39 p.

The aim of this bibliography is to provide a companion volume pertaining to the political and economic aspects of P.S. Hattingh's Bophuthatswana: a select and annotated bibliography, q.v. The 243 entries are arranged primarily in alphabetical order according to author, or title while no author is given. Treaties have been listed, together with their relevant ministerial departments. Annotations are brief, and the work is supplemented by an author index and subject guide.

504   KALLEY, Jacqueline Audrey
      A chronological and subject analysis of South
      Africa's multilateral and bilateral treaties,
      1806-1979. Johannesburg: University of the
      Witwatersrand, 1985, 677 p.

Dissertation: M.A.

This dissertation attempts to place South Africa's treaty-making powers in both constitutional and historical perspective for the period 1806-1979. It also provides a chronological list of its treaties and an index which aims to ensure easy retrieval. Section I comprises four chapters, in which the constitutional development and treaty-making powers of the British colonies, the Boer Republics, the Union of South Africa, the Republic of South Africa and the 'independent' national states of Transkei, Bophuthatswana and Venda are traced. In Section II, a chronological index is presented comprising the date of signature, date of entry into force, ratifications (if any), place of signature, signatory country (or multilateral status), title of treaty and source(s) where the text may be located. Section III provides a detailed index to both the subject and the bilateral partner. In this way a comprehensive picture of South Africa's international relations for the period under review may be ascertained.

505   KALLEY, Jacqueline Audrey
               Index to the Republic of South Africa Treaty
               Series, 1961-1975. rev. ed. Johannesburg:
               South African Institute of International
               Affairs, 1980, (South African Institute of
               International Affairs. Bibliographical
               series, no. 1), 36 p.

Does not provide references to each and every treaty to which South Africa is a party, only to those published in the South African Treaty Series, issued by the Department of Foreign Affairs. The work is divided into two sections: a chronological list which includes information such as date of entry into force; place of signature, name of bilateral partner as well as the Treaty Series number. The second section comprises a subject index following an alphabetical arrangement of both country and treaty subjects.

506   KALLEY, Jacqueline Audrey
               Index to the Union of South Africa Treaty
               Series, 1926-1960. Johannesburg: South
               African Institute of International Affairs,
               1978, (South African Institute of Interna-
               tional Affairs. Bibliographical series, no.
               5), 161 p.

As with the Index to the Republic of South Africa Treaty series q.v., this index refers only to the published Treaty Series. It follows a similar format to the former, and the two indexes should be used in conjunction.

507   KALLEY, Jacqueline Audrey
               Sanctions and Southern Africa: a bibliogra-
               phical guide. Current Bibliography on African
               Affairs, vol. 14, no. 3, 1981/82, p. 201-234

Gives salient features on important books and articles pertaining to sanctions, selected to reveal different facets of the issue. This is complemented by a select bibliography divided into theory, Rhodesia, and South Africa.

508   KALLEY, Jacqueline Audrey
          South Africa's foreign relations, 1980-1984: a select and annotated bibliography. Johannesburg: South African Institute of International Affairs, 1984, (South African Institute of International Affairs. Bibliographical series no. 12), 283 p.

Published in June 1984, this bibliography comprising 784 items, and complemented by an extensive author and subject index, is intended as a sequel to Gail Rogaly's bibliography entitled: South Africa's foreign relations 1961-1979, q.v. It is suggested that they be used in conjunction for a coverage of the Republic's foreign relations. The purpose of this work is to provide references to material on South Africa's external political relations for the period under review. While this concentrates mainly on the Republic's political relations, attention is also paid to economic factors including the role of multinational corporations, the disinvestment debate and sanctions. The effects of the new regional groupings, and their implications, both for the Southern African region and South Africa have been considered in some detail.

509   KALLEY, Jacqueline Audrey
          The Transkei region of Southern Africa, 1877-1978: a select and annotated bibliography. Boston: Hall, 1980, 218 p.

This bibliography is an expanded and updated version of the compiler's: Transkei bibliography: 1945 to independence 1976. (Johannesburg: South African Institute of International Affairs, 1976). It concentrates on geo-political and economic aspects dating from the Frontier War of 1877-1878. Also includes references for the non-specialist and general reader.

510   KANE-BERMAN, John
        Population removal, displacement, and
        divestment in South Africa. Social Dynamics,
        vol. 7, no. 2, 1981, p. 28-46

Examines the motives and implications of the government's policy of population relocation. These fall into various categories which are described and illustrated by means of case studies. Living conditions are chronicled and problems experienced by Kwazulu in particular, are listed. Concludes by assessing the impact on these removals on the homeland economies and the wider significance of influx control.

511   KANE-BERMAN, John
        Soweto: black revolt, white reaction.
        Johannesburg: Ravan, 1978, 268 p.

An in-depth investigation of the causes and details of the 1976 Soweto riots. The education language policy, the social, political and economic conditions prevailing in the township and its historical background, are seen within the context of the government's policy towards urban blacks. Black Consciousness and its manifestations are examined, and although the main focus of the work is on Soweto, attention is paid to other black communities to which the revolt spread. Details response of the white business and political establishment to the unrest.

512   KANTOR B.S. and KENNY, H.F.
The poverty of neo-Marxism: the case of South
Africa. Journal of Southern African Studies,
vol. 3, no. 1, October 1976, p. 20-40

Authors 'attempt to examine the validity of some neo-
Marxist explanations of important aspects of South
African economic history'. The paper is concerned
mainly with the contributions of Harold Wolpe and
Martin Legassick. Their critique is reviewed by Harold
Wolpe in Journal of Southern African Studies, vol. 4,
no. 2, April 1978, p. 240-256, q.v. Wolpe refutes their
thesis as ' . . . both incoherent and misplaced, and,
above all, the alternative explanations they offer
totally inadequate and incapable of advancing our
understanding of South African society'.

513   KANTOR, Brian and REES, David
South African economic issues, with
contributions by Henry Kenney and Jos Gerson.
Cape Town: Juta, 1982, 189 p.

Highlights government intervention, for political
reasons, in the markets for goods, labour, money and
credit. Chapters provide insights into sources of
economic growth, difficulties foreseen in restructuring
the constitution, racial income differences, the
monetary policy, balance of payments and exchange rate
issue, unemployment, foreign trade policy and an
evaluation of South Africa's agricultural policy.

514   KAPLAN, David
The internationalization of South African
capital: South African direct foreign
investment in the contemporary period.
African Affairs, vol. 82, no. 329, October
1983, p. 465-494

Also published in: SOUTHERN African studies - retrospect and prospect. Edinburgh: University of Edinburgh, Centre of African Studies, 1983, p. 193-247

Indicates the lack of a comprehensive study analyzing South African investment abroad. In the first section of the article, he presents an overview, and compares the Republic's direct foreign investment with that of other non-advanced capitalist countries. Substantiated by statistical data, and Table 1 provides information on the principal foreign investment of South African firms since 1976. This is complemented , in the second section, by a case study on the Anglo American group of companies.

515   KAPLAN, David
        The South African state: the origins of a racially exclusive democracy. The Insurgent Sociologist, vol. 10, no. 2, Fall 1980, p. 85-96

Author says of his article: 'The purpose of this paper is to, first, analyze why the South African state took the form of a racially exclusive democracy and second, to outline the effects of this form of state in reinforcing the racial divisions within South Africa. I will argue that the uninterrupted operation of this racially exclusive bourgeois democracy can only be explained by reference to the very particular class character of South Africa, and the precise manner in which the transition to capitalist social relations were affected. Moreover this very racial exclusivity contributed significantly to reinforcing already existing divisions between white and black workers transforming the character of their political struggles and undermining the basis for common class struggle.'

516   KAPLAN, David
        South Africa's changing place in the world
        economy. South African Review, 1, 1983, p.
        158-170

        Considers   the   Republic's   international   economic
        relations by assessing its import and export market;
        both foreign investment in South Africa, and its
        investment abroad; its relation to the international
        money markets and the status of the Rand in 1982.

517   KARIS, Thomas G.
        The resurgent African National Congress:
        competing for hearts and minds in South
        Africa IN: SOUTH Africa in Southern Africa:
        the intensifying vortex of violence, edited
        by Thomas M. Callaghy. New York: Praeger,
        1983, p. 191-236

        Provides an overview of the ANC's history, its nature
        and development into a powerful regional organization.
        The changing character of armed struggle is depicted
        and, in an attempt to assess the implications of a
        divided black opposition, he analyzes the relationship
        between Chief Gatsha Buthelezi and the   ANC.   He
        concludes with possible scenarios of the   ANC's
        position, either reform or revolutionary circumstances.
        Explores links between ANC and the Communist party in
        his article: South African liberation – the Communist
        factor. Foreign Affairs, vol. 65, no. 2, Winter
        1986/87, p 267-287.

518   KARIS, Thomas G.
        Revolution in the making. Foreign Affairs,
        vol 62, no. 2, Winter 1983/84, p. 378-406

        Focusses particularly on the African National Congress
        which he examines in depth from both historical and
        current aspects. He studies the attitude of the United
        States government towards the ANC.

519   KARUNARATNE, J.A.
          White South Africa's response to threats of
          disinvestment. Ufahamu, vol. 10, nos 1 and 2,
          Fall and Winter, 1980/81, p. 25-31

          Notes that white South Africans are almost unanimous in
          their opposition to sanctions. Identifies government
          strategy in preparing the South African public to
          accept increasing isolation, their intensive anti-
          sanction campaigns abroad, seeking of new Third World
          allies, and the enforcement of calm in black living
          areas to reassure foreign interests.

520   KEEGAN, Timothy J.
          Rural transformations in industrializing
          South Africa: the southern highveld to 1914.
          Johannesburg: Ravan, 1986, 302 p.

          Focusses on the development of the capitalization of
          white agriculture and the undermining of black
          agriculture on the highveld in the early industrial
          period. Concentrates on the making of the black rural
          working class and explores the rural origins of
          Afrikanerdom.

521   KEENAN, Jeremy
          Pandora's box: the private accounts of a
          Bantustan Community Authority. South African
          Review, 3, 1986, p. 361-371

          The operation of the local authority at Bosplaats in
          Bophuthatswana is analyzed, revealing 'how the
          government assisted in its illegal actions through both
          the direct intervention of senior government officials,
          such as the administrator/senior magistrate and through
          its indemnification of such practices'. States similar
          conditions of fraud, corruption and control are
          prevalent in other Bantustan tribal and community
          authorities.

522   KEENAN, Jeremy
The recession and its effect on the African working class. South African Review, 2, 1984, p. 133-144

Considers how the major burden of the recession in South Africa has fallen on the African working class, refuting arguments to the contrary propounded by state and capital. Assesses effects and implications.

523   KEENAN, Jeremy
Trickle up: African income and unemployment. South African Review, 1, 1983, p. 184-192

Queries data on African income, particularly that of the second half of the decade 1971-81, and refutes the claim of rising income levels. Unemployment is examined, which Keenan links to the rise in the capital: labour ratio for the period under review. In South African Review, 2, p. 318-326, he focusses on Bantustan capital intensive agricultural projects linked to central state and capital.

524   KELLEY, Robin
The role of the international sports boycott in the liberation of South Africa. Ufahamu, vol. 13, nos 2/3, 1984, p. 26-38

Demonstrates that sport has a political role to play in the struggle against apartheid. 'Not only does the movement to isolate South Africa from international sports demystify the mendacious concept of "international truce", but it has also raised the level of consciousness among the proletariat in the advanced capitalist countries'. Provides background history to the isolation movement and South Africa's efforts to re-enter international sport.

525   KENNEDY, Brian
        A tale of two mining cities: Johannesburg and
        Broken Hill, 1885-1925. Johannesburg: Donker,
        1984, 146 p.

        A comparative history of race relations in South Africa
        and Australia, drawing parallels between the early
        history and taking into account the consequences of
        industrial and urban development.

526   KENNEY, Henry
        Architect of apartheid: H.F. Verwoerd - an
        appraisal. Johannesburg: Ball, 1980, 278 p.

        In this analysis, Verwoerd's career and policies are
        examined and interpreted within the context of his
        times.

527   KEPPEL-JONES, Arthur
        When Smuts goes: a history of South Africa
        from 1952 to 2010 first published in 2015.
        Cape Town: African Bookman, 1947, 203 p.

        Based on imaginary characters with fictitious names,
        the author presents his scenario of South African
        history following the retirement of General Smuts,
        taking into account the consequences of National Party
        rule, and deep-seated tendencies prevalent in South
        African politics.

528   KIMLOCH, Graham C.
        The sociological study of South Africa: an
        introduction. Johannesburg: Macmillan South
        Africa, 1972, 180 p.

        Illustrates the relevance of sociology to an analysis
        of South Africa, by presenting a framework of
        sociological concepts which he then applies to South
        African society. The historical background to its

social evolution and its plural character are examined prior to the application of the conceptual framework. Statistical data provides an empirical foundation.

529   KITSON, David
        Interview with . . . Africa Perspective, no. 25, 1984, p. 65-75

Recounts his experiences as an underground activist - in the early 1960s providing an insight into the transition from mass to underground opposition in this period.

530   KLINE, Benjamin
        The National Union of South African Students: a case study in the plight of liberalism, 1924-77. Journal of Modern African Studies, vol. 23, no. 1, March 1985, p. 139-145

Illustrates the impotency of South African liberalism by examining the development and significance of Nusas, the subsequent response of the Nationalist government and findings of the Schlebusch Commission.

531   KOTZÉ, D.A.
        African politics in South Africa, 1964-1974: parties and issues. Pretoria: van Schaik, 1975, 276 p.

In the decade under review, significant for the emergence of new black political expression, after the bannings of the African National Congress, the Pan-African Congress and other organizations, the author identifies their structure, leadership and policies. Interrelationships, both organizationally and with the South African government are assessed. The concept of Black Consciousness, then in its formative phase, is examined, as are elections, their framework, campaigns and voting behaviour. The legislative framework, illustrating the delimitation of African participation, mainly to the homelands, is included.

532 KOTZÉ, D.A.
Bibliography of official publications of the black South African homelands. Pretoria: University of South Africa, 1979, 80 p.

Notes on the constitutional development of the homelands precede the bibliography, comprising their official publications. For each of the ten homelands, 'independent' or self-governing, the following format is utilized: hansard; estimates; official gazette; departmental reports; miscellaneous; and references.

533 KOTZÉ, D.A.
The black political experience outside the national states and TBVC countries. South Africa International, vol. 15, no. 2, October 1984, p. 76-83

This paper was presented by Professor Kotzé, Head of the Department of Development Administration and Politics, at a symposium on blacks outside the national states and Transkei, Bophuthatswana, Venda and Ciskei, organized by the Institute for Political and African Studies at the Potchefstroom University of Christian Higher Education on 24 August 1984. Aware that he is a white discussing black political life and expression, he divides the topic into three categories: shaping of political culture; the vulnerability of the weak; and participation patterns. Concludes there is increasing turbulence, frustration and radicalization of viewpoints.

534 KOTZÉ, D.A.
Traditionalism in African local government: with special reference to the Transkei and Lesotho. Stellenbosch: University of Stellenbosch, 1968, 362 p.

Thesis: Ph D.

Researches the role of both traditional political institutions and patterns of behavior in black local government. Based on extensive fieldwork.

535   KOTZÉ, D.A.
       The Witzieshoek revolt, 1940-1950. African Studies, vol. 41, no. 1, 1982, p. 127-141

Author provides an anlysis of the confrontation between the residents of the Witzieshoek Reserve and the police, basing his reasons on inadequate planning, and poor execution of a development policy. Kotzé states that this resulted in a sense of powerlessness and deprivation amongst the population.

536   KRUGER, Daniel Wilhelmus
       The age of the generals: a short political history of the Union of South Africa, 1910-1948. Johannesburg: Dagbreek Book Store, 1958, 229 p.

Analyzes the contribution made to South Africa's political history by the three Generals who succeeded each other as Prime Minister of the Union - Louis Botha, Jan Christiaan Smuts and James Barry Munnik Hertzog.

537   KUNENE, Daniel P.
       Ideas under arrest: censorship in South Africa. Ufahamu, vol. 11, no. 3, Spring 1982, p. 204-221

First published in: Research in African Literatures, vol. 12, no. 4, 1981, the author examines this topic with reference to human rights, provisions of the censorship laws, the power of literature, writers in exile, and the plight of the 'silenced generation'.

538   KUPER, Hilda
           Indian people in Natal. Pietermaritzburg:
           Natal University Press, 1960, 296 p.

As an anthropologist, Kuper observes the Indians of the
Durban area, specifically Merebank, Springfield and
Newlands in a study which she has divided into three
sections: the background of South African Indians,
changes and relevant associations developing within the
caste system; kinship among the Durban Hindu from the
aspects of structure, behaviour and ritual; while Part
Three concentrates on Hindu religion, ceremonies and
trance, as well as health.

539   KUPER, Leo
           An African bourgeoisie: race, class and
           politics in South Africa. New Haven: Yale
           University Press, 1965, 452 p.

Kuper focusses on the upper occupational strata
demonstrating those who would be leaders in South
African society, given change in its racial policies.
Divided into four main sections, Part I sets black
perspectives on political change within the context and
restraints of South African society; Part II studies
class manifestations associated with those occupations
selected for examination; Part III specifically
analyzes the occupational milieu of the intellectuals -
teachers, clergy, nurses, lawyers, doctors,
journalists, social workers and senior civil servants;
secondly concentrates on the traders, providing a case
study in African-Indian relations. Part IV focusses on
the milieu of voluntary associations, while in the
conclusion the author assesses the specific role of the
bourgeoisie and argues that there are alternatives to
racial civil war.

540   KUPER, Leo
           Passive resistance in South Africa. London:
           Cape, 1956, 256 p.

Focusses primarily on the 1952 passive resistance campaign, which the author places within the scope of an analytical study of South African race relations. Germane to the understanding of this campaign is background on the ideology of this form of resistance seen against the framework of South African politics.

541   KUPER, Leo
        The pity of it all: polarisation of racial
        and ethnic relations. London: Duckworth,
        1977, 302 p.

Although Algeria, Rumania, Burundi and Zanzibar are the principal societies under scrutiny, numerous references occur to the South African situation.

542   KUPER, Leo
        Race, class and power: ideology and
        revolutionary change in plural societies.
        London: Duckworth, 1974, 345 p.

Kuper regards his work as an examination of situations of extreme racial and ethnic conflict, and seeks to develop appropriate theoretical perspectives. Contains numerous references to South Africa. Reviewed by Robin Jenkins in Race and Class, vol. 17, Summer 1975, p. 104.

543   KUPER, Leo
        Race, class and power: some comments on
        revolutionary change. Comparative Studies in
        Society and History, vol. 14, 1972, p. 400-
        421

Applies his theories of revolutionary change to class and plural societies. Contains numerous references to South Africa, which the author states has been in a revolutionary situation for several generations, without revolutionary change.

544   KUZWAYO, Ellen
Call me woman. Johannesburg: Ravan, 1985, 266 p.

An autobiographical work of an erstwhile teacher who returned in her sixties to study for a higher qualification in social work at the University of the Witwatersrand. Active in community life and president of the Black Consumer Union of South Africa, she depicts life in Soweto interwoven with observations on political history. Appendix lists black women qualified as medical doctors (1947-1981) and lawyers (1967-1982).

545   LABOUR preference, influx control and squatters: Cape Town entering the 1980s; edited by Dudley Horner. Cape Town: Southern Africa Labour and Development Research Unit, 1983, (Southern Africa Labour and Development Research Unit. Saldru working paper, 50), 121 p.

Contains the following papers: influx control in the Cape Peninsula by Martin West; Nyanga East squatters: a sample survey by Delia Hendrie; case studies in influx control in the Western Cape by Martin West; Nyanga squatter diary July 1981 - December 1982 by Stephen Devereux; the Coloured Labour Preference policy: a chronology by Delia Hendrie; Africans in the Western Cape 1900 to 1982: a chronology by George Ellis.

546   LABOUR, townships and protest: studies in the social history of the Witwatersrand, compiled and introduced by Belinda Bozzoli. Johannesburg: Ravan, in association with the University of the Witwatersrand, Institute of African Studies, 1979, 342 p.

Selected from research papers presented at the History Workshop held at the University of the Witwatersrand in February 1978, entitled: The Witwatersrand: labour, townships and Patterns of Protest. Illustrative of local history, the concept of which is elucidated upon by the editor in her introductory chapter, these papers are arranged in three parts: township life and patterns of protest; cultural alternatives to hegemony; and worker experience and action. Reviewed by Baruch Hirson in an article entitled: Marxists, neo-Marxists and labour history in South Africa. Journal of Commonwealth and Comparative Politics, vol. 21, no. 1, March 1983, p. 80-85.

547   LACEY, Marian
        Working for Boroko: the origins of a coercive labour system in South Africa. Johannesburg: Ravan, 1981, 422 p.

By examining the apartheid system from the early Nineteenth Century to early 1930's when it was redefined as Trusteeship, the author reveals the close interrelationship between a coercive labour system and the growth of capitalism. Demonstrates that economic growth was at the expense of those working for a 'place to sleep'. Records the dissent and frustration of those suffering from exploitation. Included is an examination of the disenfranchisement of the Cape Africans; farmers and farm labourers; mine owners and migrant labour; the influx of blacks to the cities; and the 'poor white' problem. Much of the work is based on the evidence and findings, both published and unpublished of a series of commissions.

548   LA HAUSE, Paul
        Drinking in a cage: the Durban System and the 1929 beer hall riots. Africa Perspective, no. 20, 1982, p. 63-75

This brief case study of the 1929 beer boycott is examined within the context of capital accumulation and class struggle in Durban.

549   LAMBERT, Rob and LAMBERT, Lynne
         State reform and working class resistance,
         1982. South African Review, 1, 1983, p. 218-
         250

         Provides details of trade union activity during 1982
         and participation in strike activity, which illustrate
         'the permanence of working class gains in response to
         the real concessions granted by Wiehahn'. Useful tables
         depict a comparison of strikes, 1973-82; level of trade
         union involvement, 1982; regional breakdown of strikes,
         1982; and main strike demands, 1982.

550   LAPCHICK, Richard E. and URDANG, Stephanie
         Oppression and resistance: the struggle of
         women in Southern Africa. Westport:
         Greenwood, 1982, 197 p.

         Apartheid is overviewed in the introduction, thereafter
         this work is divided into two parts. Initially examines
         the effects of apartheid on women in both South Africa
         and Namibia, with a focus on conditions evident in
         rural and urban settings, employment, health, problems
         experienced in the work situation, and the lack of
         health facilities and social security. The second
         section concentrates on the role of women in the
         struggle for national liberation in Zimbabwe, Namibia
         and South Africa, with the latter concentrating on
         women against apartheid.

551   LAURENCE, John
         Censorship by skin colour. Index on
         Censorship, April 1977, p. 40-43

         Elucidates on this type of censorship which he discerns
         on two levels - that of black exclusion and of black
         viewpoint.

552   LAURENCE, John
           Race, propaganda and South Africa. London:
           Gollancz, 1979, 215 p.

           Examines the effects of propoganda by attempting to
           gauge effects had South Africa's plans for secretly
           gaining access to the West's major news sources not
           been subverted, its spread over the past fifteen years
           on public opinion, foreign policy and black/white
           relations in the nations of the West, and within all
           sectors of South African life.

553   LAURENCE, Patrick
           The Transkei: South Africa's politics of
           partition. Johannesburg: Ravan, 1976, 136 p.

           Presents an alalysis of the historical and political
           process which culminated in 'independence'. The role
           and thinking of Kaiser Matanzima is assessed in this
           study, which traces Transkei's development from the
           earliest times, which Laurence sets against the
           background of both Afrikaner and African nationalism.

554   LAW and justice in South Africa, edited by John Hund.
           Cape Town: Centre for Intergroup Studies in
           association with the University Press of
           America, 1986, 272 p.

           Intended as a companion to Legal ideology and politics
           in South Africa by John Hund and Hendrik van der Merwe,
           q.v., this series of essays explores questions on law,
           justice and the role played by ideology in securing law
           and order in the South African context. Contents
           include: Heribert Adam - Engineering compliance;
           Laurence Boulle - Administrative justice; Geoff
           Budlender - Lawyers, poverty and social justice; D.M.
           Davis - Legality and struggle; John Hund - Township
           justice; Vincent Mntambo - Legal positivism; Mathole
           Motshekga - Witchcraft trials; Paul Pretorius -

Industrial justice; A.J.G.M. Sanders - Natural law; Nico C. Steytler - Access to justice; Raymond Suttner - Ideology and the judiciary; Paul van Warmelo - My legal philosophy. The South African Freedom Charter is appended, together with an historical interpretation by A.J.G.M. Sanders.

555   LAW and politics in Southern Africa, edited by Sheldon Leader. Journal of Southern African Studies, vol. 12, no. 1, October 1985, p. 1-135

In this special issue, comprised mainly of papers delivered at a conference held at the Institute of Commonwealth Studies during April 1984, the editor has defined the organization of material into those which concentrate on strategies towards the law, the interaction between state, law and custom, and thirdly these concerned with the links between law and the gap between appearance and reality in ideologies. Among others, Harold Wolpe presents analytical considerations of political strategies and the law, while Dennis Davis and Bob Fine concentrate on historical observations. Albie Sachs in an article on South Africa's reconstruction focusses on the right of all the country's inhabitants to self-determination as an issue both in international law and domestic politics. Christopher Forsyth examines the Appellate Division of the Supreme court since 1950 while Sandra Burman and Martine Huvers discuss divorce regulations in the light of Dutch Reformed Church attitudes and National Party legislation.

556   LEACH, Graham
        South Africa: no easy path to peace.
        Bergvlei: Century Hutchinson, 1986, 266 p.

Written by the British Broadcasting Corporation's Southern African Radio Correspondent, this book is intended 'towards enlightening the general reader who wishes to understand more of the complicated situation which lies behind the daily news headlines about South Africa'. Leach places his study within its historical perspective by providing information on its racial mixture and its heritage stemming from the Boers, British and the blacks. Focusses on constitutional modifications, the changing nature of apartheid, and dissent amongst the Afrikaners. He chronicles the struggle for black freedom and highlights the Uitenhage shootings and the subsequent state of emergency. The plight of the squatters at Crossroads, the protracted search for a settlement in Namibia, Pretoria's relations with black Africa, and the American call for sanctions are discussed prior to an assessment of the chances for peaceful change.

557   LEE, R.H.
        The role of the private sector as a catalyst
        for change in South Africa. African Affairs,
        vol. 82, no. 329, October 1983, p. 455-463

        Distinguishes between the concepts of reform and change
        and provides an overview of the catalytic role played
        by the private sector, particularly in the field of
        housing and industrial relations.

558   LEEUWENBERG, Jeff
        Transkei: a study in economic regression.
        London: Africa Bureau, 1977, 33 p.

        Illustrates the extreme poverty prevalent in Transkei.
        Based on the findings of a survey, which are presented
        after introductory chapters briefly outline the
        administrative structure and aspects of Transkeian
        economy.

559   LEFORT, René
       The 'black' press in South Africa.
       International Social Science Journal, vol.
       33, no. 1, 1981, p. 99-121

       Invalidates the argument that South Africa has a free
       press and illustrates that 'all in all, the black press
       represents first and foremost a source of profit and an
       instrument of political manipulation for the wealthy
       and powerful minority'. Examines structures,
       legislation, titles and circulation of the South
       African press, complemented by useful tables. Devotes
       the major part of the study on the black press taking
       cognizance of political divisions and social evolution,
       the revival of black challenge, content, independent
       newspapers, and the clandestine press. Concludes by
       assessing the role of the black press in the liberation
       struggle.

560   LEGASSICK, Martin
       Class and nationalism in South African
       protest: the South African Communist Party
       and the "Native Republic" 1928-34. Syracuse,
       N.Y.: Syracuse University, Eastern African
       Studies Program, 1973, (Eastern African
       Studies, 15), 67 p.

       Primarily a detailed political history which discusses
       the formulation, implementation, and partial
       abandonment of the "Native Republic" policy. This was
       adopted in 1929 at the seventh annual conference of the
       Communist Party of South Africa. It called for 'a South
       African Native Republic, as a stage towards a workers'
       and Peasants' Government, with full protection and
       equal rights for all national minorities'. He places
       this policy within the South African political economy
       of the period, presents a critique of pertinent
       ideologies and problems and extends his analysis to the
       Afro-American situation.

561   LEGASSICK, Martin
        Legislation, ideology and economy in post-
        1948 South Africa. Journal of Southern
        African Studies, vol. 1, no. 1, October 1974,
        p. 5-35

        Chronologically studies the development of post-1948
        racial policy, which the author relates to economic
        trends as manifest by capitalist production and its
        productive cycle in South Africa.

562   LEGASSICK, Martin
        Race, industrialization and social change in
        South Africa: the case of R.F.A. Hoernle.
        African Affairs, vol. 75, no. 299, April
        1976, p. 224-239

        Demonstrates the relationship between South African
        liberal thought and segregationism by examining the
        writings of Alfred Hoernle, both in the period 1909-
        1917 and in 1939.

563   LEGASSICK, Martin
        South Africa: capital accumulation and
        violence. Economy and Society, vol. 3, no. 3,
        August 1974, p. 252-291

        South African modes of production and aspects of their
        economic inter-relationship are analyzed within the
        framework of the country's authoritarian and racially
        discriminatory social structure. This is discussed in
        terms of mercantile colonial conquest, primitive
        accumulation in mining and farming as well as
        capitalism in secondary industry. Evaluates
        consequences for strategies of social transformation.

216

564   LEGASSICK, Martin
South Africa: forced labor, industrialization
and racial differentiation IN: The POLITICAL
economy of Africa, edited by Richard Harris.
New York: Schenkman, 1975, p. 227-270

In this study focussing both on South Africa's economic
growth into a modern industrial state and the marked
disparity between black and white wealth, Legassick
addresses the issues under the following headings: the
world commodity market and colonial systems of forced
labour; South Africa in the era of mercantile
colonialism; South Africa in the mining era, 1875-1924
- gold, maize and segregation; the mining economy;
secondary industrialization and the white worker;
secondary industrialization in a forced labour economy;
development and underdevelopment in Southern Africa -
South Africa as an imperialist power.

565   LEGASSICK, Martin
South Africa in crisis: what route to
democracy? African Affairs, vol. 84, no 337,
October 1985, p. 587-603

Explores the implications of apartheid and capitalism
for future developments in the country, with comment on
the economy in crisis, the creation of mass movements
and political connotations. See further comment on his
article by J.D. Brewer and Tom Young in African
Affairs, vol. 85, no. 339, April 1986, p. 283-297

566   LEGER, Jean and VAN NIEKERK, Phillip
Organisation on the mines: the NUM
phenomenon. South African Review, 3, 1986, p.
68-78

Illustrates the upsurge in union activity and continuing industrial action by assessing the changing structure of the mining industry and the gold mines in particular. Reviews the development of the National Union of Mineworkers to date.

567   LEGUM, Colin
       The end of apartheid. Washington Quarterly, vol. 5, no. 1, Winter 1982, p. 169-178

In this Special Report, Legum gives his reasons for stating that the end of apartheid rule is in sight, and that South Africa has entered a period of transition. He elaborates on seven identified characteristics of this period: a time of change; government indecision; continuing repression when the government is seeking to be less repressive; growing divisions within Afrikanerdom; growing black confidence; change in the balance of internal power; growing uncertainty among whites on their future. An assessment of South Africa's choice of reform or revolution concludes this survey.

568   LEGUM, Colin
       Southern Africa in South Africa: the impact of regional events on domestic politics IN: SOUTH Africa in Southern Africa: the intensifying vortex of violence, edited by Thomas M. Callaghy. New York: Praeger, 1983, p. 153-161

Indicates that 'South Africa is clearly not an "island" lodged in the Southern African region but an integral part of a regional subsystem . . .'. Changes in power relations within neighbouring states have encouraged resistance and also altered the perspective of those whites striving to maintain the status quo. The failure of the Constellation of States concept within the region and Prime Minister Botha's subsequent attempts at internal reform and its effects, are analyzed.

569   LEISTNER Gerhard Max Erich
Towards a new order in South Africa. South
African Journal of African Affairs, nos 1/2,
1976, p. 10-18

Traces briefly the evolution of South Africa's separate
development policies, prior to evaluating issues
emanating from the resultant close economic union
between South Africa and the homelands. Presents a
possible future scenario of institutional arrangements.

570   LEKOTA, 'Terror' (and others)
UDF and AZAPO: evaluation and expectations.
Work in Progress, 35, 1985, p. 12-17

United Democratic Front leaders, 'Terror' Lekota and
Trevor Manuel were interviewed by Karen Jochelson,
while Susan Brown interviewed AZAPO president, Ishmael
Mkhabela, in order to ascertain progress made during
1984 and to comment on aims for 1985.

571   LELYVELD, Joseph
Move your shadow: South Africa, black and
white. Johannesburg: Ball in association with
Michael Joseph, 1986, 390 p.

An insight into contemporary South Africa is provided
by a journalist working for the New York Times, after
his second term of duty since the mid-1960s. The effect
of apartheid on both blacks and whites is documented in
what the author describes 'essentially . . . a book of
personal experience and observation'. Reviewed in New
Republic, 23 December 1985, p. 32-34 by George M.
Frederickson.

572   LE MAY, Godfrey, H.L.
Black and white in South Africa: the politics
of survival. London: BPC, 1971, 126 p.

Provides an account of South Africa's political development and the entrenchment of Afrikaner thought. Background information on slaves and frontiers sets the framework for discussion on the growth of Afrikaner nationalism, the status of the Afrikaner, the genesis of Afrikaner supremacy, apartheid and republicanism. Concludes with a brief assessment of National Party rule after twenty years. Work is heavily illustrated.

573 LEMON, Anthony
    Apartheid: a geography of separation. (n.p.):
    Saxon House, 1976, 261 p.

The author, a Fellow and Tutor in Geography at Mansfield College, Oxford, provides an overview of the geography of apartheid in South Africa. He gives an historical background; an examination of white South Africa by viewing the economy, the towns, their political and voting behaviour (written by Professor Owen Williams); Indians and Coloureds; Black South African homelands; and concludes with scenarios for change by taking into account both internal dynamics and external pressure.

574 LEMON, Anthony
    Federalism and plural societies: a critique
    with special reference to South Africa.
    Plural Societies, vol. 11, no. 2, Summer
    1980, p. 3-24

Reviews succinctly history and current thinking relevant to federalism in the Republic prior to analyzing federal ideas in both theory and practice outside the Republic, and as indicated in the existing literature. These findings are then applied to the South African situation and mooted as a political alternative.

575   LEMON, Anthony
        The   Indian   and   Coloured   elections: co-
        optation   rejected?   South African Inter-
        national,   vol.   15,   no. 2, October 1984, p.
        84-107

Outlines   the major provisions of the new   constitution
in   order to further understand the debate between   the
boycotters   and   participants   of   the   elections.
Implications   of the election results for the operation
of   the   tricameral parliament   are   assessed.   Article
includes useful tables.

576   LEMON, Anthony
        Issues   and   campaigns in the South   African
        general   election of   1981.   African Affairs,
        vol. 81, no. 325, October 1982, p. 511-526

Examines   reasons why these elections were   interpreted
as   a   major   setback for (then)   Prime   Minister   P.W.
Botha, and heralded a split in Afrikaner unity. Reviews
campaign manifestos of opposition parties.

577   LEMON, Anthony
        State control   over the labor market in South
        Africa.   International Political Science
        Review, vol. 5, no. 2, 1984, p. 189-208

Probably   no   avowedly capitalist controls   its   labor
market   to the same degree as South   Africa.   Statutory
job   reservation   by race has been eroded   by   economic
forces,   but   customary   discrimination   remains
widespread.   State restrictions on freedom of   movement
continue   to hinder Africans in particular from selling
their labor freely.   A brief historical review of   this
legislation   is   followed   by   consideration   of   the
agricultural   labor   market   in   relation   to   current
developments   in white farming,   and   the   role   and
changing   perspectives   of   the   mining   companies   as

employers. The implications of recent changes in government control over the labor market, and their effects on the source areas are examined. (Journal abstract)

578   LEONARD, Richard W.
       South Africa at war. Westport, Conn.: Hill, 1983, 274 p.

Documents the Republic's current position and pays particular attention to the increasing opposition towards its apartheid policies. Black resistance and the history of the African National Congress is recorded, as is South Africa's military and financial involvement in regional conflicts, South Africa's relations with the Reagan Administration, and the future implications are assessed.

579   LERUMO, A. pseud.
       Fifty fighting years: the South African Communist Party, 1921-1971. London: Inkululeko Publications, 1971, 216 p.

Written in commemoration of the fiftieth anniversary of the South African Communist Party's foundation, this book comprises a collection of chronologically linked essays, first printed in African Communist, detailing the Party's history. Based largely on internal Party documentation, it essentially reflects the Party's own view of its history. However, the author, Michael Harmel, who wrote under the above pseudonym, and was the Party's chief theoretician in the 1950s playing a key role in its intellectual development, is critical of the Party in both the period 1928 to 1933, and post-war strategies employed in 1945 to 1950. Apart from this criticism, the picture portrayed is favourable. The second edition of this work was published in 1980, and appendices include Party documentation.

580   LEVER, Henry
        Ethnic attitudes of Johannesburg youth.
        Johannesburg: Witwatersrand University Press,
        1968, 192 p.

        Intended particularly for the trained social scientist,
        the student, and the serious lay reader, Lever reports
        on ethnic attitudes prevalent among a sample of 2 302
        white school children in 1959, as indicated by the
        results of a modified Bogardus social distance test.

581   LEVER, Henry
        South African society. Johannesburg: Jonathan
        Ball, 1978, 312 p.

        As Professor of Sociology at the University of the
        Witwatersrand, Johannesburg, the author presents a
        sociological study of South African society, its
        constituent groups and the social processes taking
        place. In twelve chapters he examines topics including
        an overview of the society, and theoretical
        perspectives; population, constitution and laws; ethnic
        attitudes; voting; opinions of the electorate; poverty;
        crime; the case for and against apartheid; and
        alternative geo-political solutions of the race
        problem.

582   LEVER, Henry
        The South African voter: some aspects of
        voting behaviour with special reference to
        the General Elections of 1966 and 1970. Cape
        Town: Juta, 1972, 221 p.

        Designed for the lay reader in particular, this work
        deals with the two elections in separate sections.
        Provides background information on the elections prior
        to an assessment of voting behaviour based on personal
        interviews.

583   LEVY, Norman
The foundations of the South African cheap
labour system. London: Routledge and Kegan
Paul, 1982, 367 p.

With the emphasis of this work on the cheap labour
system utilized in the gold mines in the period 1886 to
1906, Levy divides his study into three parts.
Initially he discusses origins and development of the
structure, including the wage rate, migrant labour, and
the role of the Chamber of Mines. He, thereafter,
devotes discussion to the relationship between mining
capital and the state including the implications of the
Anglo-Boer War. Part Three is concerned with the
defence of labour structure in the period 1902 to 1906.
This section includes an examination of the Transvaal
Labour Commission, Asian and Chinese labour, as well as
the racial work restrictions which developed.

584   LEWIN, Julius
Politics and law in South Africa: essays on
race relations. London: Merlin, 1963, 115 p.

By illustrating the relative power of Afrikaner
nationalism, African nationalism and economic
interests, Lewin demonstrates the triumph of the former
and prevailing apartheid policies.

585   LEWIN, Julius
The struggle for racial equality. London:
Longmans, Green, 1967, 190 p.

Comprises a selection of thirty-two documents
illustrating this struggle, and covering the period
1833 to 1964. They indicate the changing character of
the controversy concerning race.

586   LEWIS, Dave
       The South African state and African trade
       unions: 1947-1953. Africa Perspective, no.
       18, 1981, p. 35-64

       As indicated by the title, the relationship between the
       state and black trade unions in various phases forms
       the basis of this article. It concentrates on the
       struggle for trade union recognition and the state's
       refusal, during the period under review, to extend to
       them legal recognition.

587   LEWIS, Gavin
       Between the wire and the wall: a history of
       South African 'Coloured' politics. Cape Town:
       David Philip, 1986, 320 p.

       Analyzes the origins and development of Coloured
       politics. Studies the controversial issue of identity
       and 'ethnicity' prior to examining the rise of
       political elites. The main focus is on the formative
       period up to 1948 but the work concludes with a survey
       of the main political developments up to the time of
       writing. Political organization is documented in the
       book by R.E. van der Ross entitled: The rise and
       decline of apartheid: a study of political movements
       among the Coloured people of South Africa, 1880 to
       1985. Cape Town: Tafelberg, 1986, 416 p.

588   LEWIS, Jon
       Industrialisation and trade union
       organisation in South Africa, 1924-55: the
       rise and fall of the South African Trades and
       Labour Council. Cambridge: Cambridge
       University Press, 1984, (African Studies
       series, 42), 246 p.

Lewis says of his study: 'the object has been to analyse the roots of division within the South African trade union movement by establishing a link between trade union structure and the process of industrialisation which produced a fractured working class'. The achievements and failures of the many labour organizations in the period under review are chronicled and assessed. Reviewed by Ieuan L. Griffiths in International Affairs, vol. 62, no. 1, Winter 1985/86, p. 154.

589   LEWSEN, Phyllis
        The Cape liberal tradition - myth or reality.
        Race, vol. 13, no. 1, July 1971, p. 65-80

        Offers various interpretations of Cape liberalism prior to the presentation of an in-depth examination and definition of the tradition which she sets in historical perspective.

590   LEWSEN, Phyllis
        Cape liberalism in its terminal phase IN: WORKING papers in Southern African studies, vol. 3, edited by D.C. Hindson. Johannesburg: Ravan, 1983, p. 33-50

        Evaluates the significance of the Cape liberal tradition in the light of recent research by Colin Bundy, Martin Legassick and Stanley Trapido.

591   The LIBERAL dilemma in South Africa, edited by Pierre L. van den Berghe. New York: St Martin's Press, 1979, 164 p.

        Ten contributions include the following chapter headings: an introduction by Pierre L. van den Berghe; predicaments and options of critical intellectuals at South African universities by Heribert Adam;

commitment: the liberal as scholar in South Africa, by
Hilda Kuper; on the liberal definition of the South
African situation by Hamish Dickie-Clarke; the
impossibility of a liberal solution in South Africa, by
Pierre L. van den Berghe; sociology and universal
reality: South African implications, by Fatima Meer;
the magician and the missionary by Adam Kuper; the
African doctor, and his role in the community, by
Hilstan L. Watts; the political implications of a split
labour market analysis of South African race relations,
by Edna Bonacich; the politicization of ethnic
universities: experiences with South Africa's college
'brews', by Kogila A. Moodley; intellectuals and
academic apartheid, 1950-1965, by Margo Russell; and
biographical sketch and bibliography of Leo Kuper.

592   The LIBERATION struggle in South Africa IN: The
         STRUGGLE for Africa, edited by Mai Palmberg.
         rev. ed. London: Zed, 1983, p. 237-286

In a book intended for use in study circles, schools
and organizations as well as an introductory textbook,
the chapter on the South African liberation struggle
provides background information on the country's
colonization prior to tracing African resistance to
apartheid and the role of the African National
Congress. Included among the subdivisions are the
following: SACTU organizes trade unions against
apartheid; foreign capital; imperialism arms South
Africa; strikes and worker struggles; Soweto, the Black
Consciousness Movement; and Botha's Total Strategy.

593   LIJPHART, Arend
         Power-sharing in South Africa. Berkeley:
         University of California, Institute of
         International Studies, 1985, (Policy papers
         in international affairs, no. 24), 178 p.

States as his major purpose, to critically review the most important of the proposed solutions to the South African problem, and to recommend an optimal solution. He classifies the proposals into four broad categories: majoritarian, non-democratic, partionist, and consociational. Argues that the first three should be rejected. The latter includes the various consociational, semi-consociational and quasi-consociational plans. He uses the term power-sharing mainly to refer to government by a broadly inclusive coalition, but states that it may also be used as a synonym of consociational democracy. This work contains an extensive bibliography.

594   LIPMAN, Beata
        We make freedom: women in South Africa.
        London: Pandora Press, 1984, 141 p.

The author, now a journalist in Wales, conducted over thirty interviews mainly wtih black women in South Africa, where she had worked for thirty years. The interviews are divided into eight sections, each presenting a different perspective in the lives within the labouring society in South Africa and their role in the struggle for liberation.

595   LIPTON, Merle
        Capitalism and apartheid: South Africa, 1910-
        84. London: Gower, 1985, 464 p.

Focusses on the introduction of racial policies and economic forces in South Africa, stressing the increasing erosion of apartheid by economic pressures. These pressures, both promoting and opposing apartheid, are assessed with reference to agricultural, mining and manufacturing capital, the interests of white labour, and the costs and benefits of apartheid to the whites. She subsequently illustrates the changing balance of political power.

596   LIPTON, Merle
Independent bantustans? _International Affairs_,
vol. 48, no. 1, January 1972, p. 1-19

Examines South Africa's balkanization policies within
the framework of separate development. The feasibility
of independence, and the fulfilling of the conditions
for meaningful independence are assessed. Possible
reactions by the international community are itemized.

597   LIPTON, Merle
White farming: a case study of change in
South Africa. _Journal of Commonwealth and
Comparative Politics_, vol. 12, no. 1, 1974,
p. 42-61

By analyzing the modernization of agriculture in South
Africa, Lipton argues that changes have affected blacks
to their advantage. Assesses pressures for and against
the reformist and labour repressive options.

598   LIVING under apartheid: aspects of urbanization and
social change in South Africa, edited by
David M. Smith. London: Allen & Unwin , 1982,
(London research series in geography, 2),
256 p.

Focussing mainly on urbanization, this collection of
twelve papers, is aimed at illustrating the effect of
change on certain facets affecting the lives of blacks.
Contributors include John Browett who provides an
overview of unequal development in South Africa;
urbanization and social change by David M. Smith;
apartheid, decentralization and spatial industrial
change by Christian M. Rogerson; migrant labour and
frontier commuters by Anthony Lemon; urbanization in
the homelands by P. Smit, J.J. Olivier, and J.J.
Booysen; the informal sector in Johannesburg by K.S.O.
Beavon and C.M. Rogerson; urbanization, unemployment

and petty commodity production: comparative cases in
Cape Town by D. Dewar and V. Watson; informal housing
and informal employment: case studies in the Durban
metropolitan region by Gavin Maasdorp; domestic service
in Durban by Eleanor Preston-Whyte; council housing for
low-income Indian families in Durban; the black housing
crisis by J.P. Lea; and the geography of urban social
control by John Western.

599   LODGE, Tom
        The African National Congress in South
        Africa, 1976-1983: guerrilla war and armed
        propaganda. Journal of Contemporary African
        Studies, vol. 3, no. 1/2, October 1983/April
        1984, p. 153-180

The growing influence of the ANC over the past eight
years is explained and discussed through an analysis of
events and developments up to the end of 1982. A brief
epilogue summarizes subsequent events which represent a
transition in strategy.

600   LODGE, Tom
        The African National Congress, 1982. South
        African Review, 1, 1983, p. 50-54

Re-established as a real presence within South Africa
and thus similarly affecting both decision-makers and
the rest of the population, Lodge reviews activities
during 1982, and demonstrates the ANC's relevance to
the overall regional crisis.

601   LODGE, Tom
        The African National Congress, 1983.
        South African Review, 2, 1984, p. 21-25

Surveys activities for the year under review, and
suggests that the conflict will move away from armed
struggle towards underground organizational activities.

602   LODGE, Tom
The ANC after Nkomati. Johannesburg: South
African Institute of Race Relations, 1985,
(South African Institute of Race Relations.
Topical opinion), 10 p.

Traces both the development of the African National
Congress from the early 1960s and the launching of an
insurgency campaign in South Africa after 1976. Its
success in building a local political following is
noted, as is its ability to continue its operations
within the country since the signing of the Nkomati
Accord and its entrenchment in South African political
life. Decisions taken at the Kabwe Conference, Zambia
in June 1985 are listed.

603   LODGE, Tom
Black politics in South Africa since 1945.
Johannesburg: Ravan, 1983, 389 p.

The author defines the scope of his work as ' . . . the
history of resistance movements within the black
population of South Africa, from the end of the Second
World War until the present'. The work, which can be
divided into four historical phases, each coinciding
with a different decade, concentrates on resistance
which falls outside 'the legally sanctioned outlets of
political expression for black South Africans'. The
author places the history of these protest movements
within their local context in order to further clarify
the development of black political life. This book
provided the basis for Tom Lodge's doctoral thesis
entitled: Insurrectionism in South Africa: the Pan-
Africanist Congress and the Poqo Movement, 1959-1965.
(York: University of York, 1984, 447 p.) Reviewed in
Journal of Modern African Studies, vol. 23, no. 1,
March 1985, p. 162-164, by Newell M. Stultz, in Africa
Today, vol. 31, no. 2, 1984, p. 49-52, by Donald Will.

604   LODGE, Tom
        The creation of a mass movement: strikes and
        defiance, 1950-1952 IN: WORKING papers in
        Southern African Studies, vol. 3, edited by
        D.C. Hindson. Johannesburg: Ravan, 1983, p.
        91-122.

        Focusses on black resistance in urban areas, with
        especial emphasis on the Programme of Action adopted by
        the African National Congress in Bloemfontein during
        1949. Explains why support for the campaign was
        particularly evident in the cities of Port Elizabeth
        and East London.

605   LODGE, Tom
        'Mayihlome! - let us go to war': from Nkomati
        to Kabwe, the African National Congress,
        January 1984 - June 1985. South African
        Review, 3, 1986, p. 226-247

        Reviews developments in the period dating from the
        beginning of 1984 to the end of June 1985, assessing
        them from both an internal and external viewpoint.
        Implications of the eleven major decisions taken at the
        Kabwe Conference during June 1984 are analyzed and
        reveal the high level of morale within the
        organization.

606   LODGE, Tom
        The politics of refusal. Leadership South
        Africa, vol. 5, no. 1, 1986, p. 19-23.

        Concentrates on the background, origins, objectives and
        leadership of the United Democratic Front.

607   LODGE, Tom
        The second consultative conference of the
        African National Congress. South Africa
        International, vol. 16, no. 2, October 1985,
        p. 80-97

Dr Lodge, Senior Lecturer in Political Studies at the University of the Witwatersrand, Johannesburg, reports on the conference held in Kabwe during June 1985, while providing clarity on the ANC's current leadership and strategies. Stresses the importance of this conference, both in the development of the ANC and to the history of South Africa.

608 LODGE, Tom
"We are being punished because we are poor": the bus boycotts of Evaton and Alexandra, 1955-1957 IN: WORKING Papers in Southern African Studies, vol. 2, edited by P. Bonner. Johannesburg: Ravan, 1981, p. 258-303.

Germane to the understanding of black resistance, Lodge discusses the two bus boycotts within the context of the movement to mobilize campaigns designed to hasten the collapse of the existing political system.

609 LOMBARD, J.A. and VAN DER MERWE, P.J.
Central problems of the economic development of Bantu homelands. Finance & Trade Review, vol. 10, no. 1, June 1972, p. 1-46

Addresses the issue of economic viability in the homelands taking into account their economies and problems encountered in implementing development policies. Demographic patterns are assessed, and the institutional framework examined. Considerable statistical data substantiates this analysis.

610 LOMBARD, J.A.
Freedom, welfare and order: thoughts on the principles of political co-operation in the economy of Southern Africa. Pretoria: Benbo, 1978, 191 p.

Professor Lombard, of the Department of Economics at the University of Pretoria, presents his ideas on planning for the economic development of the region, which he states, can only be achieved within an orderly system of inter-relationships. Seven chapters study the issue from the following aspects - the idea of a limited government; co-operation through voluntary exchange; fundamental reforms; the problem of market failures; co-operation through consensus; the maintenance of the economic order; and international economic co-operation. Concludes with some reflections on the National Party's constitutional plans.

611   LOMBARD, J.A. and Du PISANIE, J.A.
       Removal of discrimination against blacks in the political economy of South Africa. Pretoria: University of Pretoria, Bureau for Economic Policy and Analysis, 1985, 96 p.

       A memorandum prepared for ASSOCOM at the request of J.C. Heunis, Minister of Constitutional Development and Planning, for submission to the Cabinet Committee on the Political Future of Urban Blacks.

612   LOOKING at the Afrikaner today, compiled by Hendrik W. van der Merwe. Cape Town: Tafelberg, 1975, 124 p.

       The Afrikaner nation is viewed from various perspectives subsequent to an examination by Hermann Giliomee of the Afrikaner's concept of himself. Nancy C.J. Charton presents the view of the English-speaking South Africans, Dr R.E. van der Ross as Rector and Vice-Chancellor of the University of the Western Cape, represents the Coloured view, M.T. Moerane the African, and Edwin S. Munger the American and other foreigners' concepts.

613   LOPES JUNIOR, Miguéis
Capital accumulation in South Africa and
Southern Mozambique. Mozambican Studies, no.
1, 1980, p. 89-102

Factors in South African capitalism which led to the
Chamber of Mines reducing the recruitment of migrant
workers are described prior to assessing the effects of
this action, particularly on the region south of the
River Save.

614   LOTTA, Raymond
The political economy of apartheid and the
strategic stakes of imperialism. Race and
Class, vol. 27, no. 2, Autumn 1985, p. 17-34

Multinational companies and direct foreign investment
in South Africa are reviewed within the context of the
apartheid system, the specific way in which capitalism
has developed - both utilizing and transforming rural
African economy, and under the umbrella of imperialist
capital.

615   LOUW, Leon and KENDAL, Frances
South Africa: the solution. Bisho, Ciskei:
Amagi, 1986, 237 p.

Authors state that the purpose of their book 'is not
only to show that South Africans can have a free and
just society, but also to provide an explicit and
detailed blueprint of how it can be achieved'. The
study is divided into four parts in order to explain
South Africa's predicaments. Part 1 provides historical
background concentrating on black South Africans and
the rise of both Afrikanerdom and apartheid. Current
political and economic issues are analyzed in Part 2
including white capitalism, black socialism, political
unrest, and the political status quo, taking into
consideration the tricameral parliament, political

parties and pressure groups. The redistribution of wealth is discussed prior to the presentation of an alternative model - a detailed political, legal system based on the Swiss confederation.

616   LUBBE, G.
       Islam in South Africa: enemy or ally?
       Bulletin on Islam and Christian - Muslim
       Relations in Africa, vol. 3, no. 1, 1985, p.
       1-15

       Unseen

617   LUCKHARDT, Ken and WALL, Brenda
       Organize or starve. London: Lawrence and
       Wishart, 1980, 520 p.

       Documents the history of the South African Congress of Trade Unions. Includes an index of international organizations and solidarity actions, trade unions and organizations and contains many illustrations.

618   LUCKHARDT, Ken and WALL, Brenda
       Working for freedom: black trade union
       development in South Africa throughout the
       1970s. Geneva: World Council of Churches,
       1981, 118 p.

       In this study of trade union history, the authors examine aspects pertaining to the conditions of workers. This includes industrial relations, non-racial trade unions, the growth of black trade unions, the economic crisis of the 1970s, and the consequences of both the Wiehahn and Riekert Commissions. Reviewed by William F. Lye in Africa Today, vol. 31. no. 4, 1984, p. 35-38.

619   LUNDALL, Paul (and others)
        Directory of South African trade unions: a
        complete guide to all South Africa's trade
        unions, by Paul Lundall, Ighsaan Schroeder
        and Gordon Young. Cape Town: Southern Africa
        Labour and Development Research Unit, 1984,
        285 p.

Supersedes the first SALDRU directory compiled by
Shirley Miller in 1982, q.v., which although outdated,
has been drawn on for the present work. Divided into
four sections: analysis, which includes a contribution
by R.G. Young entitled: South African trade unions - a
growing force; a chronology of industrial relations and
allied legislation, unions by size of membership,
industrial sector and geographical area. The Directory
is alphabetically arranged, and precedes a section on
federations. An extensive index complements this work.

620   LUTHULI, Albert John Mvumbi
        For freedom in South Africa: statements ...on
        receipt of the Nobel Peace Prize. New York:
        United Nations, Centre against Apartheid,
        1981, 26 p.

Commemorates the twentieth anniversary of the
presentation of the Nobel Peace Prize to Albert
Luthuli, by reproducing his acceptance speech entitled:
Africa and freedom. Extracts of other speeches by
Gunnar Jahn: Why we honour him; Dean Natvik Pedersen:
Champion for peace; and Johan B. Hygen's Burden to
bear, are included.

621   LUTHULI, Albert John Mvumbi
        Let my people go: an autobiography.
        Johannesburg: Collins, 1962, 256 p.

Traces the life and significance of the contribution
made by Chief Luthuli as President of the African
National Congress to the liberation struggle in South
Africa.

622   McCARTHY, Jeff and SWILLING, Mark
       Transport and political resistance: bus
       boycotts of 1983. South African Review, 2,
       1984, p. 26-44

Concentrates on bus transport, arguing that structural
pressures together with the Durban and East London bus
boycotts have resulted in a crisis for the transport
system. The relationship between the state, transport
monopolies and capital is assessed, as is the role of
the Welgemoed Commission. Concludes that workers and
the state are on a collision course.

623   MACRAE, Phyllis
       Race and class in Southern Africa. African
       Review, vol. 4, no. 2, 1974, p. 237-278

The growth of the different classes in both South
Africa and the then Rhodesia forms the basis of this
article, with particular focus on relations between the
black and white working classes. Reveals that the case
for solidarity has been weakened by discrepancies in
earnings, standard of living and political power.
Discusses relations between the capitalist oligarchies
and both black and white labour in an effort to
determine their future options.

624   MacCRONE, I.D.
       Race attitudes in South Africa: historical,
       experimental and psychological studies.
       Johannesburg: Witwatersrand University Press,
       1965, 328 p.

Divided into three main parts, the author introduces
the study with an historical account of European
settlement, tracing both struggles with and attitudes
towards the blacks. He continues by devoting a section

to the theory and measurement of attitude towards race, which he complements by presenting his own measurements and results. Part Three comprises a psychoanalytical interpretation of prejudices.

625   McGRATH, Mike
       Economic   growth   and   the   distribution   of
       racial incomes in the South African   economy.
       South Africa International, vol. 15, no. 4,
       April 1985, p. 223-232

In this   paper   an   attempt is made   to   provide   some insights into the historical effects of economic growth on the distribution of incomes in South Africa. It will begin   by   examining the issue of   economy-wide   income inequality   and   will then examine the incomes   of   the racial groups and their relative growth since   1946/47. The   incidence of poverty and urban-rural   inequalities are then examined. The concluding section speculates on possible future trends.   The main emphasis is placed on income   inequalities   between   whites   and   Africans, although   the   other racial groups are also   discussed. (Author's summary)

626   MACSHANE, Denis (and others)
       Power!   Black   workers,   their unions and the
       struggle   for   freedom   in   South   Africa,   by
       Denis Macshane,   Martin Plaut and David Ward.
       Nottingham: Spokesman, 1984, 195 p.

Concentrates   on   the   black working class   and   their unions,   highlighting   the   increase in   the   level   of organization.   Based   on   research   and   personal interviews, the authors provide detailed information on the status of unions up to the mid-1980s,   organization and   structure,   health and safety,   the role of   women workers,   differences,   politics   and the importance of international solidarity. Addresses of major unions are included in the appendices, which contain useful policy statements: the workers' struggle - where does FOSATU stand? An address by Joe Foster; the General Workers Union and the Municipal and General Workers Union on the United Democratic Front; the United Democratic Front on the Unions; CUSA on political organizations; labour movement relations with South African trade unions; and international policy statement adopted by FOSATU Central Committee, April 1984.

627   MAFEJE, Archie
        Soweto and its aftermath. Review of African
        Political Economy, no. 11, January/April
        1978, p. 17-30

Analyzes strengths and shortcomings in the strategies employed by the student movement during the 1976 riots, and assesses implications of changing internal conditions for the exiled liberation movements.

628   MAGUBANE, Bernard Makhosezwe
        The mounting class and national struggles in
        South Africa. Review, vol 8, no. 2, Fall
        1984, p. 197-231

Magubane elucidates the articles's objectives. 'First the aim is to give a brief resume of the reawakening of the working-class movement and to highlight the struggles this class has waged recently. Secondly, I want to put into perspective the politics of armed struggle and its dialectics with national and class struggle. Finally, I will discuss the recent "reforms" by the apartheid regime in order to show that they are completely irrelevant to the demands of the oppressed majority of the people.'

629   MAGUBANE, Bernard Makhosezwe
        The political economy of race and class in
        South Africa. New York: Monthly Review Press,
        1979, 364 p.

In this study of racism in South Africa, based on a socio-historical perspective, the author's intention is to depict the exploitation of black labour. Going back some three hundred years, he records the impact of white domination '. . . to indicate the necessity for transforming the system of oppression so that we may help establish and create a society in which our children and our children's children will be free from exploitation, deprivation, and ignorance'. Reviewed by Baruch Hirson in an article entitled: Marxists, neo-Marxists, and labour history in South Africa. Journal of Commonwealth and Comparative Politics, vol. 21, no. 1, March 1983, p. 80–85.

630   MAGUBANE, Peter
       June 16: the fruit of fear. Johannesburg: Skotaville, 1986, 122 p.

       Compiled to commemorate the tenth anniversary of June 16 1976, this is a pictorial essay with a text by Harry Mashabela exercepted from his book: Black South African people on the boil (1976-1986), q.v. As noted by Bishop Desmond Tutu in the foreword '. . . Peter's skills have been used to bring to the notice of a wider audience a remarkable record of what has happened in a beautiful but sad and divided land in the traumatic upheaval of the uprisings since June 16th 1976'.

631   MAGYAR, Karl P.
       Federation vs. confederation in Southern Africa: the neglected economic dimension. International Affairs Bulletin, vol. 7, no. 2, 1983, p. 16-24

       Professor Magyar investigates differences between federation and confederation within the regional context and maintains that although the constellation of states idea heralded a new direction, it represented a limited concept. Advocates 'a confederation of a variety of ethnically mixed states, tied together by a limited economic "commission" constituted by representatives of the confederal members (who) will not be able to exercise superior political authority over any units, while managing their own economic viabilities and cohesion'. Envisages the ultimate inclusion of South Africa's neighbouring states in a new order, vital to regional stability.

632   MAHLENGU, Mankikola
        Women against apartheid. Ufahamu, vol. 11,
        no. 3. spring 1982, p. 24-31

The text of an address delivered to the Third Annual African Activist Association Conference, May 1981, in which the author describes the situation and roles of women in South Afric within the apartheid system. Author concludes by describing opposition to this system.

633   MAHOMED, I.
        Interview with . . . , Chairperson Anti- P.C.
        Committee. Africa Perspective, no. 23, 1983,
        p. 46-57

Based on a question-and-answer format, Dr Mahomed's own role and political position is assessed. In his discussion on the Anti-President's Council, which was established before the United Democratic Front, he explains its relationship to the UDF and the steps taken in opposition to the Presidents Council.

634   MAKATINI, John
        The imperialist game is lost. Ufahamu, vol.
        11, no. 3, Spring 1982, p. 16-21

Permanent African National Congress Representative to the United Nations presents an assessment of conditions in South and Southern Africa which illustrate his point that 'the apartheid regime and its imperialist allies are now frantically preparing for a last stand'. Paper presented to the Third Annual African Activist Association Conference, May 1981.

635   MALAN, T. and HATTINGH, P.S.
       Black homelands in South Africa. Pretoria:
       Africa Institute of South Africa, 1976,
       255 p.

A survey covering all general aspects of homeland development, followed by details concerning each of the individual homelands. Succinct biographical information on several leaders is presented.

636   MALHERBE, Paul N.
       Multistan: a way out of the South African
       dilemma. Cape Town: Philip, 1974, 172 p.

Provides an alternative in South African politics by suggesting the Multistan concept. This he defines as 'setting aside a portion of the country in which racial laws are repealed, thus giving South Africa a region which resembles other multiracial societies'. Zululand and Kwazulu are seen as a prototype, and he examines the economic, social and political consequences of the concept, and possible reactions.

637   MALHERBE, Paul N.
       A scenario for peaceful change in South
       Africa. Cape Town: College Tutorial Press,
       1986, 61 p.

Defines the political position at the time of writing and identifies contributions made to change by the various political parties. Thereafter presents his formula for effecting a peaceful process of change in the Republic.

638   MANDELA, Nelson
        I have done my duty to my people and to South
        Africa: statement from the dock, 7 November
        1962. New York: United Nations, Centre
        against Apartheid, 1982, 14 p.

Alhaji Yusuff Maitama-Sule in the preface to this publication claims that these are amongst the most notable statements made in humanity's struggle for freedom and racial equality. Published in an attempt to actively promote the campaign for Mandela's release as well as all other South African political prisoners.

639   MANDELA, Nelson
        No easy walk to freedom: articles, speeches
        and addresses. London: Heinemann, 1965,
        189 p.

Encompassing the period 1953 to 1963, eleven articles, a conference speech and documentation emanating from both the 1962 Pretoria and 1963 Rivonia trials are reproduced under the following headings: streams of African nationalism; living under apartheid; the fight against apartheid - our tactics and theirs; resistance from underground, which includes the struggle for a national convention; on trial.

640   MANDELA, Nelson
        The struggle is my life. rev. ed. London:
        International Defence and Aid Fund for
        Southern Africa, 1986, 278 p.

Originally published in 1978, this revised and up-dated
version of Nelson Mandela's speeches and writings is
augmented by historical documents. It also includes
accounts of prison conditions, and of Mandela himself.

641   MANDELA, Winnie
        Part of my soul: Winnie Mandela, edited by
        Ann Benjamin. Harmondsworth: Penguin, 1985,
        164 p.

The compiler records, in Winnie Mandela's own words,
her life, her views and feelings. This is balanced by
comment from her friends and love letters between
Winnie and Nelson Mandela. Title varies in the New York
edition published in 1985 by Norton entitled: Part of
my soul went with him, 164 p.

642   MANDY, Nigel
        A city divided: Johannesburg and Soweto.
        Johannesburg: Macmillan, 1984, 447 p.

Provides an analysis of metropolitan Johannesburg
within the South African context and is illustrative of
urbanization problems in general. Mandy has divided
this study into five parts. Part One presents the
historical background, tracing Johannesburg's
development from its establishment in 1886 as a mining
camp to a metropolitan city. Part Two concentrates on
the racial issues and legislation which have shaped
South African society, and ways in which Johannesburg
was affected. Case studies are presented. Part Three is
devoted to Soweto, Johannesburg's black residential
satellite - its evolution, the West Rand Administration
Board and the 1976 riots, its needs in the post 1977
period, the position of permanent urban blacks and an
assessment of Soweto's situation at the time of
writing, is presented. Part Four considers the status
of Greater Johannesburg, and the problems of managing
the metropolitan system conclude the study in Part
Five.

643   MANGANYI, N.C.
        Being black in the world. Johannesburg: Spro-
        cas/Ravan, 1973, 77 p.

        A collection of essays depicting aspects of the black
        experience, significant to the South African society as
        a whole.

644   MANN, Michael
        Shifts in dominant ideology in contemporary
        South Africa. Africa Perspective, New Series,
        vol. 1, nos. 1 and 2, 1986, p. 68-83

        Author's abstract is as follows: "Certain observers of
        the South African situation have pointed to recent
        transformations in dominant ideology. It is the
        contention of this paper that these changes should not
        be seen as involving a movement from one particular
        ideology to another. Rather, they might be more
        adequately construed as shifts in the emphases placed
        upon specific elements of a single discourse which
        comprises a wide and indeed contradictory diversity of
        constituents, instead of a radical break, then, between
        two ideologies, a differential appropriation and
        suppression of components of the same discourse is
        posited. This latter process, it is suggested, is
        affected by the fluctuating interests and objectives of
        various social forces. Ideological changes are thus not
        held to reflect any immanent tendency within the realm
        of discourse towards truth or greater understanding.
        They are dependent rather upon evolving social and
        historical circumstances.

645   MANN, Michael and SEGAL, Simon
        The transport industry: carrying apartheid's
        burden. Work in Progress, 38, 1985, p. 19-23

246

Conflicts between government, business and transport monopolies are examined, with bus companies often being regarded as an extension of apartheid policy. Summarizes the findings of the Welgemoed Commission.

646   MARAIS, D.
Constitutional development of South Africa.
Johannesburg: Macmillan, 1985, 100 p.

Provides a brief outline of South Africa's constitutional development from the time of Jan van Riebeeck up to 1985. Reviewed in Politikon, vol. 13, no. 1, June 1986, p. 104-106

647   MARAIS, J.S.
The Cape Coloured people, 1652-1937.
Johannesburg: Witwatersrand University Press, 1957, 296 p.

A study of race relations with particular emphasis on the Coloureds of the Cape Colony. Chapter headings include origins; the Griquas; the colonization of the North-West; the colonial Hottentots, 1795-1828; emancipation; its aftermath; the Kat River Settlement; missionary institutions since emancipation, and latter day phases.

648   MARAIS, Jaap
Where the HNP stands: South Africa International, vol. 16, no. 3, January 1986, p. 129-134

A translation of the full transcript published in Die Afrikaner, of a television interview focussing on Jaap Marais, leader of the Herstigte Nasionale Party (HNP) conducted by Willem de Klerk, editor of the Sunday newspaper Rapport. Marais makes the claim that the National Party (NP) has entirely lost its character and that the HNP is now the true NP.

649   MARCUS, Tessa
        Assessing "resettlement" IN: SOUTHERN African
        studies - retrospect and prospect. Edinburgh:
        University of Edinburgh, Centre of African
        Studies, 1983, p. 367-378

        Provides an explanation of the policy and its
        implications, clarifying theoretical perspectives
        raised by other authors on this subject.

650   MARÉ, Gerhard
        African population relocation in South
        Africa. Johannesburg: South African Institute
        of Race Relations, 1980, 110 p.

        Within an on-going programme of research undertaken by
        the South African Institute of Race Relations
        documenting details of relocation, this work provides a
        categorization and preliminary analysis of reasons why
        this occurs and is likely to continue. Explains the
        relationship between the different categories
        illustrated by case studies.

651   MARÉ, Gerhard
        Africans under apartheid in the 1980s. South
        African Review, 1, 1983, p. 72-82

        Describes the implications for blacks of their
        exclusion from the new political dispensation. Ethnic
        fragmentation, the fate of those residing outside the
        homelands, alternatives to parliamentary incorporation
        and the idea of a confederation are discussed.

652   MARÉ, Gerhard
        The new constitution: extending democracy or
        decentralising control? South African Review,
        3, 1986, p. 208-222

Briefly sketches the historical background leading to the steady erosion of democracy in South Africa prior to examining the 'extension' claimed to be taking place. Takes into account the consolidation of the new political allies brought together in the tricameral parliament, measures taken by the state to bring economic interests within the orbit of relevant state institutions, the establishment of second and third tier government, and the growth of extra-parliamentary political and economic organizations.

653   MARKS, Shula
        The ambiguities of dependence in South Africa: class, nationalism, and the state in Twentieth-Century Natal. Johannesburg: Ravan, 1986, 171 p.

Written against the background of South Africa's segregationist policies, the author states that her essays focus around the following themes: the ambiguity of the state, the ambiguity of nationalism, and the ambiguity of class and class consciousness. Each case revolves around an episode in the life of an individual: the Zulu king Solomon kaDinizulu, the nationalist leader John Dube, the trade unionist George Champion and Kwazulu's leader Mangosuthu Buthelezi. Attention should be drawn to a related 1986 publication co-edited with Stanley Trapido entitled: The politics of race, class and nationalism in Twentieth Century South Africa.

654   MARQUARD, Leo
        A federation of Southern Africa. London: Oxford University Press, 1971, 142 p.

Marquard enlarges on the concept and practicalities of implementing federalism in Southern Africa, as an alternative to racial conflict and a means of ensuring peaceful co-existence. His plan includes the division of the Republic into eleven regions and the inclusion of Botswana, Lesotho, Swaziland and Namibia into a federation.

655   MARQUARD, Leo
       Liberalism in South Africa. Johannesburg: South African Institute of Race Relations, 1965, 53 p.

Author indicates that this is no academic analysis or historical outline but '. . . rather, it is an attempt by a South African liberal to examine and to re-state his own beliefs, particularly with reference to present-day South Africa.' Provides a definition of liberalism, its status and role in South Africa, and the increasing attack on liberal organizations and individuals.

656   MARQUARD, Leo
       The peoples and policies of South Africa. 2nd ed. Cape Town: Oxford University Press, 1960, 247 p.

In a general overview, Leo Marquard depicts South Africa from the viewpoint of its historical background, the people, government, administration, the colour bar, politics, policies and parties, education, religion, the High Commission Territories and the mandated territory of South West Africa.

657   MARSHALL, Geoffrey
       Parliamentary sovereignty and the Commonwealth. Oxford: Clarendon Press, 1957, 277 p.

A Research Fellow of Nuffield College, Oxford, provides a theoretical and analytical examination of the doctrine of legislative supremacy in which problems of sovereignty in the Commonwealth are discussed. In Part

3 of the work, South Africa - its courts and the constitution, is used as a case study in parliamentary sovereignty.

658   MASHABELA, Harry
          Black South Africa: a people on the boil (1976-1986). Johannesburg: Skotaville, 1986, 120 p.

A journalist presents his personal account of events in the decade under review.

659   MATHEWS, Anthony S.
          The darker reaches of government: access to information about public administration in three societies. Cape Town: Juta, 1978, 245 p.

Author states that his objective in writing this book 'was to provide the reader with a comprehensive survey, not too encumbered with detail or technical elaboration, of the laws, practices and institutions that either support or diminish secrecy in government administration in America, Britain and South Africa'. With reference to the latter, he takes into account the Official Secrets Act; classification; general legislation limiting access to information; breach of confidence; and copyright law. As with all these countries, this analysis is placed within its socio-political context. He concludes with reform proposals necessary to open government.

660   MATHEWS, Anthony S.
          Freedom, state security and the Rule of Law: dilemmas of the apartheid society. Cape Town: Juta, 1986, 312 p.

This three part work initially examines the Rule of Law and thereafter the South African security system with reference to relevant legislation and judicial decisions. Part 3 evaluates the Republic's security system in the light of the Rule of Law. The previous title: Law, order and liberty in South Africa. Cape Town: Juta, 1971, 318 p.

661   MATHEWS, Anthony S.
        Responsibility of a free press in South
        Africa. South African Outlook, September
        1974, p. 149-151

Text of a paper delivered at a symposium organized by the South African Society of Journalists in 1974, the anniversary of the foundations for a free press laid by Thomas Pringle and John Fairbairn 150 years previously. This commemoration came at a time when free press in South Africa was more threatened than ever previously.

662   MATIVO, Kyalo
        South Africa: history of oppression and
        struggle. Ufahamu, vol. 11, no. 3, Spring
        1982, p. 74-92

Places the 1976 outbreaks in Soweto and elsewhere in the country in historical perspective. Poses the question of original occupancy of the country tracing the colonial conquest and the ultimate imposition of apartheid in all its manifestations.

663   MATTHEW, Nell
        Housing South Africa's black population,
        Optima, vol. 33, no. 1, 15 March 1985, p. 29-
        37

Identifies the confusion evident in the causes of the housing problem and approaches to be adopted. Notes that the urban black population is in almost all respects representative of a Third World situation, but with the added constraints of apartheid. Elucidates on the inhibiting factors of influx control and the non-availability of serviced land. Concludes by commenting on the governments' 'controlled self-help housing approach'.

664   MATTHEWS, Jacqueline
        Economic integration and co-operation in Southern Africa IN: SOUTH Africa in the world economy, edited by Jacqueline Matthews. Johannesburg: McGraw-Hill, 1983, p. 237-257

Investigates the problems of economic integration within the Southern African region against a theoretical background in which reference to the European Economic Community is made. Reviews six relevant categories, three of which involve economic integration, viz the Southern African Customs Union, the Rand Monetary Area and the Preferential Trade Area. The others concern economic co-operation, namely the Southern African Development Co-ordination Conference, the Constellation of Southern African States and the Lomé Convention.

665   MATTHEWS, Jacqueline
        Foreign trade IN: SOUTH Africa in the world economy edited by Jacqueline Matthews. Johannesburg: McGraw-Hill, 1983, p. 157-176

In the sphere of foreign trade, South Africa's interdependence with the international community is particularly evident. Professor Matthews has divided this chapter into three sections. She initially examines the Republic's foreign trade policy and institutional arrangements prior to considering imports and exports for the period 1975 to 1980 for which statistical tables are provided. In the third section, regional aspects are examined such as trade agreements with African countries and trends in African trade and prospects for the future.

666 MATTHEWS, Jacqueline
South Africa's external economic relations.
Journal of World Trade Law, vol. 13, no. 6, November/December 1979, p. 495-509

Considers the Republic's economic relations from three aspects: foreign trade and policy; institutional links with world organizations, and South Africa's relationship with the neighbouring states. Comments on the complexity of South Africa's relations, advancing the theory that the withdrawal of capital will hamper progress made in the employment sector, and the impact of sanctions would also affect its many trading partners, local population and neighbours.

667 MATTHEWS, Z.K.
Freedom for my people: the autobiography of Z.K. Matthews; Southern Africa 1901 to 1968, a memoir by Monica Wilson. Cape Town: Philip, 1981, 253 p.

The early part of the autobiography was recorded by Dr Harold Isaacs (later of the Massachusetts' Institute of Technology) and reproduced in a shortened form. This has been supplemented with chapters by Monica Wilson on his twenty-four years at the University of Fort Hare and five years in Geneva. These include comment by his colleagues in various fields - teaching, academic, political and ecumenical evidence of both the Court record of the Treason Trial, and from the files of the World Council of Churches.

668   MAY, Henry John
          The South African constitution. 2nd ed. Cape
          Town: Juta, 1949, 447 p.

          Considers South African constitutional law from the
          aspects of executive government, parliament, provincial
          government and councils, judicial system, government of
          blacks, and foreign affairs. Appendices include the
          Statute of Westminster, 1931; Status of the Union Act,
          1934; Royal Executive Functions and Seals Act, 1934;
          and the South Africa Act, 1909.

669   MAYLAM, Paul
          A history of the African people of South
          Africa. Cape Town: Philip, 1986, 259 p.

          States that the purpose of his book is to offer an
          outline of the history of the African people in south
          Africa . . . those people who belong to the Nguni or
          Sotho language families as well as to the Venda and
          Lemba, and secondly as a wider objective to synthesize
          findings of recent research. Divides his work into
          three parts: the precolonial era, from the Third
          Century to circa 1830; 1830-1900; and the Twentieth
          Century encompassing land, labour and African politics
          for the period 1900 to 1936. The control and
          confrontation during the period 1936 to 1976 and
          conditions in Botswana, Lesotho and Swaziland are
          examined.

670   MAYSON, Cedric
          A certain sound: the struggle for liberation
          in South Africa. New York: Orbis, 1985,
          145 p.

          A British Methodist minister, who came to South Africa
          in 1953 and faced charges of high treason before
          leaving the country, recounts his experiences of
          contemporary South Africa - the tensions, violence and
          injustice experienced by blacks.

671   MAZRUI, Ali A. and TIDY, Michael
Nationalism and new states in Africa: from
about 1935 to the present. Nairobi:
Heinemann, 1984, 402 p.

Afrikaner and African nationalism in South Africa: p.
160-184

Explains the conflict between these two competing forms
of nationalism within the framework of Nationalist
Party governments and policy during the period 1948 to
1978, drawing attention to apartheid laws and the
failure of the homelands policy, prior to examining
African nationalism - the failure of Gandhi-ism, and
the significance of the 1976 Soweto revolt to the rise
of Black Consciousness. Observes South African foreign
policy by discussing the need for dialogue with black
Africa, the effect of the Angolan intervention in the
1975 to 1976 period, closer ties with Israel, and
Western investment in the Republic.

672   MBEKI, Govan Archibald Mvunyelva
South Africa: the peasants' revolt.
Harmondsworth: Penguin, 1964, 156 p.

Describes daily life under the apartheid system, and
the struggle against the Bantu Authorities Act which
culminated in the Pondo Revolt of 1960. Concludes with
a chapter on the constitution and elections. Appendices
include Proclamation no. R. 193, 1962: Regulations for
the Administration and Control of Townships in Bantu
Areas; the Freedom Charter, adopted at the Congress of
the People, Kliptown, South Africa, on 26 June 1955;
Regulation 12 of Proclamation no. R. 400 of 1960 and a
list of men from Pondoland sentenced to death.
Reprinted by the International Defence and Aid Fund for
Southern Africa in 1984.

673   MBEKI, Thabo
        Domestic and foreign policies of a new South
        Africa. Review of African Political Economy,
        no. 11, January/April 1978, p. 6-16

        Paper originally presented by the author, representing
        the African National Congress, at a conference in
        Ottawa in February 1978. He examines, through the
        viewpoint of class and capitalism, present-day South
        Africa as a necessary prerequisite in the presentation
        of policies on a new South Africa.

674   MBEKI, Thabo
        The struggle inside South Africa. Africa
        Report, vol. 30, no. 1, January/February
        1985, p. 59-60

        The African National Congress' Secretary for Political
        Affairs reflects on the unrest in South Africa and the
        intensification of the liberation struggle.

675   MDANTSANE: transitional city, edited by Gillian Cook
        and Jeff Opland. Grahamstown: Rhodes
        University, Institute of Social and Economic
        Research, 1980, (Rhodes University Institute
        of Social and Economic Research. Occasional
        Papers, no. 25), 92 p.

        Focusses on Mdantsane, the dormitory town for the
        preponderance of East London's labour force. Highlights
        the relationship between the two towns, the origins and
        development of the former, the journey to work,
        characteristics of the employees, and the economic
        potential of the area.

676   MEER, Fatima
        Factory and family: the divided lives of
        South Africa's women workers. Durban:
        University of Natal, Institute for Black
        Research, 1985, 105 p.

        Exposes the daily life of almost 1 000 black woman
        factory workers in the Durban/Pinetown area.

677   MEER, Fatima
        Portrait of Indian South Africans. Durban:
        Aron House, 1969, 236 p.

        Based primarily on life as experienced in Durban, this
        illustrated study depicts the society from historical,
        social, economic, religious, and cultural perspectives.

678   MEER, Fatima
        Race and suicide in South Africa. London:
        Routledge and Kegan Paul, 1976, 318 p.

        A sociological study of suicide in Durban utilizing
        both court records, statistics and case studies
        providing a theoretical model and the human dimension
        respectively.

679   MEER, Y.S. and MLABA, M.D.
        Apartheid: our picture. Durban: Institute for
        Black Research, 1982, 296 p.

        Recording the effects of apartheid on blacks, this
        study is largely based on questionnaires and field
        research 'This is an account of capitalism at its
        worst; capitalism compounded by racism'. All aspects of
        life are covered, including the effect of migrant
        labour on family life.

258

680   MEER, Y.S.
        Law and the regulation of labour in South
        Africa: an attempt at reform. Warwick:
        University of Warwick, 1980, 216 p.

        Dissertation: LLM

        Concentrates on the legal regulation of labour since
        1948, tracing the origins of laws crucial to the
        political, ideological and economic situations
        prevalent at the beginning of South Africa's
        'industrial revolution'. Changes to labour legislation
        at various stages are examined, as are reasons for
        their introduction. Focusses particularly on Wiehahn
        and Riekert reforms. Meer argues that 'the form of
        legal regulation of labour under apartheid capitalism
        is determined by the anarchic manner of capitalist
        production; that this dictates that such labour
        regulation cannot but assume a repressive form; but
        that the nature of this repression is adapted within
        certain bounds to changing circumstances'.

681   MEILLASSOUX, Claude
        Apartheid, poverty and malnutrition. Rome:
        Food and Agriculture Organization, 1982, (FAO
        economic and social development paper, 24),
        101 p.

        Unseen

682   MENAUL, Stewart W.B.
        The border wars: South Africa's response.
        Conflict Studies, no. 152, 1983, (entire
        issue: 19 p.)

        In this study 'the capacity of South Africa to respond
        to and cope with a guerilla war on the Namibian border
        is examined in the context of increased violence within
        the Republic itself'. South Africa's security is

examined from various aspects including the African National Congress; the Namibian issue; training and operational bases in Angola and the war with UNITA. Provides succinct information on the South African and Namibian armed forces and their operations in the area. Appendices include statistical information on South Africa's army, navy and airforce.

683   MICHELMAN, C.
        The Black Sash of South Africa: a case study in liberalism. London: Oxford University Press for the Institute of Race Relations, 1975, 198 p.

Provides a history of the female, white organization and its opposition to the Nationalist Party policies. Chronicles its development as part of the white liberal establishment, its protest against the political and legal implications of apartheid, and the task of the advice offices in working for the rights of blacks. Attitude towards Black Consciousness and Black Power is assessed.

684   MILLAR, Thomas Bruce
        South Africa and regional security. Johannesburg: South African Institute of International Affairs, 1985, (Bradlow series, no. 3), 28 p.

Provides an analysis of Southern African issues, concentrating on South Africa and its role as a regional power. The author concludes by illustrating that although its internal and external policies are 'the joint and common policies of a single government', different approaches are employed by various state departments. Appendix A includes texts of treaties of non-agression and good neighbourliness with Transkei, Venda and Ciskei, on security matters with Swaziland and the Accord of Nkomati.

685   MILLER, Shirley
       Trade unions in South Africa 1970-1980: a
       directory and statistics. Cape Town: Southern
       Africa Labour and Development Research Unit,
       1982, (Southern Africa Labour and Development
       Research Unit, Saldru working paper, 45),
       278 p.

Intended only as an information document, this work
does not assess operations of the unions under
discussion. Although dealing almost exclusively with
their numerical strength, the author points out that
this is not the only indicator of their strength.
Grouped according to their affiliation as at 31
December 1981, much of the information was obtained as
a result of questionnaires. Includes agreements
recognizing unions.

686   MOERDIJK, Donald
       Anti-development: South Africa and   its
       bantustans. Paris: Unesco, 1981, 194 p.

Outlines the political and economic development of
South Africa from its origins prior to discussing the
government's policy of separate development as manifest
in the granting of 'independence' to sections of its
territory.

687   MOHAMMED, Dahiru
       The economics of apartheid: creation of a
       neocolonial dual economy in South Africa.
       Nigerian Journal of International Affairs,
       vol. 8, no. 2, 1982, p. 80-96

Unseen

688   MOKGATLE, Naboth
       The autobiography of an unknown South
       African. Berkeley: University of California
       Press, 1971, 350 p.

       Gives an account of an African political activist who
       died in exile in London. He was a member of the South
       African Communist Party in Pretoria in the 1930s and
       40s. The book chronicles both his political and trade
       union activities in Pretoria, and gives personal
       details of his family and community life.

689   MOLEAH, Alfred Tokollo
       The Republic of South Africa and revolution:
       an examination and assessment of theories on
       preconditions of revolution and their
       applicability to the Republic of South
       Africa, 1910-1964. Ann Arbor: University
       Microfilms International, 1973, 344 p.

       Thesis: Ph.D. (New York University)

       Based on an extensive theoretical framework defining
       revolution, its preconditions and obstacles, the author
       then applies this to the South African situation.
       Provides information on the Republic's historical
       background, its political development founded on racial
       lines, the condition of blacks and their politics.
       Concludes that although conditions for revolution are
       ripe, revolutionary leadership, organization and
       ideology have been missing. The revolutionary
       potential, however, remains.

690   MOLLER, Valerie and SCHLEMMER, Lawrence
       Contract workers and job satisfaction: a
       study of job aspirations, motivations and
       preferences among migrants in Durban. Durban:
       University of Natal, Centre for Applied
       Social Sciences, 1981, 140 p.

Based on interviews covering a wide spectrum of topics and set within a theoretical framework, this is a study of male migrant workers living in Durban. These are estimated to make up some 40% of the workforce. The study focusses mainly on the issue and perceptions of job satisfaction.

690   MOLTENO, Frank
The historical significance of the bantustan strategy. <u>Social Dynamics</u>, vol. 3, no. 2, December 1977, p. 15-33

By analyzing the reserve and bantustan strategies: economically, politically and on an ideological level, the author seeks to promote an understanding of these policies, and reveals their changing roles within both the racial system and class relations. Paper initially presented at the Eighth Annual Congress of the Association for Sociology in Southern Africa held at Kwaluseni in 1977.

692   MOLTENO, Frank
The uprising of 16 June: a review of the literature on events in South Africa, 1976. <u>Social Dynamics</u>, vol. 5, no. 1, June 1979, p. 54-76

Says of his review essay: For the uprising to be understood, it is necessary to move beyond the official, newspaper, and more or less 'popular' interpretations which abound. The aim of this article is to review certain attempts which have been made to capture what actually happened, why and how. The paucity of serious analyses to have been made so far is remarkable, as is the time most of them have taken to be produced and their relative lack of theoretical depth.

693 MOODIE, Thomas Dunbar
Power, apartheid and the Afrikaner civil
religion. Cambridge, Mass.: Harvard
University, 1971, 365 p.

Thesis: D. Phil.

Moodie states that the purpose of this study is two-
fold: although in total disagreement with the system,
he aims to provide a clearer insight into Afrikaner
ideology and logic, and secondly to demonstrate the
importance of belief systems of the Afrikaner civil
religion in their 1948 political victory.

694 MOODIE, Thomas Dunbar
The rise of Afrikanerdom: power, apartheid
and the Afrikaner civil religion. Berkeley:
University of California Press, 1975,
(Perspectives on Southern Africa, no. 11),
328 p.

As background, the author initially provides the reader
with a commentary on the Afrikaner concept of civil
faith, summed up by Moodie as 'a constellation of
symbols held fairly universally and consistently by
Afrikaners at least since the end of the Anglo-Boer War
in 1902'. The role and implications of civil theology
and the Afrikaner Broederbond are examined, as well as
cultural, economic and political thinking culminating
in the policy of separate development.

695 MOOLMAN, J.H. and LEISTNER, Gerhard Max Erich
Bophuthatswana hulpbronne en ontwikkeling
(Bophuthatswana and development). Pretoria:
Africa Institute of South Africa, 1974, 2
vols.

Surveys Bophuthatswana from various aspects, including ethnic history and cultural background, constitutional development, environmental factors, consolidation proposals and health services.

696   MORRIS, M.
        Apartheid, agriculture and the state: the farm labour question. Cape Town: Southern Africa Labour and Development Research Unit, 1977, (Southern Africa Labour and Development Research Unit, Saldru working paper, no. 8), 56 p.

A revised version of a paper originally delivered at the Saldru Farm Labour Conference during September 1976. Discusses state intervention within the context of the relations between farmers and black farm labourers. Takes cognisance of conflict over labour as capitalization of agriculture spread.

697   MORRIS, M.
        The development of capitalism in South African agriculture: class struggle in the countryside. Economy and Society, vol. 5, 1976, p. 292-343

Defines 'countryside' in this context as the geographical area officially classified as the 'white rural districts' and states that the purpose of his paper is to attempt an analysis of the contradictions within agriculture and between the capitalist countryside and the towns in the Twentieth Century, after the capitalist modes of production had already come to dominate much of South African agriculture. Focusses particularly on the transition from the stage of capitalist labour tenancy to that of capitalist settled wage labour.

698   MORRIS, M.
The state and the development of capitalist
social relations in the South African
countryside: a process of class struggle.
Brighton: University of Sussex, 1982, 326 p.

Thesis: Ph.D. (Politics)

Eight chapter headings are as follows: Introduction –
South Africa's place in the imperialist chain; the
early transition to capitalism in the countryside; the
success of the Junker bourgeois revolution in the
countryside (1901-1920); the Prussian path and the
relations of production in the countryside; the effects
of the bourgeois revolution in the countryside on the
form of state; uneven capitalist development and the
contradiction of capitalist landlord economy; the 1940s
labour shortage crisis and the contradictions within
the bourgeoisie; apartheid and the capitalist
countryside.

699   MORRIS, Pauline
A history of black housing in South Africa.
Johannesburg: South Africa Foundation, 1981,
158 p.

Urban black housing, the historical processes, influx
demand and supply of houses, the crisis in housing
shortage, and guidelines for the future form the basis
of this study.

700   MORRIS, Pauline
Soweto: a review of existing conditions and
some guidelines for change. Johannesburg:
Urban Foundation, 1980, 264 p.

Aims at providing a framework for actions leading to an improvement of the quality of life in Soweto by presenting all available information and identifying major constraints on the community. This study provides historical background to the status of urban blacks in Soweto, both its physical and social structure, administration, financial base, transport services, economic activity, housing, pre-school and formal education, health services and recreation. Concludes by illustrating the need for its integration into the metropolitan system, a more reasonable allocation of resources, an efficient administration, education, personal security, and the opportunity for self-expression and choice.

701   MOSS, Glenn
        'Total strategy'. Work in Progress, 11, 1980,
        p. 1-11

Views the concept from various perspectives and isolates and elaborates on six major dynamics which have given rise to this response. These he has identified as the changes in the economic structure over the previous decade; changes in the nature of dominant class formation, and the relationship between these classes and the state; as a response to the renewed iniatives of the dominated classes; the changing nature of class formation amongst the dominated; Western and North American initiatives; and a changed balance of forces within the region.

702   MOTALA, M.E.S.
        Theories of the rule of law in South Africa,
        with special reference to the control of the
        movement of labour. Warwick: University of
        Warwick, 1981, 323 p.

Dissertation: M. Phil

Initially examines theories of the law as systematized in South African liberal and radical scholarship and thereafter the historical development of the laws which regulated the movement of black unskilled labour from the earliest Nineteenth Century Cape Colony laws to about 1960. Concludes that the law is a complex and contradictory phenomenon and is derived from and part of contradictory social relations.

703   MOTLHABI, Mokgethi
        The theory and practice of black resistance to apartheid: a social-ethical analysis. Johannesburg: Skotaville, 1984, 326 p.

Covering the period 1948 to 1978, the author critically compares the African National Congress, the Pan-Africanist Congress and the Black Consciousness Movement, taking into account their goals, strategies and theories. He evaluates their activities highlighting the moral significance of the South African struggle and proposes alternatives for a social-ethical viewpoint.

704   MÜLLER, A.L.
        Minority interests: the political economy of the Coloured and Indian communities in South Africa. Johannesburg: South African Institute of Race Relations, 1968, 62 p.

Outlines the political status of Indians and Coloureds prior to examining their economic position. The interrelationship between political and economic aspects is assessed, revealing the dominance of the former in determining their way of life. This is reinforced by identifying the causes and consequences of government policy.

705   MUNGER, Edwin S.
           Afrikaner and African nationalism: South
           African parallels and parameters. London:
           Oxford University Press for the Institute of
           Race Relations, 1967, 142 p.

           Compares and contrasts the origins and development of
           the two nationalisms placing them within their
           political perspectives in the course of South African
           history.

706   MUNGER, Edwin S.
           Notes on the formation of South African
           foreign policy. Pasadena: Grant Dahlstrom,
           1965, 102 p.

           Introductory notes compiled by a Professor of Geography
           at the California Institute of Technology, on
           institutions and individuals contributing to the
           formulation of foreign policy. This, he reveals, is
           concentrated in the hands of a few people.

707   MURRAY, Colin
           Struggle from the margins: rural slums in the
           Orange Free State IN: STRUGGLE for the city:
           migrant labour, capital and the state in
           urban Africa, edited by Frederick Cooper.
           Beverly Hills: Sage, 1983, p. 274-318

           Describes as background, germane to the understanding
           of the mass removals and subsequent 'internal
           refugees'; reserves and farms, influx control and urban
           relocation pertaining to the Orange Free State.
           Illustrates the effects by providing the history of
           rural slums, and various experiences of those involved.

269

708   MURRAY, Martin
The formation of the rural proletariat in the
South African countryside, the class struggle
and the 1913 Natives' Land Act IN: SOUTHERN
African studies - retrospect and prospect.
Edinburgh: University of Edinburgh, Centre of
African Studies, 1983, p. 303-340

Capitalist accumulation in the South African
countryside forms the introduction to this study which
considers provisions of the 1913 Natives' Land Act and
the implications of its implementation.

709   MUSIKER, Naomi
South African history: a bibliographical
guide with special reference to territorial
expansion and colonization, compiled with the
assistance of Reuben Musiker. New York:
Garland, 1984, (Themes in European expansion:
exploration, colonisation and the impact of
empire, vol. 5), 297 p.

1 028 annotated entries are divided into the following
eighteen sections: general histories, travel and
exploration, Cape - general history, Natal - history
and description, Zululand, Orange Free State, 1854-
1899, Transvaal, political aspects of railway
development into the interior, Anglo-Boer War, 1899-
1902, peace treaty and settlement, 1902-1910, South
Africa, 1910-1980, British colonial and imperial
policy, political parties, prime ministers since Union,
race contacts, policy and relations, missionaries,
South African population. Complemented by an
author/title index and a subject/topographical index.

710   MUSIKER, Reuben
South Africa. Oxford: Clio, 1979, (World
bibliographical series, vol. 7), 194 p.

Designed as a selective guide to the standard and basic literature ranging across all fields of knowledge and accordingly arranged, this work replaces the author's now out of print, South African bibliography. (London: Crosby Lockwood, 1970). Comprising mainly works in English published in South Africa, this bibliography is aimed at a wide spectrum of users, mentioning over 1 200 works complemented by an index of authors, titles and subjects.

711   MUSIKER, Reuben
        South African bibliography: a survey of
        bibliographies and bibliographical work. 2nd
        ed. Cape Town: Philip, 1980, 84 p.

Emphasis of this work is a bibliography of South African bibliographies, which does not purport to be comprehensive, but to serve as a guide to the main subject and regional bibliographies published within the Republic. Contains a list of the 585 bibliographies, bibliographical surveys, books and articles mentioned in the text.

712   MYERS, Desaix
        U.S. business in South Africa: the economic,
        political and moral issues. Bloomington:
        Indiana University Press, 1980, 375 p.

A comprehensive review of the pressures on American companies operating in the Republic, and their response. This study is divided into two sections, firstly, business and labour in South Africa, in which background information on the development and constraints of apartheid, the role of foreign capital and the sanctions debate is presented. In the second section, four case studies of foreign investment are examined, encompassing the oil, computer and electronics, minerals, and motor industries within the Republic. Appendices include, among others, a list of laws affecting labour in South Africa, companies that have signed the Sullivan Principles and the actions of various colleges or universities that have decided to sell stock in corporations operative in the Republic.

713   MZIHELA, Sipo Elijah
        Nazism and aparthied: the role of Christian
        churches in Nazi Germany and apartheid South
        Africa.   Ann Arbor: University Microfilms
        International, 1981, 233 p.

Thesis: Ph D (New York University)

Published: New York: Vantage Press, 1983, 245 p.

Compares and contrasts the condition of German Jews under Nazi rule to that of blacks in South Africa under the   National   Party.   Assesses   the   role   of   the 'Confessing Church' which opposed nazism and attempts to determine what role a similarly orientated church could play in South Africa towards ending apartheid. Arranged in three parts, this work examines the rise and consolidation of the Nazis, prior to evaluating their   stand on Christianity. The same methodology is applied to the Afrikaners in Part Two, while Part Three presents similarities and differences between nazism and   apartheid.   Reviewed   by   Leslie   Rubin   in Africa Today, vol. 31, no. 2, 1984, p. 45-47.

714   NAIDOO, Indres
        Robben Island: ten years as a political
        prisoner in South Africa's most notorious
        penitentiary, by Indres Naidoo as told to
        Albie Sachs. New York: Random House, 1983,
        278 p.

A South African, of Indian descent presents a personal account of imprisonment. Arrested in 1963 'for his activities as a member of Umkhonto we Sizwe, his book is divided into two main sections: the chains bound and the chains loosened. He chronicles the changes brought about in conditions on Robben Island which he emphasizes came through organized resistance on the part of the prisoners. Reviewed by Peter LaSalle in Africa Today, vol. 31, no. 2, 1984, p. 65-66.

715   NATAL and KwaZulu: constitutional and political options, edited by Lawrence J. Boulle and Lawrence G. Baxter. Cape Town: Juta, 1981, 211 p.

Comprises all the papers presented to the Workshop on Constitutional Issues in Kwazulu and Natal, organized by the University of Natal's Department of Public Law on 27 and 28 October 1980. The maintenance of Natal as a political entity and the necessity for all permanent residents to enjoy full political rights were the concepts basic to this discussion of constitutional issues.

716   NATIONAL FORUM COMMITTEE
        Let's fight the organ grinder: an Azanian perspective on the Nkomati Accords. Race and Class, vol. 26, no. 3, Winter 1985, p. 47-62

A shortened version of a paper presented at the National Forum Summit, Pietermaritzburg on 22 April 1984, in which reasons for Mozambique's participation in the Accords are identified, and the consequences of the United States 'constructive engagement' are analyzed and contrasted to Soviet policy. The authors state 'the Nkomati Accords demonstrate that the Botha regime has accepted the US blueprint for Southern Africa'. Implications for other countries within the region are noted.

273

717   NATTRASS, Jill
       The dynamics of urbanisation in South Africa.
       Durban: University   of   Natal,   Development
       Studies   Unit,   1983,   (University of   Natal.
       Centre   for   Applied   Social   Sciences,
       Development   Studies Unit working paper,   no.
       2), 23 p.

       Discusses   economic growth and urbanization   indicating
       ways   in   which it could affect urban   patterns,   given
       that   most future migrants will be   Black.   Legal   and
       economic constraints are assessed.

718   NATRASS, Jill
       The   South   African economy: its growth   and
       change.   Cape Town: Oxford University Press,
       1981, 328 p.

       Intended as a first-year university textbook, this work
       explains the relationship between South Africa's   rapid
       economic   growth and the inequalities prevalent   within
       the society. Provides a description of the land and its
       people   and South Africa's economic development   during
       the   period   1860-1977 prior to discussing   the   labour
       supply,   historical   background   to   the   racial
       segmentation of the labour market, capital accumulation
       and   economic   growth,   agriculture,   mining,
       industrialization,   the   economies of the black states,
       and the role of the state. Professor Nattrass concludes
       with   the   implications of economic growth   for   socio-
       political   change   and   suggestions   for   alternative
       economic   political   systems.   Contains   extensive
       statistical   data.   Reviewed   by   Aaron   Segal   in
       Africa Today, vol. 31, no. 2, 1984, p. 63.

719   NAUDÉ, Beyers
       Where   is South Africa going?   Africa Report,
       vol. 30, no. 3, May/June 1985, p. 4-9

The General-Secretary of the South African Council of Churches, unbanned after eight years, assesses the unrest prevalent in the Republic and repressive legislation which have affected all facets of life. Attitudes and feelings of both whites and blacks are considered and Naudé concludes by suggesting a series of measures which American policy-makers could implement and therefore assist in minimizing increasing violence.

720   NCUBE, Don
        The influence of apartheid and capitalism on the development of black trade unions in South Africa. Johannesburg: Skotaville, 1985, 176 p.

The complex and varied forces shaping the origins and development of black trade unions are examined within the framework of the dominant factors - capitalism and apartheid.

721   NEAME, L.E.
        The history of apartheid: the story of the colour war in South Africa. London: Pall Mall, 1962, 200 p.

Traces, from the earliest times, the various stages in the practice of discrimination by colour, until the Bantustan policies created by Hendrik Verwoerd. Assesses possibilities of apartheid policies succeeding, but concludes that only wishful thinking can believe in the ultimate control of the black majority remaining in the hands of the white minority.

722   NEL, P.S. and VAN ROOYEN, P.H.
        Worker representation in practice in South Africa. Pretoria: Academica, 1985, 170 p.

Analyzes the origin and application of changes in legislation implemented after the Wiehahn and Riekert Commissions. Theoretical concepts such as industrial democracy, worker participation and representation precede an examination of practical aspects pertaining to the development of worker representation. The study of trade union policy and structure, the collective bargaining process, stikes, work councils, the disciplinary code and grievance procedure forms the basis of this work.

723   NELSON, John Douglas
Some external aspects of internal conflict within South Africa: a study of the place of international activities in the development of the ANC. Ann Arbor: University Microfilms International, 1975, 248 p.

Ph. D. (George Washington University)

Author states in his introduction: 'Although this examination of the international activities of the African National Congress has been developed within an historical framework, an attempt has been made to utilize some of the historical concepts appropriate to aspects of this topic. No body of theory exists that attempts to form a comprehensive overview of the international aspects of internal conflict. The literature that is suitable in this area is discussed in Chapter I. In Chapter II the history of the ANC and its international activities from 1912 - 1949 is discussed. Chapter III is primarily limited to a survey of the international aspects of the conflict; and Chapters IV and V deal with the development of the ANC and its international activities as a part of its total revolutionary effort.'

724   NGUBANE, Jordan Khush
       An African explaiⁿs apartheid. London: Pall
       Mall, 1963, 243 p.

       South Africa is viewed from the standpoint of a Black
       liberal   who   examines   the   origins   of   Afrikaner
       nationalism,   conflict   between   the   African   National
       Congress and the Pan Africanist Congress,   the role   of
       communism and provides his own alternative to apartheid
       policies.

725   NGUBO, Anthony
       The   development of African political protest
       in   South Africa,   1882-1910:   an   analytical
       approach.   Ann Arbor: University   Microfilms
       International, 1973, 192 p.

       Thesis: Ph D (University of California at Los Angeles)

       Provides   an analysis of the socio-political conditions
       and   ideological currents leading to the   formation   of
       pre-Union   religious   and   political   movements.
       Concentrating   on the Cape colony,   the   author   states
       that the study focusses on the problem of institutional
       and social integration, discontinuity and interactional
       patterns between black and white communities within the
       framework   of   their   historical   foundations   and
       development.

726   NICOL, Martin
       Riches from rags: bosses and unions in the
       Cape clothing industry, 1926-1937. Journal of
       Southern African Studies,   vol. 9,   no. 2,
       April 1983, p. 239-255

       Traces   the   relationship between   the   Cape   Wholesale
       Clothing   and   Shirt Manufacturers Association and   the
       Garment   Workers'   Union of the Cape Peninsula   in   the
       decade prior to the formation of an industrial   council

in 1936. Illustrates the role of the Minister of Labour, and, as Nicol states '. . . the point, . . . that while the Pact government did make concessions to white wage earners, they were not of such a magnitude to undermine seriously the processes of capital accumulation'.

727   NIEUWOUDT, Lieb
       Agriculture IN: SOUTH Africa and the world economy, edited by Jacqueline Matthews. Johannesburg: McGraw-Hill, 1983, p. 1-24

South Africa's contribution to world trade is relatively small, however it is one of the only six food exporting countries. Discusses the structure of agriculture and marketing policies prior to considering exports and imports.

728   The 1983 constitutional referendum and the future of South Africa: two views, by David Welsh and Marinus Wiechers. South Africa International, vol. 14, no. 3, January 1984, p. 427-439

In view one - South Africa after the vote - Professor Welsh assesses the prospects for the new constitution and the significance of the referendum results, with particular application to the Progressive Federal Party, the Afrikaners, the business community and black attitudes. Marinus Wiechers in View Two - votes for change or retardant? - reaction to the results of the referendum are monitored and its effect on long-term constitutional development is assessed.

729   NKOMO, Mokubung O.
       Apartheid education in crisis. TransAfrica Forum, vol. 3, no. 1, Fall 1985, p. 71-84

The effect of apartheid education on blacks is assessed, stating that their struggle for both social justice and educational equity should be seen in the overall struggle to dismantle the apartheid system. Addresses the issue of educational segregation by providing a brief background, noting financial expenditures and wastage in African schools.

730   NKOMO, Mokubung O.
        Student culture and activism in black South African universities: the roots of resistance. Westport: Greenwood, 1984, (Contributions in Afro-American and African studies, no. 78), 209 p.

Illustrates the development of official culture at black universities by presenting an historical examination of the state's role. He includes political and socio-economic aspects. Compares these universities to others in South Africa, prior to discussing the nature of student culture and activism providing insights into education and resistance to oppression.

731   NOLUTSHUNGU, Sam C.
        Change and reform in South Africa. International Journal, vol. 35, Autumn 1980, p. 646-662

Defines P.W. Botha's concept of reform. Traces the outline of its programme indicating weaknesses within the policy which he reveals '. . . bids fair to achieve nothing more than a new model apartheid'.

732   NOLUTSHUNGU, Sam C.
        Changing South Africa: political considerations. Manchester: Manchester University Press, 1982, 219 p.

In this extensive treatise, the author concentrates mainly on the contemporary class and racial stratifications within the South African society. Working from the premise that a peaceful option for shedding racialism still remains, Nolutshungu focusses on the political rather than the economic underpinnings for conflict. His contention that the South African state will not easily shed its racial character, nor will it be capable of deracializing the economy, is based upon the lack of understanding on the part of the state on the depth of the political foundations of black opposition. The longstanding oppression/ subordination milieu will not enable greater fluidity between class divisions to diminish racial identities, thus creating a new alignment along racial lines. The entrenchment of black opposition is not conducive to peaceful change.

733   NOLUTSHUNGU, Sam C.
        External intervention in South Africa IN:
        DECOLONIZATION and dependency: problems of
        development of African societies, edited by
        Aguibou Y. Yansane. Westport: Greenwood,
        1980, (Contributions in Afro-American and
        African Studies, no. 48), p. 173-195

        Speculates on possible interventionist options which
        Africa, the Soviet Union, China, and the United States
        could employ against South Africa. With reference to
        economic measures, the author considers how private
        business withdrawals and, possibly boycotts, are likely
        to become foreign governmental policy designed to
        foster change in South Africa.

734   NOLUTSHUNGU, Sam C.
        South Africa in Africa: a study in ideology
        and foreign policy. Manchester: Manchester
        University Press, 1975, 326 p.

Focussing mainly on the period 1945 to 1975, Nolutshungu divides his subject into South African policies towards, and relations with both colonial and post-colonial Africa. While the author sees the interweaving of both foreign and domestic policies, he limits discussion on the latter unless it clearly bears on the former. In the second part of the work, he includes an examination of the 'outward-looking' policy, the Customs Union Area, relations with Malawi; and Zambia, and the rest of Africa. Illustrates that the aim of South Africa's Africa policy remained constant, despite decolonization, and was 'to establish an African political context which was ideologically and organizationally favourable to white minority rule in South Africa'.

735   NYQUIST, Thomas E.
African middle class elite. Grahamstown: Rhodes University, Institute of Social and Economic Research, 1983, 303 p.

See also his earlier work entitled: Toward a theory of the African upper stratum in South Africa. Athens, Ohio: Ohio University, Center for International Studies, 1972, (Ohio University. Center for International Studies. Papers in international studies. Africa series, no. 15), 57 p. Based on research conducted during 1966 to 1967, and again in 1975, the object of this study to ascertain the mores of the upper stratum and potential black leaders living in the Grahamstown area. Indicates their position of sociological marginality who measure their success against white standards. Assesses the psychological and behavioural implications. Fieldwork was carried out in Grahamstown townships during 1966 and 1967.

736   NZO, Alfred
South Africa: imperalist manoeuvering and the
tide of liberation. Ufahamu, vol. 10, nos 1
and 2, Fall and Winter 1980/81, p. 19-23

Assesses the status of the liberation struggle at the
time of writing, noting the mounting unrest, worsening
economic crisis and rising unemployment.

737   NZO, Alfred
Stepping up the fight against the racist
enemy. World Marxist Review, vol. 26, no. 9,
September 1983, p. 20-26

Growing opposition to the apartheid regime by different
strata within South African society itself, and a
growing spirit of militancy is indicated by the author.
The African National Congress' role in completing the
decolonization process on the continent and in
establishing democracy is assessed.

738   NZULA, A.T. (and others)
Forced labour in colonial Africa, by A.T.
Nzula, I.I. Potekhin and A.Z. Zusmanovich,
and edited by Robin Cohen. London: Zed, 1979,
218 p.

Several sections of this work, first published in
Moscow during 1933, are specifically on South Africa.
Includes detailed development of the black trade unions
and a review of peasant agriculture in this first
sustained Marxist analysis produced on twentieth
century African society. In his lengthy introduction,
Cohen includes a biographical sketch of Nzula, the
first African General Secretary of the Communist Party
of South Africa, both on his work in South Africa and
in Moscow.

739   OBERY, Ingrid and JOCHELSON, Karen
       Consumer boycotts: industry and government,
       'two sides of the same bloody coin.' Work in
       Progress, 39, 1985, p. 9-30

Comment on the nature and goals of the boycott, a
manifestation of protest politics which the organizers
assert 'goes beyond previous campaigns'. Obery reports
on the boycott in the Eastern and Western Cape, while
Jochelson examines developments in Pretoria and
Johannesburg.

740   OBERY, Ingrid
       Long road to unity: trade union talks.
       Work in Progress, 37, 1985, p. 22-26

Assesses problems and obstacles encountered in the path
towards a united federation of trade unions.

741   ODENDAAL, André
       Vukani Bantu: The beginnings of black protest
       politics in South Africa to 1910. Cape Town:
       Philip, 1984, 391 p.

Boards edition under the title: Black Protest Politics
in South Africa published in both Cape Town: Philip,
1984 and Totowa, N.J.: Barnes and Noble, 1984. In this
history of black political life, the author traces the
emergence and development of those organizations which
preceded and were amalgamated into the African National
Congress in 1912.

742   OJO, Olusola
       South African-Arab relations. Ufahamu, vol.
       11, no. 3, Spring 1982, p. 121-132

Indicates difficulties experienced in writing the article due to the secrecy surrounding many aspects of the relationship. Highlights issues such as economic, oil and military cooperation, examines implications for Afro-Arab relations, and concludes by suggesting ways in which this cooperation could be ended.

743   O'MEARA, Dan
        The Afrikaner Broederbond, 1927-1948: class vanguard of Afrikaner nationalism. Journal of Southern African Studies, vol. 3, no. 2, April 1977, p. 156-186

Given the organization's secret nature, O'Meara attempts to clarify the history, functions and role of the Bond, within the context of Afrikaner nationalism.

744   O'MEARA, Dan
        'Muldergate' and the politics of Afrikaner nationalism. Supplement to Work in Progress, 22, April 1982, 19 p.

Originally delivered as a 1980 seminar paper in the Department of Political Science at the University of Dar Es Salaam, the journal editors have reproduced it 'because of its importance in the analysis and understanding of the recent break away of the Treurnicht group from the National Party. Not only does O'Meara provide essential background to the latest crisis in both party and government, he also provides a methodology for interpreting what is happening in the National Party as an indicator of a generalised crisis of the capitalist state in South Africa. The contemporary importance of this is that it enables one to identify the various class interests at work, not only within party and government, but within the capitalist ruling class as a whole. The identification of these interests allows for an assessment of the content of the 'reform' initiative which the alliance of the P.W. Botha led military group is attempting to implement - and which has been rejected by the Treurnicht led alliance'.

745   O'MEARA, Dan
The 1946 African mine workers' strike. Journal of Commonwealth & Comparative Politics, vol. 13, no. 2, July 1975, p. 146-173

Examines the significance and effects of the strike. The author's theory relates the changes in the structure of production and composition of the labour force to the political struggles of the 1920s and 1930s. Assesses the contribution of the strike to changes in the class basis of black opposition and African nationalism, and subsequent ramifications generated within the sphere of white politics.

746   O'MEARA, Dan
Volkskapitalisme: class, capital and ideology in the development of Afrikaner nationalism, 1934-1948. Cambridge: Cambridge University Press, 1983, 281 p.

Author sums up the aim of his book '. . . seeks to explore the material conditions, contradictions and struggles in the development of capitalism in South Africa which gave rise to "Afrikaner nationalism" as the (differentiated) form in which specific class forces came to be organised in the crucial formative period, 1934 to 1938. In doing so it aims both to remedy a lack in the Marxist literature on South Africa, and to lay to rest the myriad myths in the conventional understanding of Afrikaner nationalism'.

747   O'MEARA, Patrick
        South Africa: no new political dispensation.
        Current History, vol. 83, no. 491, March
        1984, p. 105-108, 131

        O'Meara, Professor of Political Science at Indiana
        University, assesses the consequences of the 1983
        constitutional referendum and the bombing of the
        airforce headquarters in Pretoria on 20 May 1983.

748   O'MEARA, Patrick
        South Africa: the politics of change.
        Current History, vol. 80, no. 464, March
        1981, p. 111-114, 134

        Assesses the government's changes and reforms agains
        the background of escalating black demands.

749   OMER-COOPER, J.D.
        History of Southern Africa. Cape Town:
        Philip, 1986, 320 p.

        Written by a Professor of History at the University of
        Otago, New Zealand in an analytical-cum-narrative
        style, this work centres around the origins of
        contemporary South African society and both its
        internal and external stresses.

750   OMOND, Roger
        The apartheid handbook. Harmondsworth:
        Penguin, 1985, 229 p.

        Using a system of question and answer, this work seeks
        to clarify the many manifestations of apartheid in both
        theory and practice. It illustrates how apartheid
        affects every facet of peoples' lives from legal
        considerations to personal choices. Forty such
        categories are explained in this work.

751 OPPENHEIMER, Harry Frederick
Political and economic change in South Africa. Address to the Chicago Council on Foreign Relations, 30 March 1983. Supplement to Optima, vol. 31, no. 2, 15 April 1983, 12 p.

Defines his stance as an opponent of the apartheid policy and stresses the need for the dismantling of racial discrimination in all its facets. Examines economic growth as a factor in promoting peaceful change and itemizes some of the changes in government policy, with particular regard to the constitution, which he criticizes as making no provision for black representation. Notes the role of Reagan's constructive engagement policy in promoting change in the Republic.

752 OPPENHEIMER, Harry Frederick
The press and society. Communications in Africa, vol. 1, no. 4, December 1972, p. 1-5

Discusses and defines the relationship between press and society, with particular emphasis on the functions and duties of the latter in South Africa.

753 OPPENHEIMER, Harry Frederick
Recent changes in South Africa. South Africa International, vol. 16 no. 1, July 1985, p. 24-28

Text of an address delivered to the South Africa Club in London on 17 April 1985, in which he stresses the need for peaceful reform and gives reasons why the changes already instituted by the government have not alleviated discontent and unrest among the blacks.

754   ORKIN, Mark
       The struggle and the future: what black South
       Africans really think. Johannesburg: Ravan,
       1986, 78 p.

       Based on a nation-wide survey conducted in September
       1985, this report reveals the wide spread support held
       by urban black South Africans, for some form of
       disinvestment as a means of helping to bring apartheid
       to an end.

755   ORLIK, Peter B.
       South African Broadcasting Corporation: an
       instrument   of Afrikaner political power.
       Journal of Southern African Affairs, vol. 3,
       no. 1, January 1978, p. 55-64

       Reviews the history of broadcasting in South Africa,
       illustrating the key role it played in the Briton/Boer
       power struggle. Initially a symbol of British cultural
       dominance, after its ultimate takeover 'it   was
       converted into a well-ordered vehicle for the further
       propagation and ultimate triumph of the Afrikaans and
       their Afrikaner Nationalist Party'.

756   OWEN, Ken
       A   fundamental   shift   in   South   African
       politics, Africa Notes, no. 53, 31 January
       1986, (entire issue: 6 p.)

       Enlarges on the re-emergence of the African National
       Congress and its new strategy devised at its June 1985
       congress held in Kabwe, Zambia. Identifies a framework
       within which the emergence of prerevolutionary. or
       revolutionary conditions can be assessed.

757   The OXFORD history of South Africa, edited by Monica
       Wilson and Leonard Thompson.   Oxford:
       Clarendon, 1969-1975, 2 vols.

Volume One covers South African history until 1870, whereas Volume Two focusses on the period 1870 to 1966. The latter volume contains the following contributions: Economic development by D. Hobart Houghton; The growth of the peasant communities by Monica Wilson; Farming, 1866-1966 by Francis Wilson; The growth of towns by David Welsh; The subjection of the African chiefdoms, 1870-1898 by Leonard Thompson; Great Britain and the Afrikaner Republics, 1870-1899 by Leonard Thompson; The compromise of Union by Leonard Thompson; Afrikaner nationalism by René de Villiers; African nationalism, 1910-1964 by Leo Kuper; South Africa and the modern world, by Jack Spence. Volume Two is reviewed in an article by Shula Marks entitled: Liberalism, social realities and South African history. Journal of Commonwealth Political Studies, vol. 10, no. 3, November 1972, p. 243-249. It is also reviewed by Anthony Atmore and Nancy Westlake in their article: A liberal dilemma: a critique of the Oxford History of South Africa. Race, vol. 14, no. 4, October 1972, p. 107-136.

758   OZGUR, Ozdemir
        Apartheid: the United Nations and peaceful change in South Africa. Dobbs Ferry: Transnational, 1982, 240 p.

        Dr Ozgur as Political Affairs Officer at the Centre on Apartheid, of the United Nations, comprehensively and analytically examines the relationship between South Africa and the United Nations.

759   PALMER, Mabel
        The history of the Indians in Natal. Cape Town: Oxford University Press for the University of Natal, 1957, (Natal regional survey, vol. 10), 197 p.

Provides historical background by outlining the position in Natal during the middle of the nineteenth century, circumstances in India and British policy towards both emigration and immigration. Chronologically divides subsequent history under the following chapter headings: the arrival of the Indians, 1860-70; reforms and subsequent events, 1874-93; Gandhi in Natal; anti-Asiatic agitation, 1915-26; after the Cape Town Agreement, 1927-46; passive resistance; Indian education and culture. She concludes by assessing the position at the time of writing and providing a scenario for the future.

760   PARKER, Frank J.
        South Africa: lost opportunities. Lexington:
        Lexington Books, 1983, 290 p.

A general political history, based mainly on newspaper articles and secondary sources provides a survey of both internal and external policies during the period 1977 to 1982, with an emphasis on the former. Foreign policy issues discussed include the 1977 United Nations arms embargo, nuclear co-operation with the West; the Namibian settlement issue; and the debate over United States corporate involvement in South Africa. Reviewed by Newell M. Stultz in Journal of Modern African Studies, vol 23, no. 1, March 1985, p. 162-164.

761   PATON, Alan
        Hofmeyr. London: Oxford University Press,
        1964, 545 p.

A biography of Jan Hendrik Hofmeyr, highlighting his academic career, Principalship of the University of the Witwatersrand at twenty-four, administrator of the Transvaal at twenty-nine, prior to detailing his political career, into which is woven South Africa's political history.

762   PATTERSON, Sheila
The last trek: a study of the Boer people and
the Afrikaner nation. Westport: Greenwood,
1957, 336 p.

Traces the development of the Boers into the Afrikaner
nation, and their nationhood into nationalism. Divides
her work into the past, present and the future with
chapters detailing the birth of the language,
upbringing and education, social structure and cultural
life. Demonstrates the necessity for the Afrikaner to
adapt and radically revise basic values in order to
survive.

763   PERLMAN, J.M.
The state and African working class in the
Pretoria-Odi area: population relocation,
state management and class restructuring.
Johannesburg: University of the Witwaters-
rand, 1982, (Dissertation series, 1), 103 p.

Examines the policies, practices and structures through
which the South African state has attempted to regulate
the residence, movement and employment of Africans in
this area.

764   PERSPECTIVES on South Africa: a collection of working
papers, edited by T. Adler. Johannesburg:
University of the Witwatersrand, African
Studies Institute, 1977, 366 p.

Initially presented as seminar papers at the
Universities of Oxford and Sussex, these contributions
reflect the changing nature of South African
historiography in the investigation of the country's
political economy. With an emphasis on class
categorization, this compilation includes the following
papers: Capitalism and apartheid - a critique of some
current conceptions of cheap labour power, by M.L.

Morris; Capitalist development in South Africa - class conflict and the state, by David Kaplan; The political economy of white labour in South Africa, by Robert Davies; The exercise of control in the diamond industry of South Africa - some preliminary remarks, by Duncan Innes; The South African social formation in the early capitalist period circa 1870-1939 - some views on the question of hegemony, by Martin Fransman and Robert Davies; Class Consciousness among the colonized workers in South Africa, by Fozia Fisher. Concludes with a select bibliography on work written since 1970 on South Africa's political economy.

765   PHAHLE, Roseinnes
        We don't want no education. Ufahamu, vol. 11,
        no. 3, Spring 1982, p. 134-168

Reprinted from Solidarity, no. 4, October 1980. Describes the 1980 school boycotts, identifying causes, nature and significance of these active struggles. Illustrates how pupils linked education grievances to the general conditions experienced by their parents. Discusses these community-based struggles and the fragmentation occurring among the black working class.

766   PHILLIPS, Norman Charles
        The tragedy of apartheid: a journalist's
        experiences in the South African riots. New
        York: McKay, 1960, 217 p.

As indicated by the title, a journalist recounts his experiences of the 1960 Sharpeville, Langa and Nyanga riots, which he places within their historical background. Recalls a meeting with Albert Luthuli, and gives his impression of schools, farms, the police, the Broederbond and Hendrik Verwoerd.

767   PIKE, Henry R.
A history of communism in South Africa.
Germiston: Christian Mission International of
South Africa, 1985, 601 p.

As stated on the cover . . . 'These pages are written
from the viewpoint of an American Conservative Baptist
Missionary not sympathetic to the evil ramifications of
apartheid and considers one man one vote a suicide
answer to South Africa's problems. He is totally
opposed to the left, radical right, pseudo-liberalism
and every shape and form of Marxist-Leninism. The final
chapter is a different approach to the menace of
communism in South Africa. The volume will be a pure
delight to the conservative Christian.' Copiously
illustrated, a selection of the thirty three chapter
headings read as follows: South Africa and financial
conspiracy; the many-sided onslaught continues; Russia,
Cuba, China, Yugoslavia and Breytenbach; a Czech secret
agent: the murder of Dr Verwoerd; communist trouble and
a red clergyman.

768   PILLAY, Vella
The role of gold in the economy of apartheid
South Africa. New York: United Nations, 1981,
(United Nations. Centre against Apartheid.
Notes and documents, 11/81), 29 p.

Examines the gold mining industry, which together with
other mining operations, constitute the basis of the
South African system in which migrant labour plays a
noteworthy role. Indicates that the monetary surpluses
earned by the gold mining industry are necessary to
support the militarist social structure which
characterizes South Africa's industrial development.

769   PILLAY, Vella
           Transnational   corporations: allies   or
           instruments of apartheid.   New York: United
           Nations,   1980,   (United   Nations.   Centre
           against Apartheid.   Notes   and   documents,
           28/80), 17 p.

           Paper presented to the United Nations Symposium on
           Transnational Corporations in South Africa and Namibia
           on 6 to 7 November 1980.   Examines   the role of
           multinational corporations which the author states are
           central to the evolution and maintenance of   the
           apartheid system.

770   PIRIE, Gordon
           'More of a blush than a rash': changes in
           urban race zoning. South African Review, 3,
           1986, p. 186-194

           Reviews Group Areas policy, noting amendments and
           changes bearing on territorial racial zoning.

771   PIRON, Johan
           Recognition   or rejection?   A primer   on
           recognition in South Africa. Johannesburg:
           FSA Management Consultants, 1982, 143 p.

           Written by a Professor at the University of South
           Africa's School of Business Leadership, this work is
           intended as an introductory text on recognition within
           South Africa's industrial relations practice. Provides
           details on the mechanics of recognition and related
           issues placed within the broader spectrum which has
           promoted the unions to concentrate on the recognition
           issue. The second edition was published by Macmillan
           in 1984.

772   PLATZKY, Laurine
            Reprieves and repression: relocation in South
            Africa. South African Review, 3, 1986, p.
            381-397

Writing on behalf of the newly-formed National Committee Against Removals, the author presents an overview of forced relocation. Illustrates that despite the 1985 announcement by the Minister of Cooperation, Development and Education that they would be suspended, six of the eight categories of relocation continue.

773   PLATZKY, Laurine and WALKER, Cherryl
            Review of relocation. South African Review,
            1, 1983, p. 83-96

Reviews the various categories of population removals under the following headings: consolidation of the homelands; removal of black spots; influx control; farm removals; and urban relocation. Details responses to the relocation policy.

774   PLATZKY, Laurine and WALKER, Cherryl
            The surplus people: forced removals in South
            Africa. Johannesburg: Ravan, 1985, 446 p.

This study has resulted from work on the Surplus People Project. As stated by the authors, it has been written to illustrate how the government's policy of forcibly removing millions of blacks, fits into the apartheid system. Explains how the bantustan concept, influx control and forced population removals are interwoven to maintain the white minority's political and economic power. The effects of relocation on individual and communities are chronicled by means of case studies.

775   PLURALISM in Africa, edited by Leo Kuper and M.G. Smith. Berkeley: University of California Press, 1969, 546 p.

Based on papers delivered to a colloquium organized by the African Studies Center, University of California, 1966, this work concentrates on 'the nature and social consequences of pluralism, and with problems of social cohesion and change in plural societies'. Contains numerous references to South Africa, and of relevance are chapters by Hilda Kuper: "Strangers" in plural societies: Asians in South Africa and Uganda (p. 247-282); and by Max Gluckman: The tribal area in South and Central Africa (p. 373-409).

776   POGRUND, Benjamin
The South African press. Index on Censorship, Autumn 1976, p. 10-16

Presents an assessment of the South African press, highlighting the legislation introduced by the Nationalist Government, limits on reporting, and the contradictions which are depicted by the relatively free press. Implications of the Press Code of Conduct are presented, and Pogrund concludes by stating that the prospects for the press in South Africa 'remain distinctly unhappy'.

777   POLITICAL alternatives for Southern Africa: principles and perspectives, edited by D. J. van Vuuren and D. Kriek. Durban: Butterworths, 1983, 639 p.

Also published in Afrikaans under the title: Politieke alternatiewe vir Suider Afrika.

This work is divided into three main parts subsequent to a philosophical and theoretical introduction on constitutional systems. Part I explores theoretical alternatives with contributions on the ideologies of capitalism, conservatism, socialism, communism, national, pluralism and democracy. Part II studies forms of state, authority, government and its institutions. It contains chapters on constitutions, the unitary state, federal forms of government confederal cooperation, economic relations in the Southern African region, development banking in the regional distribution of economic growth, partition, the Westminster system, consociational democracy, the executive authority, the judiciary and constitutional change, party systems and electoral systems, local authorities and the role of the press. Part III concludes this in-depth study with evaluations of constitutional proposals for Southern Africa.

778   POLLAK, Oliver B. and POLLAK, Karen
        Theses and dissertations on Southern Africa:
        an international bibliography. Boston:
        Hall, 1976, 236 p.

Lists material accepted for higher degrees between 1884 and 1974, listed by subject, Southern African country, chronologically, and thereafter alphabetically. Subject division is as follows: anthropology, ethnology, folklore, religion and sociology; economics; education; fine arts; geography; history; linguistics, literature and communications; political science and international affairs.

779   POLLAK, Richard
        Up against apartheid: the role and the plight
        of the press in South Africa. Carbondale:
        Southern Illinois University Press, 1981,
        157 p.

The relationship between the government and the media, particularly the English-speaking press forms the basis of this study, presented by the former editor of More, a journal which specializes in media analysis. Contains sections on the 'Muldergate Scandal', the Press Council, as well as press legislation. The role of the South African Broadcasting Corporation as a government tool is assessed.

780   POSEL, Deborah
        Language, legitimation and control: the South African state after 1978. Social Dynamics, vol. 10, no. 1, June 1984, p. 1-16

Analyzes the content and role of the new terminology 'both as a means of legitimating a new technocratic style of politics and as an instrument of control in itself', prior to discussing the relationship between the state's old and new languages of legitimation in order to ascertain the reason for the persistence of their existence and to determine their possible effects on the ideological efficacy of the new discourse.

781   POSEL, Deborah
        Rethinking the race-class debate in South African historiography. Social Dynamics, vol. 9, no. 1, June 1983, p. 50-66

        See also: SOUTHERN African studies - retrospect and prospect. Edinburgh: University of Edinburgh, Centre of African Studies, 1983, p. 1-30

Argues that revisionist historiography has provoked debate with liberal opponents stressing that either race or class has analytic primacy, and apartheid is either functional or dysfunctional to the growth of capitalism. In order to clarify the problem, she deals with the analytic shortcomings as evidenced in Harold Wolpe's Capitalism and cheap labour-power in South

Africa: from segregation to apartheid, and secondly, in Saul and Gelb's book entitled The Crisis in South Africa (q.v.). Concludes by proposing revised conceptualizations.

782   POTGIETER, P.J.J.S.
        Index to literature on the South African race problem and the policy of separate development (apartheid). Potchefstroom: Potchefstroom University for Christian Higher Education, 1977, 660 p.

Compiler defines the scope of the work as covering the entire South African racial and national problem. The policy of separate development, its implementation and results form the nucleus of the work. It is set within its worldwide context, and includes alternative policy suggestions. It encompasses the period 1910 to 1975, and is limited to items in English, Afrikaans, Dutch, German and French. It excludes United Nations documentation, which is effectively indexed by their own bibliographies. Contains only certain categories of South African official gazettes. The work comprises three main parts: a subject index, and an author index precede the extensive master index.

783   POTHOLM, Christian P.
        Four African political systems. Englewood Cliffs: Prentice-Hall, 1970, 308 p.
        South African political system, p. 91-137

Provides an overview of the system, modelled as it was at the time of writing, on the British Westminster framework. States it is based on the goals of survival, the continuation of the form of decision-making and the maintenance of the status quo. Examines political participation based on colour prior to assessing the capabilities of the system which assist the white minority in maintaining its position.

784   POTTER, Elaine
       The press as opposition: the political role
       of South African newspapers.   London: Chatto
       and Windus, 1975, 228 p.

       Explores   the role of the press within   South   Africa's
       political   system and assesses the relationship between
       the press and the government.   Study commences with the
       year the National Party came to power - 1948, recording
       the   effect   on   the   press.   Examines   the   ownership
       structure,   newspaper readership,   restraints on   press
       freedom, and the role of both the English and Afrikaans
       press.

785   PRAAT   met   die ANC (Conversations   with   the ANC):
       interviews   conducted   by   Gerrit   Olivier.
       Johannesburg, Taurus, 1985, 102 p.

       Contributions,   mainly   in   Afrikaans,   recording
       impressions   of conversations with,   or information   on
       the   African   National Congress.   Contributors   include
       Nico   Smith,   Piet Muller,   Anton   Steenkamp,   Eric   le
       Grange,   Hennie Bester,   Hans Müller, Phillip Verster,
       Harald   Pakendorf,   Johan   Olivier,   Tom   Lodge,   Annan
       Oosthuysen and Carel Anthonissen.

786   PRICE, Robert M.
       Pretoria's Southern African strategy. African
       Affairs,   vol.   83, no. 330, January 1984, p.
       11-32

       A comprehensive South African regional strategy emerged
       after   the   Portuguese coup d'etat of 1974,   which   the
       author   analyzes   in some detail   illustrating   in   his
       study   'the interconnectedness,   internal coherence and
       overall   thrust of what might otherwise be thought of as
       simply   tactical   and even contradictory   responses   to
       circumstance'.   Implications   of the strategy   and   its
       objectives are assessed.

787   PRINCE, Melody Anne
'Watchman, what of the night?' The political
ideas of R.F.A. Hoernle and E.H. Brookes and
their contribution to the theory and practice
of South African liberalism. Leicester:
University of Leicester, 1983, 195 p.

Dissertation: M.Phil

Prince's objective is the identification of the common
factors contained in the various manifestations of
liberalism which she evaluates as a means of promoting
political and social change. Liberalism is examined
through the writings of two of South Africa's leading
twentieth century liberal thinkers, albeit with varying
interpretations. Contradictions are assessed to account
for the apparent failure of liberal ideas in producing
a consistent approach to a practical problem.

788   PRINSLOO, M. Wilhelm
Political restructuring, capital accumu-
lation, and the 'coming corporatism' in South
Africa: some theoretical considerations.
Politikon, vol. 11, no. 1, June 1984, p. 20-
42

This article explores the theoretical correlation
between consociationalism and corporatism, and relates
recent tendencies in the political economy and the
restructuring, along consociational lines, of forms of
political representation and state intervention in
South Africa with corporatist developments. Different
dimensions of the concept corporatism are analysed, and
the author emphasises the way in which corporatist
arrangements effect the balance of class forces in
social formations. The author concludes by arguing that
consociationalism and corporatism are complementary
models of political domination, and suggests that

corporatism can be used to secure conditions for capital accumulation and to legitimate the social reproduction of capitalist relations in South Africa. (Journal abstract).

789   PRIOR, Andrew
       Political culture and violence: a case study
       of the African National Congress of South
       Africa. Politikon, vol. 11, no. 2, December
       1984, p. 12-20

Since the late 1950s political theorists have developed theoretical perspectives of factors contributing to changes in a political culture. This article discusses the way these perspectives assist in understanding a shift in the African National Congress of South Africa's view of violence as a political tactic. Specifically it examines the way institutional formation, political developments, and alliances, contributed to the legitimation of violence. It concludes with a discussion of developments which are causing this legitimation to be re-assessed. (Journal abstract)

790   PRIOR, Andrew
       South African exile politics: a case study of
       the African National Congress and the South
       African Communist Party. Journal of
       Contemporary African Studies, vol. 3, no.
       1/2, October 1983/April 1984, p. 181-196

The issue of an alliance between the two organizations is discussed and the author deduces that mutual involvement has been extensive, and elaborates on their relationship.

791   PROLETARIANIZATION and class struggle in Africa, edited
        by Bernard Magubane and Mzongola Ntalaja. San
        Francisco: Synthesis, 1983, 182 p.

Bernard   Magubane   contributes   a   chapter   entitled:
Imperialism   and the South African working class.   It is
subdivided   as follows: the geopolitics of   the   class
struggle;   the matrix of class formation,   from slavery
to proletarianization;   the discovery of diamonds   and
gold;   imperialism and   the white working   class;   the
black industrial proletariat;   mass   insurgency,   1950-
1960;   the South African Congress of Trade Unions;   the
class struggle deepens, 1970-1982.

792   PROVINCIAL and municipal government and administration:
        selected   readings,   edited and introduced by
        J.J.N.   Cloete.   Pretoria: van Schaik, 1978,
        260 p.

Intended   both   for the student   and   practioner,   this
compilation   provides   information   on   the   provincial
system;   municipal   government   and   administration,
including urbanization and planning, local authorities,
government   by commission,   voters and   voting   system,
councillors,   councils and office-bearers;   committees;
personnel administration; and control.

793   The   PSYCHOLOGY   of   apartheid: a   psychosocial
        perspective on South Africa, edited by H.I.J.
        van der Spuy with D.A.F. Shamley. Washington,
        D.C.:   University   Press   of   America,   1978,
        116 p.

This   subject is analyzed in three essays examining the
psychodynamics   of   apartheid,   the   developmental
psychology   of   the   Afrikaners,   and   methods   of
administering psychotherapy to the nation.   The   essays
are   based   on nine empirical studies   covering   topics
such   as   personality   patterns of white   and   coloured

South Africans, the incidence of emotional disturbance in the Cape Peninsula, protesting South African students, changes in racial prejudice, and the effect of minority group membership on South African children. Concludes with a study of child development and scenarios for the future.

794   PUTTING a plough to the ground: accumulation and dispossession in rural South Africa, 1850 - 1930, edited by William Beinart, Peter Delius and Stanley Trapido. Johannesburg: Ravan, 1986, 458 p.

Focusses on the transformation of much of the South African countryside into capitalist, white-owned farms and its effect on the rural population. Comprises the following contributions: Introduction, by W. Beinart and P. Delius; The origins of capitalist agriculture in the Cape Colony: a survey by R. Ross; Vagabond Hollanders and runaway Englishmen: white poverty in the Cape before Poor Whiteism by C. Bundy; The Natal sugar industry in the Nineteenth Century, by P. Richardson; Abel Erasmus: power and profit in the Eastern Transvaal, by P. Delius; white settlement and black subjugation in the South African Highveld: the Tlokoa heartland in the North Eastern Orange Free State, ca. 1850 - 1914, by T Keegan; Settler accumulation in East Griqualand from the demise of the Griqua to the Natives Land Act, by W. Beinart; irrigation, agriculture and the state; the Harts Valley in historical perspective, by K. Shillington: Putting a plough to the ground: a history of the tenant production on the Vereeniging Estates, 1896 - 1920, by S. Trapido; Competition and cooperation in Middelburg, 1900 - 1930, by R. Morrell; Lynch law and labourers: the ICU in Umvoti, 1927 - 1928, by H. Bradford.

795   QUARTERLY economic review of South Africa
        1982 -
        London: Economist Intelligence Unit

From the second quarter 1986, this publication changed its name to Economist Intelligence Unit, Country Profile: South Africa and Country Report: South Africa. Analyzes current trends in the economy, including political developments pertinent to its understanding. Appendices illustrate quarterly economic activity, while an annual supplement provides basic information relevant to the following sectors: government and general, population, employment, currency, national accounts, agriculture, mining, energy, manufacturing, transport and communications, finance, foreign trade and payments, trade and exchange regulations.

796   RACE and ethnicity: South African and international perspectives, edited by Hendrik W. van der Merwe and Robert A. Schrire. Cape Town: Philip, 1980, 237 p.

Comprises a selection of papers originally presented at the 1979 University of Cape Town Summer School Lecture Series entitled: Group Identity and National Interests, and supplemented by contributions from Robert Schrire and Nathan Glazer, and a conclusion by Professor Gwendolen Carter, this work is divided into three sections. Part I examines the theory of ethnic and group identity and discrimination, with papers by Robert Schrire, Nathan Glazer, Johannes Degenaar and D.A. Kotze. Part II provides Southern African perspectives, including contributions by J.L. Boshoff, Hendrik W. van der Merwe, Mlahleni Njisane, Eddie Brown, Rene de Villiers, Ellen Kuzwayo, Gibson Thula, David Welsh and Gerhard Tötemeyer. International perspectives comprise Part 4, including papers by Richard A. Salem, Lionel Morrison and Gwendolen Carter.

797   RACE discrimination in South Africa: a review, edited by Sheila T. van der Horst assisted by Jane Reid. Cape Town: Philip in association with the Centre for Intergroup Studies, Cape Town, 1981, 247 p.

Change in South Africa is examined within various contexts: politically by Robert A. Schrire; the role of the law by John Dugard and W.H.B. Dean; employment by Sheila T. van der Horst; education by Franz Auerbach and David Welsh; urban housing by Pauline Morris and Sheila T. van der Horst; health by J.J.O. Reid; state social pensions, grants and social welfare by Hansi Pollak; religion by Piet Meiring, J.A. van Wyk and Patrick Giddy; recreational facilities, sport, and voluntary organizations by Judy Cornell and Oscar Wollheim.

798   RACE Relations Survey
        1984 -
        Johannesburg: South African Institute of Race
        Relations
        Formerly: Survey of Race Relations in South
        Africa, 1951/52-1983, and previously
        published with the Institute's Annual Report,
        1946/47-1950/51.

An in-depth annual survey of South African affairs, providing comprehensive coverage of all aspects of national life. Should be referred to for the following topics: politics, including political organizations, opinion surveys, political violence, business and politics; constitution and local government; population and race classification; the economy; business; employment; labour relations; urbanization; social segregation; housing; transport; removals; homeland affairs; homeland development; education; health; welfare; security; international relations; the media; religious organizations; sport; legislation. It is complemented by an extensive subject index and a select index of persons mentioned.

799   RANDALL, Peter
        A taste of power. Johannesburg: Sprocas,
        1973, (Study Project on Christianity in
        Apartheid Society. Sprocas publication, no.
        11), 225 p.

        In this final, co-ordinated report emanating from the
        commissions appointed by the Study Project on
        Christianity in Apartheid Society, the material is
        organized under three main headings: towards the new
        society, report on Sprocas, selected documents, all
        underscoring the urgent need for radical change in both
        the redistribution of power and resources.

800   RANTETE, Johannes
        The third day of September: an eye-witness
        account of the Sebokeng Rebellion of 1984.
        Johannesburg: Ravan, 1984, (Storyteller
        series, no. 1), 44 p.

        Provides a personal account of police activities in
        Sebokeng on the day which has been named 'Bloody
        Monday' by the inhabitants.

801   RATCLIFFE, Simon
        The shifting dominance: the foundations of
        the armaments industry during the 1960s.
        Africa Perspective, no. 25, 1984, p. 24-39

        Reviews the production of armaments and the growth of
        repressive apparatus which he analyzes against a
        background of class forces in the 1950s and 1960s.

802   RAZIS, V.
        The American connection: the influence of
        U.S. business on South Africa. London:
        Pinter, 1986, 246 p.

The effects of the American corporate presence on South African economic growth and the process of political reform are analyzed. Razis' thesis is that this presence will strengthen the evolution of a liberal democratic system in the Republic through the requirements of free enterprise. The author is a lecturer in the Department of Business Science at the University of Cape Town.

803   RAZIS, V.
        Swords or ploughshares? South Africa and political change: an introduction. Johannesburg: Ravan, 1980, 162 p.

        Utilizing an approach which is both interdisciplinary and which incorporates different theoretical perspectives, the author presents an introductory text, determining where possible the nature of change and the possibilities for conflict resolution in South Africa. Compares and contrasts the theories and writings of Pierre L van den Berghe, Heribert Adam and Michael O'Dowd.

804   REAGAN, Ronald
        The United States and human rights in South Africa. Africa Report, vol. 30, no. 1, January/February 1985, p. 52

        Excerpts referring to the need to decry racism in South Africa, from a speech delivered on 10 December 1984 commemorating International Human Rights Day.

805   REDDY, Enuga S.
        UN and apartheid: decades of resistance. Africa Report, vol. 30, no. 5, September/ October 1985, p. 56-60

        Reviews United Nations action and achievements in the condemnation of apartheid over the past forty years.

806   REFORM and response: selected research papers on
        aspects of contemporary South Africa, edited
        by Linda Cooper and Dave Kaplan. Cape Town:
        University of Cape Town, Department of
        Economic History, 1983, 192 p.

        Four student research essays on contemporary issues and
        based heavily on primary data comprise this work. Vaun
        Cornell examines the community council system,
        critizing as a case study the Cape Town Community
        Council; Cindy Postlethwayt traces the history of the
        South African Indian Council from 1964 to 1982; Janet
        Cherry focusses particularly on the SA Cape Corps in a
        study on the increasing role of the military; Helen
        Zille analyzes the government's industrial
        decentralization policy.

807   REGEHR, Ernie
        Perceptions of apartheid: the churches and
        political change in South Africa. Scottdale:
        Herald Press, 1979, 309 p.

        Author states, as his aim, an examination of ways in
        which political perceptions have been formed, and the
        role of the church in this process. Highlights events
        and experiences which have shaped perceptions. The
        influence of both the Dutch Reformed Church, and the
        multiracial churches is traced. Addresses the problem
        of violence, discusses the rise of Black Consciousness,
        Black Theology, the role of the World Council of
        Churches, and the promotion of political change.

808   REGISTER
        (1978?) -
        London: Committee on South African War
        Resistance

The Committee, formed in 1978 by exiled South African war resisters, publishes this bulletin on the South African army and its activities.

809   REID, B.L.
       The Anti-Republican League of the 1950's. South African Historical Journal, vol. 14, 1982, p. 85-94

       Places the formation of the League in its historical and political setting. It was a non-party organization uniting all anti-Republicans, especially in Natal where 30 000 people signed the covenant. It spread to the Eastern Cape and the Transvaal but lost support by supporting the Federal against the United Party, and was disbanded in 1959.

810   RELOCATION: the Churches' report on forced removals. (n.p.): South African Council of Churches and Southern African Catholic Bishops' Conference, 1984, 64 p.

       Initially provides a general overview of forced removals in South Africa and assesses their status in the Bantustans. Theological considerations are identified and the work is complemented by various tables.

811   RENSBURG, Ihron
       People's education: creating a democratic future, an interview by Ingrid Obery. Work in Progress, 42, May 1986, p. 8-13.

       As secretary of the National Education Crisis Committee, Rensburg elucidates on its origins, programmes, and the education crisis in South Africa.

812   REPORTS of commissions and committees of inquiry, 1910–
       1976, compiled by Patricia E. Scott and staff
       members of the Department of National
       Education, Library Services Branch. Pretoria:
       The Department, 1979 (Bibliography of South
       African Government Publications, vol. 4),
       46 p.

An extensive chairman and keyword index access. 970
entry numbers. An additional mimeographed supplement
(items 971–1 044) covers the period 1977 to 1978, 14 p.
Notable commissions since 1978 include the
following, published mainly in: South Africa
(Republic). Parliament. R.P. Series:

1978:   Report of the Commission of Inquiry into
         Legislation Affecting the Utilisation of
         Manpower (Excluding the Legislation
         Administered by the Departments of Labour and
         Mines). Chairman: P.J. Riekert. Pretoria:
         Government Printer, 1979, (R.P. 32/1979).

1978–79: Report of the Commission of Inquiry into
         Alleged Irregularities in the Former
         Department of Information. Chairman: R.P.B.
         Erasmus. Pretoria: Government Printer, 1978,
         (R.P. 113/1978). See also: its Interim
         Report, and Supplementary Report, (R.P.
         63/1979).

1979–81: Report of the Commission of Inquiry into
         Labour Legislation. Chairman: N.E Wiehahn.
         Pretoria: Government Printer, 1979–1981,
         (R.P. 47/1979, R.P. 27/1981, R.P. 28/1981).

1980:   Report of the Commission of Inquiry into the
         Riots at Soweto and Elsewhere, from the 16th
         of June 1976 to the 28th February 1977.
         Chairman: P.M. Cillie. Pretoria: Government
         Printer, 1980, (R.P. 55/1980).

1980:   Report of the Commission of Inquiry into reporting of Security Matters regarding the South African Defence Force and the South African Police Force. Chairman: M.T. Steyn. Pretoria: Government Printer, 1980, (R.P. 52/1980).

1981:   Report of the Commission of Inquiry into the Mass Media. Chairman: M.T. Steyn. Pretoria: Government Printer, 1981, (R.P. 59/1981).

1981:   Report of the Main Committee of the Human Sciences Research Council Investigation into Education. Provision of Education in the RSA. Chairman: J.P. de Lange. Pretoria: HSRC, 1981.

1981:   Kommissie van Ondersoek na Veiligheidswetgewing (Commission of Inquiry into Security Legislation). Verslag. (Report). Chairman: P.J. Rabie. Pretoria: Government Printer, 1981, (R.P. 90/1981).

1983:   Report of the Commission of Inquiry into South African Council of Churches. Chairman: C.F. Eloff. Pretoria: Government Printer, 1983, (R.P. 74/1983).

1983:   Commission of Inquiry into the Structure and Functioning of the Courts. Chairman: G.G. Hoexter. Pretoria: Government Printer, 1983, (R.P. 78/1983).

1985:   Report of the Investigation into Education in the Vaal Triangle following upon the Occurences of 3 September 1984 and thereafter. By Tjaart van der Walt. Pretoria: Government Printer, 1985, (R.P. 88/1985).

1985: Report of the Commission Appointed to Inquire into the Incident which Occurred on 21 March 1985 at Uitenhage. Chairman: Donald Daniel Victor Kannemeyer. Pretoria: Government Printer, 1985, (R.P. 74/1985).

813 RESISTANCE and ideology in settler societies IN: (WORKING papers in) Southern African studies, vol. 4, edited by Tom Lodge. Johannesburg: Ravan, 1986, 222 p.

Includes among others, contributions by Tom Lodge on the Poqo Insurrection (1961-1968), Raymond Suttner on black customary law, John Wright on the ideology and the invention of the term Nguni, Helen Bradford on the Industrial and Commercial Workers' Union, and Mirjana Roth on the Natives Representatives Council, elections under the Representation of the Natives Act, 1937 to 1948.

814 The RESPONSIBILITY for education and training IN: BLACK advancement in the South African economy, edited by Roy Smollan. Johannesburg: Macmillan South Africa, 1986, p. 73 - 116.

Other chapters in this assessment include their contribution to the economy; difficulties besetting advancement and various organizational programmes and case studies.

815 RHOODIE, Nic J. and VENTER, H.J. Apartheid: a socio-historical exposition of the origin and development of the apartheid idea. Cape Town: Haum, 1959, 268 p.

Aims to investigate the origins of the Afrikaners' concept of apartheid, and to sketch its development to the 1940s 'when it crystallised into the synthesis or whole known as apartheid'. Stresses ideological aspects.

313

816 RHOODIE, Nic J.
Apartheid and racial partnership in Southern
Africa: a sociological comparison between
separate ethno-national development in South
Africa and racial partnership in the former
Federation of Rhodesia and Nyasaland, with
special reference to the principles and
motives involved in these policy systems. 2nd
ed. Pretoria: Academica, 1969, 429 p.

Part 1 is concerned with South Africa's apartheid
policy. The author traces its evolution, nature, and
basic principles. Examines the motives for separate
development in detail, and from various aspects -
political, constitutional, economic, socio-cultural,
racial and ideological. He thereafter examines the
position in the Rhodesian Federation prior to offering
a comparative overview and evaluation. Concludes with
an assessment of the future of separate development
within the Republic of South Africa.

817 RHOODIE, Nic J.
The Coloured policy of South Africa:
parallelism as a socio-political device to
regulate white-Coloured integration. African
Affairs, vol. 72, no. 286, January 1973, p.
46-56

Presents an analysis of the government's parallel
development policy in which the Coloureds are promised
separate nationhood, paralleling that of the whites.
Provides a scenario of their political future.

818 RICH, Paul B.
Ideology in a plural society: the case of
South African segregation. Social Dynamics,
vol. 1, no. 2, December 1975, p. 167-180

The 'revisionist' view of South African history has an advantage in understanding the role of values in terms of class structures, as opposed to liberal orthodoxy that sees 'race' as an autonomous variable: a view that is both static and unhistorical. The problem of explaining these values, however remains, for class analysis can be accused of economic determinism. Pluralism may, therefore, be of use as a supplement to class analysis by interpreting vlaues in a subjective sense. Class becomes only one of a number of forms of political consciousness (i.e. religious, 'tribal' or ethnic) and the analysis shifts to a market of competing political ideologies. This view is explored empirically by the example of the rise of a segregationist ideology in South Africa in the twentieth century. (Author's abstract)

819   RICH, Paul B.
       Insurgency, terrorism and the apartheid
       system in South Africa. Political Studies,
       vol. 32, 1984, p. 68-85

Analyzes the development of guerrilla insurgency and the subsequent government responses based on their 'total strategy' policy. The concepts of terrorism and guerrilla warfare are analytically discussed and distinguished into separate concepts, prior to examining their implications. These Rich divides into loss of economic confidence, the sapping of white morale and the mobilization of black political consciousness.

820   RICH, Paul B.
       Liberalism and ethnicity in South African
       politics, 1921-1948. African Studies, vol.
       35, no. 3/4, 1976, p. 229-251

Traces developments in liberal ideological thinking during the period under review. The author demonstrates the implications for liberals in South Africa, of their failure to recognize the salience of group interests and the challenge of nationalism.

821   RICH, Paul B.
        The origins of apartheid ideology: the case of Ernest Stubbs, C 1902-1932. African Affairs, vol. 79, no. 315, April 1980, p. 171-194

Rich says of his paper: '(it) seeks to pinpoint key aspects in the careers of a Native Affairs official, whose views reflected certain crucial features contained in South African industrialization in the twentieth century and the development of white capitalist settler agriculture'. Comments particularly on Stubbs' essay entitled: Tightening coils: an essay on segregation, in which he propounded the argument for racial partioning in South Africa.

822   RICH, Paul B.
        White power and the liberal conscience: racial segregation and South African liberalism, 1921-60. Manchester: Manchester University Press, 1984, 192 p.

Based on part of the author's Ph.D. thesis (1979), this work concentrates on the formative phase of South African liberalism post the First World War until the general election of 1953. Illustrates the failure of the liberals to project their political values and presents ideas and attitudes of leading liberals. Contains information on the Joint Councils, the Institute of Race Relations, the white Natives' Representatives, the Liberal Party and the Christian Institute.

823   RICHARDSON, Peter
       Chinese indentured labour in the Transvaal
       gold mining industry, 1904-1910   IN:
       INDENTURED labour in the British Empire,
       1834-1920, edited by Roy Saunders. London:
       Croom Helm, 1984, p. 260-290

       Concentrates on the status of mining and labour after
       the Anglo-Boer War and the prevailing political and
       economic climate. Details reasons for and the
       implications of Chinese labour importation.

824   RIGA, David
       Political machinations of the racist regime.
       International Affairs (Moscow), August 1985,
       p. 92-96

       Describes South Africa's 'organic crisis' - as
       occurring simultaneously on economic, political and
       ideological levels, and gives an assessment of the
       Botha government's reform proposals.

825   The RIGHT to the land, edited by T.R.H. Davenport and
       K.S. Hunt. Cape Town: Philip, 1974, (Documents
       on Southern African History), 90 p.

       A collection of documents spanning three centuries
       illustrating the problem of land ownership and
       occupation. The work is divided into four parts: the
       imposition of European tenures; the expansion of white
       settlement and the establishment of reserves; African
       land tenure - traditional and transition, ownership and
       occupation of land by blacks and Asians in urban areas.

826   The ROAD to South African freedom: the programme of the
       South African Communist Party, adopted inside
       South Africa, 1962. London: Ellis Bowles,
       (1962), 53 p.

                                                     317

This programme was adopted at the fifth National Conference of the South African Communist Party in 1962, and was first published in African Communist.

827   ROBERTS, Michael and TROLLIP, A.E.G.
        The South African opposition 1939-1945: an essay in contemporary history. London: Longmans, Green, 1947, 240 p.

A political history concentrating exclusively on the Afrikaans-speaking opposition of the day, and relevant party politics. Attempts to explain why there were several political organizations in existence, with common opposition to the government's war policy and committed to a Republican ideal, yet in rivalry for the support of Afrikaans-speaking South Africans.

828   ROBERTSON, Hector Menteith
        South Africa: economic and political aspects. Durham, N.C.: Duke University Press, 1957, (Duke University. Commonwealth Studies Center. Publications, 2), 192 p.

In three lectures, originally delivered to the Duke University Commonwealth Studies Center in 1956, Professor Robertson examines the South African economy, highlighting the role of race relations. He subsequently discusses trends prevalent at that time with particular reference to migrant labour within the apartheid system, and concludes with information on the removal of the Cape Coloureds from the common voter's role.

829   ROBERTSON, Janet
        Liberalism in South Africa, 1948-1963. Oxford: Clarendon Press, 1971, 252 p.

318

In attempting to provide a new synthesis of South African history, the author states, as her intention to describe and analyse what happened to South African liberals in the period under review. This includes information on both black liberals and their developing views within the African National Congress, and the white liberals - the Liberal Party members and those within the United and Progressive parties. Furthermore, extra-parliamentary groups such as the Black Sash and Torch Commando are considered for their liberal values.

830   ROELOFSE, J.J.
       Towards rational discourse: an analysis of the Steyn Commission of Inquiry into the Media. Pretoria: van Schaik, 1983, 95 p.

Provides a summary of the findings and recommendations of the Steyn Commission published in 1982, upon which the author briefly elaborates when necessary. Presents a framework for evaluating the Report '. . . because I believe that the commissioners have failed to adequately provide the proper criteria for evaluating South African society, namely the criterion of the freedom of the individual and freedom of expression'.

831   ROGALY, Gail Lynda
       South Africa's foreign relations, 1961-1979: a select and partially annotated bibliography. Johannesburg: South African Institute of International Affairs, 1980, (South African Institute of International Affairs. Bibliographical series, no. 7), 462 p.

2 656 entries, alphabetically arranged by author or title where no author is present are followed by a well-organized subject index of over 100 pages in length, enabling information retrieval on the various aspects of South Africa's foreign relations since the

advent of the Republic. These include its bilateral relations with other states, relations with international organizations, the Southern African question and specific issues such as the involvement of multinational corporations, nuclear development, sports relations and boycott. For a comprehensive coverage of South Africa's foreign relations, this should be used in conjunction with J.A. Kalley's: South Africa's foreign relations, 1980-1984, q.v.

832   ROGERS, Barbara
        D.I.V.I.D.E. and rule: South Africa's bantustans. Rev. ed. London: International Defence and Aid Fund for Southern Africa, 1980, 136 p.

Subsequent to a theoretical discussion on the concept of balkanizing South Africa, Rogers provides a detailed study of the homelands including the government's policy of relocation. The 'independence' of Transkei, Bophuthatswana and Venda is recorded, as is the rejection by the international community. Includes maps and illustrations.

833   ROGERS, Howard
        Native administration in the Union of South Africa: being a brief survey of the organisation, functions and activities of the Department of Native Affairs of the Union of South Africa. Johannesburg: University of the Witwatersrand Press, 1933, 322 p.

Departmental organization, both prior and subsequent to Union, is observed in the introduction. Thereafter the functions and powers of the Administration are detailed, as is the role of the Native Affairs Commission. Various early systems of local government operative amongst the blacks are considered, including the Glen Grey Council system and the Transkeian Territories Council System. Special funds, land administration, agricultural development and taxation, urban blacks and recognition of indigenous law are the topics of subsequent chapters.

834   ROGERSON, Christian M. and BEAVON, K.S.O.
A tradition of repression: the street traders of Johannesburg IN: PLANNING for small enterprises in Third World cities, edited by R. Bromley. Oxford: Pergamon, 1985, p. 233-245

The authors trace and evaluate the development and changing nature of street trading in Johannesburg, paying particular attention to the attitudes of the local municipality and the national state. Despite repressive measures which later led to a decline in street-trading, it has persisted in various forms and may be considered inseparable from the material conditions experienced under the apartheid system.

835   ROHERTY, James M.
Managing the security power base in South Africa. South Africa International, vol 15, no. 2, October 1984, p. 56-65

Focusses on the State Security Council and its supporting elements in an attempt to assess the functioning of the national security management system. The role of the 'political generals' and the development of intelligence by the principal agencies are examined in this analysis of one of the elements in the 'total national strategy'.

836   The ROOTS of rural poverty in Central and Southern Africa, edited by Robin Palmer and Neil Parsons. London: Heinemann, 1977, 430 p.

Two chapters pertain to South Africa: Martin Legassick's Gold, agriculture, and secondary industry in South Africa, 1885-1970: from periphery to submetropole as a forced labour system, (p. 175-200) and Colin Bundy's The Transkei peasantry, c. 1890-1914: 'passing through a period of stress' (p. 201-220).

837   ROPP, Klaus von der
       Power sharing versus partition in South
       Africa. Australian Outlook, vol. 35, no. 2,
       August 1981, p. 158-168

Indicates the need for a constructive Western policy, given South Africa's economic and strategic significance. Comments on the policies of President Carter prior to assessing domestic conditions. Describes South Africa as between the need for revolution from above and the probability of revolution from below. Examines the merits and possible problems in two basic concepts propounding a new political order: consociationalism and geographical partion.

838   ROTBERG, Robert I.
       Suffer the future: policy changes in Southern
       Africa. Cambridge, Mass: Harvard University
       Press, 1980, 311 p.

Divided into four main parts, viz South Africa, Namibia, Zimbabwe and Southern Africa. With reference to the former, Rotberg closely examines the internal political position, the response of the underprivileged, and pressures, both internal and external, for change on the Republic. The Republic's economic strengths and vulnerabilities are assessed, focussing on employment, foreign trade, manufacturing, mining, fuel and power, agriculture, foreign investment and lending. Attention too, is devoted to the uranium and nuclear industries.

839   ROUX, Edward
       Time longer than rope: a history of the black
       man's struggle for freedom in South Africa.
       London: Gollancz, 1948, 398 p.

       A political history dating from the earliest times,
       which has as its focus the struggle for racial freedom
       in South Africa.

840   ROYAL INSTITUTE OF INTERNATIONAL AFFAIRS
       A survey of proposals for constitutional
       development. London: The Institute, 1980,
       88 p.

       Comprehensively reviews constitutional ideas propounded
       by the South African government, political groups and
       academics. Includes contributions on segregation or
       integration; alternative options such as consociational
       democracy, federation or confederation, and concludes
       with an examinatin of the parameters of change. This
       includes discussion, amongst others, on the
       government's Twelve-Point Plan, the Presidents Council,
       the Constellation of States concept, and constraints.
       Annex comprises a white opinion poll on political and
       economic questions. Maps relevant to constitutional
       development conclude this analysis.

841   SAMPSON, Anthony
       Black and gold: Tycoons, revolutionaries and
       apartheid. London: Hodder Stoughton, 1987,
       263 p.

       The thrust of Sampson's analysis is directed towards
       the controlling power network in the Republic, with
       particular emphasis on the Anglophone business
       community, the stance of multinational corporations,
       the Afrikaner political elite and black organizations
       such as the ANC and UDF.

842   SASH
        1 - , 1956 -
        Johannesburg: Black Sash

        Comments critically on events and structures
        in apartheid South Africa.

843   SAUL, J. and GELB, S.
        The crisis in South Africa: class defense,
        class revolution. New York: Monthly Review
        Press, 1981, 156 p.

        Originally   published   in: Monthly Review,
        July/August 1981.

        Examines the historical background to the apartheid
        system, the contending parties and their options for
        change. Includes discussion on the balance of class
        forces, the defensive strategies employed by the white
        minority to defend the system and their policy towards
        advocates of South Africa's transformation. Authors
        conclude with suggestions as to how those engaged in
        producing change could best focus their energies.

844   SAUL, John S.
        South Africa: apartheid and after. Boulder:
        Westview, 1986, 210 p.

        Professor of Social and Political Science at York
        University, Toronto describes South Africa's current
        economic, social and political systems, which he places
        in historical perspective. Class and racial
        hierarchies, competing nationalisms, ethnic
        identification, religious and similar world views are
        highlighted. Saul illustrates how these factors have
        been drawn into the political arena and shaped by
        forces that will ultimately determine South Africa's
        future.

845   SAUNDERS, Christopher
Historical dictionary of South Africa.
Metuchen, N.J.: Scarecrow, 1983, (African
historical dictionaries, no. 37), 241 p.

Compiled by a Senior Lecturer in History at the
University of Cape Town, this aphabetically arranged
dictionary provides succinct information on all facets
of South African political, social and economic
history. It is complemented by a chronology dated from
circa 3rd century to August 1982, and a bibliography
relevant to the scholar of South African history.

846   SCHLEMMER, Lawrence
Black worker attitudes: political options,
capitalism and investment in South Africa.
Durban: University of Natal, Centre for
Applied Social Sciences, 1984, 49 p.

Explores the attitudes of black industrial workers to
political and strategic issues, in particular to the
disinvestment debate, and capitalism. 'Very basically
it poses the question of how radical, or ready for
confrontation, black workers are at the present time'.
Based on fieldwork carried out during May 1984.

847   SCHLEMMER, Lawrence
Privilege, prejudice and parties: a study of
patterns of political motivation among white
voters in Durban. Johannesburg: South African
Institute of Race Relations, 1973, 85 p.

Presents findings of a survey illustrating attitudes,
opinions, and white political motivations relating to
voting preferences in Durban. Attempts to clarify
patterns and trends in political sentiments and to
assess implications for party strategy. Appendix
includes a copy of the questionnaire.

848   SCHLEMMER, Lawrence
           Theories of the plural society and change in
           South Africa. Social Dynamics, vol. 3, no. 1,
           June 1977, p. 3-16

           Theories of the plural society are examined critically
           and the conclusion is reached that cultural
           differentiation in society is not, in itself, the major
           factor accounting for perpetuation of cleavages in
           plural societies. It is argued that a composite
           paradigm based on these theories is useful in ordering
           and combining elements of class culture and ethnicity
           in attempting to explain the cleavages in plural
           societies. The argument is carried further with the
           suggestion that the popular participation within ruling
           groups characteristic of plural societies results in a
           responsiveness in policy to rank-and-file corporate
           group interest. This factor unleashes forces in the
           political economy which are worthy of being
           distinguished from conventional notions of class,
           status and power in homogeneous societies. This factor
           is given the term 'popular social communalism', a
           process in which class, identity and power are combined
           and articulated to serve the overall interests of a
           corporate group. Recent changes in South Africa are
           examined in the light of this concept and the prospects
           for a devolution of power are briefly considered.
           (Author's abstract)

849   SCHMIDT, Elizabeth
           Decoding corporate camouflage: U.S. business
           support for apartheid. Washington, D.C.:
           Institute for Policy Studies, 1980, 127 p.

           Says Ronald V. Dellums in the foreword to this book
           '. . . the case against corporate collaboration with
           institutional racism and government-sponsored violence
           is presented with damning documentation in this study
           by Elizabeth Schmidt.' She analyzes the Sullivan
           Principles and the strategic role of the Sullivan

signatories in the motor vehicle, computer and energy industries, as well as in the military apparatus, bank loans to the Republic, and as a progressive force for white South Africa. Comments on the semblance of reform and apartheid's new strategies, including the role of both the Wiehahn and Riekert Commissions.

850   SCHMIDT, Elizabeth
        One step - in the wrong direction: the Sullivan Principles as a strategy for opposing apartheid. Ufahamu, vol. 11, no. 3, Spring 1982, p. 236-244

Considers the employment code within the South African context. Queries whether United States' corporations are agents or obstacles to change and provides a critique of the Sullivan Principles. Assesses reaction of black South Africans to their implementation

851   SCHOEMAN, B.M.
        Van Malan tot Verwoerd (From Malan to Verwoerd). Cape Town: Human & Rousseau, 1973, 261 p.

Not intended as an in-depth study of the period under review, this work highlights events significant to South Africa's political history. As a journalist, this study was written from his own personal experiences and conversations.

852   SCHOEMAN, B.M.
        Vorster se 1 000 dae (Vorster's 1 000 days). Cape Town: Human & Rousseau, 1974, 282 p.

Concerns political problems experienced during the late 1960s in the National Party which led to the formation of the Hertzog group.

853   SCHOEMAN, Elna
        The Namibian issue, 1920-1980: a select and
        annotated bibliography. Boston: Hall, 1982,
        247 p.

An expanded and updated version of the compiler's
earlier work entitled: South West Africa/Namibia: an
international issue, 1920-1977: a select bibliography
(Johannesburg: South African Institute of International
Affairs, 1978), the main focus of this work is on
Namibia's international status. Includes references to
the most important primary services, such as United
Nations documents and resolutions, documentation, of
the International Court of Justice commission reports,
relevant proclamations and government notes. Comprises
a chronology, the bibliography of 1 326 entries, an
author index and an extensive subject guide.

854   SCHOEMAN, Elna
        South Africa and the United Nations: a select
        and annotated bibliography. Johannesburg:
        South African Institute of International
        Affairs, 1981, (South African Institute of
        International Affairs. Bibliographical
        series, no. 8), 244 p.

This bibliography comprises over 1 000 annotated
references to documentation and relevant literature
pertaining to the United Nations, its specialized
agencies and South Africa. All United Nations
resolutions pertaining to South Africa are extensively
indexed (these are updated in J.A. Kalley's
bibliography on South Africa's foreign relations,
q.v.). Contains a useful subject guide and author
index.

855   SCHOEMAN, Elna
The Southern African Development Coordination
Conference (SADCC): a select and annotated
bibliography. Johannesburg: South African
Institute of International Affairs, 1986,
(South African Institute of International
Affairs. Bibliographical series, no. 14),
131 p.

Focussing on a recently established regional economic
organization, this bibliography refers the user to
relevant literature in over 400 items. SADCC's
objectives, structure, prospects, progress and
constraints are investigated, but authors also pay
attention to South Africa's destabilization of the
region and the dependency issue. Information retrieval
is accessed by extensive author and subject indexes.

856   SCHOEMAN, Karel
Bibliography of the Orange Free State until
31 May 1910. Cape Town: South African
Library, 1984, 226 p.

Compiled by the head of the Bibliographical Section at
the South African Library, this bibliography contains
2 536 unannotated entries. It covers works published
until the end of 1983 on historical, political,
economic and cultural development in this geographical
area, now known as the province of the Orange Free
State. Manuscript material is excluded from the eleven
main sections which are complemented by both the author
and a subject index.

857   SCHOLTZ, Gert Daniël
Die ontwikkeling van die politieke denke van
die Afrikaner. (The development of Afrikaner
political thought). Johannesburg: Perskor,
1967-, 8+ vols.

Offers a detailed examination of Afrikaner political thought within the following time frames based on documentary evidence. Vol. 1, 1652–1806; vol. 2, 1806–1854; vol. 3, 1854–1881; vol. 4, 1881–1899; vol. 5, 1899–1910; vol. 6, 1910–1924; vol. 7, 1924–1939; vol. 8, 1939–1948.

858   SCHREINER Olive
        Women and labor. 5th ed. New York: Stokes, 1911, 299 p.

A section of a larger treatise on the subject, destroyed during the Anglo-Boer War, Schreiner includes chapters on women and war, sex differences, and her objections to viewing women only in their child-bearing capacity.

859   SCHRIRE, Robert
        Time running out? The Rockefeller Commission on United States policy towards Southern Africa. South Africa International, vol. 12, no. 2, October 1981, p. 343-356

Provides an in-depth analysis of the reasons for compiling this study and its recommendations. The basic premise of the report is that the United States must remain actively engaged in South Africa in order to exert a constructive influence.

860   SEBE, Lennox L.W.
        Challenges. Cape Town: Via Afrika, (198?), 245 p.

Records statements and speeches delivered by Dr Lennox Sebe in his capacity as Chief Minister prior to the 'independence' of Ciskei.

861   SECHABA
        1 -   , January 1967 -   Monthly
        Lusaka: African National Congress of   South
        Africa

The official organ of the African National Congress of
South Africa comprising comment on all aspects of life
within   the Republic.   Contains a regular section
entitled ANC International, signifying solidarity with
the movement.

862   SEEDAT, Aziza
        Crippling a nation. London: International
        Defence and Aid Fund for Southern Africa,
        1984, 110 p.

Written by a South African doctor, now in exile, who
relates the ill-health of some South African blacks to
the apartheid system. Concludes that the implementation
of adequate health services for all South Africans
would necessitate the destruction of the system.

863   SEEGERS, Annette M.
        South African liberation: touchstone of
        African   solidarity IN: AFRICAN security
        issues: sovereignty,   stability   and
        solidarity, edited by Bruce E. Arlinghaus.
        Boulder: Westview, 1984, p. 185-202

Security issues emanating from the interaction between
black African states and the Republic form the basis of
this contribution. This interaction is examined from
various aspects, including the roots of the conflict
between them; the period 1963-1972 in which the effects
of the liberation struggle on South Africa's internal
and external policies are assessed; and chronicles
measures from 1973 onwards against South Africa, and
its reactions towards them.

864   SEIDMAN, Ann and MAKGETLA, Neva Seidman
Outposts of monopoly capitalism: Southern
Africa in the changing global economy.
Westport, Conn.: Lawrence Hill, 1980, 370 p.

Authors seek to place the theoretical issues propounded
in their earlier work entitled South Africa and U.S.
multinational corporations, q.v., in a global context
and to '. . . illuminate the way the struggle for
liberation in Southern Africa fits into the larger
process of social transformation taking place
throughout the world today'. This is explored in three
main parts: intensified transnational competition; the
renewed scramble for Africa; and towards the
transformation of Southern Africa.

865   SEIDMAN, Ann and SEIDMAN, Neva
U.S. multinationals in South Africa. Dar es
Salaam: Tanzania Publishing House, 1977,
251 p.

Explores the political economy of Southern Africa and
its increasing linkage with multinational companies
based in the United States. Records growing industry in
South Africa, the role of state capitalism, revealing
the effect on black wages and on neighbouring states in
the Southern African region. Substantiated by extensive
tables.

866   SEIDMAN, Judy
Face-lift apartheid: South Africa after
Soweto. London: International Defence and Aid
Fund for Southern Africa, 1980, 87 p.

Illustrates how the South African government adapted
its policies after the 1976 uprisings in the spheres of
race relations, politically and economically. However,

as evidenced by the continuing unrest in the country, Seidman bases her thesis on the fact that the apparent concessions conceal increased repression of the black majority, and the underlying apartheid structure remains unaltered.

867   A SELECT bibliography of South African history: a guide for historical research, edited by C.F.J. Muller, F.A. van Jaarsveld and Theo van Wijk. Pretoria: University of South Africa, 1966, 215 p.

This work is divided into three main parts: a general section including aids to research, historiography and general histories; material classified according to specific periods in history; and thirdly, by subject. Part III covers a range of subjects, with economic, constitutional, administrative and legal history receiving detailed attention. A supplement, edited by the same compilers, was published in 1974, while in 1979, together with Maurice Boucher, a revised and enlarged version was published under the title: South African history and historians.

868   SERFONTEIN, J.H.P.
Brotherhood of power: an exposé of the secret Afrikaner Broederbond. London: Collings, 1979, 278 p.

Based on Broederbond documents and his own personal investigations, the author, a journalist, provides insights into the history and workings of the all-male secret Afrikaner Broederbond. Details of its organizational structure, aims and philosophy are presented as 'the custodian of the soul of Afrikaner nationalism'. Concludes by assessing prospects for the future of the organization.

869   SERVICING the nation: local and regional government
       reform, edited by M. Bennett, A.J. Mason and
       L. Schlemmer. Durban: Indicator Project South
       Africa, 1986, 72 p.

In ten sections the following facets are discussed:
unrest, African local government and the Regional
Services Council Act, by L. Schlemmer; Regional
Services Councils' structures by M. Bennett; financial
origins of Regional Services Councils by O. Gorven;
financial implications of the Croeser tax package - the
financing of Regional Services Councils by D. Solomon;
black local authorities by E. Lear; centralization vs
decentralization using the Cape Town City Council as a
case study by R. Cameron; squatter problems by C.
Fourie; the centralization of power at regional levels
under the guise of devolution by J.S.H. Gildenhuys; P.
Mansfield presents the view that it would be more
prudent to go back to the drawing board and hold
negotiations with representative black leaders before
proceeding with Regional Services Councils. Schlemmer
presents a concluding assessment taking into account
both positive and problematic features.

870   SETAI, Bethuel
       The political economy of South Africa: the
       making of poverty. Washington, D.C.:
       University Press of America, 1977, 200 p.

Author states as follows: this book is a
multidisciplinary study of how poverty among Africans
in South Africa was created. It is written from an
economic historical approach inasmuch as historical
events are important in understanding the current
poverty of the Africans . . . The analysis emphasizes
rivalries concerning land and basic freedoms between
the Africans, the Boers and the British, and presents a
clear and interesting trend among the dynamics of these
groups . . . And because on analysis stresses economic

relationships we present and analyze factors that led to the emergence of the African working class. We also provide, in an enlightened manner, the economic causes of and justification for the Boer War . . .

871   SHELTON, Garth L.
        Theoretical perspectives on South African foreign policy making. Politikon, vol 13, no. 1, June 1986, p. 3-21

The author, incorrectly cited in the journal as Sheldon, is a member of the Department of International Relations, University of the Witwatersrand. His work is abstracted as follows: During the last three years political scientists have emphasised the role of the security establishment in the South African foreign policy decision making process. Since the signing of the Nkomati Accord, however, the use of the 'security establishment dominant model' for the explanation of foreign policy behaviour has become inadequate. This article is a contribution towards the articulation of a skeletal model which will clarify the apparent contradicitons in South Africa's foreign policy decision making process.

872   SHEPHERD, George W.
        Anti-apartheid: transnational conflict and Western policy in the liberation of South Africa. Westport: Greenwood, 1977, (Studies in human rights, no. 3), 246 p.

The Professor of International and African Studies at the University of Denver's Graduate School of International Studies, analyzes the structural support for apartheid both in the United States and Great Britain. American and British non-governmental opposition is assessed, including human rights concerns, black non-governmental organizations, action regarding the arms embargo, assistance to liberation movements, sanctions, and the anti-apartheid impact on South Africa.

873   SIKAKANE, Joyce
        A window on Soweto. London: International Defence and Aid Fund for Southern Africa, 1977, 80 p.

Thirty-five brief sections depict historical background and life in Soweto. Comprises mainly personal reminiscences together with some illustrations. Note K. French's: Mpanza, Safasonke and the political history of Soweto. Johannesburg: Ravan, 1986, 288 p.

874   SIMKINS Charles E.W. and HINDSON, D.C.
        The division of labour in South Africa, 1969-1977. Social Dynamics, vol. 5, no. 2, December 1979, p. 1-12

Empirical studies of occupational structure in South Africa have tended to be unsatisfactory, detailed work on small sectors of the economy coexisting with across-the-board studies, too crudely aggregated to allow for a precise assessment of a changing situation. This study presents the results of an analysis by 'race' into 14 occupational groups of South African employment outside agriculture, domestic service and the informal sector over the period 1969 to 1977. It argues that over the period there has been a definite increase in the share of owner/manager and, more particularly, petty bourgeois occupations, with a corresponding decline in the proportion of unskilled workers. It also suggests that changes in the 'racial' division of labour are more complex than has sometimes been supposed. (Journal abstract)

875   SIMKINS, Charles E.W.
The economic implications of the Rikhoto
judgement. Cape Town: Southern Africa Labour
and Development Research Unit, 1983,
(Southern Africa Labour and Development
Research Unit. Saldru working paper, 52),
16 p.

Divides his study into five parts: an estimate of the
size of immigration into urban areas outside the
homelands following the Judgement; a discussion on the
economic implications of those now entitled to 10(1)(b)
rights and their dependents; economic implications for
employers; economic implications for government's
spending; and the conclusion in which he considers the
economic implications to be very small.

876   SIMONS, H.J.
African women: their legal status in South
Africa. London: Hurst, 1968, 299 p.

Describes the law pertaining to black women, evaluates
it within the framework of social change, and suggests
possible reforms. Divided into four parts, this work
initially traces the development of relevant policies
and legislation, illustrating the conflict of laws by
describing diverse conditions in Natal, the Cape the
Boer Republics and Transkei, among other cases. In Part
Two, marriage systems are examined in detail. Part
Three presents rights and disabilities, while Part Four
depicts the effects of a segregated society on women –
their rights in land, their position at work, in towns,
and in politics.

877   SIMONS, H.J. and SIMONS, R.E.
Class and colour in South Africa 1850-1950.
Harmondsworth: Penguin, 1969, 702 p.

Traces resistance to white domination as manifest with the national movements of Africans, Indians and Coloureds, and in the class struggles of socialists and communists. Regarded by the authors as a political sociology, they examine controversies such as the relationship between national liberation and the class struggle, choice between socialist and capitalist democracy, black power, and non-collaborationist policies with the 'Herrenvolk' and conclude by providing an analysis of the power structure. Reprinted by the International Defence and Aid Fund for Southern Africa in 1983, 625 p., this work has been described by Iain R. Smith in a review (featured in The Third World Quarterly, vol. 7, no. 4, October 1985 pp. 1 068-1 069) as a classic radical text of path-breaking importance, especially on subjects such as the 1922 Rand Revolt, the failure of the white working class to develop class solidarity across the colour line, the growth of the African National Congress and the development of both socialist and Communist movements.

878   SIMSON, Harold
       The myth of the white working class in South
       Africa. African Review, vol. 4, no. 2, 1974,
       p. 189-203

       Written by a South African political refugee who, at the time of writing this article, was living in Sweden and working at the Economic History Institute at the University of Uppsala. By presenting a class analysis, the author illustrates the idea of unification of black and white labourers as proposed by the Communist Party, which directly contradicts the analysis of production relations.

879   SIMSON, Howard
       Fascism in South Africa. African Review, vol.
       3, no. 3, 1973, p. 423-451

Focusses primarily on a Marxist analysis of the class struggles prevalent in South Africa during the 1940s. Demonstrates the role of foreign monopoly capitalism and reviews the structure and practice of apartheid. 'Finally, the intention of this paper is to destroy several myths which tend to confuse historical analysis of South Africa. Namely, that a white minority class exists; that Apartheid is the result of the struggle between Afrikaner and African nationalists, and that the "motive force proper to colonialism is none other than the colonials themselves".'

880   SIMSON, Howard
        Is the apartheid state a fascist state? A framework for analysis IN: SOUTHERN African studies – retrospect and prospect. Edinburgh: University of Edinburgh, Centre of African Studies, 1983, 75–98

Provides theoretically, a definition and explanation of a fascist state which could be addressed to the South African situation.

881   SIMSON, Howard
        The social origins of the rise of Afrikaner fascism and its apartheid policy. Stockholm: Almquist & Wiksell, 1980, (Uppsala studies in economic history, 21),234 p.

Originally presented as a doctoral thesis at Uppsala University, Department of Economic History, the author's abstract reads as follows: This study has a dual objective: firstly, to explain the social origins of Afrikaner fascism and its Apartheid policy, which has ruled South Africa since 1948; and secondly, to determine whether the Afrikaner Nationalist phenomenon falls under the categories provided by a general theory of fascism. Both subjects have been investigated in the past, mainly from an idealistic perspective and never on the basis of an adequate general theory of fascism. A distinguishing feature of this study is the use of Marxist methodology in the analysis of both objectives.

A sketch of the formation of the peripheral capitalist society in South Africa at the turn of this century revealed that the fundamental social relationship established was, that of British mining and Boer (Afrikaner) farming capital exploiting the labour of the African masses. The rapid pace of industrialization after 1933 upset the traditional cheap labour system by providing a higher paying alternative source of employment for some African workers. Hence in the 1940's, a rift developed in the power bloc between the secondary and primary industries, the latter demanding State intervention to protect their labour supply. Secondary industrialization also led to African trade unionism and political consciousness, which challenged the "colonial" social order.

The Afrikaner fascist movement grew up in the wake of the Great Depression as a reaction to the destructive effects of monopoly capitalist development on the agrarian community. The movement aimed to unite rural and urban Afrikaners of all social strata and to achieve State power. The fascist Nationalist Party narrowly won the 1948 election (in which only whites participated), by promising to uphold the material and social interests of the Afrikaner farmers and wage earners against the threat posed by the urbanization of the Africans.

The fascist regime set about implementing its Apartheid policy, which essentially meant the repression of Black (African, Coloured and Indian) trade union and political rights. In this respect, the function of Afrikaner fascism closely resembled that of European fascism, for both ruthlessly suppressed the working class to the advantage of monopoly capital. In addition, the regimes had a similar social basis and ideology.

882   SINCERE, Richard E.
        The politics of sentiment: churches and foreign investment in South Africa. Washington, D.C.: Ethics and Public Policy Center, 1984, 164 p.

Centres around the debate on foreign investment in South Africa, and whether or not its withdrawal would help or hinder the liberation struggle. Focusses primarily on the reaction of church leaders or organizations, which the author divides into the World Council of Churches, South African Churches and American Churches. Places the study within its political and economic setting.

883   SITAS, Ari
        From grassroots control to democracy: a case study of the impact of trade unionism on migrant workers' cultural formations on the East Rand. Social Dynamics, vol. 11, no. 1, 1985, p. 32-43

The first part of this paper outlines the inter-relationship between defensive combinations amongst migrant metalworkers and their unique cultural formations; it proceeds to show how in the pre-1972 period, these workers managed to exercise a remarkable degree of control over the conditions of life in the hostels. It also describes the central notions of justice operating within these cultural formations. The second part of the paper briefly outlines the reasons for urban migrant labour disorganisation in what migrants termed the 'lean years', that is, the post-1972 period. It shows how the trade union thrust on the East Rand, initially by the Metal and Allied Workers Union, facilitated the reorganisation of the hostel workers, transforming in the process the native migrant worker associations. Finally, the third part describes the new 'moral order' which has arisen on the East Rand. (Journal abstract)

884   SIWUNDHLA, Hulme T.
       White ideologies and non-European participation in the Anglo-Boer War, 1899-1902. Journal of Black Studies, vol. 15, no. 2, December 1984, p. 223-234

       Elucidates on the heavy involvement of blacks in the war. Implications and reactions are noted from both Boer and British viewpoints.

885   SIZWE, No, pseud.
       One Azania, one nation: the national question in South Africa. London: Zed, 1979, 215 p.

       Sizwe, the pseudonym of Neville Alexander, provides a critique from an independent Marxist viewpoint of customary concepts (race, ethnic groups, and the like) so often used in the analysis of South Africa's social formation. Chapter headings include the following: the National Party and the concept of nationality; the reserve strategy and the operation of capitalism; response of the opposition; the Bantustan strategy; the movement for national liberation; elements of the theory of the nation; the national question in South Africa.

886   SLABBERT, Frederik van Zyl
       The last white parliament. Johannesburg: Jonathan Ball and Hans Strydom, 1985, 175 p.

       A personal account of the author's political development and thinking. Chronicles his years in parliament, set within the events of the times.

887   SLABBERT, Frederick van Zyl and WELSH, David
        South   Africa's   options: strategies   for
        sharing   power.   Cape   Town: Philip,   1979,
        196 p.

        A   political   analysis   centering   around   the   politics   of
        negotiation   is   presented   by   the   authors.   They   analyze
        the   basis   for   conflict   in   South   Africa,   and   compare   the
        Republic's   position   with   similar   divided   societies.   By
        examining   the   dynamics   which   have   moulded   the   country's
        political   processes,   they   illustrate   the   imperative
        need   for   an   alternative   political   framework.   This   they
        outline   after   assessing   the   possibilities   for   a
        democratic   South   Africa.

888   SLOVO, Joe
        South   Africa: no   middle   road   IN: SOUTHERN
        Africa: the   new   politics   of   revolution,   by
        Basil   Davidson,   Joe   Slovo,   and   Anthony   R.
        Wilkinson.   Harmondsworth: Penguin,   1976,   p.
        106-210

        Closely   allied   to   the   African   National   Congress'
        decision   that   armed   struggle   is   the   only   way   to   end
        minority   rule,   Joe   Slovo   presents   an   analysis   of   the
        theory   of   the   South   African   revolution   focussing   on   the
        relationship   between   race   and   class,   and   its
        implications   for   prospective   armed   struggle.

889   SLOVO, Joe
        When   the   situation   is   red   hot.   World Marxist
        Review,   vol.   28,   no.   10,   October   1985,   p.   56-
        59

        A   brief   interview   with   a   member   of   the   leadership   of
        the   South   African   Communist   Party,   and   executive   member
        of   the   African   National   Congress,   in   which   he   assesses
        the   nature,   motives   and   prospects   of   anti-racist
        protest.

890   SMUTS, J.C.
Jan Christian Smuts. Cape Town: Cassell,
1952, 568 p.

Written by his son, this biography may be supplemented
by consulting the following works on Smuts: Grey steel,
J.C. Smuts: a study in arrogance, by H.C. Armstrong.
London: Barker, 1937, 406 p.; Jan Smuts: a biography,
by F.S. Crafford. New York: Greenwood, 1968, 275 p.;
Jan Smuts by Christopher Danziger. Cape Town: Macdonald
South Africa, 1978, 24 p.; Jan Smuts remembered: a
centennial tribute by Zelda Friedlander. Cape Town:
Timmins, 1970, 104 p.; Smuts the humanist: a personal
reminiscence by T.J. Haarhoff. Oxford: Blackwell, 1970,
113 p.; Smuts: fields of force by William Keith
Hancock. Cambridge: Cambridge University Press, 1968,
589 p.; Smuts: the sanguine years, 1870-1919, by
William Keith Hancock. Cambridge: Cambridge University
Press, 1962, 619 p.; Jan Christian Smuts: the
conscience of a South African, by Kenneth Ingham.
London: Weidenfeld and Nicolson, 1986, 284 p. South
African statesman: Jan Christian Smuts, by Joan Joseph.
Folkestone: Bailey, 1970, 189 p.; Jan Christian Smuts –
a bibliophile? by Jacqueline A. Kalley. Johannesburg:
University of the Witwatersrand Library, 1985, 12 p.;
One man in his time: a pictorial review of the life of
Jan Christian Smuts, May 24th, 1870 – September 11th,
1950, by Phyllis Scarnell Lean. 2nd ed. Pretoria:
(General Smuts War Veterans Foundation), 1980, 48 p.;
Jan Smuts: being a character sketch of Gen. the Hon.
J.C. Smuts, K.C., H.L.A., Minister of Defence, Union of
South Africa by N. Levi. London: Longmans, Green, 1917,
310 p.; Smuts the patriot, by Piet Meiring. Cape Town:
Tafelberg, 1975, 215 p.; General Smuts, by Sarah
Gertrude Millin. London: Faber and Faber, 1936, 2 vols;
Selections from the Smuts papers, edited by W.K.
Hancock and Jean van der Poel. Cambridge: Cambridge
University Press, 1966-1973, 7 vols.

891   SONO, Themba
           Demographic trends, growth, and geographic
           distribution of African population as an
           index of political conflict in South Africa:
           1970-2000. Journal of Southern African
           Affairs, vol. 3, no. 4, October 1978, p. 471-
           488

           Focusses on population movement, arguing that this
           factor constitutes a fundamental determinant of
           political and social change in South Africa.
           Substantiated by statistical data.

892   SOUTH AFRICA. Parliament
           White papers
           1911 - 1961
           Pretoria: Government Printer

           Usually published following commissions of inquiry,
           this series covers a wide variety of topics.

893   SOUTH AFRICA (Republic) Parliament
           White papers
           1961 -
           Pretoria: Government Printer

894   SOUTH Africa. Africa Report, vol. 31, no. 2,
           March/April 1986, p. 4 - 36

           This issue, devoted almost entirely to South Africa,
           comprises the following articles: The year of the
           Amabuthu, by Tom Lodge and Mark Swilling; 'liberation
           now, education later?', by Jakes Gerwel; organising the
           struggle: Cyril Ramaphosa, General Secretary of the
           National Union of Mineworkers, interviewed by Barry
           Streek; Elijah Barayi, President, Congress of South
           African Trade Unions, interviewed by Phillip van
           Niekerk; activism on trial, by Patrick Laurence;
           preparing for war, by Barry Streek; standing for

sanctions, by William H. Gray; using our (U.S.) leverage, by Douglas Holladay; the Mandelas and the future of South Africa, by Andrew Young; Bishop Desmond Tutu, interviewed by Margaret A. Novicki; a challenge to action (excerpts from the Kairos Document); the media blackout, by A.H. Heard; the economic pressure point, by Vivenne Walt; Zach de Beer, interviewed by Vienne Walt; business bears down, by J.C. van Zyl; the National Party's reform program, by Stoffel van der Merwe; the Soviet-South African connection, by Kurt M. Campbell.

895   SOUTH Africa. London: Amnesty International, 1986, (Amnesty International briefing, March 1986), 17 p.

Provides information on violation of human rights in South Africa, detention without trial, bannings, torture and ill-treatment. Deaths in detention, the abduction and murder of government opponents, and the existence of the death penalty are discussed. Amnesty International presents recommendations for the protection of basic human rights.

896   SOUTH Africa: a plural society in transition, edited by D.J. van Vuuren (and others). Durban: Butterworths, 1985, 510 p.

With change as the theme of this book, the authors contribute to the debate for a peaceful resolution of the country's problems by considering the issue from numerous viewpoints. Contains the following chapters: the RSA constitution - continuity and change, by L.J. Boulle; political reform, by D.J. van Vuuren; the judicial branch of government and the Hoexter Report, by H. Corder; urbanization, by P.C. Kok and W.P. Mostert; manpower development, by W. Backer; a development strategy for Southern Africa, by A.A. Ligthelm and S.F. Coetzee; recent changes in education

346

by J. de Lange; freedom of the press, by Y.M. Burns; sport and change by J.L. Olivier; church, theology and change, by J.A. Loader; white perceptions of socio-political change, by N.J. Rhoodie, C.P. de Kock and M.P. Couper; black views on socio-political change, by C.P. de Kock, N.J. Rhoodie and M.P. Couper; socio-political perspectives on change in the Coloured sector, by De Wet Schutte; Indian attitudes towards the new constitutional dispensation, by H.P. Couper, N.J. Rhoodie and C.P. de Kock; the role of blacks in political participation, by L. Schlemmer; foreign policy 1983 to 1985 – the regional context, by J. Barratt; and the federal option, by J.A. du Pisanie and L. Kritzinger.

897   SOUTH Africa: an appraisal. 2nd ed. Johannesburg: Nedbank Group Economic Unit, 1983, 280 p.

A factual report aimed at providing information 'to those who would like to weigh the advantages and risks of financial involvement in South Africa'. A statistical overview precedes contributions placing the country within a comparative context, population, manpower, training and industrial relations, physical potential, gross domestic expenditure and product, secular and cyclical patterns, mobilization of savings, balance of payments, foreign liabilities, inflation, market structures, monetary, fiscal and exchange rate policy, development strategy, politial facts and forces, and welfare.

898   SOUTH Africa and its neighbors: regional security and self-interest, by Robert I. Rotberg, (and others). Lexington: Lexington books, 1985, (A World Peace Foundation Book), 174 p.

Arising initially from some of the papers presented at a conference held during 1984 in Hilton, Natal and sponsored by both the World Peace Foundation and the South African Institute of International Affairs, this work contains the following contributions: Introduction: South Africa in its region - hegemony and vulnerability; by Robert I. Rotberg, decision-making and the military in South Africa by Robert I. Rotberg; the Soviet threat to Southern Africa by Robert Legvold; South Africa and the Soviet Union: a struggle for primacy, by Robert I. Rotberg; economic interests and security interests in Southern Africa, by Henry S. Bienan; squaring up to regional dominance: regional patterns, by Gavin G. Maasdorp; Namibia: the regional stalemate by Robert I. Rotberg; the dynamics of Southern Africa and U.S. policy by Robert I. Rotberg.

899   SOUTH Africa and the world: special international issue, edited by Peter C.J. Vale. Reality, March/May 1986, p. 4-25

Comprises the following articles: South Africa and the world - home thoughts from abroad by J.E. Spence; Nthato Motlana - an interview; South Africa and the world - unloved and lovely by Deon Geldenhuys; South Africa - implications for the West and policy options by Hedley Bull; American policy towards South Africa - an agenda beyond constructive engagement by Sanford J. Ungar and Peter Vale; recent developments in Australia's South Africa policy by David Goldsworthy; South to South - New Zealand-South African perspectives by Rupert Watson.

900   SOUTH Africa: black labour - Swedish capital: a report by the LO/TCO (Swedish Trade Union Confederation/Swedish Central Organization Study Delegation to South Africa 1975), Stockholm: LO/TCO, 1975, 193 p.

Result of a study tour undertaken by Swedish trade union federations to provide them with an insight into the apartheid society and the Swedish multinational enterprises operative in the Republic. Subsequent to an examination of political conditions in the country, the economy and labour market as well as industrial relations and the trade union movement, the study concentrates on the social and economic conditions prevalent among employees of Swedish companies and the effect of labour legislation on them. The six companies examined were Alfa Laval, ASEA, Atlas Copco, Electrolux, Sandvik and SKF.

901   SOUTH Africa: dilemmas of evolutionary change, edited by F. van Zyl Slabbert and Jeff Opland. Grahamstown: Rhodes University, Institute of Social and Economic Research, 1980, 248 p.

Select proceedings of the Workshop on Socio-economic and Constitutional Alternatives for South Africa, held in Grahamstown in 1978. Its parameters include the possibility of peaceful constitutional change, constitutional alternatives; social change needed to combat inequality; an appropriate economic system; and major obstacles which could be encountered during a transitional period. Articles on constitutional and political change are by A. du Toit, L.J. Boulle, Gibson Thula, M.I. Hirsch and William J. Foltz. M.C. O'Dowd, Stanley B. Greenberg and S.F. Archer contribute to the debate on economic change, while Michael Savage, A.S. Mathews, Gavin Maasdorp and Theodor Hanf examine social change.

902   SOUTH Africa: economic growth and political change, with comparative studies of Chile, Sri Lanka and Malaysia, edited by Adrian Leftwich. New York: St Martin's Press, 1974, 357 p.

A series of essays centering on the debate 'about the relationship between economic growth and political and social change'. With particular reference to South Africa are chapters by Michael O'Dowd - South Africa in the light of the stages of economic growth; John Rex - the plural society: the South African case; Norman Bromberger - Economic growth and political change in South Africa; Adrian Leftwich - The constitution and continuity of South African inequality; David Welsh's The political economy of Afrikaner nationalism; The future of an illusion: the myth of white meliorism by Ruan Maud; James Barber's White rule and the outward policy; and South Africa: the future of the liberal spirit by Christopher R. Hill.

903   SOUTH Africa: government and politics, edited by Denis Worrall. Pretoria: van Schaik, 1971, 366 p.

Intended primarily as an introductory textbook and general guide to the institutions of government and South African political processes, this work commences with parliamentary definitions of politics and government. Subsequent chapters provide details on parliament and the executive, the central administration, provincial and local authorities (by Ben Roux); the economy (Marcus Arkin); politics and parties (Denis Worrall); interest groups (Peter Harris); foreign policy (Gerrit Ç Olivier); the Department of Foreign Affairs (John Barratt); with a concluding chapter outlining problems and prospects with particular reference to race relations.

904   SOUTH Africa in Southern Africa: the intensifying vortex of violence, edited by Thomas M. Callaghy. New York: Praeger, 1983, 420 p.

Investigates South Africa's relationships with the other states within the Southern African region. These include Namibia, Lesotho, Swaziland, Botswana, Angola,

Zimbabwe, Mozambique, Malawi, Zambia, Zaire and Tanzania. It becomes clear that these relations are not all confrontational but South Africa's role as a destabilizing factor in the current regional framework is explored. Select items are individually indexed.

905   SOUTH Africa in the world economy, edited by Jacqueline Matthews. Johannesburg: McGraw-Hill, 1983, 271 p.

Illustrates the interdependence between South Africa and the world economy indicating the effect of external influences. The following aspects are covered: agriculture (Lieb Niewoudt); minerals and energy (Dirk Neethling); aspects of the labour market (Loet Douwes Dekker); balance of payments trends and economic policies (Roger Gidlow); industry (Anne Ratcliffe); foreign trade (Jacqueline Matthews); transport in the Southern African region (Willem Potgieter); multinational companies (Graham Muller); economic integration and cooperation in Southern Africa (Jacqueline Matthews).

906   SOUTH Africa: industrial relations and industrial sociology, edited by Ken Jubber. Cape Town: Juta, 1979, 260 p.

The editor states that the purpose of the book is to serve as an introductory text to some of the concerns and perspectives common to both industrial relations and industrial sociology. Progresses from more general to specific topics as illustrated by the contents: the socio-political structure of the South African economy, by Wolfgang Thomas; the ownership and control of large South African companies, by Mike Savage; trade unionism: South African history by Kelvin Williams; South African industrial relations legislation, by Gideon Albertyn; a framework for developing a management strategy in industrial relations, by Sam van

Coller; contemporary crises and change in South Africa's industrial-relations system, by Ken Jubber; the nature and scope of industrial sociology, by Jan Lotz; the sociology of industrial organizations, by Ken Jubber; absenteeism in Cape industries, by S.P. Cilliers; and the motivation of black workers, by Gerd Wiendieck.

907   SOUTH Africa into the 1980s, edited by Richard E. Bissell and Chester A. Crocker. Boulder: Westview, 1979, 254 p.

Considers South Africa's development into the 1980s by exploring trends, patterns and relationships. Focusses initially on South African internal dynamics and sources of change, with contributions by John Seiler who provides the Afrikaner nationalist perspective, Steven F. MacDonald's insight into the black community, and an assessment of black labour by Roy Godson. Part Two concentrates on external linkages and pressures, investigating the regional military balance and linkages in the African, American and European context. Contributions include chapters by Chester A. Crocker, I. William Zartman, W. Scott-Thompson, and Brett Silvers, Bruce J. Oudes, Lawrence G. Franko, and Richard E. Bissell.

908   SOUTH Africa: public policy perspectives, edited by Robert Schrire. Cape Town: Juta, 1982, 374 p.

Comprises eleven articles providing an analysis of the South African government's most important policies – towards individuals, groups, the economy, and internationally towards other states. In Part One – The State and the individual: the following contributions are contained: the administration of justice and due process by Jerold Taitz; political control and personal morality by André du Toit. Part Two – The State and intergroup relations: the policies of control: blacks in the common areas by David Welsh; the homelands: political perspectives by Robert Schrire; and the Coloured people and the limits of separation by Wolfgang Thomas. Part Three - The State and the economy: Government policies affecting the distribution of income, 1940-1980 by Norman Bromberger; the regulation of labour by R.M. Godsell; and industrial decentralisation and the economic development of the homelands by Gavin Maasdorp. Part Four - South Africa and the international system: South Africa's relations with Africa by G.C. Olivier; South Africa and the West by Deon Geldenhuys; and South and the changing international community: interpreting the future in the light of the past, by Peter C.J. Vale.

909   SOUTH Africa: sociological analyses, edited by A. Paul Hare, Gerd Wiendieck, and Max H. von Broembsen. Cape Town: Oxford University Press, 1979, 430 p.

Various aspects of South African society are depicted from the following perspectives: culture, religion, the family, education, economy and labour, law and crime, social stratification and colour, political sociology, social structure and social change, concluding with a chapter on problems and opportunities in research with particular reference to social research and race relations. For a review of this work by Bernard Magubane see Contemporary Sociology, vol 2, no. 1, January 1982, p. 90-91.

910   SOUTH Africa: sociological perspectives, edited by Heribert Adam. London: Oxford University Press, 1971, 340 p.

Fifteen authors, of varying political persuasion, and only six of whom are professional sociologists, analyse the major South African social structures within their historical context, current functioning, and possible development. Selected for their relevance to political change and discussed within a comparative framework, the following topics are covered: the race crisis placed in historical perspective (Jordan K. Ngubane); a comparative analysis of similar phenomena (Stanislav Andreski); racial segregation as divided into three categories (Pierre L. van den Berghe); research on race relations (J.W. Mann); white power elite (Heribert Adam); African nationalism (Gwendolen M. Carter and Fatima Meer); urbanization (Ellen Hellmann); religion and social control (Philip Mayer); education (by Kogila Adam, and H.F. Dickie-Clark); legal system control as evidenced by the security laws (A.S. Mathews); Afrikaner nationalism and its socio-cultural background (Richard B. Ford); labour and race (G.V. Doxey); and a study of white power (Kurt Danziger). Includes a comprehensive bibliography on South Africa from 1960.

911   SOUTH Africa: the cordoned heart, edited by Omar
       Badsha. Cape Town: Gallery Press, 1986,
       204 p.

Francis Wilson, head of the School of Economics at the University of Cape Town concisely presents the major findings of the Second Carnegie Inquiry into Poverty and Development in Southern Africa. This complements a selection of 400 photographs held at an exhibition marking the Inquiry's culmination. Twenty-eight photographic essays by twenty South African photographers illustrate aspects of poverty and its concomitant effect on the people.

912   SOUTH Africa: the limits of reform politics. Journal
       of Asian and African Studies, vol. 18, no.
       1/2, January/April 1982, (entire issue)

Comparative considerations are presented by Heribert Adam in an article entitled: ethnic politics and crisis management - comparing South Africa and Israel, and by Theodor Hanf in his: lessons that are never learnt - minority rule in comparative perspective. Strategies and preconditions of reform are assessed in three contributions. Frederik van Zyl Slabbert's sham reform and conflict regulation in a divided society; Oscar Dumisani: Dhlomo on the strategy of Inkatha and its critics, and Lawrence Schlemmer in: build up to revolution or impasse? Theoretical aspects are addressed by Hermann Giliomee in: constructing Afrikaner nationalism, and Hamish Dickie-Clark concentrates on ideology in recent writings on South Africa.

913   SOUTH Africa: the privileged and the dispossessed, edited and annotated by Geoffrey Davis and Michael Senior. Paderborn: Schoningh, 1983, (Texts for English and American studies, no. 12), 145 p.

A series of essays depicting contemporary South Africa and arranged under various headings: Perspectives includes contributions by Arnold Helfet, Monica Wilson, Sipho Sepamla, and Nelson Mandela. The urban black is studied by Alan Paton, Gladys Thomas, Mongane Wally Serote, Sipho Sepamla, Mtutuzeli Matshoba, Elsa Joubert and Oswald Mbuyiseni Mtshali. Elsla Joubert and Mtutuzeli Matshoba write on the African homelands, while Athol Fugard, John Kani, Winston Ntshona, E.V. Stone and Sipho Sepamla discourse on the law. The section on Afrikaners comprises a National Party explanatory text and Willem de Klerk writes on Afrikaner history. Stages in resistance includes contributions by James Matthews, Steve Biko, Donald and Wendy Woods and Bernard Levin. Being white is examined by Nadine Gordimer and André Brink; support or boycott policies are examined by R.W. Johnson and Julius K. Nyerere, while the section, towards liberation, contains contributions by Willem Wilhelm and E.V. Stone.

914 SOUTH Africa: the road ahead, compiled by G.F. Jacobs. Johannesburg: Jonathan Ball, 1986, 300 p.

The compiler, former United Party Member of Parliament and former head of the Business School at the University of the Witwatersrand, presents the writings of nineteen prominent South Africans. His intention is to provide a forum to those 'of proven ability outside the political arena who have a keen understanding of the problems that exist in our society and of some of the steps that should be taken to resolve them'. Contributors include Jannie Geldenhuys, Simon Brand, Lawrence Schlemmer, Hendrik Marais, Mangosuthu Buthelezi, Gavin Relly, Zach de Beer, Michael O'Dowd, Ike van der Watt, Marina Maponya, Truida Prekel, Ken Owen, F. van Zyl Slabbert and Stoffel van der Merwe.

915 SOUTH African capitalism and black political opposition, edited by Martin J. Murray. Cambridge: Mass.: Schenkman, 1982, 733 p.

This extensive work is divided into six main parts, all further subdivided. Based on a theoretical framework, Frederick A. Johnstone discusses white supremacy; and Mike Morris the development of capitalism, European settlement in the period spanning the seventeenth to nineteenth centuries; Martin J. Murray analyzes European, Dutch and British commercial interests; and A. Atmore and S. Marks, the imperial factor in the nineteenth century. Thirdly, the development of capitalist production processes, mining, demand for labour and transformation of the countryside is scrutinized as follows: Alan Jeeves on control of migratory labour on the gold mines in the Kruger and

Milner eras, Robert Davies for the period 1901 to 1913, examines mining capital, the state and unskilled white workers, and Colin Bundy the emergence and decline of a South African peasantry. In the fourth part, entitled: the consolidation of monopoly capitalism 1914-1948 - the state apparatus, class struggle and political opposition, the development of capitalism in agriculture is the focus of a contribution by M.L. Morris; the politics of industrial protection, 1910 to 1939 by D.E. Kaplan; the development of black political consciousness, 1910 to 1948 by Martin J. Murray; the 1946 African miners' strike and the political economy of South Africa by Dan O'Meara. Fifthly, monopoly capitalism in the period 1948 to 1980 is discussed by Ruth Milkman in her article, apartheid, economic growth and United States foreign policy; legislation, ideology and economy in post-1948 South Africa by Martin Legassick; United States business and South Africa by Mohamed A. el-Khawas; the historical significance of the Bantustan strategy by Frank Molteno; a socio-economic analysis of conditions in Soweto by Stephen S. Hlope; and the political economy of the migrant labour system by J. Kombo Moyane. The concluding section is organized as follows under the heading of the growth of black political consciousness, class and national responses to the apartheid regime: colour caste and ruling class strategy in the South African class struggle - the case of the 'Coloured people' and collaborationist politics by Frank Molteno; the Nationalist Party in command - apartheid and political challenge, 1948 to 1976 by Martin J. Murray; trade unionism and the struggle for liberation by David Hemson; Soweto and its aftermath, by Archie Mafeje.

916   SOUTH African communists speak, 1915-1980. London: Inkululeko Publications, 1981, 495 p.

Edited by Brian Bunting, though formally not credited to him, and based largely on material from the Party's theoretical journal, the African Communist, this collection documents the Party's history for the period under review. Contains some internal Party documentation, previously published, half of which focusses on the Party's development prior to 1980, and subsequent to 1953.

917   SOUTH African dialogue: contrasts in South African thinking on basic race issues, edited by N.J. Rhoodie. Johannesburg: McGraw-Hill, 1972, 611 p.

Thirty-five contributors, covering all shades of the political spectrum, examine South Africa's racial policies under the following headings: the general race relations structure; the fabric of apartheid; the Bantu homelands; white alternatives to apartheid; race relations and the South African economy; the urban African; the Coloured and Asian South Africans; the church and education in an apartheid society; the verkramp/verlig dichotomy; and apartheid and international relations.

918   SOUTH AFRICAN INSTITUTE OF RACE RELATIONS Quarterly countdown 1986 - Johannesburg: The Institute

Aimed at monitoring the government's performance, the information is categorized into the following typologies: an identification of moves away from apartheid and towards equality; forthcoming steps; expected changes that have been delayed; provides an analysis of changes including political rights; immigration, education, labour, land ownership and occupation, social segregation, business and professions; health and welfare; concentrates on instances where discrimination has been extended; and lists discriminatory laws still in existence.

919   SOUTH AFRICAN INSTITUTE OF RACE RELATIONS
    South Africa in travail: the disturbance of 1976/77, evidence presented by the S.A. Institute of Race Relations to the Cillié Commission of Inquiry into the riots at Soweto and other places during June 1976. Johannesburg: The Institute, 1978, 143 p.

Memoranda submitted on both Soweto and the Western Cape include a chronology of events, the controversy over the medium of instruction in schools, political and socio-economic background. Appendices contain the Memorandum from Bantu Scholars fund to Regional Director Bantu Education Department.

920   SOUTH AFRICAN INSTITUTE OF RACE RELATIONS. Conference, 50th, Johannesburg, 1980
    Towards economic and political justice in South Africa. Johannesburg. The Institute, 1980, 142 p.

As a companion volume to: Resolving racial conflict in South Africa: some outside views, this collection includes papers under the following heading: the economics of rising expectations with keynote addresses by Francis Wilson on suggested directions for the future, and Jill Nattrass on guidelines for the private sector. The political structure is examined by Lawrence Schlemmer in his political structures for multi-racial societies, and David Welsh in his planning for a multi-racial democracy in Azania/South Africa. In the final plenary session, negotiable priorities are presented by Franklin Sonn, Willem Kleynhans, H. Mall, H. Ntsanwisi, Theuns Eloff, Obed Kunene, Helen Suzman and Stoffel van der Merwe.

921   SOUTH AFRICAN INSTITUTE OF RACE RELATIONS. <u>Council</u>
<u>Meeting 51st, Johannesburg, 1981</u>
Resettlement. Johannesburg: The Institute,
1981, 66 p.

As part of its research programme on resettlement, the
Institute chose to highlight this issue by selecting it
as the topic for the fifty-first conference. This study
comprises four papers: Gerhard Maré defines
relocation, its processes and policies prior to
assessing the scale of relocation; C.E.W. Simkins
examines the economic implications of resettling
Africans; Dr C.J. Jooste, Director of the South African
Bureau for Racial Affairs questions whether the
emerging states in Southern Africa have acquired their
land in accordance with international law, and secondly
whether the land is adequate, taking nation and state
building into consideration. Dr Oscar D. Dhlomo,
KwaZulu Minister of Education and Culture and
Secretary-General of Inkatha, presents a paper on
KwaZulu and its stance and problems associated with
resettlement in Natal.

922   SOUTH African Journal on Human Rights
Vol. 1 - , 1985-   3 p.a.
Braamfontein: Ravan

Published under the auspices of the University of the
Witwatersrand's Centre for Applied Legal Studies and
Lawyers for Human Rights, this journal is intended both
to mobilize human rights opinion and to enlist more
lawyers in this cause. Aims at providing a source of
information on the state of human rights in Southern
Africa, and a forum of ideas on issues affecting
justice in the region.

923   SOUTH African Labour Bulletin
vol. 1 - , 1974 -   8 p.a.
Johannesburg: The Bulletin

This journal supports the independent labour movement in South Africa, providing a forum for analyzing, debating and recording the aims and activities of this movement.

924   SOUTH African labour scene in the 1980s, edited by Deon Johannes Geldenhuys. Johannesburg: South African Institute of International Affairs, 1980, (South African Institute of International Affairs. Study Group series), 61 p.

In a focus on socio-political issues affecting multinational corporations in South Africa, the following papers centre on labour matters: international labour bodies and its relevance to South Africa (L.C.G. Douwes Dekker); the development of trade unionism in South Africa and its implications for trade unionism (Ronald C. Webb); experience with the implementation of the Sullivan Code and prospects for the future (Frank R. Golino); the EEC code and future prospects (H. Erath); labour order in the eighties (P.J. van der Merwe). In addition, papers presented to a Corporate Members Seminar entitled: The South African Economy in the Political and Economic Environment of the 1980s: A Debate on the Role of Capital and Labour, are included. Michael C. O'Dowd offers the case for dismantling constraints on market forces, while Jill Nattrass argues the case for state interference in the market.

925   SOUTH African labour: special issue, edited by Roger Southall. Labour, Capital and Society, vol. 18, no. 2, November 1985, (entire issue)

Contains the following contributions: Political unionism and working class hegemony: perspectives on the South African Congress of Trade Unions, 1955-1965, by Rob Lambert; the emergence, struggles and achievements of black trade unions in South Africa from

1973 to 1984, by Johann Maree; monopoly capital and industrial unionism in the South African motor industry, by Roger Southall; work, worker organization and labour market segmentation in South African foundries, be Eddie Webster; moral formation and struggles amongst migrant workers on the East Rand, by Ari Sitas.

926   SOUTH African News Summary
        vol. 1 -   , 1984 -   Quarterly
        Westville (Natal): Duncan Stuart

        Intended as an objective aide memoire recording events in the Southern African region, and drawn from a wide spectrum of material. The information is presented within the following categories: economy, infrastructure, economic activities, population pressures, environment and conservation, politics, homelands and the national states, South Africa's neighbours, outside world, national security, and diplomacy. In addition, principal events and trends are highlighted.

927   SOUTH African parties and policies, 1910-1960: a select source book, edited with an introduction by D.W. Krüger. Cape Town: Human and Rousseau, 1960, 471 p.

        Relevant documents illustrate the following facets in South Africa's political history: leaders views of the new South Africa constituted in 1910; party principles and programmes; the development of constitutional independence and the symbols of nationhood; the Indian problem; Cape Coloured representation; and the 'native' problem.

928   SOUTH Africa's apartheid policy under siege. New York: Foreign Policy Association, 1985, 12 p.

Among the topics examined by the editors of the Foreign Policy Association, are the clashes between the South African police and blacks, pressure for United States disinvestments and its policy options; the Republic's invasion of Botswana; its relations with Angola and Namibia and a survey of its domestic reforms.

929   SOUTH Africa's foreign policy and international practice as reflected in speeches, parliamentary speeches, parliamentary statements and replies - 1983, edited by Wim Booyse. South African Yearbook of International Law, vol. 9, 1983, p. 186-258

Main headings include the following: the onslaught against South Africa; South Africa's regional relations; regional co-operation; Namibia; and South Africa's relations with the United Nations.

930   SOUTH Africa's foreign policy and international practice during 1980 as reflected in speeches, and in parliamentary statements and replies, edited by Nel Marais. South African Yearbook of International Law, vol. 6, 1980, p. 179-228

Information is arranged under the following headings: the onslaught against South Africa; co-operation in Southern Africa; Constellation of States in Southern Africa; trade and economics; the United Nations and Namibia.

931   SOUTH Africa's foreign policy and international practice during 1981 as reflected in speeches, and in parliamentary statements and replies, edited by Nel Marais. South African Yearbook of International Law, vol. 7, 1981, p. 171-203

Select policy speeches covering a wide range of topics: the external campaign against South Africa; regional co-operation in Southern Africa; relations with Africa and the United Nations; and the Namibian issue. Concludes with a series of short statements pertaining to South Africa's relations with Transkei, Mozambique, Angola and Zimbabwe.

932   SOUTH Africa's foreign policy and international practice during 1982 as reflected in speeches, and in parliamentary practice and replies, edited by Nel Marais. South African Yearbook of International Law, vol. 8, 1982, p. 214-270

Comprises various sections: the concept of confederation; regional economic cooperation; Soviet intervention in Southern Africa; Namibia; the Republic and the United Nations; and comment on international affairs.

933   SOUTH Africa's impending socialist revolution: perspectives of the Marxist worker's tendency of the African National Congress. London: Inqaba Ya Basebenzi Publications, 1982, - p.

Inqaba Ya Basebenzi, a small group of Trotskyite former African National Congress members, finally expelled for ideological reasons, provide the rationale and justification for their beliefs. Propound that the revolution in South Africa should be based on a working class programme rather than nationalist ideology. They criticise the African National Congress and particularly the Communist Party of South Africa, for what they see as an ahderence to a two stage theory of revolution.

934   SOUTH Africa's minorities, edited by Peter Randall. Johannesburg: Study Project on Christianity in Apartheid Society, 1971, (Study Project on Christianity in Apartheid Society. Sprocas occasional publication, no. 2), 77 p.

Comprises a collection of papers presented originally as working documents for the Social Commission of the Study Project on Christianity in Apartheid Society, containing information on the major non-black groupings in South African society - Indians, Afrikaners, English-speaking whites and Coloureds. Contributions are by H.W. van der Merwe, Fatima Meer, W.A. de Klerk, C.O. Gardner and M.G. Whisson.

935   SOUTH Africa's regional political economy: a critical analysis of reform strategy in the 1980s, by William Cobbett (and others). South African Review, 3, 1986, p. 137-168

Authors state as the aim of this paper, the description, anticipation and critical analysis of the state's evolving regional strategy. Identify the major components as new controls on labour movement and settlement, regional development policies, notably industrial decentralization, and local and second tier government reforms and corresponding constitutional changes. The debate and the possibility of establishing a federal system is a central issue addressed by this paper.

936   SOUTH Africa's urban blacks: problems and challenges, edited by G. Marais and R. van der Kooy. Pretoria: University of South Africa, School of Business Leadership, Centre for Management Studies, (197-), 370 p.

Sixteen contributors, both black and white, analyze the
socio-economic and political conditions experienced by
South Africa's urban blacks. Options open to policy-
planners are assessed, while the concluding chapter
summarizes and integrates the approcahes of the
different disciplines. Substantiated by extensive
statistical data and tables.

937   SOUTHALL, Anthony J.
        Marxist theory in South Africa until 1940.
        York: University of York, 1978, 78 p.

        Dissertation: M.A.

        Examines why the economy did not collapse given the
        belief that institutionalized racism constrained
        growth; why a white labour aristocracy was encouraged
        contrary to the concept of class, not race; under-
        estimation of black nationalism's potency.

938   SOUTHALL, Roger J.
        African capitalism in contemporary South
        Africa. Journal of Southern African Studies,
        vol. 7, no. 1, October 1980, p. 38-70

        As stated by Southall: 'The objective of the present
        paper is to focus upon the current development of
        African capitalism. This will necessitate a brief
        survey of the evolution of state policy towards African
        enterprise, and will consequently include reference to
        the attempt to create a subordinate capitalist class in
        the bantustans. However, because the outlines of this
        latter aspect are now relatively well established in
        the literature, the particular purpose of this analysis
        will be to emphasise the recent efforts to promote
        African capitalism within the urban areas of 'white'
        South Africa, and to assess its significance for the
        future.'

939   SOUTHALL Roger J.
Buthelezi, Inkatha and the politics of compromise. African Affairs, vol. 80, no. 321, October 1981, p. 453-481

Evaluates both the role of Mangosuthu Buthelezi and Inkatha in South African politics. See also: Wessels de Kock's Usuthu! Cry Peace! Cape Town: Open Hand Press, 1986, 192 p.

940   SOUTHALL, Roger J.
Consociationalism in South Africa: the Buthelezi Commission and beyond. Journal of Modern African Studies, vol. 21, no. 1, March 1983, p. 77-112

Offers consociationalism as a political alternative for the Republic, subsequent to defining and enlarging on the concept. Provides a summary of the findings of a commission established on the initiative of Gatsha Buthelezi, Chief Minister of the Kwazulu Homeland. This report, entitled The Buthelezi Commission: the requirements for stability and development in Kwazulu and Natal (Durban 1981, 2 vols. q.v.), recommended a consociational structure of government for both Kwazulu and Natal combined. This was rejected by the National Party, and the implications for Inkatha are assessed.

941   SOUTHALL, Roger J.
Independence for the Transkei IN: SOUTHERN Africa since the Portuguese coup, edited by John Seiler. Boulder: Westview, 1980, p. 137-154

Explores the implications and issue of granting 'independence' to a homeland, the process of which Southall states, was accelerated by the Portuguese coup of 1974 and the subsequent decolonization of Angola and Mozambique. The role of Transkei within the South African political economy is scrutinized.

942   SOUTHALL, Roger J.
       South   Africa's   Transkei: the   political
       economy   of   an   'independent'   Bantustan.
       London: Heinemann, 1982, 338 p.

       Approaches   South Africa's balkanization policy from   a
       neo-Marxist   perspective,   examining Transkei as a   case
       study   of   the Bantustan strategy and illustrating   how
       its policy continues to exploit the oppressed majority.
       Provides historical information on Transkei's evolution
       to 'independence',   class formation, and the continuing
       role of Transkei as a labour reservoir necessary to the
       development of South African capitalism.

943   SOUTHERN   Africa   in perspective: essays   in   regional
       politics,   edited by Christian P. Potholm and
       Richard   Dale.   New York: Free Press,   1972,
       418 p.

       Part Two: the South African Nexus, (p. 18-94) contains,
       inter   alia,   analyses   of both Afrikaner   and   African
       nationalism   by Denis J.   Worrall and Inez   Smith   Reid
       respectively,   while   Christopher   Hill   assesses   the
       future of separate development in South Africa which he
       places in historical context.

944   SOUTHERN   Africa in the 1980s,   edited by Olajide Aluko
       and Timothy M. Shaw. London: Allen and Unwin,
       1985, 327 p.

       Based   on   papers   delivered   to   an   international
       conference   held   at the University of Ife during   mid-
       December   1980,   the   following   items   are   relevant,
       particularly to South Africa: the strategic importance
       of South Africa to the United States,   by Larry Bowman;
       the   EEC   and South Africa,   by   Humphrey   Asobie;   oil
       sanctions and South Africa, by Olusola Ojo; white power
       and the regional military industrial complex by Timothy
       M. Shaw and Edward Leppan; South Africa's situation and

strategic opportunities in Africa by Sam C.
Nolutshungu; South Africa's role in Southern Africa in
the year 2000 by Timothy M. Shaw. Reviewed by Roger
Tangri in Journal of Modern African Studies, vol. 23,
no. 3, 1985, p. 530-531.

945   SOUTHERN AFRICA LABOUR AND DEVELOPMENT RESEARCH UNIT
        Farm labour in South Africa: a review
        article. A report on the proceedings of a
        conference, 20 to 24 September 1976,
        University of Cape Town. Social Dynamics,
        vol. 2, no. 2, December 1976, p. 93-148

        Summarizes the main aspects depicted in the fifty-five
        papers presented at the conference by academics and
        farmers, amongst others. Regional differences in
        labourer wage and working conditions were described and
        pressures for change discussed. Amongst the major
        themes presented were small-scale agriculture, the
        historical development of capitalist agriculture,
        mechanization, education and training.

946   SOUTHERN Africa Record
        no. 1 - , March 1975 - 4 p.a.
        Johannesburg: South African Institute of
        International Affairs

        Reproduces original texts, or extracts from, important
        statements made by political leaders, government
        representatives and international organizations
        relevant to international relations within the Southern
        African region.

947   SOUTHERN African Update: a Bibliographical Survey
        vol. 1 - , 1986 - 2 p.a.
        Johannesburg: University of the Witwatersrand
        Library

Emphasizing specific Southern African issues in preference to a wider regional classification, each journal comprises one main annotated feature complemented by checklists on two additional current topics. A regular section updating previous items is an important aspect of this journal. Topics include international pressure against apartheid - boycotts, disinvestment and sanctions, and information on trade unions and church-state relations, the Namibian settlement issue, church and politics, and transport within the region.

948   SPECIAL issue on women. Africa Perspective, July 1979, (entire issue: 98 p.)

Draws together papers which include, among others, a study of women in the South African labour force, African women in Durban's textile industry, and an analysis of the family, and domestic labour in the capitalist social formation.

949   SPENCE, John Edward
        'The most unpopular corpse in history'.
        Optima, vol. 34, no. 1, March 1986, p. 3-22

Provides an analysis, in two parts, of changes that have occurred since 1945 to produce the contemporary international society, and how these changes have affected South Africa's standing and behaviour and have led to its increased isolation.

950   SPENCE, John Edward
        The political and military framework. London: Africa Publications Trust for the Study Project on External Investment in South Africa and Namibia (South West Africa), 1975, 114 p.

As an introduction to a larger study encompassing South Africa's economic relationships, Spence examines the constraints and factors governing its relations with the major Western powers. Includes a study of Anglo-South African defence relations, 1945 to 1970; the economic and strategic significance of the Indian Ocean; defence capabilities and the implications for Western attitudes to South Africa; and the implications of the 'outward-looking movement' to other states in Africa.

951   SPENCE, John Edward
       Reform in South Africa: a tangled web.
       Contemporary Review, vol. 244, no. 1416,
       January 1984, p. 6-15

Discusses the necessity of reform to South Africa's constitution which became particularly evident since the 1974 collapse of Portuguese rule in Angola and Mozambique. Identifies developments confirming this need but which have 'paradoxically rendered its implementation more difficult and, in the view of many observers improbable'. Against this background, Spence examines the establishment of the tricameral parliament. Presents an outline of its salient features and an assessment of its implications from both an internal and external viewpoint.

952   SPENCE, John Edward
       Republic under pressure: a study of South
       African foreign policy. London: Oxford
       University Press under the auspices of the
       Royal Institute of International Affairs,
       1965, 132 p.

Demonstrates reasons for the decline in South Africa's stature since 1948, and the resultant isolation and withdrawal from active politics of the African continent. Main chapter headings include the domestic context; the influence of economic factors; South Africa as an African power; and its role in international organizations.

953   SPENCE, John Edward
       South Africa: reform versus reaction.
       World Today, vol. 37, no. 12, December 1981,
       p. 461-468

Illustrates the connection between the constraints of domestic policy operative on the South African government, subsequent to the April 1981 elections, and the demands made by the international community.

954   SPENCE, John Edward
       South Africa: the nuclear option. African
       Affairs, vol. 80, no. 321, October 1981, p.
       441-452

An expanded and revised version of a contribution to the University of Sussex, Armament and Disarmament Information Unit, Report, vol. 2, no. 4, October/ November 1980. Examines South Africa's development to that of a near-nuclear state and the military and political constraints against a public declaration of this status. States that the current position is appropriately summarized by E. Bustin (South Africa's foreign policy alternatives and deterred needs, IN: NUCLEAR proliferation and the near-nuclear countries, edited by O. Marvah and A. Schultz. Cambridge: Ballinger, 1975, p. 223-224). When he claims 'whatever bargaining advantage Pretoria might be able to spin off from the exercise of its nuclear options could be derived more effectively . . . from publicizing its capacity to 'go nuclear' - which is highly credible - rather than from the threat of subsequently using such weapons - which is demonstrably less credible'.

955   SPICER, Michael
       Sanctions against South Africa: the changing context. Johannesburg: South African Institute of International Affairs, 1982, 9 p.

A re-examination of the sanctions debate in which the exhaustion of both negotiation and dialogue possibilities by many Western nations is noted. Given the possible imposition of sanctions, Spicer assesses their various typologies and implications.

956   SSALI, Ndugu Mike
       Apartheid and cinema. Ufahamu, vol. 13, no. 1, 1983, p. 105-133

Provides an historical survey of three films which the South African power structure permitted blacks to see, how and why they were selected. Evaluates the impact they were intended to have on the black community.

957   ST JORRE, John de
       A house divided: South Africa's uncertain future. New York: Carnegie Endowment for International Peace, 1977, 136 p.

The author, a former correspondent for the London Observer presents five essays emanating from his lengthy field trips to the Republic. He says 'what I have tried to do is to give a view of what is happening in the Republic and how the people who live there think and react'. White power structures are analyzed with particular emphasis on the role of Afrikaner nationalism. Assesses facets of black power including

373

the homelands concept, the significance of the Soweto
rising of 1976, and the role of both the African
National Congress and the Pan-Africanist Congress.
South Africa's strategy in Africa; efforts to promote
self-sufficiency, particularly with regard to armaments
and fuel, are examined. In conclusion, the author
presents a series of options open to the government in
resolving the country's problems.

958   ST JORRE, John de
        South Africa: is change coming? Foreign
        Affairs, vol. 60, no. 1, Fall 1981, p. 106-
        122

        Examines the Reagan Administration's attempt to foster
        a new relationship with South Africa on the basis of
        closer ties, aimed at countering Soviet influence
        within the region. Relationship is based on the premise
        that constructive change is taking place in the
        Republic. Provides a detailed analysis of the changes
        as well as the implications of the Namibian issue for
        the United States.

959   ST LEGER F.Y.
        The African press in South Africa.
        Grahamstown: Rhodes University, 1974, 394 p.

        Thesis: Ph D (Rhodes University)

        Based on a theoretical background, this work focusses
        particularly on the political aspects of the African
        press, but takes into consideration its organization,
        economics and cultural facets. Content analysis of the
        major African newspapers, and of the 1968 Rand Daily
        Mail forms the core of the thesis. This is complemented
        by material derived from surveys revealing journalists'
        values. Development over the period 1959 to 1971, and

means by which policy towards the press is shaped, is examined. Concludes by considering implications of his findings for the South African society as a whole. Appendices reprint questionnaires utilized in the study.

960   STADLER, Alfred W.
        A long way to walk: bus boycotts in Alexandra, 1940-1945 IN: WORKING papers in Southern African studies, vol. 2, edited by P. Bonner. Johannesburg: Ravan, 1981, p. 228-257

Provides a detailed examination of the causes and nature of the bus boycott movement, both highlighting and explaining the strength of the grassroots commitment.

961   STADLER, Alfred W.
        The political economy of modern South Africa. Cape Town: Philip, 1987, 197 p.

Argues that South African politics reflect the changing ways in which the region has been incorporated into the world economy. Traces the effects of a process of industrialization under the dominance of mining on the other sectors of the economy, and on the evolution of the class structure. Illustrates how a coercive labour system influenced the definition of political and social rights in racial terms, and influenced the development of authoritarian controls over blacks in the urban and rural areas from the 1920 onwards. Elaborates on the alternative strategies in this policy of control, and suggests that 'reform from above' attempts to reform, not end apartheid. Analyzes different strands in the reform movement, and speculates on the social and political forces which underlie political changes that began to take place from the mid-1970s.

962   STADLER, Alfred W.
         Shifting bases of legitimacy. Paper delivered
         at the Conference on Economic Development and
         Racial Domination, Bellville, University of
         the Western Cape, 1984, (University of the
         Witwatersrand. Paper, no. 32), 30 p.

This paper is concerned with understanding the most
recent phase of state reconstruction as an effort to
develop institutions which mediate the intense
conflicts generated in the society over the last decade
or so, without, it ought to be emphasised,
democratising its political institutions. The paper
rejects the claim which is widely supported by white
parties and business interests that the establishment
of representation for Indians and Coloureds in separate
houses will "broaden" the basis of government. On the
contrary, the likely effect will be to narrow the
political base of the regime. Indeed, this paper
concludes that attempted solutions to the problem of
declining support for government policy will lead to
its further deflation. For the same reason, the
explanation for the shortcomings of the new
constitution which rest on the exclusion of Africans is
based on a misconception of the processes which are
involved. (Author's abstract)

963   STASIULIS, Daiva K.
         Pluralist and Marxist perspectives on racial
         discrimination in South Africa.British Journal
         of Sociology, vol. 31, no. 4, December 1980,
         p. 463-490

The conventional wisdom on South African race relations
has been dominated by the pluralist perspective. This
paper attempts to demonstrate how the pluralist
approach, characterized as it is by institutional and
ethnological determinism and an undue emphasis upon
select racially discriminatory practises, removed from

their structural context, obscures rather than explains the nature of racial domination. Moreover, the critique offered by this school of the Marxist approach is a misguided one, directed at a strawman theory unrepresentative of actual analyses of South Africa by Marxists. An alternative approach is offered which is Marxist in orientation and which seeks to explain the pattern of racial discrimination in South African society as an integral part of the growth of capitalism in this country. An illustrative analysis from this perspective is given for the gold mining industry in South Africa. The argument is made that not only is the Marxist perspective able to generate a clearer understanding of the South African situation but also that it aids in the formulation of realistic strategies for social change. (Journal abstract)

964   STEYN, Anna F. and UYS, J.M.
         The changing position of black women in South
         Africa IN: The CHANGING position of women in
         family and society: a cross-national
         comparison, edited by Eugen Lupri. Leiden:
         Brill, 1983, p. 344-370

A synopsis of research findings conducted over the past twenty-five years by different researchers, and from which a broad pattern of change is deduced. Presents initially, a brief description of blacks in South Africa, and outlines factors which have contributed to their changing way of life. Particular reference is paid to the role of women illustrating the influence of westernization and urbanization on the position of most of them. Contains useful tables.

965   STOKES, Randall G.
         Afrikaner Calvinism and economic action: the
         Weber Thesis in South Africa. American
         Journal of Sociology, vol. 81, no. 1,
         1975/76, p. 62-81

Reviews their relationship and pursues the question of why Afrikaner Calvinism had a conservative effect on economic action, in contrast to the European case.

966 STONE, John
   Colonist or uitlander? A study of the British immigrant in South Africa. Oxford: Clarendon, 1973, 313 p.

The author summarizes the content of his book: '. . . I have attempted to answer a sociological problem posed by the British immigrant in South Africa – what accounts for his rapid integration into the structure of South African society, and his still more rapid acculturation into its norms and dominant values? The problem has been approached from four different ways: it has been seen in the light of sociological theory; viewed in terms of a comparative analysis of race relations in Britain and South Africa; considered from the standpoint of historical evidence; and finally assessed against the findings of a sample survey of post-war British immigrants.'

967 STRANGEWAYES-BOOTH, Joanna
   A cricket in the thorn tree: Helen Suzman and the Progressive Party. Johannesburg: Hutchinson, 1976, 320 p.

Interwoven in this history of the Progressive Party is the political biography of Helen Suzman, who for thirteen years was the party's sole representative in Parliament.

968 STREAK, Michael
   The Afrikaner as viewed by the English, 1795–1854. Cape Town: Struik, 1974, 231 p.

Traces the growth of public opinion on the Afrikaner and their relationship with the English both in South Africa and in Britain. Provides reasons for division amongst the English in their attitudes towards Afrikaners.

969   STREEK, Barry
        Apartheid under siege. Africa Report, vol.
        30, no. 1, January/February 1985, p. 54-58

Provides an overview of the tensions and government measures leading to the unrest experienced in the Republic during 1985 and 1986.

970   STREEK, Barry
        Disunity through the Bantustans. South
        African Review, 2, 1984, p. 259-270

Considers how the government's policy of divide and rule has resulted in the division and disorganization of blacks in particular. Illustrates that their methods of control and entrenching power in the ten bantustans has also created division between these bantustans as a whole, and democratic movements such as the United Democratic Front, National Forum or the African National Congress.

971   STREEK, Barry
        Illusion and reality in South Africa's sport
        policy. South Africa International, vol. 16,
        no. 1, July 1985, p. 29-41

Concentrates on factors within South Africa itself 'the mistakes', to use Dr Koornhof's terminology, which contribute to South Africa's continued sporting isolation, indicates that issues have changed, and that government policy as a whole is now in question. Lessons to be learnt from the stance taken by the international community are assessed.

972   STREEK, Barry and WICKSTEED, Richard
       Render unto Kaiser: a Transkei dossier.
       Johannesburg: Ravan, 1981, 378 p.

       Reveals what 'independence' has meant to Transkei
       illustrating that 'experiment in separate development
       is turning into a monster'. Among others, the following
       aspects are investigated: engineered consent in
       Transkei; a biographical account of Kaiser and George
       Matanzima; Transkei's financial dependence on South
       Africa; migrant labour, corruption; information
       control; and the role of the security police.

973   STUDENT perspectives in South Africa, edited by Hendrik
       van der Merwe and David Welsh. Cape Town:
       Philip in association with the Abe Bailey
       Institute of Interracial Studies, 1972,
       229 p.

       A compilation of essays by South African students, both
       black and white, commenting on the issue of race
       relations and student politics. Includes papers on the
       political sociology of South African universities, the
       role of English high schools, the development and role
       of the Afrikaanse Studente Bond, the emergence of a
       moderate Afrikaner student movement, the aspirations of
       NUSAS and its failure in recruiting the support of
       black militants. Views of black students - both high
       school and university are examined, as well as
       contributions emphasizing the significance of the Black
       Consciousness Movement. Concludes with a plea for
       greater cultural understanding between races.

974   STUDIES on urbanisation in South Africa, edited by E.A.
       Kraayenbrink. Johannesburg: South African
       Institute of Race Relations, 1984, 96 p.

The detrimental effect on race relations engendered by
legislation governing influx control is the theme of
this work. It comprises eleven papers by well known
contributors such as T.J.D. Fair, Charles Simkins,
Gavin Maasdorp, Jeremy Keenan, M. West, D. Dewar, P.
Green, A. Hirsch, M. Roux, P. Stewart, Sheena Duncan,
and A.W. Stadler.

975   STUDY COMMISSION ON U.S. POLICY TOWARDS SOUTHERN AFRICA
        South Africa: time running out. Berkeley:
        University of California Press, 1981, 517 p.

Funded by the Rockefeller Foundation, and chaired by
the President of the Ford Foundation, Franklin A.
Thomas, the brief of this eleven-man Commission was to
determine how best the United States can respond to
problems posed by South Africa, given its entrenched
policy of racial discrimination. Presents a summary of
the Commission's Findings and Recommendations prior to
a comprehensive analysis of the current position in
apartheid South Africa. Covers topics such as the road
to apartheid; the people; the apparatus of apartheid;
civil liberties; the workplace; housing, education and
health; the economy; the homelands, economy, black
challenge, white rule, and military strength. A summary
of South Africa's foreign relations with the rest of
Africa, Western Europe, Japan, Israel, Latin America
and the United States, a section on Communist
involvement in Southern Africa and on strategic
minerals is included. Five objectives to be considered
by the United States in their policy formulation are
presented. In brief, these include clarifying the
fundamental and continuing opposition of the United
States to the apartheid system; the promotion of power
sharing with the minimum of violence; the support of
organizations inside the country working for change;
the reduction of the economic inbalance of other
Southern African states; and the reduction of the
impact of stoppages of inputs of key minerals.

976   STUDY PROJECT ON CHRISTIANITY IN APARTHEID SOCIETY.
           Education Commission
           Education beyond apartheid. Johannesburg:
           Sprocas, 1971, (Study Project on Christianity
           in Apartheid Society. Sprocas publication,
           no. 6), 89 p.

           The Commission interprets education in three distinct
           but inter-related ways, namely becoming educated,
           society's need for the social development of the child,
           and thirdly, state and private institutions organized
           to meet the realization of the latter two points.

977   STUDY PROJECT ON CHRISTIANITY IN APARTHEID SOCIETY.
           Legal Commission
           Law, justice and society, edited by Peter
           Randall. Johannesburg: Sprocas, 1972, (Study
           Project on Christianity in Apartheid Society.
           Sprocas publication, no. 9), 100 p.

           Directed at the general public, and the legal
           profession in particular, these papers have as their
           common theme 'the debasing effect apartheid has had
           upon the law, the legal profession and the officers of
           the law.' With their focus on law operative in society,
           these papers are published under the names of the
           authors and prefaced by a joint statement by members of
           the Commission. The papers are listed under the
           following headings: the image of the law in the minds
           of white South Africans, by J.F. Croaker; apartheid
           legislation and an inherited understanding of the law,
           by Jack Unterhalter; South African lawyers and the
           liberal heritage of the law, by John Dugard; apartheid,
           the courts and the legal profession, by N.M. MacArthur;
           difficulties facing black South Africans in exercising
           their legal rights, by W. Lane and A.P.F. Williamson;
           the police in the apartheid society, by Barend van
           Niekerk; apartheid and administrative bodies, by Colin
           Kinghorn; change and methods of change, by D.B.
           Molteno. Includes a brief bibliography.

978   STUDY PROJECT ON CHRISTIANITY IN APARTHEID SOCIETY.
         Political Commission.
         South   Africa's   political   alternatives.
         Johannesburg: Ravan, 1973, (Study Project on
         Christianity   in Apartheid   Society. Sprocas
         publication, no. 10), 252 p.

         Proposals for political change in South Africa are
         assessed within clearly defined terms of reference: 'to
         enunciate   the   ethical   considerations   applying
         particularly to political life; to assess the present
         political   situation in South Africa in the light of
         these considerations; and finally, to consider the
         political and constitutional implications of (a) an
         equitable sharing of political rights and (b) a removal
         of discriminatory laws and practices in South Africa'.
         Provides a detailed two-stage Model for Transition, to
         which is appended a dissenting report by Edgar H.
         Brookes, and Denis Worrall gives his reasons for not
         signing the Report.

979   STUDY PROJECT ON CHRISTIANITY IN APARTHEID SOCIETY.
         Social Commission.
         Towards social change,   edited by   Peter
         Randall. Johannesburg: Sprocas, 1971, (Study
         Project on Christianity in Apartheid Society.
         Sprocas publication no. 6), 197 p.

         Analyzes the nature of the apartheid society and
         factors   underlying injustice.   Speculates on the types
         of basic changes which are likely to occur. Chapters
         are contributed by F. van Zyl Slabbert on cultural and
         ethnic politics; social organizations and change, by
         M.G. Whisson; change through institutional network, by
         L.   Douwes Dekker; H. Lever presents a practical
         programme to reduce inter-group tensions and Lawrence
         Schlemmer, strategies for change.

980   STULTZ, Newell Maynard
           Afrikaner politics in South Africa: 1934-
           1948. Berkeley: University of California
           Press, 1974, (Perspective on Southern Africa,
           13), 200 p.

           Based on the author's doctoral dissertation, this study
           examines the rapid growth of Afrikaner nationalism.
           Pays particular reference to the political implications
           of Jan Smuts' insistence that the Union Government
           should declare war on Germany in 1939, and the
           consequences of that decision for the 1948 elections.

981   STULTZ, Newell Maynard
           Consociational engineering in South Africa.
           Journal of Contemporary African Studies, vol.
           2, no. 2, April 1983, p. 287-317

           Defines the concept which came to be applied to the
           consideration of South Africa's racial problems by
           1973. The author, a Professor of Political Science at
           Brown University, reviews the process of constitutional
           adaptation from 1976. Includes both criticism and
           reasons for its defence in an attempt to assess the
           feasibility of applying consociationalism in the
           Republic.

982   STULTZ, Newell Maynard
           Interpreting constitutional change in South
           Africa.   Journal of Modern African Studies,
           vol. 22, no. 3, September 1984, p. 353 - 379

           An investigation of the 1983 constitution taking
           account of differing perceptions of the reform concept.
           Arguments presented by the Progressive Federal Party
           leader Frederik van Zyl Slabbert against the 1983
           constitutional bill are considered under the headings
           of unilateralism, black exclusion, concentration of
           powers and constitutional discrimination. Advances the

analytical problems evident in evaluating the changes, and assesses the status of the government in power at the time of writing.

983   STULTZ, Newell Maynard
The nationalists in opposition, 1934-1948. Cape Town: Human and Rousseau, 1974, 168 p.

Surveys a formative period in South Africa's political history beginning with the establishment of the United Party and ending with the victory of Afrikaner nationalists in an attempt to ascertain reasons for growth of the latter. Devotes considerable attention to the 1948 elections.

984   STULTZ, Newell M.
Thinking about South Africa from afar. Johannesburg: South African Institute of International Affairs, 1985, 10 p.

Debates the sanctions issue, and presents various models and approaches which could be utilized in accelerating change in the Republic. Comments on American policy towards South Africa given the introduction of anti-apartheid legislation.

985   STULTZ, Newell Maynard
Transkei's half loaf: race separation. Cape Town: Philip, 1980, 183 p.

Contributes to the debate on race separatism as a method of reducing racial conflict within the Southern African region, with specific focus on 'whether the existence of Transkei as an independent state contributes to an increase in racial justice in the region, lessens the chance for racial justice, or is irrelevant to the matter'. Compares Transkei's resources to that of 'white' South Africa, and by assessing prevalent conditions, illustrates its lack of economic viability and dependence on the Republic. Assesses the political decision-making that promoted the Transkei nevertheless to accept independence, the benefits of this action, and their distribution. Developments during the first year of independence are critically examined prior to analyzing the significance of Transkei independence and the implications of its isolation.

986   STULTZ, Newell Maynard
       Who goes to Parliament? Grahamstown: Rhodes University, Institute of Social and Economic Research, 1975, (Rhodes University, Institute of Social and Economic Research. Occasional paper, no. 19), 106 p.

Analyzes biographical data on the 1 169 men and twelve women, all whites, who made up South Africa's political elite during the first sixty years after Union in an attempt to further the understanding of Parliament itself and the political power of the country's leaders.

987   SUCKLING, John (and others)
       The economic factor, by John Suckling, Ruth Weiss and Duncan Innes. London: Africa Publication Trust for the Study Project on External Investment in South Africa and Namibia (South West Africa), 1975, 198 p.

Identifies areas in which foreign investment strengthens the economy and comprises five papers germane to the debate: the nature and role of foreign investment in South Africa by John Suckling; the role of foreign loans in South Africa's economic growth by Ruth Weiss; the role of para-statals in South Africa by Ruth Weiss; South Africa and its hinterland: the role of Africa in South Africa's economic and political strategy by Ruth Weiss; and the role of foreign trade and industrial development in South Africa by Duncan Innes. Appendix contains extensive statistical data.

988   SURPLUS PEOPLE PROJECT
           Forced removals in South Africa. Cape Town: The Project, 1983, 5 vols.

Volume 1 provides a general overview; volume 2 concentrates on the Eastern Cape; volume 3 on the Western and Northern Cape, and Orange Free State, volume 4 on Natal and volume 5 on the Transvaal.

989   SUTCLIFFE, M.O. and WELLINGS, P.A.
           Disinvestment and black worker 'attitudes' in South Africa: a critical comment. Durban: University of Natal, 1984?, 35 p.

Provides a critique of a questionnaire survey on black worker attitudes q.v. conducted by Professor Lawrence Schlemmer of the University of Natal, Durban. Discussion focusses on sampling problems and statistical errors prevalent in the report.

990   SUTTNER, Raymond
           The Freedom Charter - the people's charter in the nineteen-eighties. Cape Town: University of Cape Town, 1984, 31 p.

The twenty-sixth T.B. Davie Memorial Lecture, delivered at the University of Cape Town on 26 September 1984 at which Suttner recalls and discusses the origins of the Charter, its relevance as a popular document, several of its key clauses and its place in contemporary democratic struggles. A slightly revised edition is published in South Africa International, vol. 15, no. 4, April 1985, p. 233-252.

991   SUTTNER, Raymond
Political trials and the legal process.
South African Review, 2, 1984, p. 63-75

Characteristics of the modern South African political
trial are identified, taking into consideration the
goals of the state. The response of the accused and the
public are reviewed. Concludes by providing an
explanation of modifications under the 'new
dispensation'.

992   SUTTNER, Raymond and CRONIN, Jeremy
30 years of the Freedom Charter, with
contributions by 'Terror' Lekota (and
others). Johannesburg: Ravan, 1986, 266 p.

Present an account of the Congress of the People
campaign and the creation of the Freedom Charter, based
on interviews with, and documentation from participants. Includes an analysis of its relevance to
workers, women, education, culture, and churches. The
text of the Charter is reproduced.

993   SWAN, Maureen
Gandhi: the South African experience.
Johannesburg: Ravan, 1985, 310 p.

Critically assesses Gandhi's role in South African
Indian politics during the period 1894 to 1914,
examining both its effect on his political style, and
his own contribution. Viewed within the context of the
Natal and Transvaal Indian communities, rather than
'above them', the author finds that his 'contribution
to South African Indian politics has been greatly
overstated. The role of "leader" which is generally
attributed to him is entirely inappropriate before 1906
and must be carefully qualified for the period after
1906'.

994   SWAN, Maureen
           The 1913 Natal Indian strike. Journal of
           Southern African Studies, vol. 10, no. 2,
           April 1984, p. 239-258

           In this detailed analysis of a strike, by the Indian
           workers, unprecedented in scale, Swan attempts to
           ascertain reasons for its occurrence; its particular
           timing; its widespread nature; reasons for its lengthy
           duration; and why it necessitated such brutal
           suppression.

995   SWANSON, Maynard W.
           The "Asiatic menace": creating segregation in
           Durban, 1870-1900. International Journal of
           African Historical Studies, vol. 16, no. 3,
           1983, p. 401-442

           Investigates Natal's nineteenth century urban
           development and the mentality of colonial authority.
           The rise of the Indian community, and the attitude
           toward them by whites is assessed.

996   SWILLING, Mark
           Stayaways, urban protest and the state.
           South African Review, 3, 1986, p. 20-50

           Examines the stayaway tactic, focussing on specific
           instances in the Transvaal in November 1984, and in the
           Port Elizabeth-Uitenhage area during March 1985, which
           are compared in both instances. These were studied by
           the Labour Monitoring Group (LMP) and their findings
           are presented. Responses of the state, capital and the
           black petty bourgeoisie to this tactic are briefly
           considered.

997   SWITZER, Les and SWITZER, Donna
The black press in South Africa and Lesotho:
a descriptive bibliographic guide to African,
Coloured and Indian newspapers, newsletters
and magazines 1836-1976. Boston: G.K. Hall,
1979, 307 p.

A comprehensive guide, bringing together information on
newspapers, papers and serials 'directed primarily at,
or intended for, an African, Indian or Coloured
audience'. Divided into eight categories, over 700
entries are presented, which include details of date,
frequency, language and library holdings. Notes on
nature, history and significance are included. Leo
Switzer has further focussed on the privately-owned
commercial press, its relationship to the state, and
the role of the press in promoting dependency among the
black population in his work entitled: Media and
dependency in South Africa: a case study of the press
and the Ciskei "homeland", published as Africa series
no 47, of the Ohio University. Monographs in
international studies, 1985, 85 p.

998   SYMPOSIUM on Pertinent Issues of Local Government and
Administration in Natal. University of
Durban-Westville. Journal. New Series, 1,
1984, p. 171-254

Comprises the following articles: role of councillors
and officials in local government and administration,
by J.J.N. Cloete; financing of black local authorities
in Natal: existing and new sources of revenue, by G.S.
Nieuwoudt; personnel provisioning and utilisation at
local government level in Natal, by W.A.J. Coetzee; a
policy for urban development in Natal by, M.A.H. Smout.
The symposium was held at the University of Durban-
Westville on 28-29 November 1983 under the joint
auspices of the South African Institute of Public
Administration, (Natal Branch) and the University of
Durban-Westville.

999   TALKING with the ANC. Pretoria: Bureau for Information,
        1986, 42 p.

        Provides the South African government's interpretation
        on   the African National Congress, as well   as
        elaborating on both its, and the ANC's position on
        violence,   negotiations,   multi-party democracy, and
        foreign policy, among others. Widely distributed, this
        booklet was issued during one of the shuttle visits of
        the Emminent Persons Group between the South African
        government and the ANC.

1000   TAMBO, Oliver
        Oliver Tambo, President, the African National
        Congress, interviewed by Margaret A. Novicki.
        Africa Report, vol. 30, no. 4, July/August
        1985, p. 32-36

        Discusses objectives of the African National Congress,
        in the light of South African unrest.

1001   TAMBO, Oliver
        Racism, apartheid and a new world order.
        Third World Quarterly, vol. 8, no. 3, July
        1986, p. xiii-xxii

        This Third World Lecture 1986, was delivered on
        receiving the Third World Prize for 1985, on behalf of
        Nelson and Winnie Mandela, in Kuala Lumpur, 5 May 1986.
        Pays tribute to those involved in the struggle against
        racism.

1002   TAMBO, Oliver
        Storm over South Africa. World Marxist Review,
        vol. 29, no. 1, January 1986, p. 83-89

        The President of the African National Congress comments
        on the level of the liberation struggle in South
        Africa, ANC strategies and the reaction to the state of
        emergency declared by the government.

1003   TATZ, C.M.
         Shadow and substance in South Africa: a study
         in land and franchise policies affecting
         Africans, 1910-1960. Pietermaritzburg:
         University of Natal Press, 1962, 238 p.

         Illustrates the connection between territorial
         segregation and deprivation of black political
         representation in the fifty years after Union. As the
         origins are evident in the period prior to 1910, an
         analysis of both the colonial franchise laws pertaining
         to blacks and the Report of the South African Native
         Affairs Commission of 1903 to 1905 are included in this
         chronologically arranged examination. It covers the
         foundation of the union's land policy, 1910 to 1913;
         attempts at uniform land segregation, 1913 to 1920;
         Hertzog;s 'solution' of the 'Native Problem', 1921 to
         1926; his efforts to implement this policy, 1927 to
         1935; the 1936 legislation, African representation,
         1937 to 1948; the National Party and Apartheid, 1948 to
         1958; Dr Verwoerd and 'separate development' and
         reactions to this policy.

1004   TEMKIN, Ben
         Gatsha Buthelezi: Zulu statesman, a
         biography. Cape Town: Purnell, 1976, 413 p.

         Divided into two parts, this work initially provides a
         chronological account of Buthelezi's life until the
         inauguration of the KwaZulu Legislative Assembly in
         1972. Subsequently, various issues relating to KwaZulu
         and Buthelezi's role in the country's political
         history, are separately treated. Included in the
         appendix are extracts from the Inkatha's Constitution.

1005   TEMPLIN, J. Alton
         Ideology on a frontier: the theological
         foundation of Afrikaner nationalism 1652-
         1910. Westport: Greenwood, 1984, 360 p.

Concentrates on the religious aspects of early Afrikaner nationalism, tracing its development from Jan van Riebeeck's arrival at the Cape until the proclamation of Union in 1910.

1006   TERBLANCHE, H.O.
        John Vorster: OB-generaal en Afrikanervegter
        (John Vorster - Ossewabrandwag General and
        Afrikaner - fighter). Roodepoort: CUM-Boeke,
        1983, 235 p.

A detailed biography of John Vorster's early career as lawyer, promoter of Afrikaans culture, Ossewa Brandwag leader, republican and his marriage to Tini Malan.

1007   TERREBLANCHE, S.J.
        Gemeenskaparmoede: perspektief op chroniese
        armoede in die kleurlinggemeenskap na
        aanleiding van die Erika Theron- Verslag
        (Community poverty: perspectives on chronic
        poverty in the Coloured Community, in
        pursuance of the Erika Theron Report). Cape
        Town: Tafelberg, 1977, 161 p.

Highlighted by the publication of the Theron Commission, the material and spiritual poverty amongst a large part of the Coloured Community is analyzed, by an economist and member of the Commission. Reveals various lifestyles of the Coloured people ranging from the sophisticated to the poorest groups.

1008   TERRILL, W. Andrew
        South African arms sales and the
        strengthening of apartheid. Africa Today,
        vol. 31, no. 2, 1984, p. 3-13

The capabilities of South Africa's arms industry in meeting the requirements of their foreign market is examined, prior to assessing the degree to which the Republic's political influence and economic strength is enhanced by these sales. Suggests ways in which those trends could be minimized.

1009   THEIS, Nancy
        The South African black middle class: an annotated bibliography. New Haven: Yale University, Southern African Research Program, 1982, 28 p.

This bibliography is organized under the following subject headings, within which the material is alphabetically arranged and accompanied by short annotations: demographic studies; the economic position which includes standard of living, development and entrepreneurship, skilled and semi-skilled labour; urban development, including the position in both the townships and homelands; the homelands; social characteristics - religious, educational and cultural; case studies of particular elites.

1010   The THERON Commission Report: an evaluation and an early reaction to the Report and its recommendations, edited by O.D. Wollheim. Johannesburg: South African Institute of Race Relations, 1977, 39 p.

An assessment of the Report, taking cognizance of the economic, socio-cultural, and political position of the Coloured person as well as reactions by the press and public.

1011   THOMPSON, Clive
        Black trade unions on the mines. South African Review, 2, 1984, p. 156-164

Outlines the attitude of the Chamber of Mines to the emerging black unions on the mines, which have proliferated, although signs of rationalization are evident. Briefly identifies the different unions prior to describing the strategies, negotiations and disputes involving the National Union of Mineworkers.

1012   THOMPSON, Leonard M.
Afrikaner nationalist historiography and the policy of apartheid. Journal of African History, vol. 3, no. 1, 1962, p. 125-141

Reviews the contributions of historians and other academics to the Afrikaner national mythology and to the apartheid policy of the National Party, revealing an emphasis on anglophobic and negrophobic elements.

1013   THOMPSON, Leonard M.
The political mythology of apartheid. New Haven: Yale University Press, 1985, 293 p.

Places the concepts of political myth and political mythology within a theoretical framework prior to utilizing South Africa as a test case. The context within which Afrikaner nationalism was developed and propagated is examined and its racial nature highlighted. Identifies and provides accounts of specific myths such as the Slagtersnek Rebellion, and the defeat of the Zulus at the Battle of Blood River in 1838. An explanation of the adaptation and erosion of Afrikaner nationalist mythology since the 1948 gain of government control by Afrikaners. Concludes by raising general questions on the role of political mythology in the light of the South African case study. Reviewed in New Republic, 23 December 1985, p. 30-31.

1014   THOMPSON, Leonard M.
Politics in the Republic of South Africa. Boston: Little, Brown, 1966, 228 p.

Provides an insight into ways in which political power operates in the Republic. He provides a case both for and against the Government, as well as commenting on the international effects of South African policy. The political system is placed within its historical, demographic and economic background, prior to a presentation of the framework of political life and the operation of the system. Both internal and external opposition is examined in some detail.

1015   THOMPSON, Leonard M. and PRIOR, Andrew
        South African politics. Cape Town: Philip,
        1982, 255 p.

Provides a succinct introduction to South African politics centering around an analysis of political power as it actually operates within the Republic. Places this discussion within its historical, demographic, economic and international contexts. Reviewed by Lucy Mair in African Affairs, vol. 82,.no. 329, October 1983, p. 592-593.

1016   THOMPSON, Leonard M.
        The unification of South Africa, 1902-1910.
        Oxford: Clarendon Press, 1960, 549 p.

A detailed history of the movement towards Union in South Africa, based largely on primary sources. Examines the origins of the principal features of the South African Constitution, the fieldwork leading to the convening of a National Convention, its role and findings, reactions of the four colonial parliaments, approval, and enactment of the Constitution in England.

1017   TOTAL war in South Africa: militarisation and the
        apartheid state. Johannesburg: NUSAS, 1982,
        88 p.

        Examines the South African Defence Force in some depth,
        paying particular attention to its development,
        including the incorporation of women and blacks and its
        role within the 'total onslaught' concept. Includes a
        chapter on the 'war economy' in which the private
        sector's relationship with the Defence Force is
        examined, emphasizing the arms industry. The SADF
        operative in Namibia, the regional destabilization
        policy and activity within the Republic is studied as
        is its increasing influence over the educational
        system.

1018   TÖTEMEYER, Gerhard
        Legitimacy and viability: a critical analysis
        of the new South African constitution (Act
        no. 110 of 1983) with special emphasis on
        local government. Politikon, vol. 12, no. 2,
        December 1985, p. 59-65

        Tömeyer, a member of the Department of Political
        Studies, University of Cape Town, describes his
        contribution: 'This article seeks to analyse the
        legitimacy and viability of the South African
        Constitution Act of 1983 with special emphasis on local
        government. Ethnicity is still underpinning the
        constitutional principle of separate local authorities
        for different population groups while the black
        population remains excluded from national decision-
        making. It is asserted that the new local government
        institutions lack in viability and legitimacy, two
        intimately related concepts, with legitimacy eroding
        rapidly in the absence of viability.'

1019   TOWN and countryside in the Transvaal: capitalist
        penetration and popular response, edited and
        introduced by Belinda Bozzoli. Johannesburg:
        Ravan, 1983, (History Workshop, 2), 446 p.

        Select proceedings of the second History Workshop held
        at the University of the Witwatersrand in February
        1981, which reveal a concern for the history and
        analysis of ordinary South Africans. The work is
        divided into four parts: class relations in the
        countryside includes papers by Modikwe Dikobe, Peter
        Delius, Stanley Trapido, Malete Nkadimeng, Georgina
        Relly, Tim Keegan and Helen Bradford. In Part Two
        entitled: Life and Culture in the Towns, contributors
        include Eddie Koch, Dunbar Moodie, Tim Couzens and Ruth
        Tomaselli. Part Three covers urban organization and
        resistance in papers by Maureen Tayal, Julia Wells,
        Eddie Webster and Tom Lodge. Part Four: Literature and
        Ideology papers by Stephen Gray and Paul B. Rich are
        presented.

1020   TRADE union membership in South Africa. South African
        Review, 3, 1986, p. 97-106

        A useful compilation of information on the following
        trade unions; Azanian Confederation of Trade Unions;
        Council of Unions of SA; Federation of SA Trade Unions;
        South African Confederation of Labour; Trade Union
        Council of SA; United Democratic Front - linked unions;
        and independent unions. Membership figures are not
        vouched for accuracy by the South African Review.

1021   TRANSKEI STUDY PROJECT
        Transkei independence, by Debbie Budlender
        (and others). Johannesburg: Wages and
        Economics Commission, c/o Students
        Representative Council, University of the
        Witwatersrand, 1976, 69 p.

The intention of this work 'is to illuminate practical aspects of Transkeian "independence" and to suggest alternative reasons - not so closely linked to the white South African's concern for justice and the human dignity of Blacks - why Apartheid is appealing to White South Africans'. In this context, the significance of 'independence' is examined, as is Transkei's economy, agriculture and migrant labour, the Xhosa Development Corporation, and the creation of an elite.

1022   TRAPIDO, Stanley
        South Africa in a comparative study of industrialization. Journal of Development Studies, vol. 7, no. 3, April 1971, p. 309-319

The peculiarities of South African society, where class, ethnic, linguistic and national cleavages overlap, tend to obscure the process which have led to industrialization. This is unfortunate because a study of South African social structures may shed light on the wider problems of development. An attempt is made in the article to compare political and economic developments in South Africa with similar developments in Tsarist Russia, Imperial Germany and the American South. It is suggested, for example, that the German 'marriage of iron and rye' has a counterpart in the relationship between maize and gold in South Africa and that similar political consequences follow. The organization of the South African mining compound is considered, in its formulating effect upon the peculiar process of urbanization in South Africa. This particular form of urbanization has resulted in the creation of a very considerable surplus for investment, the implications of which are discussed. (Author's abstract)

1023   TREURNICHT, A.P.
Credo van 'n Afrikaner (Philosophy of an Afrikaner). Cape Town: Tafelberg, 1975, 109 p.

Presents his views on political, religious and moral issues affecting Afrikaner nationalism.

1024   TROUP, Freda
South Africa: an historical introduction. London: Eyre Methuen, 1972, 428 p.

An extensive historical survey encompassing conditions prior to 1652, the Dutch East India Company, the colonies, the Volk 1948-58, Union, and the Republic until 1968. Contains many maps, illustrations, drawings and cartoons.

1025   TURFLOOP testimony: the dilemma of a black university in South Africa, edited by G.M. Nkondo. Johannesburg: Ravan, 1976, 93 p.

Elucidates on the growth of Black Consciousness at the University of the North and student unrest. Presents a memorandum prepared on the behalf of the Univeristy's Black Academic Staff Association and a questionnaire and answers, presented to the Snyman Commission of Inquiry. Appendix includes a speech on Bantu Education by Ongkopotse Ramothibi Tiro, former President of the Student's Representative Council at the University, who was elected by the students to deliver the 1972 graduation address. The speech caused his expulsion by the university authorities and subsequently further unrest erupted on the campus and at other black universities.

1026   TUTU, Desmond
            Bishop Desmond Tutu: the voice of one crying
            in the wilderness: a collection of his recent
            statements in the struggle for justice in
            South Africa, introduced and edited by John
            Webster. London: Mowbray, 1982, 125 p.

            This collection of forty-three writings constituting
            Bishop Tutu's sermons and press statements during his
            tenure as General Secretary of the South African
            Council of Churches, is divided into five parts. Part 1
            is mainly theoretical, concentrating on the emerging
            church; Part 2 focusses on the struggle for justice in
            South Africa. These papers include, among others, the
            South African problem and black protest, challenge and
            invitation to white students, papers directed to the
            white South African community and the South African
            Broadcasting Corporation, as well as on the South
            African Council of Churches and the Bishop's own
            testimony. Part 3 is headed: Windows on South Africa,
            providing insight inter alia on Steve Biko, Robert
            Sobukwe, bannings, urban unrest, and pass laws. Part 4
            concentrates on freedom, including Nelson Mandela's
            release while Part 5 looks at the challenge of the
            Eighties. Includes a paper on divided churches, women
            and the church and children's rights.

1027   TUTU, Desmond
            The question of South Africa. Africa Report,
            vol. 30, no. 1, January/February 1985, p. 50-
            52

            Text of a statement made before the United Nations
            Security Council on 23 October 1984 in which he urges
            the South African authorities to hold talks with the
            authentic representatives of all sections of the black
            community.

1028   UME, Kalu E.
        The origin of apartheid in South Africa: a
        review. Journal of African Studies, vol. 8,
        no. 4, Winter 1981/82, p. 176-181

        Traces the idea of apartheid back to the second half of
        the Seventeenth Century, taking into consideration the
        role of Christianity, the origin of passes and
        legislation dating to 1853. Briefly assesses world
        reaction as evidenced by United Nations resolutions,
        and black resistance of the earliest times.

1029   UMSEBENZI: The Voice of the South African Communist
        Party,
        1981 -
        (n.p.): The Party

        Issued approximately four times per year, this
        newsletter is written in a more popular style than the
        African Communist. It is illustrated and each issue
        comprises about twenty pages.

1030   UNGAR, Sanford J. and VALE, Peter Christopher Julius
        South Africa: why constructive engagement
        failed. Foreign Affairs, vol. 64, no. 2,
        Winter 1985/86, p. 234-258

        Itemize the limitations of the United States'
        'constructive engagement' policy as advocated by
        Chester Crocker, and argue that American attempts to
        appease the Botha Government should be halted. Instead,
        a policy of effective pressure should be implemented
        against the Nationalist Government and should encourage
        non-racial opposition in South Africa. The need for a
        balanced United States policy is urged, and the authors
        propose a series of measures which could affect the
        white South African government without inflicting undue
        damage on black South Africans.

1031   UNITED NATIONS. Centre against Apartheid
         Notes and documents
         1976 –   Irregular
         New York: United Nations

         Formerly: United Nations. Unit on Apartheid,
         Notes and documents, 1971-1975

         Investigating   all   aspects   of   apartheid   and
         international action taken against it, the following
         have been listed to provide an indication of the wide
         spectrum of material. For full lists of publications,
         the user should consult: Notes and documents, 3/81 for
         the period 1976 to 1980, and thereafter annual listing
         in special issues.

         2/76:   South Africa's defence strategy, by Abdul S.
                    Minty
         6/76:   Arms embargo against South Africa: a review
                    of resolutions by the United Nations General
                    Assembly and Security Council
         9/76:   The   United   Nations Trust Fund for South
                    Africa
         19/76:   Resolutions of the Organization of African
                    Unity in relation to South Africa
         21/76:   The   South   African miners' strike of 1946,
                    by N.P. Naicker
         7/77:   The South African situation and the attitude
                    of the Church by Denis E. Hurley
         10/77:   Police   brutality   and   the   torture   of
                    political prisoners
         18/77:   Implications   of apartheid on health and
                    health services in South Africa
         1/78:   Mrs Winnie Mandela, profile in courage and
                    defiance
         19/78:   Govan Mbeki: a South African political
                    prisoner honoured by Amsterdam University,by
                    Rob Bartlema and Johan Kortenaray

22/78:	Tribute to Canon Collins:Christian action in South Africa (1948-1978)
21/79:	Children under apartheid: report of the International Seminar on Children Under Apartheid, Paris, 18-20 June 1979
25/79:	The Wiehahn Report and the Industrial Conciliation Amendment Act: a new attack on the trade union movement in South Africa, by Michael Shafer
27/79:	Repression of conscientious objectors in South Africa
16/80:	The Sullivan Principles: no cure for apartheid
20/80:	African women and apartheid in labour matters
27/80:	Mass population removals in apartheid South Africa (1978-1980), by Barbara Rogers
13/83:	The psychiatry and psychosocial pathology of apartheid 1948-1982, by John Dommisse
15/84:	State terrorism in South Africa, by I.E. Sagay
2/85:	Children in prison: South Africa, by Fiona McLachlan
4/85:	Women in apartheid society, by Fatima Meer
12/85:	Bank loans to South Africa, from mid 1982 to December 1984, by Eva Militz
1/86:	Resolutions on apartheid adopted by the United Nations General Assembly in 1985
2/86:	International Convention against Apartheid in Sports

1032   UNITED NATIONS. Centre on Transnational Corporations
Policies and practices of transnational
corporations regarding their activities in
South Africa and Namibia. New York: United
Nations, 1984, 55 p.

Reviews their investment and disinvestment policies
from the perspective of the economic and general trend
of foreign investment in the Republic. Policies and

practices in the field of employment are examined, and their role in some strategic sectors of the economy are assessed. These include the following sectors: electronics, computer, chemical, energy and military. Annex lists both those companies operating within these strategic sectors, and those that have taken measures to terminate their activities.

1033   UNITED NATIONS EDUCATIONAL, SCIENTIFIC AND CULTURAL ORGANIZATION
Apartheid: its effect on education, science, culture and information. Paris. Unesco, 1967, 205 p.

Second revised and enlarged edition published in 1972, 256 p.

A detailed examination of the consequences of South Africa's apartheid policies for education, science, culture, and the dissemination of information.

1034   UNITED STATES. Congress. House Committee on Foreign Affairs. Subcommittee on Africa
The current crisis in South Africa. Washington, D.C.: Government Printing Office, 1985, 20 p.

In order to consider South Africa's internal political position, and set against the United States policy of constructive engagement, Bishop Desmond Tutu, as sole witness, presents testimony pertinent to the deepening crisis followed by a question and answer session.

1035   UNITED STATES. Dept of State. Office of the Historian
The United States and South Africa: U.S. public statements and related documents. Washington, D.C.: The Office, 1985, 2 vols.

405

Covering periods 1948 to 1976, and 1977 to 1985 respectively, these two volumes focus on major developments in United States foreign policy towards South Africa, and are therefore not intended to be comprehensive. These collections of documents comprise foreign policy messages, addresses, statements, press briefings, conferences, congressional testimony, and United Nations documents. Each volume is preceded by a list of contents.

1036   UNITY in action: a photographic history of the African National Congress, S. Africa, 1912-1982. London: African National Congress, 1982, 156 p.

Comprises mainly photographs.

1037   UNIVERSITY OF CAPE TOWN. History Workshop,1976. (Papers). Cape Town: University of Cape Town, Centre for Extra-Mural Studies, 1977, various pagings

A collection of four papers aimed at placing disturbances in South Africa in historical perspective. Robin Hallett presents two papers (nos 1 and 3): New winds of change: South Africa, 1966-1976 and the burden of black grievances: Soweto and Cape Town, 1976. Black power: American import or logical development of black political thought in South Africa? by Michael Maughan-Brown constitutes paper no. 2, and paper no. 4 entitled: The Cape of Storms again: an account of the unrest in the Cape Peninsula, August to September 1976 is by Elizabeth van Heyningen, Howard Phillips and David Killick.

1038   UNIVERSITY OF THE WITWATERSRAND. African Studies Institute
Seminar Papers
1972 - Irregular
Johannesburg: The Institute

A multidisciplinary collection of unpublished papers, a selection of which are published in the volumes entitled: Working papers in Southern African studies, q.v. In order to illustrate their wide-ranging scope, the following have been listed from the some 187 papers delivered to date.

1972: The political function of some religious movements in South Africa, by A.G. Schutte

1973: Black strikes, prices and trade union organisation, 1939-73, by David Hemson

1974: Major patterns of group interaction in South African society, by Michael Savage

1975: The agrarian counter-revolution in the Transvaal and the origins of segregation, by Paul B. Rich

1975: Language and religion as factors of division in the Indian Community: aspects of the South African case, by Stan Kahn

1975: The rise of Afrikanerdom as an immanent critique of Marx's theory of social class, by T. Dunbar Moodie

1976: Class in white South Africa, by Alf Stadler

1976: Ideology and capitalism in South Africa, by Alex Erwin and E. Webster

1976: The Torch Commando and the politics of white opposition in South Africa, 1951-1953 by Michael Fridjhon

1976: Liberalism and ethnicity in South African politics, 1921-1946, by Paul B. Rich

1977: Economy and society in South Africa, by Lawrence Schlemmer

1978: Political organisation and community protest: the African National Congress in the Rand townships, 1955-1957, by Tom Lodge

1978: 'Christian compounds for girls': Church hostels for African women in Johannesburg, 1907-1970, by Debbie Gaitskell

1979: Black Consciousness, by P. Horn

1979: The resistance to the extension of passes to African women 1954-1960, by Richard de Villiers

1980: Cape liberalism in its terminal phase, by P. Lewsen

1981: Political implications of industrial unrest in South Africa, by Steve Friedman

1981: Disposable nannies? The role of domestic servants in the political economy of S.A., by Jacklyn Cock

1982: The origins of a coercive labour system in South Africa, by Marian Lacey

1982: Straddling realities: the Urban Foundation and social change in contemporary S.A., by Peter Wilkinson

1983: Ideology and organization in Indian politics, 1880-1948, by Maureen Tayal

1984: The origins of the South African Reserve Bank, by Stephen Gelb

1984: The role of regional policy in South Africa, by Trevor Bell

1985: The Union, the nation and the talking crow: the ideology and tactics of the independent ICU in East London, by Colin Bundy and William Beinart

1985: A review of the Second Carnegie Commission of Enquiry into Poverty in South Africa, by Francis Wilson

1985: Class conflict, communal struggle and patriot unity: the Communist Party of South Africa, during the Second World War, by Tom Lodge

1986: Race, civilization and culture: the elaboration of segregationist discourse in the inter-war years, by Saul Dubow

1986: The disposal of the regiments: radical African opposition in Durban, 1930, by Paul la Hause

1039   UP against the fences: poverty, passes and privilege in South Africa, edited by Hermann Giliomee and Lawrence Schlemmer. Cape Town: Philip, 1985, 365 p.

Focusses on the increasing urbanization of blacks and the concomitant effect on the "homelands" from whence labour has traditionally been drawn. In this analysis of both past and present policies, and an attempt to prescribe for the future, the work comprises four main sections together with an editorial overview. The sections include rural underdevelopment; influx control and black urbanization; government policies; and the response of the private sector.

1040   URNOV, A.R.
The policy of the Republic of South Africa (English title). Moscow: Nauka Press, 1982, 150 p.

Published in Russian, this study of South Africa's foreign policy in Africa during the period 1980 to 1981 is based largely on secondary literature and documentation from the South African Communist Party, the African National Congress and works of leading members of the national liberation movement.

1041   VALE, Peter Christopher Julius
The Atlantic nations and South Africa: economic constraints and community fracture. Leicester: University of Leicester, 1980, 446 p.

Thesis: Ph.D.

In this policy-oriented study, the author examines the nature of Western interests in South Africa, particularly in the realms of trade and investment and access to strategic minerals. It explores the hypothesis that the Atlantic nations will divide as the incipient South African racial crisis deepens. This fracture will result from an uneven spread of Western interests in the abovementioned areas, which are empirically examined. At the abstract level, the study concerns itself with certain fundamental questions in the continuing debate on international political economy. (Author's summary)

1042   VALE, Peter Christopher Julius
The Botha Doctrine: Pretoria's response to the West and its neighbours. South African Review, 2, 1984, p. 188-196

Argues that alleged 'isolation' has been of a superficial nature, sheltered both by Pretoria's role in the military, economic and political policies of the Western Allies in the post-war period, and the cordon sanitaire provided by the white colonial governments of neighbouring states. Presents an explanation of the West's 'tilt' towards white South Africa in the early 1980s and the implications for the region.

1043   VALE, Peter Christopher Julius
        The compulsion to incorporate: Pretoria's Southern African policy IN: SOUTH Africa in crisis, edited by Jesmond Blumenfeld. London: Croom Helm, 1987, Chapter 10.

Explores Pretoria's involvement with Southern Africa. Vale asserts 'that regional policy is not driven by functionalism, but rather by two strains of incorporation: assertive and coercive'. He analyzes these strains of incorporation, assessing their impact on select facets of Southern African relations. Other contributions include economy in the light of international economic sanction, by Jesmond Blumenfeld; the white oligarchy, by Stanley Uys; the security forces by Simon Baynham; the constitutional options by Murray Forsyth; constitutional compromises in divided societies – a comparative comment by Adrian Guelke; is apartheid being modernised or reformed? by Merle Lipton; the black political groupings by Martin Meredith; the black trade unions, by Robin Smith; foreign policy by J.E. Spence.

1044   VALE, Peter Christopher Julius
        Pretoria and Southern Africa: from manipulation to intervention. South African Review, 1, 1983, p. 7-22

Presents historical background to South Africa's 1982 regional policy and indicates its significant move towards the use of the military option to ensure its security. Illustrates how this option became increasingly attractive due to the Republic's waning economic leverage over the region.

1045   VAN BILJON, F.J.
        State interference in South África. London: King, 1939, 322 p.

In an attempt to clarify increased state action in the South African economy, the author discusses the origin and development of these policies, and evaluates them, indicating the degree of interference. Pays particular reference to government trading, protection of manufacturing industries, agricultural development focussing on farm products and sugar economics, foreign trade policy and relations, wage and labour conditions, and oil and motor transport. Concludes by offering a synthesis and appraisal of economic policy.

1046   VAN DEN BERGHE, Pierre L.
        South Africa: a study in conflict. Berkeley: University of California Press, 1967, 371 p.

States as his objective, an analysis of South African society in its entirety, from a broad sociological perspective, illustrating the various sources of conflict which threaten the existing order. Devotes chapters to the economic system and its dysfunctions, value conflicts, external pressures and their effect on internal structures, and concludes by drawing theoretical implications based on the study.

1047   VAN DER HORST, Sheila T.
        Native labour in South Africa. London: Oxford University Press, 1942, 340 p.

Traces the developing utilization of black labour complemented by an analysis of the economic repercussions of this policy. The book is divided into three parts: Economic contact between the races before 1870, with particular reference to the British colonies of the Cape and Natal, and in the Boer Republics. In the period 1870 to 1899, the author assesses the impact of the diamond and gold discoveries on the market for black labour. Part Three focusses on the problem of competition between the races, as evidenced in the Twentieth Century. She takes particular cognisance of the supply of unskilled labour in the gold mining industry, the 'Poor White' problem and the colour bar.

1048   VAN DER VYVER, J.D.
Human rights: aspects of the dual system applying to blacks in South Africa. Comparative and International Law Journal of Southern Africa, vol. 15, no. 3, 1982, p. 306-318

Evaluates, from a human rights standpoint, South Africa's variety of dual or plural systems, and focusses particularly on how blacks are affected.

1049   VAN HELTEN, Jean Jacques
Empire and high finance: South Africa and the international gold standard 1890-1914. Journal of African History, vol. 23, no. 4, 1952, p. 529-548

Demonstrates the impact of the 1886 discovery of Witwatersrand gold on the operation of the international gold standard. Author suggests that South African gold eased international liquidity problems by facilitating an expansion of the gold base and money supplies. Considers in detail the resultant London network of brokerage, insurance, refining and marketing facilities, and the role of the Bank of England in particular.

1050   VAN JAARSVELD, F.A.
        The awakening of Afrikaner nationalism, 1868-
        81. Cape Town: Human & Rousseau, 1961, 258 p.

        Traces the origins and development of the Afrikaner
        national consciousness into nationalism which the
        author perceives as a reaction to the Imperial Factor
        in South Africa. Accordingly provides background
        information detailing imperial actions and subsequent
        Afrikaner reaction.

1051   VAN NIEKERK, W.P. and HEATH, E.T.
        An investigation into the Mdantsane/East
        London bus boycott. Port Elizabeth:
        University of Port Elizabeth, Institute for
        Planning Research, 1984, (University of Port
        Elizabeth, Institute for Planning Research,
        Special publications, no. 8), 99 p.

        Identified as one of the major contemporary
        problems of this area, the boycott is analyzed in-
        depth providing general information and related
        problems, a chronological outline, reasons for
        the boycott, and suggested solutions. Based
        extensively on personal interviews.

1052   VAN ONSELEN, Charles
        Studies in the social and economic history of
        the Witwatersrand, 1886-1914. Johannesburg:
        Ravan, 1982, 2 vols.

        In these two volumes, the author sets the social history
        of Johannesburg within the context of the industrial
        revolution which transformed the Witwatersrand at the
        turn of the century. He concentrates on the period 1886-
        1914 and demonstrates the effect of industrialization on
        the ordinary lives of the city's inhabitants over which
        the ruling classes asserted their control. Volume 1: New
        Babylon, the liquor sellers, the prostitutes and cab

414

drivers form the basis of the work, while Volume 2, New Nineveh, is concerned with domestic labour, Johannesburg's Afrikaners, and the Witwatersrand's lumpenprotelarian army.

1053   VAN SCHOOR, M.C.E. and VAN ROOYEN, Jan J.
        Republieke en republikeine. (Republics and republicans). Cape Town: Nasionale Boekhandel, 1960, 244 p.

Explores the long history of republicanism within Afrikaner thought and tradition liking it to Dutch and British concepts.

1054   VAN VUUREN, Nancy
        Women against apartheid: the fight for freedom in South africa, 1920-1975. Palo Alto: R & E Research Associates, 1979, 133 p.

Evaluates and describes the status of women in South Africa for the decades from the nineteen twenties to the mid seventies. Appendices include the Suppression of Communism Act, 1950; the Native Laws Amendment Act, 1952; and the Freedom Charter, 1955. Study contains extensive statistical data.

1055   VAN VUUREN, Willem
        Domination through reform: the functional adaption of legitimizing strategies. Politikon, vol. 12, no. 2, December 1985, p. 47-58

Van Vuuren, head of the Department of Political Science at the University of the Western Cape, abstracts his article as follows: This article offers a framework for the critical analysis of reform as a factor for stabilizing existing relations of domination in South Africa. For this purpose it presents a working definition of domination and focuses on two interacting areas of the government's reform strategy. On the one hand it considers reform as manifested in a formal process of constitutional change, and on the other hand, it views reform as reflected in shifting ideological stances.

1056   VAN WYK, Koos
        Elite opinions on South African foreign policy. Johannesburg: Research Project on South Africa's Foreign Relations, 1984. (Research Project on South Africa's Foreign Relations. Occasional paper, no. 1), 51 p.

The author presents a comprehensive and empirical survey of elite opinion on South African foreign policy. The seven elite groups which he anaylzes are politicians, bureaucrats, the media, academics, businessmen, blacks, coloureds and Indians.

1057   VATCHER, William Henry
        White laager: the rise of Afrikaner nationalism. London: Pall Mall, 1965, 309 p.

Focusses on the evolution of the Afrikaner nationalist movement and factors contributing to its development, which the author has placed in political perspective. The role and known focus on the Afrikaner Broederbond are presented, and the impact of Nazism, and the roles of both the Afrikaner press and Dutch Reformed Church are examined.

1058   VAWDA, Shahid
        Worker action in the post-1973 period: a preliminary analysis. University of Durban Westville, Journal. New Series, 1, 1984, p. 117-138

As indicated by the title, this analysis concentrates on the development of trade unions, both non-racial and black, and the subsequent implications for industrial relations. Relevant labour history issues are included. The role of workers is emphasized and the argument propounded for a reassessment of working class life, culture and organizations, and their contribution to the Republic's development.

1059   VERWOERD, H.F.
Verwoerd speaks, 1948-1966, edited by A.N. Pelzer. Johannesburg: APB Publishers, 1966, 735 p.

A selection of Dr Verwoerd's speeches dating from 1958 when he assumed the Prime Ministership of South Africa, to the end of 1962, although other important speeches have been included. They have been translated into English where necessary, and their focus is on the evolution of Dr Verwoerd's separate development policies.

1060   VICKERY, Kenneth P.
'Herrenvolk' democracy: egalitarianism in South Africa and the U.S. South. Comparative Studies in History and Society, vol. 16, 1983, p. 309-328

Concentrates on the Nineteenth and early Twentieth Century during which time there were periods comprising certain parallels in the histories of the two regions under discussion. Highlights movements for increased democracy among the whites and greater oppression for the blacks. Lower-class South African whites were more successful than their American counterparts in attaining economic gains and security. Reaction to the presence of Imperial Britain is noted and discussed.

1061   The VOICE of the miner. Mozambican Studies, no. 1,
1980, p. 75-88

Illustrates, through the medium of interviews and songs
translated by Alpheus Manghezi, the socio-economic
impact on Mozambican migrant labour to South Africa.

1062   VOICES of liberation in Southern Africa: the perimeter
of the white bastion; statements by leaders
of liberation movements in Rhodesia,
Mozambique, Angola, and Namibia, with some
views of leaders of independent African
countries, edited by Wolf Roder. Waltham
Mass.: African Studies Association, 1972,
95 p.

Provides insights into the status of the liberation
struggle and illustrates the interrelationship among
white minority and colonial governments, highlighting
South Africa's role.

1063   VOLLENHOVEN, Sylvia
South Africa at the crossroads. Third World
Quarterly, vol. 8, no. 2, April 1986, p. 486-
506

Charters events in the Republic which culminated in the
declaration of a state of emergency in July 1985,
analyzing the underlying causes of the continued
unrest. She pays particular attention to the exclusion
of blacks from politics, the educational system and the
impact of unemployment. Outlines the forms of the 1983
constitution which generated extra-parliamentary
opposition such as the United Democratic Front and the
National Forum.

1064   VOSLOO, W.B. (and others)
Local government in Southern Africa, by W.B.
Vosloo, D.A. Kotzé, and W.J.O. Jeppe.
Pretoria: Academica, 1974, 291 p.

Surveys general characteristics of local government
institutions and administration in order to provide a
comparative study of trends prevalent in Southern
Africa. Two chapters are devoted to South Africa, where
local government is studied in both the white and black
areas of the country.

1065   VUKANI MAKHOSIKAZI COLLECTIVE
South African women speak. London: Catholic
Institute for International Relations, 1985,
266 p.

This book was written by a Johannesburg-based women's
collective comprising Jane Barrett, Aneene Dawber,
Barbara Klugman, Ingrid Obery, Jennifer Shindler and
Joanne Yawitch. It relfects the lives of black working
class women under apartheid. Based on numerous
interviews, this study concentrates on their struggle
to make ends meet, taking rising rents and high costs
into consideration. The need for adequate housing,
child care facilities and the fight for a society free
from class exploitation and racial and sexual
oppression forms the basis of this work.

1066   WALKER, Cherryl
Women and resistance in South Africa. London:
Onyx Press, 1982, 309 p.

Walker clarifies the scope of her work by stating that
it traces the development of a women's movement in
South Africa, within the context of the national
liberation movement, from 1910 to the early 1960s. The
book's main focus is the Federation of South African
Women and its history during the period 1954 to 1963,

but she also provides information on the growth of political organizations among women. Divided into two parts, 1910 to 1939 and 1939 to 1953, this survey is set 'against the background of the economic changes restructuring their position in society'. Takes into consideration contributions of the African National Congress, the Communist Party of South Africa, the South African Indian Congress, as well as certain trade unions and grassroots organizations.

1067   WALSHE, Peter
        Church versus state in South Africa: the case
        of the Christian Institute. London: Hurst,
        1983, 234 p.

Details the activities, development and influence of the Christian Institute from its founding in 1963 until it was banned in 1977. Demonstrates its increasing involvement in the Black Consciousness Movement including Black Theology, which harmonized with the Institute's evolving liberation theology.

1068   WALSHE, Peter
        The rise of African nationalism in South
        Africa: the African National Congress 1912–
        1952. London: Hurst, 1970, 480 p.

Describes the evolution of African nationalism within the complexities of South Africa's racial structure. Policies, attitudes and organization of the ANC from its foundation until the Defiance Campaign of 1952 are recorded in depth in an attempt to illustrate its alternative to apartheid.

1069   WARWICK, Peter
        Black people and the South African War, 1899–
        1902. Cambridge: Cambridge University Press,
        1983, (African studies series, 40), 226 p.

Chronicles the role, significance and experiences of blacks participating on both sides of the Anglo-Boer War. Illustrates ways in which they were affected, providing insights into the war's social history.

1070   WASSENAAR, A.D.
        Assault on private enterprise: the freeway to communism. Cape Town: Tafelberg, 1977, 154 p.

Defines Marxist principles, and by providing a comprehensive analysis of the South African economy, attempts to demonstrate that the country, which proffers to be anti-communist, is adopting various facets of communism by stifling a free economy.

1071   WATSON Graham
        Passing for white: a study of racial assimilation in a South African school. London: Tavistock, 1980, 130 p.

Focusses on the Colander High School in Cape Town, officially a 'white' school but one in which Coloureds passed as white. Author examines the social structure in the school, its relationship to the government's apartheid policies, and to the community. Attitudes of the teachers and roles of the Principal and Vice-Principal are assessed in this sociological study.

1072   WEAVER, Tony
        The President's Council. South African Review, 1, 1983, p. 114-121

Analyzes the structure and role of the Council and its proposals which the author sees as the symbol of restructuring the state. He elaborates on the idea that '. . . They represent an attempt to enlarge and recast class alliances which form the dominant bloc in South African society . . .'.

1073   WEBSTER, Eddie
Cast in a racial mould: labour process and trade unionism in the foundries. Johannesburg: Ravan, 1985, 299 p.

Analyzes the nature of work and worker resistance in the metal industry which lies at the core of South Africa's manufacturing industry. It illustrates how white craft workers resisted deskilling, and more recently, how black workers have begun to organize into industrial unions.

1074   WEBSTER, Eddie
New force on the shop floor. South African Review, 2, 1984, p. 79-89

States that despite the recession, 1983 was a year of advancement for the emerging unions. Provides an analysis of the structures, organizational achievements and potential role of these unions in the post-Wiehahn period.

1075   WEINBERG, Eli
Portrait of a people. London: International Defence and Aid Fund for Southern Africa, 1981, 199 p.

Records the campaigns of the African National Congress and allied organizations in a series of photographs.

1076   WEISS, Marianne
South Africa: economics and politics. A selected bibliography. Hamburg: Institute für Afrika-Kunde in conjunction with the Stiftung Deutsches Übersee-Institut, 1977, (Dokumentationsdienst Afrika, Reihe A, 15), 169 p.

The Africa Documentation Center defines their reasons for publishing this bibliography as taking cognisance of the problems and changes within the region that affect South Africa by providing an idea of the bourgeoning studies on the Republic. 1 047 references emphasize the political, economic, and social conditions of the blacks within South Africa's political system; the system of domination; role of the opposition, both black and white; and the possibilities of political change. Entries are briefly annotated, and a useful innovation for users in the Federal Republic of Germany, is the use of library codes indicating the location of each document.

1077   WEISSMAN, Stephen
        Dateline South Africa: the opposition speaks.
        Foreign Policy, 58, Spring 1985, p. 151-170

Weissman participated in a 1984 Congressional Foreign Affairs Committee staff study mission to South Africa, and in this article expresses his own views on United States lack of action against apartheid. Concerned with the government's attempt to relocate the inhabitants of Mgwali, a 'black spot' as part of a wider pattern, Weissman notes increased organization of resistance in the form of the United Democratic Front, the African National Congress and the trade unions. Presents a resumé of attitudes towards the disinvestment controversy.

1078   WELLS, Julia
        Passes and bypasses: freedom of movement for African women under the Urban Areas Act of South Africa IN: AFRICAN women and the law: historical perspectives, edited by Margaret Jean Hay and Marcia Wright. Boston: Boston University, African Studies Center, 1982, p. 126-150

Focusses on the shift of state dominance from the international to national capitalist interests, mainly from mining to secondary industries. Illustrates how women's freedom from pass laws served the interests of the latter until the ascendancy of agricultural interests ended this freedom in 1948.

1079   WELLS, Julia
Why women rebel: a comparative study of South Africa's women's resistance in Bloemfontein (1913) and Johannesburg (1958). Journal of Southern African Studies, vol. 10, no. 1, October 1983, p. 55-70

Women's anti-pass resistance is illustrated by two case studies which occurred fifty year's apart. Provides details of the political background and a summary of events relating to the two episodes, prior to analyzing reasons for the commitment. Both case studies are more extensively examined in her Ph D thesis entitled: The history of South African Women's resistance to Pass Laws 1900-1960. (Columbia University-Teachers College, 1982).

1080   WELSH, David
Constitutional changes in South Africa. African Affairs, vol. 83, no. 331, April 1984, p. 147-162

Gives reasons why the National Party instituted a new constitution for South Africa. This initiated significant changes in the political system but ensured the control of political power to the whites. Welsh, Professor of African Government at the University of Cape Town, describes the provisions of the Constitution Act. Does not purport to assess in any detail the prospects for its operation but in his view there is little chance for success.

424

1081 WELSH, David
   The cultural dimension of apartheid. <u>African</u>
   <u>Affairs</u>, vol. 71, no. 282, January 1972, p.
   35-53

   Illustrates, by chronicling its development from the
   earliest times, how cultural segregation has been part
   of the technique of domination and a response to the
   assumed threat posed by a growing class of accultivated
   Africans.

1082 WELSH, David
   The roots of segregation: native policy in
   colonial Natal, 1845-1910. Cape Town: Oxford
   University Press, 1971, 381 p.

   Author substantiates his theory that 'it is a myth that
   apartheid is the exclusive product of Afrikaner
   nationalism: its antecedents are to be found in Natal
   rather than in any of the other provinces'. He divides
   the period under review into two distinct sections. In
   the first to 1876, Welsh assesses the role and
   significance of Sir Theophilus Shepstone's policies of
   African administration. In remaining chapters, he
   attempts to account for the survival of Shepstone's
   policies. The attitude of the colonists, the
   contribution of the missionaries, particularly to black
   education, and the change in the black social structure
   forms part of this study.

1083 WELSH, David
   South Africa: power, process and prospect.
   Cape Town: University of Cape Town, 1982,
   27 p.

   See also: <u>Journal of Contemporary African</u>
   <u>Studies</u>, vol. 2, no. 2, April 1983, p. 319-
   351.

In his inaugural lecture delivered on 14 April 1982, Professor Welsh 'plunges into the thickets of academic controversies in the field of Southern African studies' and provides a substantiated review of its historiography. Pays particular attention to the issue of race.

1084   WENTZEL, Wilfred
         Poverty and development in South Africa
         (1890-1980): a bibliography. Cape Town:
         Southern Africa Labour and Development
         Research Unit, 1982, (Southern African Labour
         and Development Research Unit. Saldru working
         paper, 46), 170 p.

Undertaken specifically for the second Carnegie Inquiry into Poverty and Development, the compiler says of his choice of material on poverty 'to let these speak for themselves in places, to offer limited guidance in others and to keep analytical judgement in suspense for the time being'. Entries range from the unannotated to those with fairly extensive annotations and are arranged in the ten categories which follow, together with further chronological subdivisions: general - non-South African; general - South African; agriculture; education; health and nutrition; housing; living standards; unemployment; urbanization (relocation); welfare (social services). Many commissions of inquiry are cited but there are no additional author or subject indices.

1085   WEST, Martin
         Bishops and prophets in a black city: African
         independent churches in Soweto Johannesburg.
         Cape Town: Philip, 1975, 225 p.

426

Based on two years of fieldwork among the independent churches. A preliminary general survey of 252 churches was conducted from which three different types of churches were selected for specific study and comparison. Leadership is analyzed in some detail, as is the membership of the congregation, revealing reasons for joining their churches. Networks of cooperation between individual and different churches are discussed, from both informal and formal contact aspects, and especial attention is devoted to the African Independent Churches' Association. Concludes by summarizing the attractions of the movement and placing it in perspective, especially to its urban environment.

1086   WEST, Martin
From pass courts to deportation: changing patterns of influx control in Cape Town. African Affairs, vol. 81, no. 325, October 1982, p. 463-477

Describes the 'Coloured Labour Preference Area' policy instigated in the Western Cape by Dr W.M.M. Eiselen as Secretary for Native Affairs in 1955. The resultant implications for the large numbers of black people who live and work in the area, and who are deemed illegal, are examined. Particular attention is paid to the relevant legislation, and the methods of enforcement, including deportation to Transkei. Shows that despite these measures, the tide of black urbanization has not been stemmed.

1087   WHEARE, K.C.
The Statute of Westminster and Dominion status. 5th ed. London: Oxford University Press, 1953, 347 p.

The statute and legal status of South Africa, p. 239-254; the statute and the entrenched sections of the South Africa Act, p. 339-34

1088   WHITE South African elites, a study of incumbents of top positions in the Republic of South Africa, by Hendrik W. van der Merwe (and others). Cape Town: Juta, 1974, 190 p.

Co-authored by Hendrik W. van der Merwe, M.J. Ashley, Nancy C.J. Charton and Bettina J. Huber, this study focusses on formal leadership as a basis for further research on South Africa's political process. Based on a survey completed by approximately 1 000 people, their values, careers, and attitudes are assessed in relation to the wider South African society.

1089   WHITESIDE, A. and PATEL, C.
        Agreements concerning the exmployment of foreign black labour in South Africa. Geneva: International Labour Office, 1985, 55 p.

Reprints texts of agreements with neighbouring states which provide migrant labour, prior to offering a comparative study of those treaties.

1090   WHO's Who of Southern Africa
        1907 –   Annual
        Johannesburg: Argus

Incorporating the South African Who's Who and the Central African Who's Who, this compilation provides an illustrated biographical record of prominent South Africans, Namibians, Zimbabweans as well as those from neighbouring countries and Mauritius. Also contains official guides, information on university incumbents and obituaries. The 1986/87 edition lists trade unions, their officials and affiliations, active political groups, together with official statements of their politicies, aims and objectives, and an introduction by Tom Lodge. The groups include the

African National Congress, the Afrikaner
Weerstandsbeweging, Azapo, Inkatha, Pan Africanist
Congress, the United Democratic Front and all political
parties represented in Parliament.

1091   WICKENS, R.L.
        Industrial and Commercial Workers' Union of
        Africa. Cape Town: Oxford University Press,
        1978, 222 p.

African trade unionism in South Africa is the focus of
this monograph. Traces the historical development of
the trade union in question, and discusses recognition,
the problem of trade unionization of unskilled workers,
in particular that of rural migrants and discrimination
against skilled workers, both in employment and in
trade union rights.

1092   WILKINS, Ivor and STRYDOM, Hans
        The super-Afrikaners. Johannesburg: Ball,
        1978, 450 p.

The historical development, strategies and significance
of the secret organization, the Afrikaner Broederbond,
is documented in detail, revealing its 'remarkable
campaign to harness political, social and economic
forces in South Africa to its cause of ultimate
Afrikaner domination'. Appendix contains 7 500 (about
60%) names and addresses of Broederbond members.

1093   WILKINSON, Peter
        Housing. South African Review, 1, 1983, p.
        270-277

Surveys developments in township housing after the 1976-77 'township revolt' under the following headings: self-help as an alternative to conventional housing provision; home ownership and the question of occupational tenure; and private sector involvement in the provision of African housing, the Viljoen Committee Report. Assesses the implications.

1094   WILLAN, Brian
        Sol Plaatjie: a biography. Johannesburg, Ravan, 1984, 436 p.

A biography of the first Secretary of the African National Congress, and a leader of his people. Also the author of the first novel in English by a black and a diary of the Siege of Mafeking.

1095   WILLIAMS, Donovan
        African nationalism in South Africa: origins and problems. Journal of African History, vol. 11, no. 3, 1970, p. 371-383

Traces the roots of African nationalism back to the events on the Cape Eastern Frontier during the nineteenth century. The Port Elizabeth/East London/ Alice triangle have subsequently remained a significant area for nationalist ideas and action.

1096   WILSON, Francis
        Labour in South African gold mines, 1911-1969. Cambridge: Cambridge University Press, 1972, (African studies series), 218 p.

Investigates the relationship of labour to the development of the gold mining industry, which the author places within the context of the industry's organization and financial structure. Appendices contain much statistical information.

1097   WILSON, Francis
Migrant labour: report to the South African
Council of Churches. Johannesburg: South
African Council of Churches and SPRO-CAS,
1972, 281 p.

Determines the nature and causes of South Africa's
extensive system of migrant labour. Provides in-depth
information on the utilization and consequences of
migrant labour in agriculture, mining, industrial
centres and rural areas. Compares the situation in the
Republic to the nature and extent of migrant labour in
the United States, Western Europe, South America, and
the rest of Africa. Discusses alternative strategies
available to South Africa in eliminating 'this cancer
from our society'. Substantiated by numerous tables and
statistical data.

1098   WOLDRING, Klaas
The prospects of federalism in Southern
Africa. African Review, vol. 3, no. 3, 1973,
p. 453-478

Also published in: Kroniek van Afrika, vol.
13, no. 2, 1973, p. 133-157

Presents several approaches to federal government prior
to tracing the history of federation attempts in
Southern Africa. South Africa's Africa policy is
interpreted as an attempt to maintain the status quo.
Woldring's federal suggestions are placed within a
political framework. Robert Molteno critically comments
on this contribution in the article following (p. 479-
489) entitled: Southern Africa - is federation a road
to liberation?

431

1099   WOLPE, Harold
            The analysis of the forms of the South
            African state IN: SOUTHERN African studies -
            retrospect   and   prospect.   Edinburgh:
            University of Edinburgh, Centre of African
            Studies, 1983, p. 47-71

            States that his purpose is to identify important gaps
            in the analysis of the state, through the examination
            of two opposing viewpoints that of fascist or a police
            state, and a 'racially exclusive bougeois democracy'.

1100   WOLPE, Harold
            Capitalism and cheap labour power in South
            Africa. Economy and Society, vol. 1, no. 4,
            November 1972, p. 425-456

            Identifies and explains differences between apartheid
            and segregation, by referring to the changing relations
            of capitalist and pre-capitalist modes of production.

1101   WOLPE, Harold
            The changing class structure of South Africa:
            the African petit-bourgeoisie IN: RESEARCH in
            political economy, edited by P. Zarembka. 1
            Greenwich, Conn.: Jai Press, 1977, p. 143-174

            Summarizes   briefly,   as background,   the   general
            political strategy of both the South African Communist
            Party and the African National Congress derived from
            their analysis of South Africa's social formation.
            Thereafter discusses the African   petit-bourgeoisie
            under the following sub-sections: the period 1948 to
            the mid 1960s; its considerable increase in size,
            conditions of development, and political position.

1102   WOLPE, Harold
            The deepening crisis in South Africa. Marxism
            Today, vol 26, January 1983, p. 7-11

Notes that since the 1973 strikes of the black industrial workers, South African capitalism has entered into a period of crisis which has permeated into the economic, political and ideological spheres. Defines the parameters of this crisis, examines the state's response, in particular the 'Total Strategy' concept and analyzes the effect of this response on the state and on class relations.

1103   WOLPE, Harold
       Industrialism and race in South Africa IN: RACE and racialism, edited by Sami Zubaida. London: Tavistock, 1970, p. 151-17

The emergence in South Africa of an advanced industrial economy has provided the basis for the propositions which have become central to much of the recent analysis of that society. In brief, the thesis asserts that there is a contradiction between economy and polity, between the processes of industrialization and the (racial) political system. According to one version of the thesis, the 'logical imperatives' of industrialization will transcend the contradiction by urging '. . . the polity forward beyond its (racial) ideology'. According to a second version, the power of the polity to resist and even mould the economic pressures that are contradictory to it will result in a revolutionary struggle by the non-white masses. The main purpose of this paper is to examine some of the implications and limitations of the propositions common to both versions, but, before doing so, it is necessary to set out the argument more fully. At the end of the paper, an alternative approach will be briefly considered. (Author's introduction)

1104   WOLPE, Harold
       The Solomon Mhalengu Freedom College. Ufahamu, vol. 11, no. 3, Spring 1982, p. 32-39

Places in context reasons for establishing the school in Tanzania, the content of teaching, and progress made in resolving some of the problems experienced.

1105   WOLPE, Harold
        Strategic issues in the struggle for national liberation in South Africa. Review, vol. 8, no. 2, Fall 1984, p. 232-248

        In this article, says Wolpe, my object is to identify major phases in the structuring of the political terrain since the present regime came to power in 1948, and to discuss connections with class alliances and strategic issues.

1106   WOLPE, Harold
        Towards an analysis of the South African state. International Journal of the Sociology of Law, 8, 1980, p. 399-421

        Author states that the object of his paper 'is to subject the Poulantzian and "state derivation" based work to a critical examination in order to open the way towards a radical reformulation of the theoretical means through which the substantive analysis of the South African state and politics may be more fruitfully approached.'

1107   WOLPE, Harold
        The 'white working class' in South Africa. Economy and Society, vol. 5, 1976, p. 196-240

        . . . in this paper, concepts of the 'white working class' commonly found in the literature are critically analyzed and an alternative conceptualization which begins from the mode of production is outlined. The paper ends with a brief analysis of the changes in the relationship between the white working class and the state (Author's abstract).

1108   WOMEN and changing relations of control, by Jacklyn
        Cock (and others), South African Review, 1,
        1983, p. 278-299

        Collectively compiled by Jacklyn Cock, Merle Favis,
        Avril Joffe, Shirley Miller, Kathy Sachwell, Jenny
        Schreiner, Ginny Volbrecht and Joanne Yawitch, this
        article concentrates on state intervention with regard
        to women, both in the work-place and in the household.
        Discusses in detail the process whereby women have been
        drawn into wage labour, and the complexities involved
        in the changing position of black women. Includes some
        useful tables.

1109   WOODS, Donald
        Biko.   New York: Paddington   Press,   1978,
        288 p.

        Attempts objectively to depict the life of Biko despite
        his grief and outrage over his death. Gives his
        personal memories before tracing events subsequent to
        Biko's trial which culminated in Biko's death and
        inquest.

1110   WOODWARD, Calvin A.
        Reform   or revolution in South Africa.   Round
        Table, 282, April 1981, p. 101-115

        Addresses this question from the viewpoint of the split
        in the National Party, an analysis of the counter-
        revolutionary strategy as applied by the Botha
        government and a discussion of the dynamics that will
        determine its success or failure. Takes into
        consideration black opposition and the government's
        capacity to negotiate for constitutional reform.

1111   WOODWARD, Calvin A.
        Shift in voters' loyalty in South African
        elections. Round Table, 284, October 1981,
        p. 381-391

        Provides an assessment of the April 1981 elections,
        which the author then links to the issue of reform.
        Elaborates on the fundamental realignments evidenced by
        the general election, and their significance for South
        Africa's future political history.

1112   WOODWARD, Calvin A.
        Understanding revolution in South Africa.
        Cape Town: Juta, 1983, 70 p.

        Initially considers revolution and counter-revolution
        from a theoretical viewpoint prior to applying it to
        the South African situation. Analyzes local perceptions
        of revolution, reactions to the strategies employed by
        the Nationalist government, thereafter assessing
        prospects for avoiding revolution in the Republic.
        Speculates on the type of society likely to evolve
        should the ruling party's policies be fully
        implemented.

1113   WORKING in South Africa, edited by Ken Dovey, Lorraine
        Laughton and Jo-Anne Durandt. Johannesburg:
        Ravan, 1985, 397 p.

        Comprises 129 interviews with a broad spectrum of
        people depicting their daily experience of work in
        apartheid South Africa.

1114   WORKING papers in Southern African studies.
        Johannesburg: Ravan, 1977 -
        vol. 1 edited by P. Bonner
        vol. 2 edited by P. Bonner
        vol. 3 edited by D.C. Hindson
        vol. 4 edited by T. Lodge

Multidisciplinary in character, the papers contribute to the debate on the nature of Southern African societies and represent a selection presented to the African Studies Seminar of the African Studies Institute at the University of the Witwatersrand. Select items individually indexed.

1115   WRIGHT, Harrison M.
        The burden of the present: liberal-radical controversy over Southern African history.
        Cape Town: Philip, 1977, 137 p.

Professor of History at Swarthmore College, Pennsylvania, considers the nature of South African historiography as expounded by the liberal school, and that of the radical. Methodology, approach, tendencies and possible implications of the controversy are assessed. Focusses mainly on historians, South African by birth, education or residence.

1116   WYNNE, Susan G.
        South African political material: catalogue of the Carter-Karis collection. Bloomington: Southern African Research Archives Project, 1977, 811 p.

Commissioned by the Southern African Research Archives Project, in order to facilitate access to material collected by Gwendolen M. Carter and Thomas Karis during their field trips to South Africa in 1963 and 1964. The collection appears on seventy-one reels of microfilm and its strength lies in material issued by African, Indian, and Coloured political, cultural and labour organizations. Material has been arranged according to a specifically-designed classification scheme, and access is further facilitated by an extensive index comprising mainly personal names and corporate bodies.

1117   YAWITCH, Joanne
         Betterment: the myth of homeland agriculture.
         Johannesburg: South African Institute of Race
         Relations, 1981, 102 p.

Works from the premise that the reserves and
consequently, reserve agriculture, cannot be understood
in isolation from processes that have affected South
Africa as a whole. The study, part of the Institute's
wider research project on relocation, is arranged as
follows: the relationship of both migrant labour and
the racial allocation of land to reserve agriculture;
the historical development of betterment and
agricultural planning culminating in an examination of
the Tomlinson Report, the findings of which are
summarized. Thereafter the practical aspects of
planning are discussed, as well as those pertaining to
relocation. Fieldwork, the results of which comprise
the body of this publication, was conducted in
Praktiseer, Sekhuthune, Thabamoopo, Seshego and
Sekgosese.

1118   YAWITCH, Joanne
         Women and squatting: a Winterveld case study
         IN: WORKING Papers in Southern African
         studies, vol. 2, edited by P. Bonner.
         Johannesburg: Ravan, 1981, p. 199-227

Focusses on the political economy of black women in
South Africa, and utilizes as a case study conditions
at Winterveld. This is an area approximately thirty-
five kilometres outside Pretoria and within the
'borders' of Bophuthatswana. It houses a vast
population of 'squatters'.

1119   YOUNGE, Amanda
         Housing policy and housing shortage in Cape
         Town: 1942-1980. Africa Perspective, no. 21,
         1982, p. 9-28

The author traces the desperate housing shortage in Cape Town to the state's attempts to utilize housing as a means of dividing and controlling the black working classes. Segregation along ethnic lines is examined in the state's policy of providing 'economic' housing to the wealthier sections of the 'coloured' working class, while destroying the squatter settlements. The system of differential provision has ensured that the poorest groups have suffered more severely, and that the local authorities have thus increased their control over the lives of the city's workers.

1120   YUDELMAN, David
The emergence of modern South Africa: state, capital, and the incorporation of organized labor on the South African gold fields, 1902-1939. Westport, Conn.: Greenwood, 1983, (Contributions in comparative colonial studies, no. 13), 315 p.

With particular emphasis on the production of gold in South Africa, the author seeks to place the issue of the Union's racial policies within a wider framework. He summarizes his work as 'a history concerned with the nature of the relationship between a modern state and big business, and with the dynamics of the process through which decisions were made and power exerted.'

1121   YUDELMAN, David
Industrialization, race relations and change in South Africa: an ideological and academic debate. African Affairs, vol. 74, no. 294, January 1975, p. 82-96

Analyzes contributions to, and implications of the academic debate over economic growth and social change.

1122   YUDELMAN, David
        Lord Rothschild, Afrikaner scabs and the 1907
        stike: a   state-capital   daguerrotype.
        African Affairs,   vol. 81,   no. 323,   April
        1982, p. 257-269

        Drawing on a chapter from his book: The emergence of
        modern South Africa: capital, organized labor and the
        state on the gold mines, 1902-39, q.v., the author
        examines   the   1907 white miners' strike on   the
        Witwatersrand within the context of the emerging state-
        capital relationship.

1123   ZILLE, Helen
        Restructuring the industrial decentralisation
        strategy. South African Review, 1, 1983, p.
        58-71

        Details   the new strategy for regional development   and
        illustrates   how it deviates from traditional apartheid
        policy. The necessity for this restructuring,   and its
        economic, political and ideological aims are analyzed
        in an attempt to ascertain the likelihood of its
        successful operation.

BARAYI, Elijah, 894
BARBER, James, 45, 52, 53, 54,
  55, 56, 57, 58, 902
BARKAT, Anwar M., 59
BARKER, Anthony, 192
BARRATT, Charles John Adkinson
See:
BARRATT, John
BARRATT, John, 3, 21, 60, 195,
  196, 896, 903
BARRELL, Howard, 61
BARRETT, Jane, 1065
BARTLEMA, Rob, 1031
BASKIN, Bo, 135
BAX, Douglas, 33
BAXTER, Lawrence G., 715
BAYNHAM, Simon, 1043
BEAVON, K.S.O., 598, 834
BEINART, William 62, 86, 192,
  794, 1038
BEKKER, Simon, 63, 64, 173
BELL, Trevor, 65, 66, 1038
BENBO
See:
BUREAU FOR ECONOMIC RESEARCH
  RE BANTU DEVELOPMENT
BENCH, Bryan, 67
BENDER, Gerald J., 14
BENDIX, Sonia, 460
BENJAMIN, Ann, 641
BENNETT, M., 869
BENSON, Mary, 68, 69
BENYON, John A., 193
BERGER, Iris, 70
BERMAN, John Kane-
See:
KANE-BERMAN, John
BERNSTEIN, Hilda, 71
BERRIDGE, Geoff R., 60
BESTER, Hennie, 785

BHANA, Suendra, 72, 259
BIENEN, Henry S., 483, 895
BIESHEUVEL, Simon 446
BIKO, Stephen Bantu
See:
BIKO, Steve
BIKO, Steve, 75, 76, 77, 78,
  85, 913
BISSELL, Richard E., 79, 907
BLACK RENAISSANCE CONVENTION,
  1984, 83
BLACK SASH, 842
BLOCH, Graeme, 88
BLOCH, Robin, 89
BLUMENFELD, Jesmond P., 90,
  1043
BOESAK, Allan, 33, 91, 92
BÖHMER, E.W., 93
BÖHNING, W.R., 81
BONACICH, Edna, 591
BONNER, Philip, 34, 299, 461,
  608, 960, 1114, 1118
BOOTH, D.G., 94
BOOTH, Joanna Strangewayes-
See:
STRANGEWAYES-BOOTH, Joanna
BOOYSE, Wim, 929
BOOYSEN, A.P., 258
BOOYSEN, H., 258
BOOYSEN, J.J., 598
BOOYSEN, Susan, 95
BOSCH, David, 33
BOSHOFF, J.L., 796
BOSTON UNIVERSITY. African
  Studies Center, 1078
BOTHA, P. Roelf, 96
BOTHA, P.W., 97, 98, 258
BOTTARO, Jean, 99
BOUCH, Richard, 100
BOUCHER, Maurice, 867

BOUILLON, Antoine, 37
BOULLE, Laurence J., 101, 199, 200, 554, 715, 896, 901
BOWMAN, Larry W., 102, 944
BOZZOLI, Belinda, 103, 177, 382, 546, 1019
BRADFORD, Helen, 104, 794, 813, 1019
BRAHME, G., 35
BRAND, Simon, 3, 914
BRANDEL-SYRIER, Mia, 105
BREWER, John D., 106, 107
BREYTENBACH, Willie J., 108, 109, 487
BRICKHILL, Jeremy, 114
BRINK, André, 22, 913
BRITISH ANTI-APARTHEID MOVEMENT 28
BRITISH DEFENCE AND AID FUND FOR SOUTHERN AFRICA, 227
BROEMBSEN, Max H. von, 909
BROMBERGER, Norman, 902, 908
BROMLEY, R., 834
BROOKES, Edgar H., 111, 112, 113, 978
BROOKS, Alan, 114
BROTZ, Howard, 115
BROUARD, Pierre, 116
BROUGHTON, Morris, 117
BROWETT, John, 598
BROWN, Douglas, 118
BROWN, Eddie, 796
BROWN, Michael Maugham-
See:
MAUGHAM-BROWN, Michael
BROWN, Susan M., 194, 207, 570
BRUTUS, Dennis, 119
BUCKLAND, Peter, 120
BUDLENDER, Debbie, 121, 1021
BUDLENDER, Geoff, 554

BUIS, Robert, 122
BULL, Hedley, 195, 899
BUNDY, Colin, 123, 124, 125, 794, 836, 915, 1038
BUNTING, Brian, 126, 127, 128, 129, 130, 916
BUNTING, Sidney Percival, 131
BURCHELL, David E., 132
BUREAU FOR ECONOMIC RESEARCH RE BANTU DEVELOPMENT, 133, 134, 610
BURMAN, Sandra, 555
BURNHAM, Walter Dean, 195
BURNING, Jill, 274
BURNS, Y.M., 896
BUSTIN, E., 954
BUTHELEZI COMMISION, 136
BUTHELEZI, Manas, 83
BUTHELEZI, Mangosuthu Gatsha, 85, 137, 198, 258, 914
BUTHELEZI, Qedusizi, 138
BUTHELEZI, Sipho, 82
BUTLER, Jeffrey, 139, 154
BUZAN, Barry, 140

C.I.I.R.
See:
CATHOLIC INSTITUTE FOR INTER-NATIONAL RELATIONS
CACHALIA, Firoz, 141
CALLAGHY, Thomas, 376, 517, 568, 904
CALLINICOS, Alex, 142
CALPIN, G.H., 143, 144
CAMERON, R., 869
CAMERON, Trewhella, 458
CAMPBELL, Kurt M., 894
CANON COLLINS MEMORIAL LECTURE, 227
CARNEGIE ENDOWMENT FOR

ELOFF, Theuns, 920
EMDON, Erica, 296
ENGLISH-SPEAKING SOUTH AFRICA:
AN ASSESSMENT. Conference,
Grahamstown, 1974, 297
ENSOR, Linda, 206, 299
ERASMUS, R.P.B., 812
ERATH, H., 924
ERWIN, Alex, 1038
ESTERHUYSE, Willie, 110
ETHICS AND PUBLIC POLICY
CENTER, 882
EVANS, Gavin, 300
EWING, Winifred Crum, 466

F.A.O.
See:
FOOD AND AGRICULTURE
ORGANIZATION
FAIR, T.J.D., 974
FATTON, Robert, 303, 304
FAVIS, Merle, 1108
FEIT, Edward, 305, 306, 307
FENRICK, Joseph C., 308
FERGUSON, Ed, 119
FICK, Johan, 237
FIG, David, 309
FINE, Alan, 310
FINE, Bob, 555
FIRST, Ruth, 311, 312
FISHER, Foszia, 83, 764
FOLKESTONE, Joan Joseph, 890
FOLTZ, William J., 14, 315,
483, 901
FOOD AND AGRICULTURE
ORGANIZATION, 681
FORD, Richard B., 910
FOREIGN POLICY ASSOCIATION,
928
FORSYTH, C.F., 451

FORSYTH, Christopher, 555
FORSYTH, Murray, 1043
FOSTER, D.H., 199
FOSTER, Joe, 626
FOUNDATION FOR FOREIGN
AFFAIRS, 3
FOURIE, C., 869
FRANKEL, Philip, 316, 317,
318, 319
FRANKO, Lawrence G., 907
FRANSMAN, Martin, 764
FREDERIKSE, Julie, 320
FREDMAN, Sandra, 321
FREDRICKSON, George M., 322,
571
FREER, Pamela A., 323, 324
FRENCH, K., 873
FREUND, W.M., 325, 326
FRIDJOHN, Michael, 1038
FRIEDLAND, Elaine Alice, 327,
328
FRIEDLANDER, Zelda, 890
FRIEDMAN, Stephen, 329, 330,
1038
FRIEDRICH EBERT STIFTUNG, 84,
435
FUGARD, Athol, 913

GAITSKELL, Deborah, 176, 461,
1038
GANN, Lewis H., 333
GARDINER, Michael, 288
GARDNER, C.O., 934
GASTROW, Sheila, 334
GELB, Stephen, 335, 843, 1038
GELDENHUYS, Deon Johannes,
266, 336, 337, 338, 339,
340, 341, 342, 343, 344,
345, 346, 899, 908, 924
GELDENHUYS, Jannie, 914

452

NUSAS
See:
NATIONAL UNION OF SOUTH
  AFRICAN STUDENTS
NXASANA, Harold, 83
NYERERE, Julius, 913
NYQUIST, Thomas E., 733
NZO, Alfred, 736, 737
NZULA, A.T., 738

O.A.U.
See:
ORGANIZATION OF AFRICAN UNITY
OBASEKI, Nosakhare O., 315
OBERY, Ingrid, 739, 740, 811,
  1065
O'CONNELL, M.C., 86
ODENDAAL, Andre, 741
O'DOWD, Michael, 901, 902,
  914, 924
OHIO UNIVERSITY. Center for
  International Studies, 367
OJO, Olusola, 742, 944
OLIVIER, Gerrit, 785,
OLIVIER, Gert Cornelius, 903,
  908
OLIVIER, J.J., 598
OLIVIER, J.L., 896
OLIVIER, Johan, 785
OLIVIER, N.J.J., 258
O'MEARA, Dan, 232, 233, 234,
  299, 743, 744, 745, 746, 915
O'MEARA, Patrick, 374, 747,
  748
OMER-COOPER, J.D., 749
OMOND, Roger, 750
OOSTHUYSEN, Annami, 785
OPLAND, Jeff, 675, 901
OPPENHEIMER, Harry Frederick,
  751, 752, 753

ORGANIZATION OF AFRICAN UNITY,
  1031
ORKIN, Mark, 754
ORLIK, Peter B., 755
ORPEN, Christopher, 202
OUDES, Bruce J., 907
OWEN, Ken, 756, 914
OZGUR, Ozdemir, 758

PACHAI, Bridglal, 259
PAKENDORF, Harald, 195, 465,
  785
PALMBERG, Mai, 592
PALMER, Mabel, 759
PALMER, Robin, 836
PARKER, Frank J., 760
PARNELL, Sue, 413
PARSONS, Neil, 836
PATEL, C., 1089
PATON, Alan, 761, 913
PATTERSON, Sheila, 762
PAX CHRISTI, 151
PEDERSEN, Dean Natvik, 620
PELZER, A.N., 1059
PERLMAN, J.M., 763
PHAHLE, Roseinnes, 765
PHELPS-STOKES FUND, 431
PHILLIP, Kate, 288
PHILLIPS, Howard, 1037
PHILLIPS, Norman Charles, 766
PHIMISTER, Ian, 299
PIKE, Henry R., 767
PILLAY, Vella, 768, 769
PINNOCK, Don, 211
PIRIE, Gordon, 770
PIRON, Johan, 771
PLATZKY, Laurine, 772, 773,
  774
PLAUT, Martin, 177, 626
POGRUND, Benjamin, 192, 776

RICHARDSON, Peter, 461, 794, 823
RIEKERT, P.J., 812
RIGA, David, 824
RIIA
See:
ROYAL INSTITUTE OF INTERNATIONAL AFFAIRS
ROBERTS, Michael, 827
ROBERTSON, Hector Menteith, 828
ROBERTSON, Janet, 829
ROCKERFELLER FOUNDATION, 975
RODER, Wolf, 1062
ROELOFSE, J.J., 830
ROGALY, Gail Lynda, 831
ROGERS, Barbara, 832, 1031
ROGERS, Howard, 833
ROGERS, John, 142
ROGERSON, Christian M., 598, 834
ROHERTY, James M., 835
ROODT, Monty, 288
ROPP, Klaus von der, 837
ROSBERG, Carl G., 34
RÖSEMAN, W.A., 465
ROSS, R., 794
ROTBERG, Robert I., 139, 195, 838, 898
ROTH, M., 813
ROUX, Ben, 903
ROUX, Edward, 839
ROUX, M., 974
ROYAL INSTITUTE OF INTERNATIONAL AFFAIRS, 44, 840, 952
RUBIN, Leslie, 393
RUSSELL, Margo, 591

S.A.C.C.
See:
SOUTH AFRICAN COUNCIL OF CHURCHES
S.A.I.I.A.
See:
SOUTH AFRICAN INSTITUTE OF INTERNATIONAL AFFAIRS
S.A.I.R.R.
See:
SOUTH AFRICAN INSTITUTE OF RACE RELATIONS
S.A.L.D.R.U.
See:
SOUTHERN AFRICA LABOUR AND DEVELOPMENT RESEARCH UNIT
SACC
See:
SOUTH AFRICAN COUNCIL OF CHURCHES
SACHS, Albie, 35, 555, 714
SAGAY, I.E., 35, 1031
SAIIA
See:
SOUTH AFRICAN INSTITUTE OF INTERNATIONAL AFFAIRS
SAIRR
See:
SOUTH AFRICAN INSTITUTE OF RACE RELATIONS
SALDRU
See:
SOUTHERN AFRICA LABOUR AND DEVELOPMENT RESEARCH UNIT
SALEM, Richard A., 796
SAMOFF, Joel, 841
SAMSON, D., 323
SANDERS, A.J.G.M., 200, 554
SARAKINSKY, Mike, 444
SATCHWELL, Kathy, 1108

458

SLABBERT, Mana, 211
SLOVO, Joe, 888, 889
SMALL, Adam, 196
SMIT, Dirk van Zyl, 199
SMIT, P., 192, 598
SMITH, David M., 598
SMITH, M.G., 775
SMITH, Nico, 785
SMITH, Robin, 1043
SMOLLAN, Roy, 814
SMOUT, M.A.H., 998
SMUTS, J.C., 890
SOLE, Kelwyn, 194
SOLOMON, D., 869
SONN, Franklin, 920
SONO, Themba, 891
SOUTH AFRICA. Parliament, 892
SOUTH AFRICA (Republic).
Bureau of Information, 999
SOUTH AFRICA (Republic). Dept.
of National Education,
Library Services Branch, 812
SOUTH AFRICA (Republic).
Parliament, 893
SOUTH AFRICA FOUNDATION, 41,
487, 699
SOUTH AFRICAN COMMUNIST PARTY,
13, 131, 826, 916, 1029,
1040
SOUTH AFRICAN COUNCIL OF
CHURCHES, 810, 1097
SOUTH AFRICAN INSTITUTE OF
INTERNATIONAL AFFAIRS, 3,
24, 266, 337, 342, 344, 345,
346, 372, 503, 505, 506,
508, 684, 831, 854, 855,
924, 946, 955, 984
SOUTH AFRICAN INSTITUTE OF
INTERNATIONAL AFFAIRS.
Conference, Hilton, Natal,

1984, 898
SOUTH AFRICAN INSTITUTE OF
INTERNATIONAL AFFAIRS.
Conference, Rustenburg,
1978, 195
SOUTH AFRICAN INSTITUTE OF
INTERNATIONAL AFFAIRS.
International Political
Outlook Conference, 1st,
Johannesburg, 1981, 411
SOUTH AFRICAN INSTITUTE OF
PUBLIC ADMINISTRATION, 998
SOUTH AFRICAN INSTITUTE OF
RACE RELATIONS, 116, 168,
206, 287, 290, 291, 329,
392, 436, 437, 438, 439,
440, 602, 650, 655, 704,
798, 847, 918, 919, 974,
1010, 1117
SOUTH AFRICAN INSTITUTE OF
RACE RELATIONS. Conference,
50th, 1980, 920
SOUTH AFRICAN INSTITUTE OF
RACE RELATIONS. Conference,
52nd, 1982 257
SOUTH AFRICAN INSTITUTE OF
RACE RELATIONS. Council
Meeting, 51st, Johannesburg,
1981, 921
SOUTH AFRICAN LIBRARY, 856
SOUTH AFRICAN SOCIETY OF
JOURNALISTS. Symposium,
1974, 661
SOUTHALL, Anthony J., 937
SOUTHALL, Roger J., 925, 938,
939, 940, 941, 942
SOUTHERN AFRICA IN THE WORLD.
Conference, Johannesburg,
1981, 411
SOUTHERN AFRICA LABOUR AND

464

180
UNIVERSITY OF THE WESTERN
CAPE, 251
UNIVERSITY OF THE WESTERN
CAPE. Conference, 1984, 962
UNIVERSITY OF THE
WITWATERSRAND,763
UNIVERSITY OF THE
WITWATERSRAND. African
Studies Institute, 546, 764,
1038, 1114
UNIVERSITY OF THE
WITWATERSRAND. Centre for
Applied Legal Studies, 408,
922
UNIVERSITY OF THE
WITWATERSRAND. Development
Studies Group, 409
UNIVERSITY OF THE
WITWATERSRAND. History
Workshop, 2nd, 1981, 1019
UNIVERSITY OF THE
WITWATERSRAND. History
Workshop, 3rd, 1984, 382
UNIVERSITY OF THE
WITWATERSRAND. Library, 947
UNIVERSITY OF THE
WITWATERSRAND. School of
Law, 27
UNIVERSITY OF THE
WITWATERSRAND. Students
Representative Council, 1021
UNTERHALTER, Elaine, 194
UNTERHALTER, Jack, 977
URBAN FOUNDATION, 700
URBANISATION CONFERENCE, 1982,
257
URDANG, Stephanie, 550
URNOV, A.R., 1040
USSALEP

See:
UNITED STATES - SOUTH AFRICA
LEADER EXCHANGE PROGRAM
UYS, J.M., 964
UYS, Stanley, 1043

VALE, Peter Christopher
Julius, 899, 908, 1030,
1041, 1042, 1043, 1044
VAN ASWEGEN, H.J., 458
VAN BILJON, F.J., 1045
VAN COLLER, Sam, 906
VAN DEN BERGHE, Pierre L.,
591, 910, 1046
VAN DER HORST, Sheila T., 196,
797, 1047
VAN DER KOOY, R., 936
VAN DER MERWE, Hendrik W., 18,
453, 457, 612, 796, 934,
973, 1088
VAN DER MERWE, P.J., 609, 924
VAN DER MERWE, Stoffel, 894,
914, 920
VAN DER POEL, Jean, 890
VAN DER ROSS, R.E., 110, 612
VAN DER SPUY, H.I.J., 793
VAN DER VYVER, J.D., 1048
VAN DER WALT, Tjaart, 812
VAN DER WATT, Ike, 914
VAN HEERDEN, Willem, 465
VAN HELTEN, Jean Jacques, 461,
1049
VAN HEYNINGEN, Elizabeth, 1037
VAN JAARSVELD, F.A., 277, 1050
VAN JAARSVELD, J.A., 867
VAN NIEKERK, Barend, 977
VAN NIEKERK, Phillip, 566, 894
VAN NIEKERK, W.P., 1051
VAN ONSELEN, Charles, 1052
VAN ROOYEN, Jan J., 1053

Methodological principles 16
Morogoro Conference 16
Pan Africanist Congress conflict 724
Pictorial record 17, 1036, 1075
Plaatjie, Sol 1094
Press clippings 15
Programme of Action, 1949 604
Rand townships 1038
Rural struggle 123
Western Cape 432
South African Communist Party relationship 518, 790
Speeches 23
United States policy towards 518
Violence 789
Women's League 1066

AFRICAN NATIONALISM 10, 18, 34, 80, 83, 85, 91, 92, 105, 142, 146, 148, 150, 154, 170, 194, 196, 203, 223, 268, 304, 305, 306, 307, 313, 327, 331, 347, 349, 392, 401, 450, 498, 531, 546, 584, 585, 603, 639, 671, 703, 705, 725, 745, 757, 839, 877, 910, 919, 943, 1037, 1068, 1095

AFRIKANSE STUDENTEBOND 973

AFRIKANER BOND
History 225

AFRIKANER BROEDERBOND 34, 693, 694, 746, 868, 1057, 1092
Bibliography 709
Functions 743, 868
History 743, 868, 1092
Members
names and addresses 109
Significance 1092
Strategies 1092
Structure 868

AFRIKANER NATIONALISM 9, 34, 42, 146, 148, 154, 159, 170, 196, 203, 241, 268, 277, 278, 279, 299, 313, 356, 399, 416, 417, 441, 450, 457, 612, 615, 629, 671, 693, 694, 705, 724, 743, 744, 746, 757, 762, 827, 844, 851, 852, 857, 868, 881, 902, 907, 910, 912, 927, 943, 957, 965, 968, 980, 983, 1005, 1012, 1013, 1023, 1050, 1057, 1092

AFRIKANER VOLKSWAG 798

AFRIKANER WEERSTANDSBEWEGING 798
Biographies 1090

AFRIKANERS 399, 457, 572, 612, 762, 934
Attitudes 399, 457, 917, 934
Calvinism 693, 694, 965
origins
myth of 279

Status quo 227
Theory 283

ARAB COUNTRIES
Foreign relations 742

ARMAMENTS
Capability 760
Industry 801, 1008

ARMED FORCES
See also:
SOUTH AFRICAN DEFENCE FORCE

ARMED FORCES 1043
Statistics 682

ARMS EMBARGO
Bibliography
United Nations
documentation 39, 1031

ASIANS
See:
INDIANS

AUSTRALIA
Foreign policy 899

AWB
See:
AFRIKANER WEERSTANDSBEWEGING

AZACTU
See:
AZANIAN CONFEDERATION OF TRADE
UNIONS

AZANIAN CONFEDERATION OF TRADE
UNIONS
Membership 1020

AZANIAN PEOPLES' ORGANIZATION
798
Biographies 1090
Evaluation 570

AZAPO
See:
AZANIAN PEOPLES' ORGANIZATION

B.O.S.S.
See:
BUREAU FOR STATE SECURITY

B.P.C.
See:
Black Peoples' Convention

BANK LOANS 1031

BANKING
Bibliography 73

BANNINGS 189, 250, 314, 895,
1026
Mandela, Winnie
banning orders 191
Organizations 93
Persons 93

BANTU AUTHORITIES ACT
Struggle against 672

BANTU EDUCATION ACT, 1953
Analysis 427

473

BANTU LABOUR ACT, 1953
  Analysis 282

BANTUSTANS
See:
HOMELANDS

BARAYI, Elijah
  Interview 894

BASUTOLAND
See also:
Lesotho

BASUTOLAND
  Migrant labour 461

BEER BOYCOTT, 1929
  Durban 548

BENSO
See:
BUREAU FOR ECONOMIC RESEARCH
RE BLACK DEVELOPMENT

BIBLIOGRAPHIES 710, 711, 910,
  947
  African National Congress
    499
  Afrikaner Broederbond 709
  Agriculture 73, 1084
  Apartheid 214, 215, 218,
    782
    legal aspects 216
  Arms embargo 39
  Banking 73
  Black Sash 709
  Blacks 1009
  Bophuthaswana 404, 503

Carter-Karis Collection
  1116
Chrome 24
Church and state 947
Ciskei 173
Constitutional history
  867
Demography 73
Disinvestment 947
Dissertations 778
Economic development 73
Economic history 867
Economics 73, 1076, 1084
Education 73, 1084
  blacks 29, 502
Energy 73
Finance 73
Forced removals 325, 1084
Foreign relations 508, 831
  United States 221, 294,
  308
Health 73, 1084
Historiography 867
History 269, 308, 709,
  845, 867
Homelands 168, 308
  official publications 532
Housing 1084
Industrial relations 73
Kuper, Leo 591
Labour 73
Liberalism 709
Manganese 24
Migrant labour 290
Mineral dependency 24
Mining 73
Namibian settlement issue
  853, 947
Official publications
  homelands 532

discrimination removal
611
Rikhoto Judgement 875
Western Cape
chronology 545
Women 71, 83, 176, 358,
550, 594, 632, 814, 948,
964, 1031, 1065, 1108,
1118
church hostels 1038
freedom of movement 1078
labour 83, 1031
bibliographies 274
biographies 360
domestic 176,178, 360,
913, 948, 1038, 1052
Durban 598
factory 676, 948
legal status 71, 876
liberation struggles
71, 550, 594, 632, 1066
passes 1078
resistance to 1038
squatters
Winterveld 1118
Working class 281
culture 461
emergence 870
fragmentation 765
Pretoria-Odi area
state regulation 763
recession
effect 522

BOER REPUBLICS
Great Britain and 757
Treaties 504
Treaty-making 504

BOESAK, ALLAN
Philosophy 91

BOPHUTHATSWANA
See also:
HOMELANDS

BOPHUTHATSWANA 18, 139
Bibliographies 404, 503
Bosplaats accounts 521
Constitution
analysis 201
text 201
Development 486
Education 288
General survey 133, 186,
695
Land tenure 486
Local authority accounts
521
Political parties
documents 18
Trade unions 204

BORDER AREA
East London district
attitudes 456

BORDER INDUSTRIES 65, 171,
192, 254, 424, 598, 806,
935, 1038, 1123

BOSS
See:
BUREAU OF STATE SECURITY

BOTHA, Louis
Political contribution 536

BOTHA, P.W.
  Biography 252, 340
  Crisis period, 1984-85
  comparison with
    B.J.Vorster 343
  Decision-making 341
  Foreign policy-making 337
  Leadership style 340, 375
  Namibian policy 482
  Prime Ministership 399
  Speeches and writings 36

BOTSWANA
  Invasion 394, 928

BOURGEOISIE
  Blacks 8, 209, 444, 539,
    735, 1009, 1101
  Radicalization 461

BOYCOTTS
See also:
RESISTANCE

BOYCOTTS 913
  Black universities 18
  Bus 608, 622, 913, 960,
    1051
  Consumer 739
  Mdantsane/East London 1051
  Reasons 378
  Schools
    black 765, 1019
  Sport 94, 472, 524

BPC
See:
BLACK PEOPLES' CONVENTION

BRAZIL
  Anglo-American interests
    309

BRITISH ANTI-APARTHEID
MOVEMENT 28

BRITISH EMPIRE
  South Africa's role 348

BROADCASTING
See also:
MASS MEDIA
SOUTH AFRICAN BROADCASTING
  CORPORATION

BROADCASTING 12
  History 755
  State domination 12, 384,
    755

BROEDERBOND
See:
AFRIKANER BROEDERBOND

BROOKES, Edgar H.
  Liberalism
    analysis of thought 787

BUNDY, Colin
  Liberalism
    analysis of research 590

BUREAU OF ECONOMIC RESEARCH RE
BANTU DEVELOPMENT
  Dissolution 423

BUREAU OF STATE SECURITY
See also:
STATE SECURITY COUNCIL

BUREAU OF STATE SECURITY
Activities
in Great Britian 53

BUS BOYCOTTS
See:
BOYCOTTS

BUTHELEZI COMMISSION REPORT
136
Comment on 120
Constitutional law
implications 200
Summary 940

BUTHELEZI, Mangosuthu Gatsha
653
Biographies 139, 1004
Role 939
Speeches 137

C.O.S.A.T.U.
See:
CONGRESS OF SOUTH AFRICAN
TRADED UNIONS

C.P.
See:
CONSERVATIVE PARTY

C.U.S.A.
See:
COUNCIL OF UNIONS OF SOUTH
AFRICA

CALVINISM 92
Afrikaner nationalism
relationship 416
Economic action
relationship 965

CANTON SYSTEM
Model 615

CAPE
Agriculture
class transformation 125
Blacks
disenfranschisement 547
Influx control 185, 545,
1086
Liberalism 589, 590, 1038
Race
attitude towards 326
Rural struggle 432
Shebeens 211
Squatters 185, 545
Trade unions 726
Unrest, 1976-1977 919, 1037

CAPE ACTION LEAGUE 798

CAPE COLONY
Capitalist agriculture
origins 794
Resistance
development 725
Whites
poverty 794

CAPE PROVINCE
See:
CAPE

CAPE TOWN
City council 869
Colander School
racial assimilation 1071
Community council 806
Housing 1119

CAPE WHOLESALE CLOTHING AND
SHIRT MANUFACTURER'S
ASSOCIATION
Garment Worker's Union
relationship 726

CAPITALISM 103, 141, 142, 156,
203, 401, 595, 615, 777,
841, 865, 881, 915
African National Congress
841
Afrikaner nationalism 746
Agriculture 915, 945
class struggle 696, 697,
698, 708
class transformation 125,
708
Apartheid 565, 595, 938
relationship between 229,
561
Class formation 103, 229,
515, 764
Corporatism 788
Crisis 1102
Development 915
Energy 169
Ideology 103, 203, 1038
Labour 1100
black 846
white 229
Legitimation of social
order 962
Migrant labour
recruitment 613
Mining 359, 464
Modes of production 1100
Monopoly 464, 712, 849,
864, 915, 925
Mpondo chiefdom
effect on 62

Race 8, 19, 363, 515, 963
Rural areas
class struggle 696, 697,
698, 708
Settler 246
State 764
formation 103, 229

CAREERS 19

CARNEGIE CORPORATION
Inquiry into Poverty and
Development in Southern
Africa, 1982-1985 99, 911,
1038
bibliography on poverty
1084
Investigation into Poor
White Problem, 1929-1932
99

CARTER, Gwendolen Margaret
Analysis of views on South
Africa 429

CARTER-KARIS COLLECTION
Bibliography 1116

CENSORSHIP 537, 551
Press 354, 383, 414
legislation 354, 414

CHAMBER OF MINES
Role in labour system 583

CHAMPION, George 653

CHANGE
See also:
POLITICAL ALTERNATIVES

President's Council
 membership 1
Social conditions 183
Socio-economic status 448
Sociological study
Johannesburg 285, 286
Sparks Estate, Durban 256
Theron Commission of
 Inquiry
  analysis 1007, 1010

COMMISSIONS OF INQUIRY 812

COMMITTEES OF INQUIRY 812

COMMONWEALTH
 Eminent Persons Group
  report 191
 Heads of Government Meeting
 Nassau, 1985 43
 Parliamentary sovereignty
 657
 Withdrawal from 348

COMMONWEALTH ACCORD ON SOUTH
 AFRICA 191

COMMUNISM 203, 724, 777
 History 767

COMMUNIST PARTY OF SOUTH
 AFRICA
See:
SOUTH AFRICAN COMMUNIST PARTY

COMMUNITY COUNCILS 447, 806
 Cape Town 806

COMMUNITY DEVELOPMENT
 Black perspectives on 18

CONFEDERATION 195, 631, 651,
 777, 840, 932

CONFLICT
 Resolution 361, 393
 Sources 1046

CONGRESS ALLIANCE 223
 Education programme 288,
 467

CONGRESS MOVEMENT
 Documentary history 331

CONGRESS OF SOUTH AFRICAN
TRADE UNIONS 145, 197
 Barayi, Elija
 interview 894
 Launch 197

CONGRESS OF THE PEOPLE
CAMPAIGN 992

CONSAS
See:
CONSTELLATION OF SOUTHERN
AFRICAN STATES

CONSCIENTIOUS OBJECTION
 Churches attitude 151
 Repression 1031

CONSERVATISM 777

CONSERVATIVE PARTY 798

CONSOCIATIONALISM 101, 195,
 393, 475, 593, 777, 837,
 840, 981

488

DEFENCE
    Capability 333, 950, 975
    Homelands 376
    Legislation
     historical analysis 367
    Relations 950
     Great Britain 950
    Strategy 483, 1031
    White papers 892, 893

DEFIANCE CAMPAIGN 540
    Documentary history 331

DE LANGE COMMITTEE OF INQUIRY,
    1981 812
    Comment on 120, 166, 167,
    501

DELAGOA BAY HINTERLAND
    Migrant labour 194, 461
    Production 194
    Trade 194

DEMOCRACY 777

DEMOCRATIC PARTY 465

DEMOCRATIC SOCIALISM 203

DEMOCRATIC WORKERS' PARTY 798

DEMOGRAPHY 392, 581, 795, 897
    Bibliography 73
    Blacks
     politcal conflict 891
    Pressures 926
    Urbanization 172

DEPARTMENT OF FOREIGN AFFAIRS
    903

DEPORTATIONS 189

DESTABILIZATION POLICIES
    Southern Africa 98, 187,
    315, 328, 338, 370, 394,
    578, 904, 1017

DETENTIONS 189, 250, 314, 895
    Security legislation 250

DEVELOPMENT
    Economic 3
     bibliography 73
     blacks' perspective on 18
    Homelands planning 3
    Separate development 3
    Southern Africa 896

DEVELOPMENT BANK OF SOUTHERN
AFRICA 423

DIAMONDS AND DIAMOND INDUSTRY
    Control 764
    Discovery
     effect on class struggle
     791
    Kimberley hinterland
     effect on 461

DINIZULU, King Solomon ka 653

DISINVESTMENT
See also:
DIVESTMENT
SANCTIONS

DISINVESTMENT 380
    Bibliography 947

Blacks
  attitude towards 487, 754,
  846, 989
  Multinational corporations
  1032
  United States 135
  West 312

DISSERTATIONS
  Bibliography 778

DIVESTMENT
See also:
DISINVESTMENT
SANCTIONS

DIVESTMENT 249

DOMESTIC WORKERS 176, 178,
  360, 913, 948, 1038, 1052
  Bibliographies 274
  Biographies 360
  Durban 598

DOMINION STATUS 1087

DRC
See:
DUTCH REFORMED CHURCH

DRUGS AND DRUG ABUSE 211

DUBE, John 653

DUIGNAN, Peter
  Analysis of views
    on South Africa 429

DURBAN
  Bus boycotts 622
  Domestic workers 598
  Factory labour 676
  Housing
    Indian 598
    informal 598
  Indians 677
  Migrant workers
    job satisfaction 690
  Suicide
    sociological study 678
  Whites
    voting preferences 847

DUTCH REFORMED CHURCH
See also:
CHURCH AND POLITICS
RELIGION
THEOLOGY

DUTCH REFORMED CHURCH 693, 694
  Afrikaner nationalism
    impact 1057
  Change 807
  Divorce laws and 555

DU TOIT, S.J.
  Role 225

E.C.
See:
EUROPEAN COMMUNITY

EAST GRIQUALAND
  Settler accumulation 794

EAST LONDON
  Bus boycotts 622, 1051

EXECUTIVE 179, 361, 668, 777, 903

F.O.S.A.T.U.
See:
FEDERATION OF SOUTH AFRICAN TRADE UNIONS

FACTORY LABOUR
  Women 676, 948

FAGAN, H.A.
  Race relations 115

FARM LABOUR 696, 945

FASCISM 129, 879, 880, 881, 1099

FEAR 34
  Determinant in politics 77

FEDERALISM 195, 450, 574, 631, 654, 777, 840, 896, 935, 1098
  Blacks' perspectives on 18

FEDERATION OF SOUTH AFRICAN TRADE UNIONS
  Membership 1020
  Policy statements 626

FEDERATION OF SOUTH AFRICAN WOMEN 194
  History, 1954-1963 1066

FEDSAW
See:
FEDERATION OF SOUTH AFRICAN WOMEN

FINANCE
See:
ECONOMY

FISHING INDUSTRY
  Interests
    in Chile 309

FOOTBALL HISTORY 1019

FORCED REMOVALS 248, 325, 389, 399, 470, 510, 545, 649, 650, 772, 773, 774, 798
  Bibliographies 325, 1084
  Churches' report on 810
  Ciskei 362
  Effect on
    Coloured family life 211
    Coloured gangs 211
    Homeland economics 510
    Kwazulu 510
  Kwazulu 921
  Orange Free State 707
  Pretoria-Odi area 763
  Sophiatown 443, 1019
  Surplus People Project 988
    analysis 389

FOREIGN INVESTMENT 516, 592, 614, 838, 987
  Abroad 516
  Churches' reaction 882
  Electronics industry 712
  Minerals 712
  Motor industry 712
  Multinational corporations 1032
  Oil industry 712
  and Rural black economy 614
  West 1041

KADALIE, Clements
Biography 498

KAIROS DOCUMENT 153
Excerpts 894

KANGWANE
See also:
HOMELANDS

KANGWANE
General survey 134

KANNEMEYER COMMISSION OF
INQUIRY, 1985 812
Analysis 407

KIMBERLEY
Compounds 461
Diamond discoveries
effect on hinterland 461
Labour history 461

KITSON, David
as underground activist 529

KOK, Adam
Biography 80

KOTANE, Moses
Biography 128

KOZA, Daniel
Biography 395

KUPER, Leo
Bibliography 591
Biography 591
Pluralist thought analysis
64, 449

KUZWAYO, Ellen
Biography 544

KWAMASHU
Inkatha membership 106, 107

KWAZULU
See also:
BUTHELEZI, Mangosuthu Gatsha
HOMELANDS
INKATHA
'NATAL OPTION'
ZULUS

KWAZULU 18
Buthelezi Commission Report
136, 940
Buthelezi, Mangosuthu
Gatsha
role 1004
Development 85
Homelands policy 139
Nqutu district
socio-economic study 175
Political options 715

LABOUR
See also:
MIGRANT LABOUR

LABOUR 34, 83, 84, 156, 441,
442, 583, 795, 797, 798,
897, 900, 905, 923, 924, 925
Bibliography 73
Blacks 83, 84, 192, 213,
280, 281, 299, 301, 359,
383, 470, 471, 474, 487,
546, 547, 597, 629, 897,

900, 906, 907, 923, 924,
961, 1038, 1047, 1052,
1073
  motivation 906
Bureaux 421
Changes 141
Cheap labour 420, 583, 1100
  capitalism critique 764
Chinese 583, 823
Conditions 192
Constraints 192
Domestic 176, 178, 360,
  913, 948, 1038, 1052
Farm 597, 696, 945
Foundries 925, 1073
Gold mines 461, 583, 1096,
  1120
Indians 583
International policies
  relevance 266
Internatioal politics
  towards South Africa 84
Kimberley 461
Legislation 84, 702, 812
Metal industry 925, 1073
Modernization effects
  Western Transvaal 240
and Political economy 441
and Politics 26
Prison 301
Racial division 230, 265,
  267, 591, 874, 910
Regulation 680
  legislation 702
  Pretoria ODI area 763
Riekert Commission of
  Inquiry 812
  analysis 419, 421, 444,
    474, 680
Sociological analysis 909

State and 230, 577
Trends 324
Utilization 914
Whites
  and capitalism 229, 230
Wiehahn Commission of
  Inquiry 812
Women
  blacks 176, 178, 676, 1031
  class consciousness 70
  Zulu tributary labour 194

LABOUR HORIZONS 1956,
Conference, Johannesburg,
1985 26

LABOUR PARTY
See also:
COLOUREDS
POLITICAL PARTIES

LABOUR PARTY 1, 183, 798
  Constitution 183
  Constitution, 1983
    participation 198
  President's Council
    membership 1

LABOUR RELATIONS
See also:
INDUSTRIAL RELATIONS

LABOUR RELATIONS 26, 310, 493,
  722, 798, 914
  History 104
  Race and 917

MANGANESE
Dependency on South African
supply
bibliography 24

MANGOPE, Lucas
Biography 139

MANPOWER
See:
LABOUR

MANUEL, Trevor
Interview
on United Democratic Front
570

MA-RASHEA GANG 382

MARSHALL PLAN CONCEPT 380

MARXISM
See also:
IDEOLOGY

MARXISM
Afrikaner nationalism
interpretation 746
Law interpretation 453
Race relations
interpretation 963
Theory 937

MARXIST SOCIOLOGY 497

MASOPA
Biography 80

MASS MEDIA
See also
BROADCASTING
PRESS
SOUTH AFRICAN BROADCASTING
CORPORATION
TELEVISION

MASS MEDIA 12, 164, 798, 1033
Liberation struggle 164,
559
Propaganda 552
State control 12, 164
Steyn Commission of Inquiry
812
analysis 384, 830

MATANZIMA, George
Biography 972

MATANZIMA, Kaiser
Biography 972
Role in Transkei
'independence' 553, 972

MATTHEWS, Z.K.
Biography 667

MBEKI, Govan
Biography 1031
and Rural struggle 123

MDANTSANE 675
Bus boycott 1051
East London
relationship 675

MEDIA
See:
BROADCASTING

508

MASS MEDIA
PRESS
SOUTH AFRICAN BROADCASTING
 CORPORATION
TELEVISION

METAL INDUSTRY
    Labour 925, 1073
    Trade unions 1073

MIDDELBURG
    Agriculture
     cooperatives 794

MIGRANT LABOUR
See also:
LABOUR

MIGRANT LABOUR 81, 86, 442,
    471, 547, 583, 629, 828,
    870, 915, 1039, 1096, 1097
    Anthropological
     perspectives 86
    Basutoland 461
    Bibliography 290
    Conditions of 81
    Delagoa Bay hinterland 194,
     461
    Dependency reduction 81
    Durban
     job satisfaction 690
    Family life effect 679
    Gold mines 81, 485, 768,
     915, 1096
    Historiography 359
    Kinship 461
    Lesotho
     plight of families 86
    Mozambique 311
     recruitment reduction 613

socio-economic impact 1061
Nqutu district 194
Pondoland 62
Recruitment reduction 613
Retrenchment 479
Rhodes University Project
 86
Swaziland 81
Trade unions
 effect on
  cultural formation 883
  moral formation 925
Transkei 942, 972, 1021
Treaties 504, 1089
Women
 bibliography 274

MILITARIZATION 2, 151, 315,
    318, 368, 372, 483, 484,
    871, 898, 1017

MINERALS 905
    Dependency
     bibliography 24
    Foreign investment in 712
    Strategic minerals 975
    West and 1041

MINES AND MINING 442, 795, 838
    and Apartheid 768
    Bibliography 73
    Capitalism 359
    Chinese indentured labour
     823
    Class struggle and 791
    Control 299

509

Economy and 718
International gold standard
1049
Johannesburg
 comparison with Broken
 Hill, Australia 525
Labour 299, 359, 461, 583,
 1096, 1120
  culture and identity 1019
  migrant 81, 485, 768,
   915, 1096
  married quarters 461
Racial discrimination
 class explanation 491
Resistance 299
Sale policies 350
Strikes
 1907 1122
 1946 745, 915, 1031
Trade unions 566, 1011

MINING CAPITAL
 Labour issues 23?
  unskilled whites 230, 915
 Monopolies 464
 State
  relationship 583

MINORITIES
See also:
MINORITY GROUP CONCERNED

MINORITIES 934
 Anxieties 34

MISSIONS
 Education 132, 427

MKHABELA, Ismael
 Interview
  on Azapo 570

MMA-POOE, Nkgono
 Biography 461

MONOPOLY CAPITALISM 135, 312,
 369, 405, 464, 614, 712,
 760, 769, 802, 849, 864,
 865, 870, 900, 905, 915,
 924, 1032
  Consolidation 1914-1948 915
  and Industrial unionism 925

MOROGORO CONFERENCE, 1969
 Decisions and resolutions
  16, 23

MOTLANA, Nthato
 Interview 195, 899

MOTOR INDUSTRY
 Foreign investment in 712
 Multinational corporations
  369

MOZAMBIQUE
See also:
NKOMATI ACCORD

MOZAMBIQUE
 Foreign relations 47
 Migrant labour 311
  recruitment reduction 613
  socio-economic impact 1061
 South African invasion 394

MPANDE, Cetshwayo ka
 Biography 80

510

MSWATI II
  Biography 80

MULDERGATE SCANDAL
See:
INFORMATION SCANDAL

MULTINATIONAL CORPORATIONS
  312, 614, 769, 841, 864,
  870, 905, 1032
  Black labour 487
  Motor industry 369
  and Rural black economy 614
  and Socio-political issues
   924
  Sweden 900
  United States 135, 405,
   712, 760, 802, 849, 865,
   915
   and change 135, 802
  West 312

MULTI-RACIALISM
  Planning for 920
  Political structure 920
  Progressive Party programme 917

MUNICIPAL AND GENERAL WORKERS'
UNION
  Policy statement
   on United Democratic Front
   626

MUTLOATSE, Mothobi
  Speeches and writings 36

MZILIKAZI
  Biography 80

N.A.F.C.O.C.
See:
NATIONAL AFRICAN FEDERATED
CHAMBER OF COMMERCE

N.F.
See:
NATIONAL FORUM

N.P.
See:
NATIONAL PARTY

N.U.M.
See:
NATIONAL UNION OF MINEWORKERS

N.U.S.A.S.
See:
NATIONAL UNION OF SOUTH
AFRICAN STUDENTS

NAFCOC
See:
NATIONAL AFRICAN FEDERATED
CHAMBER OF COMMERCE

NAIDOO, Jean
  Funeral oration
   by Neville Alexander 19

NAMIBIA
  Foreign relations 928
  Settlement issue 379, 556,
   656, 682, 898, 929, 930,
   931, 932
   bibliographies 853, 947
   effect on South African
    domestic politics 482

511

South African Defence
Force in 301, 482, 1017

NATAL
Agriculture
colonial 298
Buthelezi Commission Report
136
analysis 120, 200, 940
Coal industry
colonial 298
Colonial native policy 1082
Economic history 298
Gandhi, Mahatma 759
Harbour 298
Indians 298, 759, 995
anthropological study 538
strike, 1913 994
Local authorities
financing 998
Peasants
impoverishment 298
Political options 615, 636,
715
Protest politics
women, 1959 194
Railway development 298
Social history 298
Sugar industry
colonial 794
Urban development 998
Woolled sheep industry 298

NATAL INDIAN CONGRESS 490, 798

NATAL NATIVE CONGRESS
Self-help
ideology of 194

'NATAL OPTION' 615, 636, 715

NATIONAL AFRICAN FEDERATED
CHAMBER OF COMMERCE 444

NATIONAL CONVENTION, 1909 1016

NATIONAL EDUCATION CRISIS
COMMITTEE 811

NATIONAL FORUM
Composition 61, 207
Meetings 263
Organizational structure
207
Perceptions of United
Democratic Front 207
Prospects 263
Relations 263
Strategies 61

NATIONAL FORUM COMMITTEE 798

NATIONAL MANPOWER COMMISSION
310

NATIONAL PARTY
See also:
POLITICAL PARTIES

NATIONAL PARTY 34, 115, 146,
465, 572, 798, 852, 913,
915, 983
Cape
history 100
Coloured policy 917
Congress, Durban, 1985 97
Decision-making 9
Interest groups
impact on 397, 398
Mass media control 12, 164

PASS SYSTEM 211
  Labour 420
  Women 1078
    resistance 1038, 1079

PASSIVE RESISTANCE
  Ideology 540
  Indians 72, 490, 540, 759,
  1019

PC
See:
PRESIDENT'S COUNCIL

PEASANTS
  Agarian transformation 125,
  794
  Agricultural sector 125,
  708, 738, 794, 915
  Community growth 757
  and Ethiopianism 194, 839
  Proletarianization of 125,
  708, 794, 915
  Transkei 836

PEBCO
See:
PORT ELIZABETH BLACK CIVIC
  ASSOCIATION

PEDI POLITY
  History 245

PEOPLES' CONGRESS PARTY 798

PFP
See:
PROGRESSIVE FEDERAL PARTY

PHELPS STOKES LECTURES, 1939
  431

PHILIP, Dr John 194

PLAATJIE, Sol
  Biographies 461, 1094

PLATINUM
  Dependency on South African
  supply
    bibliography 24

PLURALISM 64, 96, 101, 361,
  449, 466, 475, 528, 542,
  644, 775, 777, 818, 848, 963

POLICE FORCE
See:
SOUTH AFRICAN POLICE FORCE

POLICY STATEMENTS 946

POLITICAL ALTERNATIVES
See also:
INDIVIDUAL POLICY
  CONCERNED

POLITICAL ALTERNATIVES 9, 11,
  96, 101, 193, 195, 199, 208,
  275, 321, 361, 450, 475,
  476, 574, 593, 615, 636,
  637, 651, 715, 724, 777,
  799, 837, 840, 887, 896,
  901, 902, 914, 917, 978,
  981, 1043

POLITICAL ECONOMY 6, 312, 325,
  441, 870, 961
  Bibliography 764

517

PORT ELIZABETH BLACK CIVIC
ASSOCIATION 206

PORTS
See:
HARBOURS

POST-APARTHEID
Foreign relations 140
Scenarios 11, 42, 140, 184,
264, 844, 914

POSTS AND COMMUNICATIONS
Bibliography 73

POULANTZAS, Nicos
Theory 177
analysis 1106

POVERTY
See also:
HEALTH
MALNUTRITION

POVERTY 99, 126, 470, 581,
625, 681, 870
Bibliography 1084
Cape Colony
whites 794
Carnegie Inquiry 99, 911,
1038, 1084
Coloureds 1007
Photographs 911
Transkei 558, 836

POVERTY DATUM LINES
Bibliography 291
History 121
Nqutu district 175

POWER-SHARING
See also:
POLITICAL ALTERNATIVES

POWER-SHARING 593
Bibliography 593
Model for transition 978
Possibilities 11, 837, 887,
978

PREFERENTIAL TRADE AREA 664

PRESIDENT'S COUNCIL 141, 840
Report, 1984 444
Role in constitutional
process 101, 1072
Structure 1072

PRESS 12, 164, 384, 559, 752,
776, 777, 779, 784, 914
Afrikaans 354, 784
impact on Afrikaner
nationalism 1057
Blacks 130, 354, 384, 559,
959
bibliography 997
Censorship 354, 384, 414
legislation 354, 414
Change 155, 384
Ciskei 997
Coloureds 997
Commercial 12, 997
English 117, 354, 779, 784
Freedom 117, 352, 451, 661,
896
Functions 752
Indian 997
Legislation 776, 779
censorship 354
Liberation struggle and 164

523

'RUBICON' SPEECH
Delivered at National Party
Congress, 1985 by P.W.
Botha 97
Effect on economy 463

RUBUSANA, W.B.
Biography 495

RURAL AREAS 459
Capitalism
transformation 794, 915
and class struggle 696,
697, 698, 708
Class relations 1019
Foreign investments
effect on black economy
614
Monitor 459

RURAL SLUMS
Orange Free State 707

RURAL STRUGGLES 123, 124, 194
Transkei 194
Western Cape 432

RUSSIA
See:
SOVIET UNION

S.A.B.C.
See:
SOUTH AFRICAN BROADCASTING
CORPORATION

S.A.B.R.A.
See:
SOUTH AFRICAN BUREAU OF RACIAL
AFFAIRS

S.A.C.C.
See:
SOUTH AFRICAN COUNCIL OF
CHURCHES

S.A.C.P.
See:
SOUTH AFRICAN COMMUNIST PARTY

S.A.C.T.U.
See:
SOUTH AFRICAN CONGRESS OF
TRADE UNIONS

S.A.C.U.
See:
SOUTHERN AFRICAN CUSTOMS UNION

S.A.D.C.C.
See:
SOUTHERN AFRICAN DEVELOPMENT
COORDINATION CONFERENCE

S.A.D.F.
See:
SOUTH AFRICAN DEFENCE FORCE

S.A.I.C.
See:
SOUTH AFRICAN INDIAN COUNCIL

S.A.I.R.R.
See:
SOUTH AFRICAN INSTITUTE OF
RACE RELATIONS

S.A.P.
See:
SOUTH AFRICAN POLICE FORCE

S.A.S.O.
See:
SOUTH AFRICAN STUDENTS'
ORGANISATION

S.B.D.C.
See:
SMALL BUSINESS DEVELOPMENT
CORPORATION

S.P.R.O.C.A.S.
See:
STUDY PROJECT ON CHRISTIANITY
IN APARTHEID SOCIETY

SABC
See:
SOUTH AFRICAN BROADCASTING
CORPORATION

SABRA
See:
SOUTH AFRICAN BUREAU OF RACIAL
AFFAIRS

SACC
See:
SOUTH AFRICAN COUNCIL OF
CHURCHES

SACHS, Solly 299

SACP
See:
SOUTH AFRICAN COMMUNIST PARTY

SACTU
See:
SOUTH AFRICAN CONGRESS OF
TRADE UNIONS

SACU
See:
SOUTHERN AFRICAN CUSTOMS UNION

SADCC
See:
SOUTHERN AFRICAN DEVELOPMENT
COORDINATION CONFERENCE

SADF
See:
SOUTH AFRICAN DEFENCE FORCE

SAIC
See:
SOUTH AFRICAN INDIAN COUNCIL

SAIRR
See:
SOUTH AFRICAN INSTITUTE OF
RACE RELATIONS

SANCTIONS
See also:
DISINVESTMENT
DIVESTMENT

SANCTIONS 249, 379, 380, 435,
712, 894, 955, 984, 1042
Bibliographies 214, 215,
217, 507, 947

and Blacks
  attitudes 754
  labour 487
Commonwealth
  Heads of Government
  Meeting
    Nassau, 1985 43
  Oil 944
  Southern Africa
  bibliography 507
  United States 220, 249, 556
  White attitude towards 519

SAP
See:
SOUTH AFRICAN POLICE FORCE

SASO
See:
SOUTH AFRICAN STUDENTS'
ORGANISATION

SAUL, John S.
  Race - class debate
  analysis 781

SBDC
See:
SMALL BUSINESS DEVELOPMENT
CORPORATION

SCHLEBUSCH COMMISSION REPORT
  Analysis 530

SCIENCE
  Apartheid
  effect on 1033
  Bibliography 73

SEBE, Lennox L.W.
  Speeches 560

SEBOKENG REBELLION, 1984 800

SECURITY 315, 345, 483, 484,
  682, 798, 835, 914, 926
  Bureau of State Security
  activities in Great
  Britain 53
  Characteristics 345
  Legislation 189, 314, 660,
  798, 910
    change 155
    detentions 250
    Rabie Commission of
    Inquiry 812
  Regional 684, 898, 904, 907
  bibliography 947
  strategies 345, 483, 484
  State Security Council 835
  Steyn Commission of
  Inquiry, 1980 812

SEGREGATION
See also:
APARTHEID
SEPARATE DEVELOPMENT
TRUSTEESHIP

SEGREGATION 653, 910
  Apartheid
  differences 1100
  General Hertzog's bills
  opposition 194
  Ideology 818
  Inter-War years 1038
  Liberalism
  relationship between 562
  Natal Colony 1082

Origins 152, 1038, 1082
Stubbs, Ernest
theories 821

SELF-DETERMINATION
And Homelands 35

SEMINAR OF THE LEGAL STATUS OF
THE APARTHEID REGIME AND
OTHER LEGAL ASPECTS OF THE
STRUGGLE AGAINST APARTHEID.
Lagos, 1984
Declaration 35

SENZANGAKHONA, Mpande ka
Bibliography 80

SEPARATE DEVELOPMENT
See also:
APARTHEID
SEGREGATION
TRUSTEESHIP

SEPARATE DEVELOPMENT POLICIES
816
Background 450
Bibliography 782
Critique 275, 917
Economics of 22
Evolution 195, 569, 1059
Future 943
Homelands 3
Ideology
comparison with United
States 152
Origins 152
Rationale 917
Verwoerd, H.F. 1059

SHEBEENS
Cape Province 211

SHEEP INDUSTRY
Natal
colonial 298

SHEPSTONE, Sir Theophilus
Administration policies
role and significance 1082

SIMONS, H.J.
Pluralist thought
Marxist analysis 449

SLABBERT, Frederick van Zyl
Biographies 149, 886

SMALL BUSINESS
Role 914

SMALL BUSINESS DEVELOPMENT
CORPORATION 444

SMITH, M.G.
Pluralist thought
analysis 64, 449

SMUTS, Jan Christian
Biographies 890
Political contribution 536,
890

SNYMAN COMMISSION OF INQUIRY
Documentation 1025

SOBUKWE, Robert 1026

SOCIAL CHANGE 155, 238, 598,
901, 902, 909, 979, 1121

SOCIAL COMMUNICATION 83

SOCIAL DEMOCRACY
See also:
IDEOLOGY

SOCIAL DEMOCRACY 203

SOCIAL HISTORY
    Anglo-Boer War 1069
    Dictionary 845
    Witwatersrand 382, 546,
    1052

SOCIAL PENSIONS 797

SOCIAL SEGREGATION 798

SOCIAL SERVICES
See:
SOCIAL WELFARE

SOCIAL STRUCTURES 171, 475,
    844, 909, 910
    Formation 284, 885, 1101
    Periodization 194
    Race 326

SOCIAL TRENDS 459
    Equality
    search for 914

SOCIAL WELFARE 797, 798, 897
    Bibliographies 73, 1084

SOCIALISM
See also:
IDEOLOGY

SOCIALISM 19, 203, 777
    Black and 615

SOCIO-ECONOMIC CONDITIONS 226

SOCIOLOGY 528, 909
    of British immigrants 966
    History of 497
    Industrial 906
     organizations 906
    Marxist 497
    Suicide 678
    Urban 642, 735
    Working under apartheid
    1113

SOGA, Tiyo
    Bibliography 80

SOLIDARITY 798

SOLOMON MAHLENGU FREEDOM
 COLLEGE 1104

SOPHIATOWN 443
    Forced removals 443, 1019

SOTHO
    Cosmological system 390
    History 669

SOUTH AFRICA ACT, 1909
    Text 668

SOUTH AFRICAN BROADCASTING
 CORPORATION 1026
    History 755
    State control 12, 384, 755,
    779

SOUTH AFRICAN POLICE FORCE 977
    Blacks 373
    Brutality 478, 1031
    Steyn Commission of
    Inquiry, 1980 812

SOUTH AFRICAN RESERVE BANK
    Origins 1038

SOUTH AFRICAN STUDENTS'
ORGANISATION 415
    Alice Declaration, 1972 18
    Biko's thinking on 78
    Manifesto and objections 18
    Trial, 1976 76

SOUTHERN AFRICA 36
    Communist involvement 975
    Constructive Engagement
     towards 67, 212, 859, 898,
     899, 958, 1030, 1034
    Destabilization 98, 187,
     315, 328, 338, 370, 394,
     578, 904, 1017
    Development 3, 610, 896
    Economic cooperation 929,
     930, 931, 932
    Economic intergration 664,
     905
    Economic interests 898
    Economic relations 666, 777
    Foreign relations 36, 232,
     428, 904, 929, 930, 931,
     932
    Policy statements 946
    Political economy 929, 930,
     931, 932
     role in 374
    Politics 142, 232, 324, 926
    Power struggle 914

Regional structures 324
Sanctions
 bibliography 507
South African Defence Force
 involvement 1017
Soviet Union's intentions
 187, 898, 932
Transport 905
 bibliography 73, 947
 domination by South Africa
 394

SOUTHERN AFRICAN CUSTOMS UNION
    664, 734

SOUTHERN AFRICAN DEVELOPMENT
COORDINATION CONFERENCE 232,
    374, 394, 664, 898
    Bibliography 855

SOVIET UNION
    Foreign relations 894
    Southern Africa 898, 932

SOWETO 642, 700
    Administration 365
    General survey 700
    Independent churches 1085
    Living conditions 192, 544,
     700, 873
     socio-economic analysis
     915
    Political culture 317
    Political history 544, 873

SOWETO UPRISINGS
    Analysis 401, 415, 426,
     511, 592, 627, 662, 913,
     915, 919, 1037

Multinational corporations
135, 405, 712, 760, 802,
849, 865, 915
  and change 135, 802
Race federation policy 917,
Racism
  comparison 152, 1060
Sanctions 220, 249, 556
Statements of Principles of
U.S. Firms with Affiliates
in South Africa 405
White supremacy
  comparison 322

UNITED STATES - SOUTH AFRICA
LEADER EXCHANGE PROGRAM
  Blacks
    educational investigation
    findings 289

UNITY MOVEMENT
  Political history 349

UNIVERSITIES
  Black boycott 18
  Blacks
    activism 730
    student culture 730
  Political sociology 973
  Politicization 591

UNIVERSITY OF THE NORTH
  Black consciousness 1025
  Snyman Commission of
    Inquiry 1025

UNREST
See also:
VIOLENCE

UNREST
  1960 766
  <u>1976</u> 114, 401, 415, 426,
    511, 592, 627, 662, 913,
    915, 919, 1037
  Comparison of Botha and
    Vorster eras 343
  <u>1985-1986</u> 54, 320, 329,
    380, 407, 556, 615, 674,
    719, 928, 1034, 1063
  Industrial
    political implications
    330, 1038

UP
See:
UNITED PARTY

URBAN BLACKS
See:
BLACKS, Urban

URBAN FOUNDATION 444, 1038

URBAN MONITOR 459

URBANIZATION
See also:
HOUSING

URBANIZATION 196, 254, 324,
  598, 717, 757, 798, 896,
  910, 974, 1039
  Bibliographies 73, 1084
  Change 155, 598
  Demographic aspects 172
  Homelands 598
  Planning 792
  White papers 892, 893

540

USA
See:
UNITED STATES OF AMERICA

USSALEP
See:
UNITED STATES - SOUTH AFRICA
  LEADER EXCHANGE PROGRAM

VANADIUM
    Dependency on South African
    supply
      bibliography 24

VAN DEN BERGE, Pierre
    Writings and theory
      analysis 803
        pluralist thought 64

VAN DER WALT COMMISSION OF
INQUIRY, 1985 812

VAN JAARSVELD, F.A.
    Afrikaner nationalism 277

VENDA
See also:
HOMELANDS

VENDA 18
    Constitution
      analysis 201
      text 201
    Language group
      history 669
    Opposition politics 194
    Political parties
      documents 18
    Treaties 504
      non-aggression 684

VEREENIGING ESTATES
    Tenant production 794

VERKRAMP/VERLIG CONCEPTS 917

VERWOERD, Hendrik Frensch
    Biography 526
    Commonwealth withdrawal 348
    Speeches 1059

VIGILANTES
    Right-wing 408

VILJOEN COMMITTEE REPORT
    Analysis 1093

VIOLENCE
See also:
UNREST

VIOLENCE 798, 807
    African National Congress
    789
    Cinema 211
    Human burnings 237
    Impact 237
    Legitimation 789
    Minimizing possibilities
    719
    Political culture and 789
    Race relations 542
    Reasons 378
    Resistance and 223, 331
    Television 211
    Theory 304, 888
    Total National Strategy
      effect 375

WOMEN'S CHARTER, <u>1954</u> 1066

WORK COUNCILS 722

WORK SITUATION
    Sociology 1113

WORKING CLASS
  Blacks 281
  Culture 461
  Emergence 870
  Fragmentation 765
  Pretoria - Odi Area
   state regulation 763
  Recession
   effect 522

WORLD COUNCIL OF CHURCHES
    Attitude towards
     foreign investment 882
     racism 59
    Change 807

XHOSA DEVELOPMENT CORPORATION
  1021

ZULUS
    Colonial administration
    1082
    External exchange 298
    'Independence' issue 917
    Political economy
     tributary labour 194
    Political independence
     destruction, <u>1879-1884</u>
     381, 461
    Reconstruction 461
    Social system 775
    War, <u>1879-1884</u> 381